RIGHT HERE I SEE
MY OWN BOOKS

RIGHT HERE I SEE
MY OWN BOOKS

*The Woman's Building Library
at the World's Columbian Exposition*

Sarah Wadsworth

AND

Wayne A. Wiegand

University of Massachusetts Press
Amherst and Boston

Copyright © 2012 by University of Massachusetts Press
All rights reserved
Printed in the United States of America

LC 2011044229
ISBN 978-1-55849-928-7 (paper); 927-0 (library cloth)

Designed by Jack Harrison
Set in Adobe Caslon Pro with Bernhard Modern display
Printed and bound by Maple-Vail Book Manufacturing Group

Library of Congress Cataloging-in-Publication Data
Wadsworth, Sarah, 1963–
Right here I see my own books : the Woman's Building Library at the World's
Columbian Exposition / Sarah Wadsworth and Wayne A. Wiegand.
pages cm. — (Studies in print culture and the history of the book)
Includes bibliographical references and index.
ISBN 978-1-55849-927-0 (lib. bdg.) — ISBN 978-1-55849-928-7 (pbk.)
1. Libraries—Illinois—Chicago—History—19th century.
2. Woman's Building (World's Columbian Exposition, 1893, Chicago, Ill.)
3. Women authors—Exhibitions. 4. Literature—Women authors—Exhibitions.
I. Wiegand, Wayne A., 1946– II. Title.
Z732.I2W33 2012
027.0773'11—dc23
2011044229

British Library Cataloguing in Publication data are available.

. . .from Sarah
To
Beverley Wadsworth
who showed me the way
and to
Sabrina Black
and
Blaise Black
for making it fun

. . .from Wayne
To
Cori McDermott
Erin Wiegand
and
Jenelle Welling
Strong women all who have greatly enriched my life

"And right here I see my own books . . ."
—MARIETTA HOLLEY
Samantha at the World's Fair (1893)

Contents

Foreword

Long before the term "networking" was created, women had worldwide networks that arguably were stronger than comparable ones today. With handwritten letters as their primary method of communication, feminists organized large international meetings from the 1870s onward.

The International Woman Suffrage Alliance, for example, met in Berlin, Copenhagen, Liverpool, London, Paris, and Stockholm, as well as in the United States. Its last major gathering was in Budapest in 1913, just before World War I. Soon after the war ended, women had voting rights in northern Europe, Canada, Australia, and the United States—which brought an effective end to the organization. Ironically, in the Roaring Twenties, as communication became easier with telephones and radio, feminism was increasingly seen as passé.

The largest and indisputably the most important of these international gatherings was in conjunction with the four hundredth anniversary of Columbus's voyage to the Western Hemisphere. Held in Chicago, it officially began on October 12, 1892, four centuries after the Spanish fleet arrived in the Caribbean. That exploration was sponsored by Queen Isabella, who not only was a co-equal monarch with her husband, but also was more scientifically curious than he. Without her support and that of other women—including his mother-in-law—Columbus might never have sailed. Americans in the 1890s recognized that, and the first U.S. postage stamp honoring a woman was for Isabella; it was issued for this anniversary.

Women's participation in the event—variously called the World's Columbian Exposition or the Chicago World's Fair—arguably began with their experience in 1876, when the United States celebrated the centennial of its birth in Philadelphia. That event, with 180 structures on a huge fairground, attracted almost ten million visitors and exhibits from some fifty nations—but women were not included in its planning. After repeated requests, centennial officials finally allotted a small space to the American Woman Suffrage Association, headed by Lucy Stone and Julia Ward Howe. Although most of its exhibits focused on domesticity, other works by women also were displayed: among them were Rocky Mountain wildlife shown by a female taxidermist with the U.S. Geological Survey and pharmaceutical products that were prepared by students at the Women's Medical College of Pennsylvania. The event also featured books by women, including not only the expected novels and poetry, but also nonfiction on unconventional subjects such as astronomy, marble carving, and even watch repair.

Centennial authorities, however, refused to grant space to the rival National Woman Suffrage Association, which was led by Susan B. Anthony and Elizabeth Cady Stanton. The status of women at the time is clearly seen in the fact that when officers of the National decided to rent space outside of the fairground, they had to wait for Anthony's arrival: she was the only unmarried officer, and under Pennsylvania law, married women could not sign a rental contract. On the Fourth of July, Anthony led others in taking over a bandshell and reading aloud a "Declaration of Rights" modeled on the Declaration of Independence. (Stanton had written a similar one in 1848, when the world's first women's rights "convention" was held in her hometown of Seneca Falls, New York.) The 1876 rebels expected to be arrested for their disruption of the ceremonies, but instead, interested men fought each other to obtain copies of the document.

An older and presumably wiser Anthony took a more pragmatic approach to the Columbian celebration. The rival suffrage organizations had merged in 1890, but she nonetheless expected that radicals such as herself would be dismissed as they had been in 1876, and she quietly recruited women who were not part of the suffrage movement. Early in 1890, these women presented a petition to Congress asking for women on the Board of Managers for the event. Because the petition was signed by hundreds of Washington's finest ladies—including the wives of Cabinet members, Supreme Court justices, and their own wives and daughters—congressmen could not ignore it.

The eventual result was legislation creating a Board of Lady Managers that included two women from each state—and a generous appropriation of money for expenses and salaries. Although she contributed it to the cause, Bertha Honoré Palmer, who chaired the board, was entitled to an annual salary of $9,000, a munificent sum at the time. Usually known by her formal married name, Mrs. Potter Palmer, she was a rare woman who combined an elite social status with active feminism. A millionaire entrepreneur in Chicago who doubled her inheritance with keen investments, she later owned much of southwest Florida—where she conducted experiments in cattle breeding.

Palmer and her twenty-five-member executive committee found exhibits for the fair not only from all the American states, but also by women in forty-seven foreign nations. The Woman's Building in which these things were displayed was designed by a female architect and furnished by a female decorator, its murals and statues were by female artists, and an orchestra of women performed works by female composers.

The most striking portion of the event occurred in May, when the World's Congress of Representative Women convened. Led by May Wright Sewall of Indiana, it drew delegates from 126 women's organizations in twenty-seven nations. More than a dozen simultaneous sessions on a huge range of topics were held each hour of every day for a week, offering more than three hundred speakers to some 150,000 attendees. So eager were women for such networking that there were constant lines waiting to get in.

A marvel of organization, the Columbian Exposition was of tremendous significance to women—who, just a generation earlier, had little opportunity even to attend meetings, let alone be in charge of them. The explosion of ideas and personal contacts had echoing effects for years, as all across America women went back to small towns and began implementing things they learned in Chicago. A number of important organizations also grew out of the networking. Among them were the National Household Economic Association, which promoted the new field of home economics, as well as the Congress of Mothers, which evolved into the PTA. The National Council of Jewish Women and the precursor of the American Nurses Association also have roots in the exposition.

The American Library Association was seventeen years old at the time, as was the Dewey system for cataloging library books. It is this aspect of the exposition that has been well researched by Sarah Wadsworth and Wayne Wiegand in *Right Here I See My Own Books*. Wadsworth is an English professor at Marquette University, and Wiegand, currently at Florida State University, has a long list of credentials in library science. Their study focuses on the library of books by women that was on the second floor of the Woman's Building. Wadsworth and Wiegand have uncovered a wealth of detail about the library's development, as well as the collection of more than eight thousand books by women that was displayed.

The authors have combed archives, and their book contains a great deal of information that has never before been published. Their detailed research of this library adds a new dimension to our knowledge of women in the Progressive Era, feminism's most important time of change. The book also introduces a number of intriguing topics, including some previously little-known women, that merit exploration in still more study of the vast history of American women.

Keeping that continuum going remains almost as challenging today as it was in 1893, despite vastly improved communication. Given how much harder it was to organize causes in the 1890s, it is not especially surprising that when the fair ended, the contents of the Woman's Building were packed up and returned to their lenders. Despite feminist awareness that the 1893 library was unique, most of its books again were dispersed and rendered largely inaccessible. Palmer encouraged suggestions for a permanent women's museum, even pledging money for it, but after most of the exposition buildings burned in 1894, that idea came to naught.

Various feminists ever since have proposed national and international museums dedicated to women, but more than a century later, that goal—much less a congressional appropriation—remains unrealized. Wadsworth and Wiegand have generously pledged their royalties from *Right Here I See My Own Books* to this cause. We invite you to join them in supporting the National Women's History Museum.

Joan Bradley Wages, *President*
National Women's History Museum

Doris Weatherford
Author and NWHM Consultant

Acknowledgments

It's been a great experience. While doing research for his book *Irrepressible Reformer: A Biography of Melvil Dewey* (1996) at Columbia University in the early 1980s, Wayne Wiegand came across a cache of letters between Dewey (American Library Association president at the time) and Bertha Honoré Palmer, chair of the Board of Lady Managers of the World's Columbian Exposition, who in 1892 and early 1893 was putting together a library of books written by women for the exposition's Woman's Building. Because she intended for it to cover all books issued since Christopher Columbus set foot in the New World in 1492, Palmer's effort promised to create the most comprehensive collection of women's writings ever assembled. The discovery was too tempting to pass up. In subsequent years (and between other research projects) Wayne slowly accumulated data on the origins of the collection, and when he found an abbreviated author/title catalog of the library's contents in the papers of the Board of Lady Managers at the Chicago History Museum, he knew he needed an expert skilled in nineteenth-century American women's literature to analyze the collection.

Enter Sarah Wadsworth. Just completing a Ph.D. at the University of Minnesota, she agreed to join the project in 2000. Together we obtained a Carnegie-Whitney grant from the American Library Association to create a relational database of the contents of the Woman's Building Library that (unlike the abbreviated print version found at the Chicago History Museum) allows us to search by author, title, publisher, place and date of publication, state of origin, and broad Dewey Decimal number (which enables subject access). Then, in 2005, Melodie Fox came onboard and vastly improved the database while working on a graduate degree in Library and Information Studies through the University of Wisconsin–Milwaukee. Thanks to Melodie, and the team of LIS graduate assistants at the University of Wisconsin–Madison who preceded her, the database has allowed us to analyze the contents of the Woman's Building Library with much greater precision and a wider scope.

We have many people and institutions to thank for helping us complete this project. While teaching at the University of Kentucky (1976–1986), the University of Wisconsin–Madison (1987–2002), and Florida State University (2003 to 2010), Wayne benefited much from the services and materials in the collections amassed at each of these institutions over the generations. Most valuable were the collections at the Wisconsin Historical Society, which in the 1890s actively sought as much printed material from the 1893 World's Fair as the society could obtain. Wayne also thanks University of Kentucky College of Library Science dean Timothy Sineath, University of Wisconsin–Madison School of Library and Information Studies director Louise S. Robbins, and Florida State University College of Information deans Jane B. Robbins and her successor, Larry Dennis, for their support. The library and archives professionals, staff, and collections at the Chicago History Museum, the University of Kentucky, the University of Wisconsin–Madison (especially Michelle Besant and her staff), the Wisconsin Historical Society (especially James P. Danky), the University of North Carolina (especially Robert Anthony and his staff), Florida State University (especially Pam Doffek and her staff), Library of Congress, Newberry Library in Chicago, University of Minnesota, Marquette University, and Northwestern University (especially Scott Krafft) were particularly helpful.

At Marquette, Sarah benefited from two summers of support (a Summer Faculty Fellowship from the Graduate School and matching funds from the Klingler College of Arts and Sciences) that allowed her to crunch data using the new relational database and to draft chapters; a Junior Faculty Research Leave, spent reading and writing about fiction in the Woman's Building Library, and a sabbatical, devoted in part to revising and polishing the completed manuscript. Sarah would like to acknowledge Kelsey Squire, for many valuable conversations on regionalism; and she especially thanks the Department of English and her graduate research assistants over the years: Jen Anderson, Kathleen Burt, Alisa Dargiewicz, Erin Kogler, Heather Pavletic, and Matthew Van Zee. Collectively, they prepared bibliographies (Alisa, Erin, Heather, and Kathleen), tracked down elusive sources and authors (Kathleen and Matthew), proofread drafts (Kathleen and Jen), helped prepare the tables in chapter 2 (Jen), and helped to verify quotations (Jen and Kathleen). Each was a pleasure to work with.

At our request, several scholars read all or parts of the manuscript, and we owe them special thanks. Doris Weatherford read a complete late draft and gave us a number of valuable tips for improvement. In addition, we have benefited from the careful commentary of Michael D. Cohen, who graciously read a full draft at an earlier stage of its development. Angela Sorby, Faith Barrett, and Donald Ross provided perceptive and often witty suggestions for several chapters. Amy Blair, Heather Hathaway, and Jodi Melamed also offered thoughtful feedback. Edward M. Griffin, Karen Roggenkamp, Donald Ross, Danielle Tissinger, and the Early American subfield at the University of Minnesota provided helpful direction at an early stage of the analysis. Marija Dalbello at Rutgers and Jeffrey Garrett at Northwestern facilitated visits to their institutions, where we were able to present our work-in-progress. Both at Rutgers and at Northwestern, sharing our ideas, fielding questions, and discussing our findings with faculty and graduate students proved constructive.

Working with acquisitions editor Brian Halley and managing editor Carol Betsch at the University of Massachusetts Press has been a delight. Mary Bellino, the best copyeditor we've ever worked with, helped smooth out the rough edges. We are profoundly grateful for her wisdom and editorial acumen. Roberta Engleman earned our enduring gratitude by contributing a top-notch index as a special contribution to the National Women's History Museum. Thanks also to the two anonymous readers who reviewed the manuscript. Their commentary was thorough and perceptive, and we value their critiques. Thanks also go to the contributors of the special issue of *Libraries & Culture* devoted to the Woman's Building Library (Winter 2006)—Candy Gunther Brown, Bunny Gallagher, Amina Gautier, Barbara Hochman, Anne Lundin, Angela Sorby, and Emily Todd, who deserves special mention for helping this collaboration come about. And a very special thank you goes to Sabrina Black for assisting with the tables in chapter 2.

An earlier version of chapter 1 appeared in *Signs: Journal of Women in Culture and Society* 35.3 (Spring 2010): 699–722, © 2010 by the University of Chicago. All rights reserved. A portion of the material in chapter 5 appeared in *European Journal of American Studies* 2011 (2), http://ejas.revues.org/9067. We thank the publishers of both journals for permission to reprint material from our articles.

One final note. Both of us owe much to our immediate families for patience and support. Sarah thanks her husband, Marc Black, who has aided and abetted in countless ways, and dedicates this book to her mother, Beverley, and children, Sabrina and Blaise; Wayne thanks Shirl, his wife of forty-six years, and dedicates it to the women in his immediate family who have mirrored her strength.

RIGHT HERE I SEE
MY OWN BOOKS

Introduction

In *A Jury of Her Peers: American Women Writers from Anne Bradstreet to Annie Proulx* (2009), Elaine Showalter reflects on the long absence of a comprehensive history of American women's writing. (Hers is the first.) She posits several reasons for the extended delay, among them the daunting scope of a literary history encompassing nearly four hundred years of astonishing productivity. Similar obstacles impede the study of the Woman's Building Library at the 1893 World's Columbian Exposition: a collection of more than eight thousand texts written, illustrated, edited, or translated by women which (like Showalter's history but international and multidisciplinary in scope) aimed to document a comprehensive chronology of women's writing.[1]

At the same time, however, the Woman's Building Library presents unrivaled opportunities to follow the advice offered by Margaret Ezell in *Writing Women's Literary History* (1993). In this groundbreaking study, Ezell urges literary historians to "be conscious of the criteria used" to portray traditions and create canons and "actively seek to challenge and expand the range of possibilities." She writes: "Instead of trying to create a single, monolithic scheme of women's literature, in which every piece neatly fits the predetermined design or is excluded and devalued, we can recognize that the literary past is much more chaotic and diverse than we have previously implied in our literary histories." The construction and contents of the Woman's Building Library abundantly reflect both the chaos and the diversity Ezell identifies and thus provide an important site to test assumptions and correct misconceptions that have influenced our historiographies and shaped our literary histories.[2]

For over a century now, the World's Columbian Exposition has been a subject of scholarly fascination in many disciplines. Historians and popular culture analysts, especially, have found fertile ground for exploring myriad facets of late nineteenth-century American life. Yet the fair's culture of print has received surprisingly little attention, despite the fact that manifestations of print culture abounded on the exposition's grounds. Fair directors even included a literary exhibit in the Manufactures and Liberal Arts Building. There, in the building's northwest corner, many of America's six hundred publishers set up impressive book displays. Harper and Brothers, for example, spotlighted Lew Wallace's best-selling *Ben-Hur,* along with works by Bret Harte, Frank Stockton, and the ever-popular, ever-controversial Mark Twain. Charles Scribner's Sons featured "books in gorgeous bindings," Funk & Wagnalls, G. & C. Merriam, and the Century Company (which also loaned drawings and book illustrations to the Woman's and Children's buildings) displayed their dictionaries, and William Wood & Company its medical texts. Houghton Mifflin assembled a library of dark bookcases topped with busts of Longfellow, Holmes, Hawthorne, Whittier, and Stowe to showcase its prestigious Riverside Press imprint. While the Riverside backlist defined the developing literary canon dominated by male authors, the frontlist titles Houghton Mifflin displayed featured male and female writers in equal numbers. Nearby, a raft of magazine publishers—Harper, Scribner's, the *Century,* Lippincott, and Godey, among others—displayed their wares.[3]

And, along with these commercial exhibits, the exposition housed a host of small libraries, in addition to the monumental one in the Woman's Building. One of the most impressive could be found in the Children's Building, which was sponsored and managed by the fair's Board of Lady Managers. "In it are found the books of all lands," Moses Handy wrote in his *Official Directory,* "and in all languages."[4] One-fourth of the six hundred volumes were signed by their authors. The children's storyteller and author Clara Doty Bates had sought "to select the library from the child's and youth's standard," rather than choosing books thought suitable "from the point of view of the adult." Bates decorated the walls with illustrations from the popular youth magazines *St. Nicholas, Wide Awake, Youth's Companion,* and *Harper's Young People,* placed donated copies of current issues on low tables for children to enjoy, and assembled an exhibit of manuscripts, proof sheets, and artwork to illustrate the making of magazines. She also obtained original sketches, signed manuscripts, and autographed illustrations and asked local schoolchildren to send her lists of favorite authors.[5] Here visitors were allowed to handle—and thus read—the volumes—although the books were "not for the children to read so much," the monthly *World's Columbian Exposition Illustrated* advised, "but to give mothers a clue towards the establishing of a library at home, for this children's home is not to educate children, but to show mothers how children may be educated."[6] Parents, teachers, and librarians interested in the pioneering area of children's library services could peruse the shelves for guidance in selection. "Still, children from every part of the country have haunted the room . . . to lose all knowledge of outside wonders and beauties under the spell of some favorite book," Bates later reported. "They wearied of sight-seeing and pageantry, but never wearied of stories."[7]

The American Library Association assembled a model library that visiting librarians and town officials could use to develop collections in their own communities (see chapter 1). A library in the Department of Mines and Mining contained works loaned by numerous U.S. mining companies, and most state buildings included libraries of works by favorite sons and daughters. Germany's building featured a display of every periodical published in the country, as well as a library of recently printed books in exemplary bindings. France outdid its neighbor by displaying masterful reproductions of illuminated manuscripts in "superb specimens of artistic binding."[8] Yet despite this abundance of books and periodicals, the Columbian Exposition has figured only peripherally in discussions of literary history.[9]

Part of the reason is timing. The exposition took place when American literature was just becoming institutionalized as a subject of academic study ripe for canon-building. That more than a century would pass before the publication of a comprehensive literary history of American women's writing points up this fact: in 1893 a distinct, cohesive four-hundred-year tradition of women's writing was a revolutionary idea. And, as the story of the Woman's Building Library demonstrates, literature as an institution, no less than the libraries that contain it, plays a powerful role in consolidating audiences and mobilizing groups of readers. A product of a "separatist political strategy" combined with a vibrant women's culture, this library is a prime example of the kind of "female institution building" that, as the historian Estelle Freedman illustrates, "helped sustain women's participation in both social reform and political activism."[10]

In "Mothers of Literature," an article published in the exposition miscellany *The Columbian Woman* (1893), Mary Newbury Adams (cofounder of the Northern Iowa Woman Suffrage Society) succinctly surveys the conjunction of women's culture, literature, and community building leading up to this transitional period in women's history. Adams writes of the "fitting of woman to her legitimate work as religious, literary, and industrial leaders in the abbeys" of Western Europe. Under the direction of "holy women, of great endowments," the abbeys made possible a higher civilization by "introduc[ing] ingenuity and art, showing how men and women could dignify life with industry and thought." Manuscript and, later, print culture played a crucial part in this process. In the history of the abbeys, Adams observes, "we see how the best collected thought of that day which they could secure was put into literature, training those men and women in Saxon language that molded the hearts of the common people, uniting them by attraction through literature and religion, thus building the fire of patriotism." This process of uniting the learned and uneducated classes, enlightening the "common people," and, ultimately, advancing the enterprise of nation building originated, in Adams's view, with the uniquely feminine power of domesticity: "Women were the ones to unite the ancient people by fire on the hearth, to prepare them in the later time for uniting about the light of litera- ture." In many ways, the Woman's Building Library epitomizes the relationship between women and literature that Adams articulates in this quintessentially "Columbian" fusion of domestic, progressive, and antimodern ideologies. As this paradoxical mix suggests, the library can deepen our understanding of the cultural, institutional, and gender histories that intersect in the production and performance of the Columbian Exposition.[11]

The Woman's Building Library represented important components of the culture of print that evolved and helped shape history in the four centuries since Columbus landed in the New World. It was a cultural space that invited the exchange of social capital by millions of visitors to the exposition. It was also an example of what Michel Foucault calls "heterotopias": actual places that "are something like counter-sites . . . in which the real sites, all the other real sites that can be found within the culture, are simultaneously represented, contested, and inverted." In contrast to a utopia ("a placeless place"), a heterotopia has a physi- cal location, although it is nevertheless "outside of all places."[12] For our purposes, the concept of "heterotopia" provides a powerful critical lens, since the Woman's Building reflected a version of the surrounding culture that was both "real" (and pragmatic) and "unreal," or idealized. Applying this theoretical construct helps separate the image from the underlying reality and reveal distortions and inver- sions in order to interpret the actual conditions this "other space" reflects.

"Juxtaposing in a single real place several spaces, several sites that are in them- selves incompatible" (as Foucault writes), the sites of the Columbian Exposi- tion were simultaneously illusory and concrete, universal yet multifarious. An actual site within Chicago, the exposition (often referred to as the "White City" because most of its important buildings were painted white) stood at the same time distinctly apart from it, isolated yet penetrable, apparently open and acces- sible to all yet "hid[ing] curious exclusions." The World's Fair may be seen as contrasting versions of "other space": "heterotopias of indefinitely accumulating time" and those that are "linked . . . to time in its most fleeting, transitory, precar- ious aspect, to time in the mode of the festival." Exemplifying the former type, museums and libraries form "a sort of general archive" in order to "enclose in one place all times, all epochs, all forms, all tastes." With their goal of collecting "all women's writing from everywhere and every time," the Board of Lady Managers aspired to produce precisely this kind of timeless, limitless, all-encompassing archive—"a place of all times that is itself outside of time." Yet with its proximity to the exposition's carnivalesque Midway and its location within the ephemeral White City, the library also possessed characteristics of the alternative "absolutely temporary" heterotopic mode. The Columbian Exposition, with its many spectacles and exhibits, conflated these two forms of "other space": the fleeting and the infinite, the seasonal festival and the eternal museum.[13]

It is not our project to "prove" that the Woman's Building Library was a heterotopia. Rather, we invoke the concept to emphasize the unique relationship this site bears to the culture that produced it. It is tempting to interpret the library as simply a snapshot or microcosm of late nineteenth-century print culture. In fact, however, the context of the World's Fair complicates interpretation in manifold ways. Books that found their way into the library were not a random sampling of women's writing, nor were they "representative" in any straightforward way of the culture as a whole. This does not suggest that the library is less worthy of scrutiny or less significant as a cultural landmark. It does, however, force an additional layer of analysis. In approaching the Woman's Building Library, we have sought to ask not only what the library and its history reflect, but how that reflection represents an ideological "revision." In our analysis, the library's conflicting currents converged uneasily to produce a unique and often contradictory blend of the timeless and the time-bound. In pragmatic terms, the result was a peerless collection of predominantly nineteenth-century books shaped by a sociohistorical reality the library both reflects and refutes.

In *The Incorporation of America: Culture and Society in the Gilded Age,* Alan Trachtenberg argues that the White City "implied not only a new form of urban experience but a new way of experiencing the urban world"—"as *spectators.*" He writes, "The Fair was delivered to them, made available to them, . . . not as an actual place, a real city, but as a frank illusion, a picture of what a city, a real society, might look like." And, although the White City "represented itself *as* a representation, an admitted sham . . . that sham, it insisted, held a truer vision of the real than did the troubled world sprawling beyond its gates."[14] Trachtenberg's insights invite reflection on the relationship of this spectacular, theatrical performance to the real nineteenth-century city. Foucault, like Trachtenberg, emphasizes that "other spaces" improve on perceptions of reality (if only locally or temporarily) through the agency of the imagination. This capacity to project a "truer vision of the real" aptly characterizes not only the World's Columbian Exposition but also what one observer described as the "theater" of the Woman's Building, with its "stage" where various women's groups "met and conferred or differed."[15] It also informs many of the texts the Woman's Building Library archived for an evanescent posterity.

The chapters that follow examine this tension between reflecting and rejecting society at large. They also apply to the Woman's Building Library what

James Clifford (building on the work of Mary Louise Pratt) calls a "contact zone" approach, which explores relational meanings, often in situations involving imbalances of power, or "uneven reciprocity." Clifford notes, "When museums are seen as contact zones, their organizing structure as a *collection* becomes an ongoing historical, political, moral *relationship*—a power-charged set of exchanges, of push and pull." He suggests that "a contact perspective views all culture-collecting strategies as responses to particular histories of dominance, hierarchy, resistance, and mobilization."[16]

Viewing the Woman's Building Library from a contact perspective helps to foreground dynamics of gender, race, and class and reveal the impact—both positive and negative—of the complex relationships, histories, and modes of valuation that inform the collection. Chapters 1 and 2 show women adopting the framework and mechanisms of a patriarchal bureaucracy to accomplish decidedly antipatriarchal ends. In chapter 3 we examine the prominent role two New York groups played in the library's development and management. In differing ways, each helped "sway" the library toward more progressive or reformist ends. Chapter 4 offers a glimpse of the library in action and shows the sometimes surprising ways contemporary visitors responded to it as "other space." The remaining three chapters focus on the collection itself. In chapter 5 we look at the substantial body of texts authored by women who took part in the administration of the Woman's Building or had other official or professional roles connected to the exposition or its congresses. In many instances, these "Columbian Women" writers used fiction to critique society and offer their own "heterotopic" revisions of fin-de-siècle culture. In chapter 6 we explore the impact and representation of race in the library, and in chapter 7 we consider the collection within the context of regionalism, nationalism, and the shifting "center" of American culture. Seeking a middle ground between an enumerative bibliographical description and the kind of carefully engineered selection that would merely reproduce the existing canon, the three analytical chapters broadly survey the library's contents in order to interpret the site holistically. At the same time, the earlier historical chapters inform readings of a wide range of individual texts presented in these later chapters. Finally, a brief epilogue traces the library in the aftermath of the exposition and through the first decades of the twentieth century. In presenting the history of the Woman's Building Library and revealing something of its complexity and richness, we hope to open it up for others to enjoy and explore.[17]

Paradoxically, the library's wide-ranging roots, all-too-brief flourishing, and sharply arrested growth (creating a collection "frozen" in time) earn it an enduring place in the history of women's authorship. Yet in many ways, as these chapters show, the story this collection tells about women and their role in print culture is different from those articulated in conventional literary and cultural histories. While not without its own biases, the Woman's Building Library lacks the academic emphasis of those more familiar heterotopias—collections developed by research universities, scholarly organizations, prestigious publishers, and other elite cultural institutions. On its shelves stood scores of texts that fall outside the purview of traditional libraries, including many that were deliberately excluded from important archives and bibliographies. Moreover, the process through which the library developed was in many ways one of decentering and recentering, both contesting and inverting the prevailing hierarchies of book publication and dissemination. In the American section, for example, women often selected texts written and even published in their own regions, remote from the publishing establishment concentrated in the Northeast. Relatively few of the women represented were professional authors who supported themselves by their writing, and, while the collection included many now-canonical works, a large proportion of the texts were neither "literary" nor "popular." Many volumes displayed there are unknown today, their authors long forgotten and obscured by time. On many levels this collection challenges prevailing perceptions of the nineteenth-century literary world.

Finally, the Woman's Building Library provides an unrivaled opportunity to contemplate fiction by American women en masse, and for those interested in noncanonical nineteenth-century women's writing it offers an embarrassment of riches. But the library has a more elusive value as well, one recoverable only by considering the collection within the historical context of the 1890s and attempting to decipher the relation this "other space" bears to the actual place and time of the American fin de siècle. Rather than viewing the surviving compilation of titles and authors as a transparent window opening onto an unobstructed panorama of women's writing on "all lines of thought" from print's earliest days, in this book we regard the library as simultaneously a representation and a redaction of ways late nineteenth-century women conceived of women's writing and constructed it as a meaningful body of texts. Construed in this way, the Woman's Building Library can be likened to a mirror that reflects the way women's literary culture was perceived by hundreds of women on state and national women's club boards, thousands of women who aided their efforts, and hundreds of thousands of exposition visitors of both sexes who marveled at its contents and consequently formed—or revised—their notions of women's contribution to the cultures of the world. But, in true carnival fashion, the heterotopic looking-glass always possesses within it the creative possibilities of distortion and inversion as well as the mimetic powers of reflection and representation. And so the journey begins . . .

1

By Invitation Only

At 9:30 a.m. on July 21, 1893, members of the American Library Association (ALA) gathered for their seventh conference session in the Woman's Building, within the "White City" of the World's Columbian Exposition in Chicago. As guests of the Board of Lady Managers (BLM)—the group responsible for the design, construction, and exhibits of the marvelous building in which they were meeting—they sat in the middle of the rotunda on the building's ground floor. Several BLM members mingled with their ALA guests. That the ALA selected Chicago for its 1893 conference was not surprising. For two years the exposition's World's Fair Auxiliary worked hard to convince hundreds of professional associations to choose the Columbian Exposition as a site for their annual conferences; the ALA committed in 1891. Not until June 26, 1893, however, did ALA president Melvil Dewey accept an invitation from Virginia Meredith, chair of the BLM's Committee of Awards, to hold at least one of its conference sessions in the Woman's Building. "I will try and make the women specially prominent on that day," he promised, "and think we can make it be a desirable feature."[1]

What particularly interested the ALA members gathered there was the library on the building's second floor: a unique collection of printed materials written, illustrated, edited, or translated by women from all over the world. Never before had such a collection been assembled. That morning the ALA met in the rotunda to view and commemorate this landmark library. Because the rotunda rose to the full height of the building and was capped with a skylight, many of those attending could glimpse the library's entrance from where they sat.

As the assembled ALA members knew, the library upstairs—sixty feet long, forty feet wide, and twenty feet high—had several functions. Organizers intended that it exhibit books authored by women since 1492, that it serve as a comfortable and aesthetically distinctive gathering place for Woman's Building visitors, and that through resident librarians it operate as a source of information about women. The ALA, from whose membership resident librarians were drawn, hoped it would model the role women had embraced in pioneering the new professional field of librarianship. These functions were largely complementary; nevertheless, the convergence of the ALA and the BLM at the midpoint of the fair's six-month run brings into focus competing visions of culture and progress that contended within the public space of the Woman's Building and in the larger arena of the Columbian Exposition. Nowhere were these competing views more evident than in the discourses of inclusion and exclusion that informed the cultural projects of the Woman's Building Library and the American Library Association.

The women responsible for the creation of the Woman's Building Library were keenly aware of the unprecedented opportunity the building afforded to spotlight women's contribution to fine and applied arts, education, family life, service, and other fields in which women had labored. Aware that women's work had long been undervalued, they were highly attuned to the venue's enormous advantages, as well as its potential disadvantages. Although the question of whether or not women's work should be integrated into exhibits throughout the exposition had been hotly contested (see chapter 2), advocates of a special women's exhibit hall had prevailed. In the end, the decision to erect a special building to house exhibits by and about women reflected a political compromise. While upholding the underlying construction of "True Womanhood," the exhibits and events held in the Woman's Building sought to extend the range of women's domestic activities into the public sphere. As this compromise suggests, both the building's physical space and the planning and organizing that went into it became a battleground on which conflicting ideas about women and womanhood vied.

Like the debate over separate or integrated exhibits, the library's interior design reflected both a validation of the feminine values associated with separate-sphere ideology—relegating women to the privacy of the home and restricting their participation in public life—and a critique of that ideology. In order to signal the resulting combination of values—femininity, domesticity, and benevolence, but also education, progress, and professionalism—the BLM had paid special attention to the aesthetics of the room. The committee that oversaw the library's design carefully devised a decor that recalled the reassuring solidity and exclusiveness of a well-appointed private library. In taking this approach, the committee departed from architectural and decorating imperatives of (mostly male) library leaders, who in the 1890s preferred to emphasize bureaucratic efficiency and utilitarian purpose in planning library spaces. But

Candace Wheeler, the nationally known New York textile designer and interior decorator who designed it, had very particular ideas about libraries that emphasized the connection between these traditionally masculine spaces and the feminine sphere of domesticity.

In *Principles of Home Decoration* (1903), Wheeler insists that a home library is "not only to hold books, but to make the family at home in a literary atmosphere." Thus, she concludes, the color scheme "may, and should, be much warmer and stronger than that of a parlour pure and simple, the very constancy and hardness of its use indicating tints of strength and resistance." For Wheeler, "such a room is apt to be a fascinating one," in part because of its variety of uses and in part because of the family treasures it holds: "Books, pictures, papers, photographs, bits of decorative needlework, all centre here, and all are on most orderly behaviour, like children at a company dinner." Moreover, she suggests, the aesthetics of the room should blend harmoniously with its natural surroundings, emphasizing the distinctiveness of its location and environment.[2] Elsewhere in the Woman's Building, Wheeler had felt herself "constantly restrained" by the need to take a "safe" approach to interior design and decoration, but the library allowed her more scope. "I felt that both its purpose and its place demanded the use of every appropriate means of beauty," she later wrote. Noting her desire to integrate its decor with the panorama of Lake Michigan and its boundless horizon, she recalled: "After seeing the nobility of the room's proportions, and the one great window which seemed to take in all the blue of the sky and the expanse of water which lay under it, I felt that it would be an insult to this dominant color to introduce anything in this sheltered space which would be at war with it; consequently, I chose modulations of blue and green for the color treatment."[3]

The library's design apparently achieved the desired effect—that of recreating the atmosphere of a lavish home library within the public space of the Woman's Building in a manner that harmonized naturally with its physical setting. Maud Howe Elliott, daughter of Julia Ward Howe and editor of *Art and Handicraft in the Woman's Building,* praised the domestic character of the interior design: "From a purely artistic standpoint the library is the most important feature of the building, after the Hall of Honor. . . . The room has a character and individuality that we rarely find save in the house of some esthetic lover of books. . . . [T]here is no single apartment in the whole Fair where [the visitor] will find himself so pleasantly at home."[4] Equally impressed, the magazine *Art Amateur* declared it "among the very best bits of interior decoration in the Fair" and described it in terms that suggest an idealized feminine deportment, noting that "the whole effect of the room is reposeful, quiet and cheerful."[5] To BLM secretary Susan Gale Cooke, the room's color scheme "was its crowning charm,

The Woman's Building, World's Columbian Exposition, Chicago, 1893. Photographer—Harrison. Chicago History Museum. ICHi-16265. Reproduced by permission.

The Woman's Building Library. *World's Columbian Exposition Illustrated*, August 1893. Wisconsin Historical Society. WHi-82899. Reproduced by permission.

being a harmonious blending of shades of green, brown, blue and gold into a general tone that invited rest and quiet, and suggested elegant literary ease." Ellen Henrotin, a member of the BLM, pronounced it simply "the most beautiful room in the building," and the *New York Times* gushed, "The entire room in every detail breathes the spirit of decorative art." The *Chautauquan* informed its readers that "the large and well-filled library presents a cosy appearance."[6] The overwhelmingly positive response attests to the success of Wheeler's committee in using interior design to project the outward appearance and feminine values of the private, domestic sphere onto this very public space.

As is intimated by Wheeler's mention of the "nobility of the room's proportions," the exhibits and decor cultivated a high-cultural elitism along with an elegant domesticity. An elaborately carved, twelve-foot oak fireplace formed the room's focal point, its opening screened by a custom-made hanging of blue silk brocade woven with a pattern of stylized oak leaves that matched the room's portieres. At either end of the library stood two large standards framed with wings, containing a collection of autographs and documents written by such noble and notable women as Queen Mary, Queen Elizabeth, Mary Queen of Scots, Catherine de Medici, George Eliot, and Elizabeth Barrett Browning.[7] A gilded frieze encircled the walls, and affixed to the ceiling was a large painting by Wheeler's daughter Dora Wheeler Keith, depicting allegorical figures framed within large oval medallions. Enclosed within a border of Venetian scrollwork, the central oval featured mythical figures representing realms of intellectual endeavor—Science, Literature, and Imagination. Medallions in the corners, connected by images of drapery intertwined with lilies and streamers, framed the literary genres of History, Romance, Poetry, and Drama in a similar allegorical guise. To avoid straining their necks, viewers could examine the images by peering into a mirror placed atop a large dark oak table in the room's center, hand-carved with sixteenth-century designs. Visitors could repose in similarly carved antique oak chairs and sofas upholstered in dark green leather by Associated Artists of New York, a firm Candace Wheeler had founded with Louis Comfort Tiffany. Paneling of the same dark oak lined the walls above the carved walnut bookcases, on top of which, at calculated intervals, specimens of hammered brass and pottery from Rookwood—one of the first U.S. companies owned and operated by a woman—alternated (on special occasions) with graceful palms. On the walls above the glass-covered bookcases hung portraits of many women whose works appeared in the collection, including the early American novelist Charlotte Lennox and a prominent oil painting of the popular American poet Lydia Huntley Sigourney, framed autographs of women writers, and illustrations by Mary Hallock Foote, Kate Greenaway, and other women artists. Wheeler also made sure that "busts of notable women by notable women were decoratively used." Chandeliers above, painted wall panels at either end, and a Turkish carpet patterned in red and blue completed the decor. All this contrasted sharply with other libraries recently erected across the country, almost all of which exhibited busts of famous men, whose names and literary quotations were often chiseled into building cornices and whose portraits frequently hung over library fireplaces.[8]

In addition to evoking Old World stateliness and refinement, the room's decor prominently displayed artwork created by and representing American women. Thus it implicitly placed the contributions of American women within the context of European traditions, set their work alongside those of the most admired European women, and distinguished Americans among all nationalities represented as meriting heightened attention. And, while some items on display alluded to American racial and cultural diversity (see chapter 6), these allusions were mediated or interpreted through Eurocentric perspectives. In one corner a five-foot mahogany cabinet with glass sides and glass shelves showcased an early portrait of Harriet Beecher Stowe, copies of forty-two translations of *Uncle Tom's Cabin*, its two-volume first edition, the latest reprint by Houghton Mifflin, and "a beautiful silver inkstand" Stowe had received from English supporters. The inkstand stood "ten inches in height, eighteen inches wide, and twenty-eight in length," a Connecticut official proudly noted, and represented "two slaves freed from their shackles." A marble bust of Stowe (still living in 1893, but too frail to journey to Chicago) gazed serenely from a granite pedestal nearby.[9]

"Altogether I was satisfied," Wheeler concluded. "I felt that the women of all America would not be sorry to be women in the face of all that women had done besides living and fulfilling their recognized duties." Most visitors seemed to agree. In late June a Canadian fairgoer reported to her local newspaper that "a whole day devoted to this one room would repay one richly." Frances Willard, president of the Woman's Christian Temperance Union (WCTU), was effusive. Echoing the rhetoric of progress that pervaded the entire exposition, Willard identified the library as "an amazing collection of books written by women" that demonstrated a history of women in letters. To Willard, the library revealed this history by showing "what a thin, long line it was during many centuries, and how it has rapidly broadened out in a magnificent way since education has opened the door to almost every department of science and art." "Had the Board of Lady Managers accomplished nothing else than bringing these books together—the literary performances of women in all ages and all countries" she exclaimed, "it would have done a great deed." BLM member Rebecca A. Felton (who, in 1922, would become the first female U.S. senator) observed that the library's "very atmosphere became redolent with the greatness of American women in literature and fine art."[10]

As they made their way to their conference session on that midsummer morning, ALA members had ample opportunity to experience the fair's vibrant, up-to-date, eclectic, and carnivalesque atmosphere as well as its more sedate and self-consciously refined museumlike exhibits. Like everyone else visiting the White City that day, they arrived by one of several modes of transportation designed to move them swiftly and efficiently into and around the grounds. Some had come by rail, alighting by one of the thirty-five tracks leading into the Terminal Railway Station just behind the Administration Building. Others had taken steamers and disembarked from Lake Michigan. Still others had ridden in horse-drawn coaches from downtown. Some had walked the Midway Plaisance—the mile-long stretch linking Washington Park to the fair. Those who strolled along the Midway had the opportunity to view a variety of popularized anthropological exhibits. They might have gazed on provocatively draped women performing exotic dances. It was here, for example, that a dancer called "Little Egypt" introduced America to the belly dance—subsequently called the "hootchy-kootchy"—which one BLM member pronounced "highly immoral and degrading."[11] Midway pedestrians also encountered novel entertainments such as the mammoth 265-foot Ferris Wheel, which cost five cents per ride and could accommodate 1,440 people at a time.

Inside the park, ALA members could hop aboard an electric railway circling the exposition every forty-five minutes, or they could pay seventy-five cents an hour to be "wheeled about the grounds and through the buildings" in "roller chairs" with enterprising college students as guides. Elsewhere launches, small boats, and a fleet of twenty gondolas traversed the waterways, all regularly patrolled by the U.S. Navy. ALA members could enjoy the exposition's clean streets, sanitary drinking water, and 3,116 public toilets—a contrast to what they found elsewhere in Chicago.[12] Altogether, the White City was a "countersite" that corrected what its developers perceived as flaws in the modern city. The White City was cleaner, prettier, more orderly and homogeneous: an idealized "City Beautiful" codified, categorized, and neatly compartmentalized by geographical space (e.g., the Illinois Building, the East India Building) and socioeconomic sector (e.g., mines, manufacturing, agriculture).[13] With its rigid allotments of public space and a bureaucratic impulse toward social, economic, and cultural divisions, the White City was, like other heterotopias, apparently open and accessible to all, yet "hid[ing] curious exclusions."[14]

The Columbian Exposition vibrated with a diversity of world cultures never before assembled in one place. On its 686 acres, forty-seven different countries and most of the U.S. states and territories displayed some 65,000 exhibits in buildings erected specially for the fair. For all its apparent progressiveness and cosmopolitanism, however, the exposition was relentlessly exclusive even as it conveyed the image of openness and inclusiveness. In many exhibits, visitors would find little that documented the contributions of women, immigrants, the working classes, and other marginalized groups. Prejudice against these groups was made conspicuous by their absence. Buildings representing Deep South states, for example, exhibited displays that celebrated white cultures and sectional heritage but paid little attention to the cultural contributions and heritage of the millions of African Americans living in these states.[15] Although the Woman's Building Library included some works by African American women as well as numerous works by white women that addressed racial injustice (see chapter 6), the BLM had refused to cooperate with African American women who requested representation in the Woman's Building. If ALA members noticed such omissions, however, they made no public protest. Like the BLM, the ALA manifested exclusionary cultural biases in the professional practices and services it had advocated since its formation in 1876.

The Court of Honor—both its name and its architecture trumpeting the kind of enduring institutions, timeless values, and elite European lineage the White City celebrated—constituted the fair's main focal point. At the center of this resplendent enclave sparkled the Great Basin, with Daniel Chester French's sixty-five-foot *Statue of the Republic* towering above the water at the east end and Frederick William MacMonnies's *Columbian Fountain* splashing and frothing at the west. Around its banks clustered many of the fair's most magnificent edifices, including the Administration, Electricity, Machinery, Agriculture, Manufactures, and Liberal Arts buildings: a monumental mingling of the marvelous and the mundane. Every day tens of thousands packed into the buildings, walkways, and open spaces of the Court of Honor; every night many thousands remained to witness it shimmering like a fantastic mirage under a flood of artificial light, with radiant beams "playing red, emerald, and gold under the white waters" of MacMonnies's fountain. "Nothing that I have ever seen in Paris, in London, in St. Petersburg, or in Rome," wrote English journalist William T. Stead, "could equal the effect produced by the illumination of the great white palaces" at night.[16] Stead, like many others who described their experience of the White City, gives the impression of having stepped into an "unreal, virtual space," a fantasyland of realistic illusion and illusive reality that destabilized the image of solidity and timelessness its exhibits projected.[17]

Fronting the Midway, on the northwest quadrant of the exposition grounds, flanked by the Illinois and Children's buildings, stood the Woman's Building— its physical placement appropriately signposting the social position of women as embedded in the local, familial, and domestic. The fair's Department of

Horticulture had given permission to Jules Lemoine, principal gardener of the city of Paris, to use the space around the Woman's Building for a "floricultural" exhibit; as a result of his efforts, meticulously manicured landscaping circled the building, inviting fairgoers to rest on public benches amidst "gorgeous rhododendrons and azaleas" shaded by silver spruces, cedars, Japanese maples, palms, and "a single black oak at the northern entrance." (As a French visitor observed of this portion of the fairgrounds, "women, children, flowers, this is a logical progression.") Directly in front of the building, which rose up against "a backdrop of stately old oak trees," lay an ornamental lagoon, crowned with a picturesque wooded island.[18] ALA members traversing its waters by gondola could disembark on a convenient landing in front of the Woman's Building and walk up to a flower-bedecked terrace six feet above the water's edge and one hundred feet in front of its triple-arched main entrance.

Over the entrance, directly beneath a pediment decorated with nineteen-year-old Alice Rideout's bas-relief representations of Literature, Home Life, Art, and Beneficence (all considered appropriate endeavors within women's sphere), an open balcony afforded a superb view of the lagoon and the attractions beyond its banks. Higher up, above the second floor and accessible by elevator, perched the Roof Garden Café, with Rideout's twelve-foot sculpted "angels" roosting at its four corners amid potted ferns and arching palms—a "hen-coop" *American Architect* quipped, "for petticoated hens, old and young." Although only two hundred people had dined there on May 1, by October the café would accommodate more than four thousand customers daily.[19] There, visitors of diverse races and nationalities sipped tea and munched quail on toast—a favorite combination and one of the café's specialties. For café guests, the self-consciously feminine refinement of the venue and menu was only slightly marred by signs on the railings admonishing them not to spit over the sides.

With dimensions of 199 by 388 feet, a footprint of 1.8 acres, and total floor space of 3.3 acres, the Woman's Building was one of the smallest of the fair's major exhibit halls; nevertheless, it soon became a must-see attraction. As Kate Field wrote for the *Chicago Tribune* toward the end of the fair: "If popularity be a sign of approval, the Woman's Building outranks all others. I never entered its portals without being oppressed by an overflow of humanity. Every woman who visited the Fair made it the center of her orbit. Here was a structure designed by a woman, filled with the work of women. Thousands discovered women were not only doing something, but had been working seriously for many generations."[20] Other observers perceived the Woman's Building as the architectural epitome of feminine dignity and grace. BLM president Bertha Honoré Palmer confidently dubbed it "The American Woman's Declaration of Independence"—a rhetorical fusing of national and feminine identities in a pointed inversion of the patriarchal declaration of the country's founding fathers.[21] Thomas Palmer, president of the exposition's National Commission, echoed her, saying that the building represented "woman's declaration of independence; her assertion to do whatever man can do, and do it well." BLM member Virginia Meredith found the Woman's Building "chaste and delicate," "a restful and refreshing point for the eye" as one gazed along the Court of Honor, and a worker in the building reportedly confided to Maud Howe Elliott: "I call it the flying building. It seems to lift the weight off my feet when I look at those big angels."[22]

A number of others joined the chorus of approval, portraying the building in terms of femininity, American identity, or both. Elliott described it as "essentially feminine in character," noting that "it has the qualities of reserve, delicacy, and refinement." To Candace Wheeler, it was "the most peaceably human of all the buildings" and "like a man's ideal of woman—delicate, dignified, pure, and fair to look upon." *Harper's Bazar* attributed to the building "a deft and dainty touch," adding that "in some way or other it seems homelike."[23] In pronouncing "the Woman's Building and its deep significance" the "'new birth of our new soil,' the best that is American," one male author seems to have idealized femininity as the pinnacle of American identity, although, oddly, he also found the Woman's Building "gentlemanly."[24] Less impressed with the building's design (though no less reliant on stock stereotypes of feminine identity), a male architect quibbled, "Its fault is one which makes it especially suitable for the purpose for which it is to be used—it is chaste and timid."[25] Despite (or perhaps in response to) the widespread use of such stereotypes, the spirit of female solidarity encapsulated in the building's motto—*Juncti valemus* ("United We Prevail")—seemed to permeate the atmosphere.

To enter the building, visitors walked through one of four entrances leading to the Eastern and Western Vestibules and the North and South Pavilions. These areas housed large exhibition spaces surrounding the 70-by-65-foot rotunda, or Hall of Honor, where ALA members convened that morning.[26] Librarians facing the north wall viewed a mural by Mary MacMonnies titled *The Primitive Woman,* which depicted a male hunter returning from a kill to a group of children and women who carried water, tended babies, and planted crops.[27] The name of BLM president Bertha Palmer was emblazoned below the mural. Those facing the south wall could contemplate a complementary mural by Mary Cassatt titled *The Modern Woman,* with building architect Sophia G. Hayden's name inscribed underneath it. In counterpoint to the patriarchal needs-based scene depicted in *The Primitive Woman,* Cassatt's mural idealized femininity in terms of culture, leisure, and recognition, portraying women and girls playing, dancing, and listening to music, gathering apples (or as Cassatt described it, "plucking the fruits of knowledge and science"), and pursuing Fame, surrounded by a border adorned with "circles containing naked babies tossing fruit."[28] Poised between the "Primitive" and the "Modern," ALA guests had abundant opportunity to reflect on the symbolic implications of both their physical and their temporal placement at a fair equally invested in glorifying the past and heralding an even more glorious future. Gracing the center of the rotunda, an ornamental fountain designed by Anne Whitney featured a cupid amid a bunch of lilies. Whitney's statue of Leif Ericson, her specially commissioned bust of Lucy Stone, and display cases of needlework completed the scene.

Inside each entrance visitors could browse at a booth containing articles for sale: a faint yet irrepressible echo of the bustling profit-hungry bazaars along the Midway. Here they might purchase miniature models of the building itself, the official flag of the Columbian Exposition, souvenir spoons, and commemorative coins. They could buy guidebooks, collections of recipes Lady Managers compiled especially for the exposition, and other fairground publications, including *The Story of the Woman's Building*, adapted from *Three Girls in a Flat*, a novel coauthored by Laura Hayes (Bertha Palmer's private secretary) and Enid Yandell (who sculpted the caryatids on the Woman's Building) and dedicated to the BLM—"that noble body of women which is acting as advance-guard to the great army of the unrecognized in its onward march toward liberty and equality." (The title's third "girl" was Jean Loughborough, Palmer's record keeper and file clerk.)[29] Also for sale were copies of the "Distaff Series," a six-volume collection of anthologized periodical articles written by New York women, put together by the state's Lady Managers and marketed by Harper Brothers.[30] The first-floor rooms on the rotunda's east side housed exhibits of women's inventions, education, and progress. Rooms on the west side accommodated a souvenir shop, a scientific exhibit, and facilities to check coats and handbags, mail letters, and make telephone calls. Stairways located at the rotunda's four corners led up to a second floor, where cloisterlike galleries overlooking the rotunda opened through arches to a series of interior rooms.

Although one-fourth of the building's exhibit space featured American work, most of the first floor was devoted to the forty-one foreign exhibitors, including works that came from what one guidebook called "savage and half-civilized nations, such as Siam, Ceylon, and even Africa."[31] In some cases, non-Western exhibits were prepared and presented by Americans who put them on display as exotic and inferior Others. Here, for example, ALA members could peruse an exhibit titled "Woman's Work in Savagery," courtesy of the Smithsonian Institution. These exhibits offered the semblance of an inclusiveness persistently undercut by the cultural chauvinism through which they presented non-European cultures.

Above the South Pavilion—just off the galleries—librarians found the BLM's administrative headquarters and the Organization Room, which housed displays by the Daughters of the American Revolution, the WCTU, and the Association of Collegiate Alumnae.[32] A public exhibit of materials generated by nearly half of the 278 member clubs in the recently founded General Federation of Women's Clubs formed an additional attraction. "Within it," noted WCTU president Frances Willard, "lies the impressive representation of the noblest work of women."[33] On display were club yearbooks, lists and portraits of officers, and printed study guides—enabling the kinds of "textual exchanges" that, as Anne Ruggles Gere argues, had for years "strengthened bonds among women separated by distance and/or time, adding an affective dimension to their literacy practices."[34] Here, "many clubwomen from various parts of the country spent long hours, even days, studying the materials, making penciled notes, and discussing club methods with each other."[35] Absent from the room, however, was any reference to clubs such as the Knights of Labor or the American Federation of Labor. Instead, benevolent societies proudly publicized their efforts to educate working-class girls.[36] Also absent was the Colored Woman's League of Washington, D.C., founded by Hallie Q. Brown. As early as April 17, 1892, Charlotte Smith, president of the Woman's National Industrial League of America, had complained to an audience of Waverly Hall Socialists in Chicago that "working women are not represented in the [BLM] board; neither were red women and black women."[37] As these exclusions suggest, the exhibits were, to a large extent, constructions the BLM and affiliated women had fashioned in their own image.

In rooms above the North Pavilion, fairgoers found a tearoom, the Model Kitchen (run by Iowa women), and the Assembly Room, which was used primarily for lectures. Second-floor reception rooms had been planned to represent the four main geographical sections of the country: North, South, East, and West. On the east side of the rotunda, just off the galleries, lay an office for the building's superintendent, a public restroom, the Japanese Room, and the Kentucky, Cincinnati, and California Parlors, with "charming little boutiques" in between the rooms. The west side contained the North Carolina Room, the Connecticut Room, the British Nursing Exhibit, a miscellaneous exhibit room, and, separated from the adjacent records rooms by heavy blue draperies, the library—"the most elaborate apartment in the building," as Virginia Meredith noted.[38]

Before ascending to the library itself, the ALA members gathered in the rotunda that morning listened to four papers on the subject of librarianship, two delivered by women, two by men. All represented conventional topics in professional library discourse; none spoke to the gendered distinctions that the Woman's Building self-consciously profiled and its library exuberantly celebrated. Not until Melvil Dewey, ALA president, New York State Librarian, and a formidable pioneer in the public library movement the country was experiencing, introduced Mary Trautmann, first vice president of the BLM, did the ALA officially acknowledge its surroundings.[39]

"Every member of the board is proud of [the library]," Trautmann announced, "and I am particularly so, being a New York woman." She then acknowledged the preeminent role New York women had played in decorating the library and gathering books for its collections. Dewey thanked her for her remarks with a flurry of compliments. "I came out here on official business before the fair opened," he said, "and found the woman's building by far the most advanced. After the opening I came in here and found all moving as smoothly as if these women, and not their brothers, had received the business training of centuries." He reported that "a score of people" had told him that the Roof Garden Café was the "best managed" on the entire fairgrounds. "I am sure," he continued, "that the men of the A.L.A., which has always given to woman full recognition as co-workers, will share my pride in the splendid showing she has made at the world's greatest exposition." His comments tactfully concealed an attitude he expressed elsewhere that the Woman's Building Library emphasized art at the expense of professional efficiency.[40]

As he finished his remarks Bertha Palmer entered the rotunda. Librarians present had already had ample opportunity to recognize her. Against the background of the Woman's Building, her likeness had been woven into silk bookmarks, printed on playing cards and postcards, and minted into souvenir spoons available for sale all over the fairgrounds. At one time, she was told that "except the Ferris Wheel" she was the fair's most popular attraction.[41] Taking care to emphasize that an appropriate public role need not compromise a woman's domestic competence, Dewey introduced her as a "lady who is as graceful and gracious and efficient at the head of this great administrative work as at the head of one of the most beautiful, hospitable, and palatial homes for which this wonderful city is becoming famous."[42] His emphasis on Palmer's dual roles in the public and private spheres clearly resists the assumption that women's domestic prowess depends on their separation from the public sphere, just as his choice of the word "head" repudiates the oft-cited dictum that the role of head of the household belongs to men, while women's role is to be its heart.

Palmer, a native Kentuckian "whose Southern vowels flowed like wine and carr[ied] her audience with them where she will[ed],"[43] cordially congratulated the ALA for its work for the nation and praised Dewey, "who has been our good adviser and friend throughout," adding, "Through his kindly influence and mediation, we have been able to show in this building the work of expert librarians in this country, and we feel very much gratified that in this work women bear so distinguished a part." Librarianship, she believed, was one of the "new avocations that are being fitted to the intelligence, refinement, and system, and order, and many other qualities that are shown pre-eminently by women." She also noted that the collections and services evident in the library on the floor above her represented one of the best examples of this new vocation. To the assembled librarians, she said she hoped that the ALA's influence might "spread and radiate . . . all over the world." Her comments, which obviously harmonized with prevailing views of the distinct and elevated nature of womankind as well as with the ALA's educational mission and the exposition's ethos of cultural imperialism and globalizing progress, met with enthusiastic applause.[44]

Not coincidentally, on July 21, the same day the ALA met in the rotunda, Mary Lockwood, chair of the committee in charge of the Woman's Building Library, had issued a summary report to the Executive Committee of the BLM. She noted that the library contained 8,247 volumes in sixteen languages from twenty-three countries and every U.S. state and territory but nine, with more books arriving daily. She reported that 1,453 women elsewhere in the world had identified and selected the 3,467 foreign books, while 2,628 American women representing thirty-one out of forty states and territories had participated in the selection of 4,780 books by American female authors. As she enumerated state contributions, it was evident that the BLM had revised the late nineteenth-century definition of "library," expanding it to include—and even generate—cultural texts most libraries of the day chose not to collect.

To identify what was in the collection, Lockwood reported, visitors had access to a partially completed subject/author public catalog of nearly nine thousand alphabetically arranged cards containing two types of entries. One gave statistics on each author represented in the collection, including date and place of birth and death (if applicable) along with information about the author's education and life work. The other gave conventional library information on each book in the collection and contained a Dewey Decimal Classification (DDC) number representing a classification scheme Dewey himself had developed as a librarian at Amherst College between 1874 and 1876, which, in 1893, was being adopted by the increasing number of public libraries opening up in communities across the nation. In this instance, the BLM had made a deliberate decision to follow the lead of the nation's developing library profession. "The peculiar excellence of a card catalog," Lockwood noted, was "that new books can always be inserted without interference and it can be arranged and rearranged in any manner desired." Lockwood also explained that the librarians working in the room were informing visitors that at the conclusion of the exposition the BLM intended to publish a printed catalog of the library's collection, all arranged in a single DDC scheme.[45]

The Woman's Building Library was an astonishing collection, representing pioneering work of which the BLM was justifiably proud. Yet ALA visitors perusing the stacks after the meeting had adjourned could not help but notice three unusual features that distinguished it from modernizing American public libraries. First, visitors were not permitted to pull books from the shelves and page through them. As ALA members knew, "closed stacks" marked a dated philosophy of service that venerated the book as artifact: a treasure to be protected. "Open stacks," which increasingly characterized modern-day library practice, celebrated the book as a useful tool in self-education. The decision in favor of closed stacks enhanced the timeless, museumlike quality cultivated by the library's organizers at the expense of usability and service.[46]

Second, the books themselves were arranged first by the state and/or country of authors represented and then, depending on the size of the state or country's contribution, by subject. As we argue in chapter 3, this geographical organizational scheme, running counter to a basic premise of library service manifest in the uniform subject/author public catalog, reflected political divisions within the Board of Lady Managers. To Dewey and disciples of his classification system (almost all of whom were female), however, this arrangement constituted professional heresy.[47]

Third, the contents of the library frequently tested contemporary definitions of "quality." Library professionals of the late nineteenth century were adamant about their responsibility to elevate the taste of the reading public they served with books endorsed and legitimated by cultural authorities. They operated on the assumption that if their libraries made only "good" books available to readers, they would make a substantial contribution to solving problems attending immigration, industrialization, and urbanization by enabling the masses to educate themselves, thereby reducing threats to the social order. (As Theresa West, director of the Milwaukee Public Library, put it, the "central idea" of the modern library "is to help mankind into fuller, freer, more perfect life.")[48] This commitment was most evident in the model library the ALA had put together for its exhibit elsewhere on the grounds. A committee of librarians had exercised great care in selecting the five thousand volumes on display. They first computed the average percentage of the total collection found in each subject in selected American public libraries.[49] They then used the Osterhout Free Library of Wilkes-Barre, Pennsylvania, as a test collection, checked its entries against standard bibliographical guides and other library catalogs, and sent the pool of possibilities to about seventy-five libraries for a vote. The results of the vote were critiqued and revised by a panel of subject specialists, including a number of university professors. As Katharine Sharp, director of Chicago's Armour Institute Library and Library School and a Dewey protégée, noted, as a result of this rigorous process "the books now on the shelves [of the ALA model library] represent the thoughtful recommendations of experienced librarians and scholars."[50]

As casual observers discovered, however, the Woman's Building Library did not reflect the same commitment to "quality" literature. In addition to a host of cookbooks, Sunday School texts, and devotional books, the collection included many self-published and privately published texts issued in small editions, along with various kinds of ephemera, privately circulated volumes such as scrapbooks and manuscript books, and works by popular authors excluded from the ALA's model library: the sensationalist E. D. E. N. Southworth, working-girl favorite Laura Jean Libbey, mystery writers Anna Katharine Green and Mary R. P. Hatch, sentimental novelists Martha Finley, Augusta Jane Evans, Mary Jane Holmes, and Anna and Susan Warner, passionate poet Ella Wheeler Wilcox, girls' series book author Elizabeth Champney, prolific evangelist Hannah Whitall Smith, and many others. Based on statistics gathered from a sampling of American public libraries, the ALA had devoted only 15 percent of the model library to works of fiction. In contrast, fiction comprised roughly double that percentage in the American section of the Woman's Building Library.

In addition to revising contemporary definitions of "literature," the Woman's Building Library also reflected significant changes in conventional thinking about library space. Although Andrew Carnegie's turn-of-the-century philanthropy stimulated a movement that soon made the American public library a ubiquitous civic institution, in the vast majority of communities much of the impetus for starting these libraries came from women's organizations. The thousands of women's club members who visited the Woman's Building Library in Chicago and subsequently returned to their communities to help establish the public libraries Carnegie money made possible formed particular ideas about how those libraries should look, inside and out. In almost every case a small-town public library built after 1893 was located on or near the town's main street. In almost every case it boasted a manicured lawn with inviting landscaping, comfortable furniture, and attractive accessories and decorations. Rare was the public library, in fact, that did not sport fresh floral arrangements donated and regularly changed by local women's organizations.[51] All of this was done to make users feel, as Wheeler put it, "at home in a literary atmosphere." In this endeavor, women's organizations did not take their cues from the library profession (which privileged bureaucratic efficiency over aesthetics), and although they may not have directly followed the lead of the Woman's Building Library, its existence helped legitimate what they did with their own hometown public libraries.

A "captious critic," cautioned ALA member Caroline Garland (director of the Dover, N.H., public library), might argue that many practices of the Woman's Building Library are "not in accordance with advanced library ideals." Nevertheless, Garland pointed out, "it must be remembered that this is not a working library, but an exhibit, and as such should be arranged as artistically as possible." Other librarians at the July 21 meeting were not so gracious and privately pointed to the ALA library as a much better model.[52] No one, however, mentioned the contrast in the official remarks recorded that day in the rotunda. Katharine Sharp made no adverse comparisons in her published description of the ALA's model library, and no ALA member publicly criticized the arrangement of materials in the Woman's Building Library. Although the ALA's commitment to professionalizing librarianship conflicted in several ways with the BLM's commitment to gender, none of these conflicts ever became public. The women's library obviously represented a labor of love politically negotiated through the many groups of women with a shared interest in putting it all together.

Compared to the ALA's model library, in many ways the Woman's Building Library reflected a much broader view of culture that contested the genteel traditions and canonical texts the dominant patriarchy promoted, albeit in quiet, nonthreatening ways. Perhaps the willingness to let gender expand the definition of culture chilled the atmosphere for professional librarians. The latter were committed first to their profession, which for a quarter century after the organization of the American Library Association argued for a more elevated definition of culture: "The best reading for the greatest number at the least cost" was the ALA motto. While the ALA's model library reflected that motto, the Woman's Building Library, reflecting its own motto of female unity, *Juncti valemus,* allowed gender to take precedence over the "best reading." Some librarians had difficulty with this; rather than joining in the celebration of the Woman's Building Library they chose to remain silent.

The conflicting agendas of the BLM and the ALA are evident in the responses to the Woman's Building Library as well as in the competing discourses of professionalism and gender identity that informed their projects. The ALA promoted professionalism but, in doing so, advocated a narrowly construed definition of "culture." The BLM emphasized the solidarity of women ("women clasping hands with women," as one member of the BLM put it), but advocated a narrowly defined construction of feminine identity.[53] While the ALA's model library mirrored the former, the Woman's Building Library reflected the latter.

Although advertised as a unified collection of women's writing from all places and all times, the Woman's Building Library actually comprised scores of discrete "collections" sent in by state and national committees with widely varied responses to the question of inclusiveness. On one hand, the collection's inclusiveness in terms of genre, literariness, and subject matter illustrates the breadth, depth, and diversity of women's contribution to print culture (particularly in the United States) up to 1893. On the other hand, its exclusiveness in terms of the class and ethnicity of the women who contributed to it illuminates the mechanisms involved in the mediation and erasure of race and class in women's print culture. Not coincidentally, both the canon-building of the ALA and the self-conscious gender construction and negotiation of the BLM crystallized in the historical era that gave rise to the professionalization of librarianship as well as the formulation of literary history as an expression of national identity and gender politics.

2

Planning and Developing the Collection

Exactly when Bertha Palmer and her colleagues fixed on the idea of devoting part of the Woman's Building to a library of women's texts is unclear. Once conceived, however, the library took shape and gained substance on a grand scale. Organizing and assembling this monumental collection was facilitated in part by women's activities at prior national exhibitions. Still, the women involved in the Chicago World's Fair were breaking new ground as an organizing body the federal government officially formed and sanctioned. In doing so, they appropriated and adapted structures of traditionally patriarchal institutions to accomplish an agenda focused on women's interests. As we show in this chapter, the Woman's Building Library developed from the ground up with a rapidity and sense of purpose that reflect the importance the Board of Lady Managers (BLM) ascribed to the written word as a vehicle for women's continued progress and an established avenue of their advancement. At the same time, the means involved were no less significant than the end result. Even before it became a repository of women's texts and meeting place for women from all over the world, the library became a touchstone around which the BLM and its counterparts in foreign countries and individual states organized thousands of women worldwide, debated questions of gender, race, and representation, reached a series of compromises through a mixture of diplomacy and discrimination, and ultimately entered the public sphere largely on their own terms.

Before 1893 women's libraries as separate entities—whether by, for, or about women—have a thin history directly tied to women's literacy. Libraries for women in religious communities existed as early as the seventh century, when one abbot described a group of nuns collecting reading materials as industriously as bees. Eight centuries later, ten sisters established a Dominican convent in Nuremberg, Germany, that included a library. By the end of the eighteenth century female literacy had so increased that many women in Great Britain and the new United States satisfied their literary interests by frequenting circulating and subscription libraries, many of which catered to a growing urban middle-class population favoring novels. In the United States, women began to construct reading club libraries like the Female Library of Candia, New Hampshire (1795), the Ladies' Library of Dublin, New Hampshire (1799), the Ladies Library of Abington, Connecticut (1813), and the Ladies' Moral Society Library of Walpole, Massachusetts (1816).[1]

In 1841 the Great Falls Manufacturing Company of Somersworth, New Hampshire, established a library for the fifteen hundred women who worked in its textile mills, in part to occupy their free time with useful, controlled activities, and in part to keep them away from men. Women's colleges established before 1893 also developed libraries with concentrations in works by, about, and for women.[2] Women had also been collecting private libraries for generations. At the time of her death in 1826, Virginia bluestocking Jean Skipwith had accumulated an eclectic collection of four hundred volumes, with a substantial portion consisting of novels, conduct manuals, travel, history, biography, and practical works on cooking and gardening. In 1867 Sotheby's issued a *Catalogue of the Extraordinary Library, Unique of Its Kind, Formed by the Late Reverend F. J. Stainforth, Consisting Entirely of Works by British and American Poetesses, and Female Dramatic Writers* for an auction a year after Stainforth's death.[3] Another notable collector, Thomas Wentworth Higginson (a literary critic, abolitionist, and mentor to Emily Dickinson), collected approximately sixteen hundred books by and about women over a period of fifty years before donating the collection to the Boston Public Library in 1896. Considered at the time "the best of its sort in the world," the collection, known as the Galatea Collection of Books Relating to the History of Women, was particularly strong in books that addressed the social and political status of women in the nineteenth century. As Higginson explained, his collection was "*about* women" more than "by" women, unlike the "remarkable library of women's writings" he had toured at the Chicago exposition.[4]

The Woman's Building Library had another important precedent. In 1876 the Philadelphia Centennial International Exhibition distinguished itself from earlier international fairs in several ways. First and foremost, the Centennial Exhibition, which ten million guests visited between May 10 and November 10, gave the U.S. an opportunity to boast about and display its accomplishments to the rest of the world. Second, the Centennial featured a thirty-thousand-square-foot Woman's Pavilion. "Devoted exclusively to the results of women's labor," according to the *Official Catalogue*, the Woman's Pavilion housed six hundred exhibits, an art gallery, a kindergarten annex, and a library, all planned, funded, and managed by women to showcase their interests and celebrate their accomplishments. What the women involved chose to highlight there chiefly reflected domesticity and the concept of separate spheres rather than civic equality (a choice that was itself political). "It must be admitted," the *Centennial Eagle* reported in its August 8, 1876, issue, that the exhibits did not "represent woman in her competition with man [or] her labor in the great world of work, but rather the result of her leisure." In fact, the *Eagle* lamented, "some of the exhibits do not rise above the standard of a common county fair."[5]

The experience of organizing the Woman's Pavilion had hardly been positive for the women involved. They were invited to contribute to the exhibition only after the all-male board of commissioners found itself short of money and appointed a committee of thirteen women to help raise additional funds. Still they were denied space in the Main Exhibit Hall, which had been their venue of choice. The insult rankled many and even alienated some women from the exhibit intended to represent them. For example, when members of the National Woman Suffrage Association (NWSA) were denied an opportunity to read their newly structured "Declaration of Rights for Women" at the Centennial's Fourth of July festivities at Independence Hall, Elizabeth Cady Stanton branded the Woman's Pavilion "an afterthought, as theologians claim woman herself to have been." Elizabeth Gillespie, a great-granddaughter of Benjamin Franklin who had spearheaded a committee effort to raise $93,000 for the exhibit, was even more acerbic. In her estimation, the Centennial patriarchy had sent a clear message: "Get up a side show for yourselves, pay for it yourselves, and be happy." Susan B. Anthony, Phoebe Couzins, and four others protested the treatment publicly. On July 4, 1876, they marched into Independence Hall, handed a copy of their Declaration to the master of ceremonies, then marched out to Independence Square to read it to the assembled members of the public.[6]

Even though the Centennial Exhibition experience had been less than satisfactory, the Woman's Pavilion was significant in that it provided separate cultural space in which to spotlight the accomplishments of women. About its library, however, not much is known. Among a listing of exhibits, the *Official Catalogue* included a subsection for the Woman's Pavilion titled "Educational Systems, Methods and Libraries," under which appeared:

83. Hale, Sarah Josepha. Philadelphia, Pa. Books, Sec. C.
84. Fields, Mrs. Jas. T. Boston, Mass. – Books by Massachusetts Women, Sec. C.
85. Stone, Lucy, Boston, Mass. – Books. Sec. C.[7]

Sarah Josepha Hale, the editor of *Godey's Lady's Book,* wrote or edited such titles as *A Complete Dictionary of Poetical Quotations* (1849); *Flora's Interpreter; or, The American Book of Flowers and Sentiments* (1832); and *Poems for Children* (1830), which included, most famously, "Mary Had a Little Lamb." Poet, editor, and publisher Annie Adams Fields was the wife of publisher James T. Fields, of Boston's Ticknor and Fields, and the companion of Sarah Orne Jewett. Women of considerable editorial influence and professional acumen, both Hale and Fields were important women of letters who played significant roles in cultivating women readers and nurturing the careers of women writers.

Lucy Stone's exhibit was the subject of a minor controversy. In the spring of 1876, when the Women's Centennial Executive Committee issued a circular requesting contributions, Stone volunteered to put together an exhibit of printed materials on the subject of "Taxation without Representation." In it she included works by suffragist tax resisters, including the pioneering physician Harriot K. Hunt, the popular author Hannah Lee, the abolitionist Abigail Kelley Foster, and the novelist Sarah E. Wall, as well as Julia and Abby Smith's *Correspondence on Woman's Rights* (1875), along with women's rights tracts she had compiled.[8] "These were all put in a plain black walnut case, two feet square, with a glass door," accompanied by a sign labeled "Protests of Women against Taxation without Representation," Stone later recounted in *Woman's Journal.* During the summer, however, friends told Stone they had searched for her exhibit but could not find it. Assured by correspondence with pavilion officials that it was there, Stone decided to investigate for herself. "When I went to the . . . Exposition," she recalled, "I found this exhibit so high on the shelf of the library that the best eyes could not read a word there was on it, and the 'sign' was nowhere to be seen. Besides, the library was apparently a private room or office, into which the crowd looked, but did not enter." Although Stone requested that the collection be moved lower and the sign be placed over it, friends reported that the latter "never appeared." The explanation, they discovered, was that the exhibit administration "thought that anything which savored of 'protest' was not suited to the time and place" and "one of the Massachusetts Commissioners for the Centennial, agreed."[9]

Fifteen years later the cultural climate for middle-class women had shifted, owing in large part to the networking afforded by the increasing number of women's clubs that undertook cultural work through literacy practices. In the late nineteenth century thousands of women's clubs across the country engaged in a variety of projects, including musical recitals, book socials, and community beautification. Most important, however, they read and wrote, in part for self-education, in part for a sense of identity, in part for culturally sanctioned and socially useful activities to bring them together, and in part to set the cultural standards for local communities. The texts they circulated fostered a sense of connection among the members of individual clubs, between clubs, and with the larger world in which they lived. Their literary practices contributed to the construction of what Benedict Anderson has described as an "imagined community." The interaction of women's groups within the culture of print provided opportunities for self-fashioning and the exercise of power in ways the patriarchy around them regarded as beneficial and nonthreatening. A cornerstone of the shared female culture that flourished throughout the nineteenth century, women's clubs comprised one of the most important components of "social feminism."

"By assigning reading on specific topics, creating libraries, offering book reviews in their publications, requiring members to write papers as well as club histories, minutes, and a variety of other documents," Anne Ruggles Gere notes, "women's clubs pushed members to become more insightful readers and better writers." For many involved with planning the Woman's Building in the early 1890s, tracing a history of women's writing by creating a library of publications authored by women over the centuries likely seemed an obvious as well as a necessary and rewarding task. Such a library had potential to connect women to a past they had never known. Most middle-class white clubwomen had already experienced the power of self-fashioning that the culture of print made possible, and here they could reconstruct women's share in that culture on a national and even international scale through female-authored texts extending centuries back.[10] Strengthening the movement's structure and enhancing its power and scope, the General Federation of Women's Clubs had recently formed in Chicago. Nonetheless, women appeared to be absent when Chicago competed with several other cities to host the Columbian Exposition.

When a group of Chicago leaders (all male) formed themselves into a "Christopher Columbus Celebration Committee" on July 7, 1888, to push the idea, the city they represented offered a mixed picture. In 1890 it had one million people (double what it had a decade earlier), including 400,000 recent immigrants, 167,000 of whom had come from Germany, 73,000 from Scandinavia, 70,000 from Ireland. The city was also home to 14,000 African Americans. The great fire of 1871 had been devastating, but at the same time it allowed Chicago to rebuild itself. A generation later an efficient but noisy around-the-clock street railway system moved great numbers of people from home to work and back, although it also killed more than six hundred per year. And because Chicago was at a crossroads for much of the nation's commercial traffic, railroads truly made the city by facilitating the growth of industries like agricultural equipment manufacturing, mail order merchandising, grain processing, and lumber milling. Trains brought in millions of swine and cattle for the meatpacking industry and its subsidiaries, which employed 25,000 people. So important to the city's livelihood was meatpacking that an 1890s *Baedeker's* guide recommended a visit to the stockyards for those with the stomach for it. "The process of killing the cattle and hogs are [*sic*] extremely ingenious and expeditious," the guidebook offered, "and will interest those whose nerves are strong enough to contemplate with equanimity wholesale slaughter and oceans of blood." Another ugly byproduct of this industry was the stench from manure and the decaying carcasses of slaughtered animals. Many complained that too much of the refuse from these plants found its way into the Chicago River, which was often "stinking," as a result, with thick chunks of offal.[11]

Chicago also had more than its share of vice, violence, and unrest. Many of its citizens (mostly male) supported seven thousand saloons, which in 1893 served 1,673,685 barrels of beer. The city also accommodated nine hundred brothels and ten thousand prostitutes, many of whom plied their trade on the "Levee," a part of South State Street familiarly known as "Satan's Mile." Gamblers could lose their pocket money at the "Store," an establishment on the corner of Clark and Monroe. Chicago also led the nation in the rate of criminal arrests per thousand. The Haymarket Riot of May 4, 1886, in which seven Chicago policemen were killed by a bomb, reflected labor's uneasy relationship with Chicago capitalists. Many members of the working class wanted to bring the Columbian Exposition to the southwest end of Lake Michigan, just a short distance from the company town of Pullman, where angry railroad workers were threatening to strike. Perhaps their desire for social order while Chicago was competing for the fair encouraged capitalists to show a greater sense of civic responsibility toward labor.

Contrasting with all of this, however, was another Chicago, the first major city in the United States to embrace the skyscraper as an architectural innovation. And despite the city's newness and its reputation as an upstart, by the 1890s many of Chicago's cultural institutions already had histories extending back generations. The Chicago Historical Society had organized in 1856, the Chicago Academy of Sciences in 1857, the Chicago Art Institute in 1879. More recently, Louis Sullivan's Auditorium for opera had opened in 1889, and in 1891 the city established the first permanent symphony orchestra in the country. Thanks to the benefactions of John D. Rockefeller, the University of Chicago had begun its rapid rise toward world-class status. In addition, the city had a substantial stake in the culture of print. In 1892 Chicago was a major publishing center, hosting Rand McNally, Belford Clark & Co., and the A. C. McClurg Company, among others. It also boasted the Chicago Public Library (already seventh largest in the nation); the Newberry Library, containing eighty thousand volumes concentrating on the humanities and social sciences; the John Crerar Library, which would become a major library in the sciences; and the University of Chicago Library, which had recently negotiated a purchase for three hundred thousand volumes from a Berlin dealer.

City leaders looked on the Columbian Exposition as an opportunity to interrupt business as usual and put on a one-time, world-class demonstration that celebrated material progress in Chicago, the United States, and the world. Hosting a world's fair would give the city an opportunity to profile itself as a cultural center. London began the practice in 1851, attracting over six million visitors to its Crystal Palace Exhibition. New York sponsored a much less successful fair two years later, with fair managers reporting a $300,000 loss; but the 1876 Centennial International Exhibition in Philadelphia erased that memory and encouraged other American cities to compete for future fairs.

For the privilege of hosting a world's fair to celebrate the four hundredth anniversary of Christopher Columbus's landing in the New World, Chicago vied with Philadelphia, New York, and Washington, D.C., in the East, as well as Cincinnati and St. Louis in the West. Some scoffed at Chicago. "Don't pay any attention to the nonsensical claims of that windy city," Charles A. Dana advised *New York Sun* readers. "Its people could not build a world's fair even if they won it." Dana and others pointed derisively to Chicago's high crime rate, unsettled labor problems, questionable drinking water, and cultural parochialism. Few were as supercilious as the French critic Marie Blanc, however: "To laugh at Chicago is a bad habit common to all civilized America," she carped; she singled out for criticism "the shrill, nasal voice of its citizens; their trivial manners; the big feet of its women; the enormity of bad taste shown in its . . .'sky scrapers.'"[12]

Despite the fierce competition and negative criticism, however, Chicago pushed ahead. On August 1, 1889, 250 men incorporated as "The World's Exposition of 1892" and promptly assigned responsibilities to a raft of committees to raise $5 million for the fair and promote Chicago as its site. As their president they elected Lyman Gage, a First National Bank vice president and the founder of Chicago's Civic Federation; as vice presidents they elected Thomas B. Bryan, a prominent lawyer and land speculator, and Potter Palmer, a real estate promoter and the owner of the famous Palmer House hotel. Chicago's politicians and newspapers rushed to support their efforts. To raise money, businesses bought up hundreds of thousands of the committee's star-shaped stickers, inscribed with "Chicago World's Fair, 1892," and attached them to letters and packages they mailed to customers and clients around the country.[13] After deciding to locate the fair on the lakefront if Chicago's bid was successful, they hired Frederick Law Olmsted & Company as consulting landscape architects, Daniel Burnham as consulting building architect, and Abram Gottlieb as consulting engineer. The Committee on Grounds and Buildings drafted a site plan that included the main buildings, lagoons, and a canal, as well as 3,116 water closets—3.5 times more than the Centennial Exhibit. Space allocated to foreign exhibits alone exceeded the total space of any prior world's fair.

Because no women had been admitted into these inner-circle committees, Myra Bradwell, a prominent suffragist, lawyer, and founding publisher of the *Chicago Legal News,* and Emma Wallace, who (like Bradwell) was affiliated with the Chicago Woman's Club, approached the all-male group to suggest that the fair include a "woman's department." To leaders of a city quite accustomed to women's involvement in social and civic affairs, their initiative did not seem unusual. The Executive Committee for the Chicago Exposition responded by authorizing the creation of a "Women's Department," which immediately set three goals: to build a Woman's Pavilion at the fair to exhibit the work of women; to host conferences for social workers of all sorts; and to raise money by selling as many shares of fair stock as possible.[14]

Eventually, plans made in Chicago were sent to Washington, D.C., as part of Chicago's formal bid to host the exposition. Buried in an enabling legislation and appropriations bill was an amendment proposed by Congressman William Springer of Illinois authorizing "a Board of Lady Managers of such numbers and . . . duties as may be prescribed by said Commission." In offering the amendment, Springer had no intention of promoting women's suffrage, a cause that drove the politics of a very vocal and well-organized minority of American women. Rather, he wanted the commission to award prizes "for exhibits which may be produced in whole or in part by female labor."[15]

But some women had other ideas. In August 1889, a group of Chicago women with a different political agenda organized themselves as the Queen Isabella Society. They had two immediate goals in mind: to fund the construction of a statue of Queen Isabella on the fairgrounds to honor Columbus's benefactor; and, rather than a showplace for the products of women's labor, to erect a Woman's Pavilion where women attending the fair could convene. "Ideas rather than objects [ought] to be the leading feature of the Columbian Exposition," the society maintained.[16]

The discourse of mind vs. matter, or "ideas" vs. "objects," as the Isabellas phrased it, animates one of the most heated and politically charged debates concerning women's role at the exposition. The emphasis on physical displays of women's handiwork, the Isabellas argued, deflected attention from loftier ideals, aspirations, and rights. "An injustice was done women at Philadelphia by the woman's department which contained objects . . . well enough in their way, but not involving mechanical training or financially remunerative toil, and

giving no idea of the practical industrial ability many women possess and practice," declared the "Isabella Corner" of the *Woman's Tribune* in January 1891.[17]
Recognizing the social and political ramifications of women's role at the fair,
the society's members, all of whom were suffragists, determined to control
the role of the women's department at the fair, wherever Congress ultimately
decided to locate it. Within months additional chapters of the Queen Isabella
Society formed in other major cities.

In part as a result of their efforts, one senator presented a petition to his
colleagues on January 31, 1890, signed by the wives of several Supreme Court
justices and sundry other elected officials in Washington. In fact, the petition
had been orchestrated behind the scenes by Susan B. Anthony, who had led
the defiant Fourth of July march into Independence Hall at the Philadelphia
Centennial. The petition called "for the appointment of women on the board
of managers of said exhibition, in view of the fact that there will be in the
exhibition a presentation of the share taken by women in the industrial, artistic,
intellectual and religious progress of the nation."[18]

While suffragists pushed their cause, selecting a site took precedence. After
seven ballots, the House of Representatives finally chose Chicago over New
York on February 24, 1890. Two months later, President Benjamin Harrison
signed a bill approved by both houses authorizing Chicago as the official site
for the World's Columbian Exposition. To approve decisions about site design
and construction—and because many in Congress doubted Chicago's ability to
manage such a huge undertaking—the new law called for a national commission representing each state and territory. Section 6 contained the final version
of an amendment requiring the World's Columbian Commission "to appoint
a Board of Lady Managers of such numbers and to perform such duties as
may be prescribed by said Commission. Said Board may appoint one or more
members of all committees authorized to award prizes for exhibits which may
be produced in whole or in part by female labor."[19] This enabling legislation
neglected to specify how many women would occupy positions on the board,
nor did it indicate what their specific duties would be. And, like the Senate
petition presented several months earlier, it made no mention of a library.

Once the legislation passed, several women took issue with the phrase "Lady
Managers." "The title Congress gave us conveys the impression that we are
a useless ornament," one woman objected—mere "idle women of fashion."[20]
Others channeled their energies differently. Back in Chicago, two groups of
women battled for control of the board: the Isabellas and the Women's Department), a group of Chicago women involved in reform work. Opposing the
idea of a separate women's exhibit, the Isabellas wished to use the opportunity
presented by the fair to work for suffrage and equal rights for women. The

Women's Department favored a separate exhibit and advocated more general social reform. Caught in the middle, the National Commission tried to satisfy both factions.

By the summer of 1890 Chicago commissioners had settled on the exact site for the fair—three hundred acres of lakefront property bordering Jackson Park. About the same time, the National Commission began fulfilling its obligation to appoint Lady Managers: two from the District of Columbia and each territory and state, as well as eight at-large members. Although women could not vote, it was nevertheless assumed that equal numbers of Lady Managers would favor Democrats and Republicans. The governing body included a president, eight vice presidents, a vice-president at large, a secretary, a superintendent of the Industrial Department, a superintendent of State Work to monitor exhibits by women in state buildings, a chairman of the Committee on Awards, and a director of the Woman's Building. As a concession to pressure from the Chicago-based Women's Department, the commission also appointed nine additional Lady Managers from Chicago. Only one was an Isabellan; the rest belonged to the prestigious, socially active but not suffragist Chicago Woman's Club. In the end, the Board of Lady Managers consisted of 117 women and an equal number of alternates.

Lady Managers were bound into this governing body by more than gender alone. All were white, all were upper or middle class. Conversely, none were African American, Hispanic, Native American, or Asian American, and none were working class. In the *Chautauquan*'s July 1892 issue, the journalist Antoinette Van Hoesen adopted a defensive tone when she countered the "erroneous impression" that the Board of Lady Managers "is for the most part composed of ladies of leisure who have no comprehension, or sympathy with, bread-winning women": "The fact is," she declared, "that a large proportion of the Board are practical business women." One board member clarified the apparent contradiction: "Our board comprises as many workers, as much representation of the active industries of the country, as if it were composed of men. There are doctors, lawyers, real-estate agents, journalists, editors, merchants, two cotton planters, teachers, [and] artists." As the historian Jeanne M. Weimann observes, the rift reflects a "basic lack of rapport between suffragists (professional women—Isabellas) and philanthropists (clubwomen—socialites)."[21]

On October 21, 1890, the Executive Committee of the World's Columbian Exposition adopted a resolution with the same wording as the congressional legislation, authorizing a Board of Lady Managers that would award prizes for exhibits produced partly or entirely by women. On November 19, most of the delegates gathered at Chicago's Kinsley's Hall for their first meeting. "An unprecedented spectacle," Frances Willard proclaimed it: "an executive body composed wholly of women, acting with government authority." National Commission president Thomas W. Palmer said much the same thing. "This is the first time in the history of our Government," he told his audience, "that woman has been fully recognized in the administration of a great public trust like this." Shortly after Palmer finished his remarks, those assembled selected Rebecca Latimer Felton of Georgia (wife of Congressman William H. Felton) as one of two temporary "chairmen." In her comments, Felton echoed Palmer: "It is the first time in the history of the Republic that women have been recognized as competent to attend any sort of public business by the National Government."[22] That the message was repeated so often suggests at least two points: first, those present in Kinsley's Hall recognized that women had been handed a unique and historic opportunity; second, they were determined not to let the opportunity pass.

The next day the delegates reassembled to elect a president. (By that time the board had decided to reject the title "chairman" for obvious reasons.) Social power and cultural influence weighed heavily in the deliberations. So, evidently, did the lingering effects of sectionalism. As far back as 1883 the *Chicago Inter Ocean* had touted the city as a site that "would introduce the North and South anew in a city free from prejudices and animosities."[23] During her impromptu address the previous day, Felton affirmed that sentiment. After declaring, "As a Southern woman I certainly appreciate this compliment at your hands," she assured her listeners, "I know no South, no North, no East, no West. We are all dear sisters engaged in a work of loyalty and patriotism, under the grand old flag in the home of our fathers."[24]

After her speech Felton mentioned to a South Carolina delegate that, lacking time to prepare her address, she could only scribble notes on the backs of two envelopes. "Mrs. Isabella Beecher Hooker was standing nearby and heard what I said," Felton later recalled. "With characteristic impulse she turned on me, and cried out, 'Would you have us believe that you did not carefully prepare that finished speech before you came to the meeting? I am more than astonished at you!' At first I thought I could not restrain a very harsh retort, but I recollected that any dispute would quickly go to reporters and that I would be posted as having a quarrel with a member of the Beecher family—the North and South in early conflict, so I held myself down." Felton's near-altercation with the half-sister of Harriet Beecher Stowe, a member of the Isabella Society known for her "piquant remarks," reveals both the sensitivity of sectional feeling and the recognition that the role of president would require exceptional diplomacy as well as tact.[25]

For president, Mary Cantrill of Kentucky nominated the Chicago social icon Bertha Honoré Palmer. The wife of Potter Palmer, Bertha Palmer was born to a father of French descent and a mother from "one of the oldest and most aristocratic Southern families."[26] New York's Mary Trautmann nominated Mary Logan, widow of the Civil War hero John A. Logan and editor of *The Home,* a popular women's magazine. Logan, "a tall, commanding-looking woman" with "earnest black eyes, under [a] halo of snowy hair," quickly withdrew her nomination in favor of Palmer, who was then unanimously elected by voice vote. Members present also elected, as secretary, Phoebe W. Couzins of Missouri, who had accompanied Susan B. Anthony in the 1876 Centennial Exhibition protest, as well as one at-large vice president and eight others representing various parts of the country. In accepting the office, Bertha Palmer asked her audience to make the most of this tremendous opportunity: "The full benefit of this intermingling will not be felt, however," she exhorted, "unless we, each and all, are generously willing to leave for a time the narrow boundaries in which our individual lives are passed, to give our minds and hearts an airing by entering into the thoughts and aspirations of others, and enjoying the alluring vistas which open before us."[27] Palmer obviously agreed with the sentiments expressed at Kinsley's Hall the previous evening.

In many respects, Bertha Palmer was the logical choice to lead the Board of Lady Managers. In *The Great American Fair,* the historian Reid Badger refers to her as the "Lady Astor of the Middle West." An active clubwoman, she was also the sister-in-law of former President Ulysses S. Grant's eldest son and thus had a secure connection to Washington, where she was a regular visitor at the White House.[28] Known to family and friends as "Cissie," she married Chicago entrepreneur Potter Palmer in 1870 and over the years participated widely in the city's activities. Together, in 1873 they opened the Palmer House, a landmark hotel on the corner of State and Monroe with—the promotional literature advertised—"flush toilets in every room." Although not everyone was impressed (Rudyard Kipling ungraciously called it "a gilded and mirrored rabbit warren"), within a decade the Palmer House had become one of Chicago's premier hotels. During the Grant administration, it had even functioned as the President's headquarters in Chicago. In 1883 the Palmer House broke hotel industry precedent by hiring a woman as cashier.[29]

In 1882 the Palmers began to build an enormous personal residence on the corner of Lake Shore Drive and Banks Street on the city's north side. Christened "The Castle" by locals, the Palmer mansion contained a large and elaborately decorated library that included an ornate carved mantelpiece taken from an old Flemish cathedral. The library also featured a "beautifully painted" ceiling adorned with "scenes and characters from many well-known books," including Faust and Marguerite and Shakespeare's Juliet.[30] Bertha Palmer was one of America's first collectors of French impressionism (her friend Mary

Cassatt counseled her on purchases), and from time to time she opened her art collection to public viewing. On such occasions she often wore a jeweled collar of 2,268 pearls and seven large diamonds.[31]

In 1874 Palmer joined the Fortnightly Club, Chicago's oldest women's organization, where she delivered a paper titled "The Obligations of Wealth." The paper surprised many, "both for its literary merit and its lofty tone," an observer recalled in the early 1890s, adding that over the years it had "often been referred to by the members of the club."[32] Several years later Palmer joined the Chicago Woman's Club, a group concerned equally with the city's social problems and with the social standing of its own members. By 1890 the club boasted five hundred members. Palmer's club contributions often expressed "labor sympathies," as did her role in helping Jane Addams and Eliza Gates Starr establish the settlement house Hull House and her support of the Woman's Alliance, which sought to protect sweatshop workers. On the issue of suffrage, however, Palmer was a moderate much more interested in using the Columbian Exposition to promote the general welfare of women than to obtain their franchise. This fact heralded future conflict with the Isabella Society.[33]

After electing officers, the next major issue the BLM had to settle was whether to erect a separate building to house exhibits of women's work or push for the integration of all women's work displayed at the fair into general exhibits distinguished only by cultural form. At its November 19 meeting, Chicagoan Frances Shepard, a founding member of the Daughters of the American Revolution, urged a separate building. Others present balked, however; many recommended against any arrangement "that would contain a separate exhibit of the work of women." To the dismay of the Isabellas, however, the BLM reversed its position on November 26 and decided—with Palmer's support—to erect a separate building for the purpose of spotlighting women's work. "The Board of Lady Managers for the World's Fair decided not to have a separate exhibit of women's work," the *Woman's Journal* reported somewhat ambiguously, "but to have a pavilion for a special exhibit of such work as does not come under the general classification, and of such matters as will call attention to woman's progress and development." This action, Frances Willard argued, "not only infinitely advanced the interests of all women exhibitors, but . . . also vastly increased the power of the Board itself. . . . Small exhibits by women could not after this be crowded out by powerful and rich firms who could make splendid displays." On November 27 the BLM petitioned the National Commission to authorize a "Woman's Building."[34]

On December 8 Palmer informed Lyman Gage of the Chicago World's Columbian Exposition committee that the BLM wanted a separate building "in which will be placed special exhibits of woman's work, which on account of their rare merit and value the exhibitors would prefer to have placed under special care and custody of the Board." For the Building and Grounds Committee, Palmer sketched out a 200-by-500-foot building consisting of a large central gallery illuminated by a skylight and surrounded by a series of exhibit rooms on two floors. She did not designate any room as a library. The committee subsequently approved a slightly smaller building, 200 by 400 feet, to cost no more than $200,000.[35]

The decision to create a separate building just for women occasioned a mixed response from the local media. The *Chicago Herald* liked the idea and predicted that "Mrs. Potter Palmer will probably be successful in her efforts to secure a separate building for a separate exhibit of women's work." The *Chicago Evening Post* disagreed. "A Woman's Building is utterly without warrant in sound sense," it protested; a separate exhibit would be "a special building that only one visitor in every fifty thousand will care to visit."[36]

But there was another angle to the debate as well. As the literary historian Grace Farrell observes, "underlying the ideas of woman's separate sphere and woman's moral superiority was the presumption that the sexes were radically different." This presumption of difference is reflected in much of the rhetoric surrounding the Woman's Building. "The prevalent use of the singular 'woman' in the discussions of women's nature and role in society," she writes, "connoted a univalent view that all women were of a singular character with well defined attributes."[37] Farrell traces this conception of gender difference to the dominant line of feminist thought in nineteenth-century America, descending from "Catherine Beecher and others who emphasized the distinctive nature of woman, her special needs, and her unique role." "Nineteenth-century suffragists invoked the ideologies of 'woman's separate sphere' and 'woman's moral superiority' to authorize their public voice," Farrell notes. "They reasoned that to give the vote to those morally superior persons charged with the upbringing of the next generation would raise the ethical level of political discourse and insure a more moral world for the future. Such notions were useful to the woman suffrage movement because they bypassed the issue of inferiority by stressing difference."[38]

But another line of feminist thought, "a radical line stemming from Mary Wollstonecraft and Frances Wright, who based their suffragism on the principle that women and men share a common nature and thus must share common rights," challenged the former view. "A small minority of post-Civil War suffragists, including Elizabeth Cady Stanton," Farrell points out, "saw the dangers for women's progress in emphasizing gender differences." When the Fourteenth Amendment failed to include women, the latter view became increasingly marginalized, as suffrage leaders "tended to stress women's unique virtues and special responsibility to the community, rather than the identity of men's and women's public roles." The debate over a separate or integrated exhibit—like the rhetoric of singular womanhood at the Columbian Exposition (as in "*Woman's* Building")—was highly charged, ideologically and politically, and reflected this contentious division within the women's movement. The Omaha *World Herald* put it bluntly: "The woman idea is a mistake. It has always been a mistake. . . . The woman idea is a relic of barbarism. It is still what keeps conservative women from taking part in the accomplishments of this active age." Separatist women, the *World Herald* argued, "are forever injuring the cause of women in her struggle to break down the woman idea and become a responsible human creature, with the responsibilities, liberties and judgments of a proper human."[39]

The separatist view prevailed, however. According to the feminist historian Estelle Freedman, "the ideology of 'true womanhood' was so deeply ingrained and so useful to preserving social stability in a time of flux that those few women who explicitly rejected its inequalities could find little support for their views. . . . [M]ost women were not interested in rejecting their deeply rooted female identities."[40] Nearly twenty years after the Columbian Exposition, the decision to display women's work apart from men's still rankled some women. In a 1910 *Atlantic Monthly* article, the novelist Margaret Deland, who chaired the Massachusetts Board's literary committee, wrote: "How much better if the few great things . . . had been placed among their peers, and not put aside as noticeable because women did them. Such insistence upon sex in work is an insult to the work, and to the sex, too."[41] For Deland and many others, "separate" (at least in this case) was inherently unequal.

On January 29, 1891, exposition officials fixed the location of the Woman's Building.[42] A few days later, in a February 3 circular to BLM members, Palmer announced that the board had been appropriated $200,000 to erect the "women's building" and that "competitive designs will at once be invited from the women architects" all over the country. She then listed some of the building's anticipated features: "parlors where women may rest and have refreshments; a bureau of information with interpreters for foreigners; a club room for women exhibitors; ample space for the showing of all charity and reform work inaugurated or conducted by women; administration and committee rooms; an assembly hall for social meetings and such lectures and congresses as may be desired by any organization of women and approved by our House Committee, etc." She said nothing about a library. Competition instructions came out shortly thereafter. "A simple light-colored classic type of building will be favored," they specified. Architects submitting plans were advised to "follow closely" the sketch Palmer had submitted to the Building and Grounds Committee.[43]

Because fair organizers considered the appropriations proposed by Congress in February 1891 too small, Palmer and several members of the BLM Finance Committee traveled to Washington to plead Chicago's case before the appropriations committees of the House and Senate. While there, Palmer also pressed the BLM's case for a separate exhibit before the newly formed National Council of the Women of the United States, which also heard Dr. Julia Holmes Smith articulate the Queen Isabella Society's position. Council members chose not to take sides. On February 22 Palmer showed senators and congressmen drawings of a series of exhibits, including plans for the Woman's Building. She must have been persuasive. Within days, Congress increased its appropriation to the Exposition Commission by $95,000, of which the Board of Lady Managers got $36,000.[44]

The Chicago *Inter Ocean* heaped praise on Palmer's political sagacity. "More than any other," it noted, "she saved the World's Fair appropriation and vindicated the dignity of the national commission."[45] Frances Willard discerned another benefit to Palmer's victory. "Until then it had been the rich manufacturer furnishing the materials who received the award," she commented, "and the humble worker whose brain and fingers had fashioned the beautiful or useful article remained unknown." With the increased appropriation to the BLM, however, "at least one wrong is righted, and merit—not merely money—is recognized." Under Palmer's direction, the Board of Lady Managers was fast obtaining a reputation as the fair's "argus-eyed guardian, and eloquent advocate of the interests of women." Within a month, Palmer formed a BLM executive committee of twenty-four members, six each from four parts of the country.[46]

In subsequent meetings, the BLM refined its focus to create a special set of exhibits for the Woman's Building to highlight the cultural progress women had made in the four hundred years since Columbus arrived in the New World. "The decision to have a special exhibit in the Woman's Building gives a fine opportunity of emphasizing the most creditable achievements of women," the board's minutes record. Still striving toward a solution to the separate-or-integrated debate, the BLM proposed that "where there is anything [elsewhere on the grounds] of such extreme excellence that we, as a sex, feel proud of it, that we have a duplicate of it, or another piece of work from the same hand in the Woman's Building, in order to call attention to the fact that it is the work of woman." Further, the BLM announced its determination "to keep this exhibit very choice," adding, "We must keep the standard up to the highest point. No sentimental sympathy for women should cause us to admit second-rate things into this gallery." Obviously, standards of quality for what went into the Woman's Building as duplicates would be determined by the canons of the upper- and middle-class white American women responsible for making these decisions. A circular sent out shortly after the BLM's September 1891 meeting underscored its "intention to make in the Woman's Building an exhibit which will clear away existing misconceptions as to the originality and inventiveness of women . . . from prehistoric times to the present." Mindful of the building's importance as meeting place as well as exhibition hall, BLM members also resolved at the same meeting "that a special committee of seven be appointed who shall have charge of arranging for Congresses to be held in the Woman's Building during the Fair." Still, no document the BLM generated mentioned a library.[47]

The Isabellas made several other attempts to use the BLM to get their own building on the fairgrounds and erect their statue, but all efforts failed. Palmer defeated them every time and in subsequent meetings assumed what the Chicago *News* called "almost autocratic power" of the BLM—but not without public protest. Phoebe Couzins and Frances Dickinson, both BLM members, the *News* reported, "protest against the action of the Commission in giving Mrs. Palmer absolute authority in all matters relating to the Lady Managers," which they argued resulted in "destruction of [the BLM's] national character."[48] Palmer made no public response.

The Isabellas were not the only group rebuffed by Palmer and the BLM. At a meeting on November 25, 1890, Mary Logan offered a resolution drafted the previous evening at a "mass-meeting at Bethesda Baptist Chapel" by a group of "colored women of Chicago" led by Lettie Trent, a schoolteacher. By that date sixteen thousand African Americans were living in Chicago, three times as many as in 1876. Like many other African Americans looking toward the exposition, the Chicago women wanted to use the fair to demonstrate the progress their race had made since emancipation less than thirty years earlier. They also wanted fair officials to hire African American women in administrative and clerical positions in the Woman's Building. They called their organization the Woman's Columbian Association and promptly had stationery printed up with "1893 World's Fair, Chicago" in the upper left corner.[49]

Because no provision had been made by exposition officials "for securing exhibits from the colored women of this country," and because under the exposition's existing classification system, any work exhibited by African American women would be indistinguishable from others and thus rob them of "honor, fame, and credit," Trent's group appealed to the BLM "to establish an office for a colored woman whose duty it shall be to collect exhibits from the colored women of America." The BLM heard Logan read the resolution and then, without endorsement, voted to refer it to the National Commission. When someone suggested that Trent be appointed to fill a vacancy on the BLM, a "Southern Lady Manager" was overhead to say, "We will speak to negroes and be kind to them as employees, but we will not sit with them." BLM member Nancy Huston Banks then stated that she had also received a communication from Emma B. Lewis, "who represents one faction among the colored organizations." Banks moved that it be placed on file with other communications from African American women "until the proper time comes to take action upon it."[50]

After the meeting Palmer appointed several BLM members to meet with Trent. By that time, however, a third group of African American women in Chicago—the Columbian Auxiliary Association (better funded but less aggressive than Trent's Woman's Columbian Association)—had organized under the leadership of Mrs. R. D. Boone. "We do not in any way suggest a separate department in the coming exposition," Boone wrote Palmer, "but we do believe there is a field of labor among the colored people, in which members of the race can serve with special effectiveness and success."[51]

For her time Bertha Palmer was a moderate on race, class, and gender politics. Unfortunately, however, rather than dealing with the issue in public, in April 1891 she unwisely asked Kentucky's Mary Cantrill (whom one historian describes as "so soaked in Southern paternalism that she was incapable of recognizing her own discriminatory practices") to represent the interests of "colored people," hoping thereby to placate Chicago's African American women. Several months later *Woman's Journal* reported that the BLM decided to follow a National Commission ruling "that there should be no discrimination upon the score of race, and that colored women should have precisely the same chance that white women had, by being given equal opportunity, neither more nor less, to do the best work they are capable of."[52]

By this time, however, Palmer was being pressed by four different groups, all claiming to represent African American women. Her response to each was not only patronizing, it also contradicted practices that would later be implemented throughout the Woman's Building. "Nearly all of our members thought that it would be making a distinction which the Negroes themselves would not want," she wrote a BLM member on December 17, 1891, "as there is no reason why their exhibit should not be collected and entered in the general collection."[53]

One reason Palmer minimized the requests by African American women for representation on the BLM and a separate identity in the exhibits was that their causes were also being championed by Isabellans like Phoebe Couzins and Isabella Beecher Hooker. "I hear that Miss Couzins has been having conferences with these women," she wrote Mary Logan on October 11. "Of course Miss C. is using this for her own ends, but they do not realize this." In part,

Couzins and Hooker were probably using Trent, Lewis, and Boone for political purposes against Palmer; in part, Palmer was probably using Trent, Lewis, and Boone for political purposes against the Isabellans.[54] Caught in the middle as the two groups jockeyed for power and influence, the African American women faced overwhelming odds.

Forced to break the deadlock, Palmer hit upon a seemingly ingenious solution. She drew up a statement that identified "a great deal of trouble among the colored people" and on October 13, 1891, sent it to all Lady Managers. The statement obligated each signee "to do all in my power to further the interests of the colored women of my State" and to give them "all the information and assistance possible, by sending them the publications issued by the Board of Lady Managers, and in every other way striving to promote their interests." Palmer asked her colleagues to forward the signed statements to Mary Logan, who would show them to concerned groups of African Americans. Palmer was especially solicitous of Southern women. To the statement she attached a circular dated October 14 and addressed "to all interested in the colored people." The circular argued that because "discussions among the colored people" yielded no consensus, signing this commitment was essential.[55]

One by one the signed documents came in to Logan. Many contained comments. A Virginia representative assured Logan that she had "already distributed a good deal of literature" given her by the World's Columbian Association.[56] An Arkansas representative hoped her signed document would "help allay the fervor which has so unfortunately attacked our dusky sisters." A representative from Georgia was insulting. "My knowledge of the race leads me to believe that they never originate anything themselves," she wrote Logan on October 14. "There is always someone behind to push them on." Ultimately, with signed commitments in hand, Logan convinced Trent to withdraw her protest. With clear misgivings, Trent wrote on November 4, "I really thing [*sic*] unless something is done for our women that they should appeal to Congress as the State Boards will do nothing for the colored women but talk." Her words proved prophetic.[57]

Rather than appealing to Congress, the African American women made their case public by publishing in the October 24 *Boston Courant* a circular indicating that they "resent[ed] the insult" the BLM "hurled at the women of our race." The circular cited a Lady Manager from Arkansas who reported she would as soon exhibit the work of "poor white cotton pickers" as sponsor an African American women's exhibit in the Woman's Building. The circular also cited a BLM member from Georgia who agreed with her and another from Texas who maintained that "the darkies are better off in white folks' hands" and that "the Negroes in my State do not want representation." Further, the circular noted that when the representative from the District of Columbia pressed the BLM to give a delegation of African American women a hearing, Palmer replied "that if she ever brought up the colored question, she would never be forgiven for it." In effect, it concluded, "a small number of white women" had denied "five million of Negro women . . . the grandest opportunity to manifest their talent and ability."[58]

Palmer and her colleagues on the BLM bristled at this attack (Palmer called the circular "a tissue of lies"), but only mildly.[59] And although African Americans made no protest to Congress, they persisted with World's Fair officials. In a meeting of the National Board of Control held in Chicago in early December 1891, Fannie Barrier Williams—"a handsome and refined colored woman" as *Woman's Journal* described her—requested that two African Americans be appointed to some position "where they could work in the interests of their people." She argued "so logically and eloquently" that the National Board of Control instructed exposition officials to appoint "two colored people to positions on the bureau of publicity and promotion." Williams herself, active in the club movement as well as in civic affairs, received one appointment. Although Palmer addressed the BLM the same day Williams was appointed to the fair's Bureau of Publicity and Promotion, she made no reference to the appointment or to discussions that took place between the BLM and African American women in previous months. Instead, she set forth "the directions in which to exemplify the interests and occupations of women."[60]

Other BLM members followed Palmer's lead. On April 8, 1892, Hallie Q. Brown, at the time dean of women at Tuskegee Institute and a nationally noted elocutionist, sent a circular to members of the BLM. Because "no adequate opportunity is to be offered [the eight million African Americans living in the United States] for proper representation in the World's Fair," especially in the South, where African American "wage women" were not even being surveyed by state boards, she asked if it was "less than fair to request for [African Americans] a special representation?" Fewer than half the BLM members answered her. Some suggested the BLM should not interfere with state boards; others argued the African American community was itself divided. Only three Lady Managers endorsed Brown's suggestion.[61]

A May 1892 editorial in *Halligan's Illustrated World's Fair* sought to put the issue to rest. Many Lady Managers "have refused to admit the work of colored women to the Columbia Exposition," it acknowledged, but the BLM itself "has no desire to make any such discrimination." The BLM was not aware of the racial origins of its exhibitors, whose work was being selected on the basis of quality, and not skin color, *Halligan's* went on to explain. The Woman's Building sought to integrate the work of women from all over the world into its exhibits, "and it will certainly feel an especial interest in securing such a representation from the colored women of the country as will fully illustrate their rapid advancement since the emancipation of their race."[62] Reactions from the African American community to this shallow editorial are not known.

In early 1893 Palmer did hire Mrs. A. M. Curtis, an African American woman and former employee of Chicago's Provident Hospital, as Secretary of Colored Interests. "Mrs. Curtis' principal and especial duty," *Woman's Journal* noted, "will be to secure fair play for colored exhibitors in the matter of space and position." For unknown reasons, Curtis stayed only two months. She was succeeded by Fannie Barrier Williams, who, also for unknown reasons, left after a short tenure.[63]

Chicago-area African American women stung by the BLM's indifference subsequently helped fund the pamphlet *The Reason Why the Colored American Is Not in the World's Columbian Exposition,* which Ida B. Wells, Frederick Douglass, Irvine Garland Penn, and Ferdinand L. Barnett put together and published on August 30, 1893. In the pamphlet Barnett, a Chicago attorney and newspaper editor, wrote that African American women from Chicago were unable to secure a significant presence in the Woman's Building because "the Board of Lady Managers eagerly availed itself of the opportunity to say that the colored people were divided into factions and it would be impolitic to recognize [any] faction."[64] Although thousands of copies of *Reasons Why* sold in the Haitian Pavilion at the exposition, they were not available in the Woman's Building. Nor was the pamphlet included in the collection of the Woman's Building Library. How the Board of Lady Managers treated African American women up to and during the Chicago World's Fair probably reflects a political compromise Palmer felt compelled to make. Not alienating BLM members from the South may have seemed more important to her than accommodating the requests of the several groups of African American women who looked to them for support.[65]

While the BLM strove to quell opposition, Bertha Palmer had another worry. In late March 1891 she approached with a "sinking of heart" the designs that had been submitted for the Woman's Building: only fourteen women had entered into the competition, most under twenty years of age, and all but two from the South or West. Despite her misgivings, however, "with surprise and delight," as one observer reported, "she discovered the general excellence of the designs" when she opened them.[66] On March 25, 1891, the BLM awarded the first prize of $1,000 to Sophia Hayden, an architecture graduate of the Massachusetts Institute of Technology who lived near Boston.[67] Following competition specifications, Hayden's initial sketch manifested Roman and Italian influences and a Renaissance style. The plan for the building matched the neoclassical style and common cornice height of most of the other exposition buildings, including those bordering the Court of Honor. And like other buildings planned for the exposition, it would be made white by a new invention—a powered paint-sprayer—its pristine neoclassical facade contrasting sharply with the colorful eclecticism of the Midway leading up to the White City.

Hayden's initial plan sketched out a number of rooms, but none designated a library. In May Hayden visited Chicago to view the site and go over details of the building with Palmer and her BLM colleagues. At hand they had a report from the BLM Committee on Classification dated April 28, 1891, that identified categories and subdivisions of the committee's responsibilities but made no mention of a library. Nor did Nancy Huston Banks mention a library in her monthly reports on BLM activities for the May and June issues of *World's Columbian Exposition Illustrated*, although she affirmed that "here will probably be a special exhibit of such things as make a showing of woman's progress during the quadro-centennial which the exposition celebrates." "A Plan of the Woman's Building," published in the August–September issue of the *Exposition Illustrated*, did identify a library on the first floor, just off the Main Gallery between the "Bureau of Information" and "Records" rooms. It is probable, therefore, that by the time she returned to Boston on May 26, 1891, Hayden knew she would have to include a library as well as an assembly room and rooftop garden in the building's floorplan.[68]

In the Architect's Report she wrote for the BLM in April, 1894, Hayden mentioned that initially she planned a third story "to extend over a portion of the north and south wings." Eventually that third story became the Roof Garden Café. Her initial plans for the second floor included a number of "smaller rooms, designed for committee rooms," but "subsequently," she noted, without specifying exactly when, "the partitions were removed, in the south wing, as it was used for a different purpose." Here she probably referred to the library. When construction began July 7, preliminary plans placed a room marked "library" on the first floor opposite the main front entrance.[69]

At the September 9, 1891, BLM meeting, the Committee on Classification reported that the subjects of education, literature, engineering, public works, music, and drama would be dealt with under "Department L, Liberal Arts," and that the work of this department would be subdivided further into groups. Group 146 would be headed by a Press Committee, which would also assume responsibility for exhibits falling under Group 150, "Literature, Books, Libraries, and Journalism." Number 145, the "Educational Group," would deal with "Institutions and Organizations for the Increase and Diffusion of Knowledge."[70]

At an afternoon session BLM member Josephine Allen, from Oregon, offered a resolution: "Whereas, we have been assured that abundant opportunities will be given to display the work of women in the field of literature; therefore be it resolved, that the Lady Managers in their respective states endeavor to collect the meritorious literary works of the women in their states." After the motion carried, Allen offered a second: "Resolved, that the library in the Woman's Building be in charge of a librarian, that the works which are there exhibited may be examined by visitors who desire the privilege." It also passed.[71] The *Los Angeles Times* predicted that the library of the Woman's Building would "show the literary work of women beginning with the tinkling madrigal of the dainty dames of olden times, following the thin thread of romance on down to the valuable treatises upon the exact sciences, produced by the brainy women of today."[72] Now it remained for the Board of Lady Managers and its affiliates to make this prediction come true.

Once marching orders were approved, others had to be convinced to participate in constructing the library's collection. Earlier, Palmer had persuaded George Davis, the exposition's director-general, to issue a circular to each state legislature advocating the appointment of women to state commissions, thus assuring the BLM some claim on the appropriations of each state for the fair. Her hope now was that the women appointed to those commissions would assume most of the responsibility for collecting materials for the library. In a separate circular to state Boards of Lady Managers, she explained that "it is intended that this building, and all its contents, shall be the inspiration of woman's genius." By September the climate of cooperation that had been fostered by women's clubs across the nation was beginning to pay large dividends. Women's groups had organized in thirty-one states and territories to obtain World's Fair appropriations from their legislatures.[73]

In early January 1892, Palmer issued a circular outlining the work state women's boards "are asked to do in cooperation" with the BLM. Several BLM members, including Mary Logan, started giving canned speeches. "The Board proposes to extend its helpful influence throughout this vast country, across the sea, around the world," she regularly told her audiences. "It ignores politics, 'isms,' rank and race—it is women clasping hands with women." Each state was requested to compile statistics, she would explain, construct an exhibit on women's work (especially philanthropic, recreation, health, and reform work), identify individuals who could serve on juries, assist the BLM with publicity, and list subjects worthy of exhibits. Finally, she also asked women across the country "to secure for the women's library books written by women, especially such as relate to the exact sciences, to philosophy, art, etc."[74]

Besides prodding the states, Palmer moved forward on other fronts. On March 19, 1892, she wrote to the popular British novelist Mrs. Humphrey Ward (a noted antisuffragist) with a detailed description of what the BLM hoped to accomplish at Chicago. "We hope to make the exhibitions in the Woman's Building the grandest display that has ever been made of the work of women of every race and country in every department of art, science, literature, industry, and philanthropy, from the earliest times to the present day," she declared. "We hope to accomplish this by means of records and by exhibiting objects of unusual beauty or merit that have been made by women." Although she did not specify the role the library would play, by this time the bare outlines of an acquisitions policy had become evident. "If we succeed," she continued, "this collection will show the progress of women from the beginning of history to the present era, and commemorate all the great achievements of women." Palmer then asked Ward "if it would be possible for you to allow us to exhibit 'Robert Elsmere' as it appeared from your pen" for a display of manuscripts by prominent women writers. She sent similar requests to other authors, along with the heirs of Helen Hunt Jackson, from whom she requested the manuscript of *Ramona*.[75]

Later that spring Palmer expanded her campaign. In April she began efforts to compile a World's Fair "encyclopedia of the organizations conducted by women, not only in the United States, but the world." By means of circulars published in periodicals, she asked "the president of every such organization" to send a list of officers to the Rand McNally publishing house in Chicago. During a trip to New York she requested from publishers lists of women authors and female book and magazine illustrators they had published. Once she had the list, "plans were set on foot to obtain old volumes and manuscripts illustrated by women, together with historical data concerning women's share in this line of work from ancient times down to the present."[76]

To the Century Company, Palmer wrote: "As you know, one of the features of the Woman's Building is to be a library of books written by women. We are of course anxious that our country-women should be well represented there. Can you read us the names and addresses of women whose books your firm has published?" She indicated that the BLM wanted "books of fiction, poetry, biography, history, art, etc., and particularly any work written by women on any of the exact sciences." She also asked for "original manuscripts of famous books together with a portrait of the author," but she realized they would need the publishers' permission. "Can you advise us on this point?" she queried. She sent similar letters to Harper Brothers, *Cosmopolitan*, Charles Scribner's Sons, Macmillan, Appleton, Lippincott, Roberts Brothers, and Houghton Mifflin.[77]

Of the BLM member representing the District of Columbia Palmer requested "that you will visit the Congressional Library and let me know if there is anything there which will be of interest to us—books written by women or in regard to women, or old illuminations, manuscripts, or anything of that kind." She asked for a quick response: "I am very anxious to have this information as soon as possible, as the Commission expects to secure permission to use available material in this library, and we wish to put in our request at the same time if there is anything that will be useful to us." To a Missouri member of the BLM, she asked whether "the [Missouri] literary committee could send us information as to books written by women which should find a place in the women's library, also as to rare manuscripts and portraits or busts of noted women of which they may chance to know."[78]

To solicit exhibits from foreign countries, Palmer often tried to work through the U.S. State Department. In many cases she appealed to women's organizations in those countries by citing the role and contributions of women and the conditions under which they had to work in modern societies. "The very fact of the creation of the Board of Lady Managers . . . was sufficiently extraordinary to attract and hold the attention of foreign women of the best thought," she later wrote. "Consequently our invitation was at once understood . . . and met with universal reception of the warmest cordiality."[79] That summer Palmer toured Europe. Everywhere she went, she related, "we were taken seriously" by exposition officials. To many of the people she visited, she mentioned the Woman's Building Library. "Our building has been a greater help to us than any other one feature," she reported. Frances Willard later avowed: "It became the fashion abroad to be identified with Exposition work. . . . No movement has ever so universally enlisted the most influential women of Europe."[80] In the end, the only European countries not represented in the Woman's Building exhibits were Russia, Denmark, and Portugal.

In England, Queen Victoria took direct interest in the British exhibit that was being constructed for the Woman's Building. So did her daughter Princess Christian.[81] By June 1892, the first consignment of books from England had arrived—four books by the Christian writer Constance Howell accompanied by a letter saying she had been requested, the *World's Columbian Exposition Illustrated* reported, by "an auxiliary of the Board of Lady Managers to contribute the writings to the Library of women's books."[82] In the end, the British collection included volumes by (among others) Jane Austen, Mary Elizabeth Braddon, the Brontës, Rhoda Broughton, Elizabeth Barrett Browning, Fanny Burney, Marie Corelli, Maria Edgeworth, George Eliot, Elizabeth Gaskell, Felecia Hemans, Fanny Kemble, Mary Lamb, Vernon Lee, Harriett Martineau, Edith Nesbit, Margaret Oliphant, Ouida (Marie Louise de la Ramée), Ann Radcliffe, Christina Rossetti, Olive Schreiner, Mary Shelley, Mary Sherwood, Mrs. Humphrey Ward, Ellen Wood, Mary Wollstonecraft, and Charlotte Yonge. England also sent manuscripts by Jane Austen, Charlotte Brontë, Maria

Edgeworth, Fanny Burney, Elizabeth Gaskell, and George Eliot, in addition
to three pristine editions of the *Boke of St. Albans*, by Dame Juliana Berners,
which was first printed around 1480.[83]

In France, Palmer discovered a committee of women formed for the 1889
Paris Exposition who had a continued interest in the charitable and philan-
thropic work of French women. With some prompting from Palmer, the
French government agreed to appoint a Woman's Committee and appropriate
200,000 francs for its work. In the end, France's contribution to the Woman's
Building Library was the largest non-English collection. All told, it contained
nearly one thousand items, including works by Madame Récamier, Marie de
France, George Sand, and Madame de Staël. Royalty in Germany, Belgium,
Austria, and Italy took responsibility for the exhibits from their countries. In
Austria, Princess Metternich and Princess Windisgratz, seeing an opportunity to promote traditional peasant crafts and open markets for these articles
abroad, persuaded the Empress Marie Therese to head the Austrian Women's
Commission. The Viennese educator Augusta Groner sent thirteen volumes of
her own work, and newspapers urged "upon her countrywomen the immense
importance of their availing themselves of the opportunity afforded them by
cooperation with the American Woman's Board."[84] Although Groner's volumes
were not included in the library's *List of Books*, and thus were probably displayed
elsewhere at the exposition, the Austrian Women's Commission did contribute
poetry and novels, as well as works on home economics and education, to the
Woman's Building Library. The women of Bohemia collected roughly three
hundred books for the library, "all original, not one translated," and all "written exclusively by women." That compared quite favorably, remarked Josefa
Humpal Zeman, a native of Bohemia, with five hundred from Germany and
seven hundred from France, where women were more numerous and benefited
from a more consistently stable political and cultural environment.[85]

Because Spain's Queen Isabella would receive special attention at the exposition, Spanish women made efforts to collect material written by their countrywomen since 1492, including works by women who inhabited the Spanish
West Indies. Echoing an ideology that was repeated in countless forms and
contexts throughout the Columbian Exposition, Frances Willard later commended Spain's contribution to the imperialist project while denigrating the
non-Western people they colonized. "When America was peopled by naked
savages," she noted, "the Spanish women were eminent, as appears from this
extraordinary showing, in literature and art."[86] With more than five hundred
volumes on display, Spain contributed more items to the library than any other
countries except the United States and France.

Italy benefited from the efforts of Alice Howard Cady of New York, who in 1892 was visiting her sister there. Because the Italian Committee appointed by the government had "absolutely refused" to develop a woman's book collection, Cady, at her own expense, interviewed authors, "translated and published circulars in Italian, advertised printed notifications in the papers and attended to all the detail of having the Italian books transmitted from their authors." As a result, she accumulated 150 volumes, accounting for two-thirds of Italy's contribution to the library. She convinced Madame Fanny Zampini Salazar (an Italian countess who later represented her country at the exposition) to publish an appeal throughout the country, declaring it was the "patriotic duty" of Italian women engaged in literary, scientific, artistic, or educational work "to join in an exhibition wherein women from the world over would send their intellectual productions." Response was tepid. "You must not judge us by our display," Salazar demurred after she arrived at the fair, because in Italy "woman's intellectual work is not encouraged." Her fellow countrywomen, she explained, "could not overcome" a "timidity" bred by this cultural climate.[87] Eventually, the Biblioteca Nazionale in Rome sent a number of books, some dating as far back as 1587, written by women in Italian convents.

Salazar's sentiment mirrored the reactions from many corners of the globe. Mexico promised nine books but apparently never delivered them, and except for Mercedes Cabello de Carbonero, a Peruvian writer who sent her own works, Latin America was very sparsely represented.[88] Despite her public rhetoric to the contrary, Palmer felt snubbed by countries like Japan, China, Tunis, and Syria, where rulers felt women were not, as a Japanese official wrote, "sufficiently advanced to successfully undertake an enterprise of this kind."[89] Not until late fall 1892 did Japan form a Woman's Board, and then only after five months of effort by Mrs. Erastus L. Bell of Chicago. "At first," *Woman's Journal* reported, "she found only an apathetic acceptance of the statement that nothing could be done because the Japanese government had made no provision for the representation of its women." Only after Bell gained the interest of the Empress did she receive invitations to receptions at which she explained "all that it would mean for the women of their country" to form a board. Ultimately, Japan promised to send fifty books; if delivered, however, their arrival was never recorded.[90]

With the help of people like Bell and Cady, Palmer succeeded in making the Woman's Building Library more globally comprehensive. The character of the works sent from abroad, the *Chicago Daily Tribune* reported (with a tacit assumption of fiction's low status), "seems to indicate that woman has passed beyond fiction and is writing textbooks on science and philosophy," noting

that "imposing works on metaphysical subjects are being constantly received."
Largely through Palmer's "plans and efforts," *Woman's Journal* stated later, "the
claims of women have been presented before foreign governments, and as a
result women and their work are officially recognized in the exhibits from
nearly every country." Although *Woman's Journal* exaggerated the proportion of
foreign countries represented, the library did receive contributions from many
nations, including some in Asia, South America, and the Middle East (see
table 2.1). A circular to all foreign women's World's Fair committees soliciting

TABLE 2.1

Approximate number of items contributed to the
Woman's Building Library by participating countries

Country	Number of items
United States	4,866
France	985
Spain	533
Great Britain	507
Germany	326
Bohemia	283
Italy	227
Norway	159
Sweden	149
Belgium	116
Holland	62
Austria	23
Peru	5
Portugal	3
Turkey	3
Canada	2
China	2
Greece	2
Arabia	1
Brazil	1
Cuba	1
Finland	1
Japan	1
Poland	1
Total	**8,259**

SOURCE: Edith Clarke, *List of Books Sent by Home and Foreign
Committees to the Library of the Woman's Building, World's
Columbian Exposition, Chicago, 1893* (Chicago, 1894).

information on exhibit space asked first: "How many books will be sent to the Woman's Library?"[91]

As word circulated through the state and foreign exposition committees that the BLM was assembling a library for the Woman's Building, Palmer began receiving inquiries from authors about including their titles. When Fanny Byse of Lausanne, Switzerland, told Palmer about her new book, *The New Continent*, for example, Palmer thanked her for her offer to donate a copy but told her she would first have "to secure the endorsement of the Swiss Commission of women . . . as the rule has been established that all exhibits . . . from foreign countries must first receive the approval of the Woman's Commission of that country."[92] In every case for which documentation can be found, Palmer's response to such queries was consistent with this one.

The success of the library, however, rested largely on the response of women in the United States. Works by foreigners, the *Los Angeles Times* suggested, were "but a matter of curiosity; the work of American women will make an exposition in itself." By the fall of 1891 Palmer could report to her colleagues, "The organization of state boards has been slowly perfected and we have at present thirty-seven States, two Territories, Alaska and the District of Columbia in which there are committees composed of able and influential women." Palmer recognized that although these women were primarily responsible to their states, the discoveries they made about native daughters in the course of doing state work would inevitably benefit the library as a representative collection of authors and texts. "Reams of circulars were printed and sent out from the headquarters at Chicago," the Connecticut Woman's Board of Managers reported later, "recommending, urging, outlining, planning, suggesting," and asking questions. "Tons of letters went flying back and forth. Nothing was left untouched in these plans. The heavens above and the earth beneath, and the waters under the earth were to be searched."[93]

As the soliciting, collecting, and shipping of books progressed, the question of how to assess literary value remained unresolved, and probably deliberately. Because the BLM declined to put into place any formal mechanism for vetting and admitting contributions to the library, it was left to the literary committees of the various state and foreign boards to identify what was "choice" and what was "second rate," and then to acquire and convey to the exposition the selected literary productions of each region. Inevitably, these contributions varied in completeness and character according to the diverse criteria used to determine inclusion. These criteria ranged from the broadly inclusive to the highly selective to the seemingly haphazard.

New York, which claimed to uphold the original ideal of comprehensiveness, sought to contribute works by all authors who were born in the state or had lived there at any time.[94] "The aim of this Exhibit was to make a record of literary work, limited, through necessity, both by sex and locality, but, as far as possible, accurate and complete, and to preserve this record in the State Library in the Capitol at Albany," New York BLM member Blanche Bellamy noted. "It includes twenty-five hundred books, beginning with the works of Charlotte Ramsay Lennox, the first-born female author of the province of New York, published in London in 1759, closing with the pages of a translation of Herder, still wet from the press, and comprising the works of almost every author in the intervening one hundred and forty years." But not only books, Bellamy added. "It includes also three hundred papers read before the literary clubs of the State, a summary of the work of all writers for the press, and the folios which preserve the work of many able women who have not published books."[95] Massachusetts, in contrast, confined itself (at least in principle, if not in practice) to one book per author of what it considered the best works. Connecticut considered only authors *born* in state.[96] Some states probably sent whatever happened to turn up; nine states and territories sent nothing at all (see table 2.2).

In her home state of Illinois, Palmer persuaded the legislature to appropriate $80,000 (one-tenth of the state's entire appropriation for the exposition) to an Illinois Woman's Exposition Board. This board quickly established three goals: to collect "samples" of work done by Illinois women; to demonstrate "the best methods and results in all the common and everyday duties of life"; and to identify "new avenues of activity and the broadening opportunities for self-advancement and self-support" open to the state's women. The board organized Columbian County Clubs in every county except Cook County, which already had numerous organizations; and its Committee on Literature set about collecting works by Illinois women that appeared in books, newspapers, and magazines.[97]

The Illinois State Building benefited directly from these efforts. Two committee members took responsibility for decorating the building's reception room and library, following Candace Wheeler's lead in making users feel "at home in a literary atmosphere." It contained a white maple mantel furnished by the Jacksonville Women's Club, a hand-carved bookcase from the Sterling Women's Club, a carved easel from Ford County, and a painted ceiling and frieze with designs adapted from bookplates by William Caxton and other early printers. On them Illinois women artists depicted "Music," "Teaching," "Industrial Arts," "Drama," "Progress," and "Youth." The Illinois Woman's Exposition Board eventually identified 150 female authors spanning the state's short literary history, whose works they also placed in the library of the Illinois Building, and they produced a catalog of works by Illinois women writers that utilized two classification systems (one alphabetical, one with subject

Table 2.2

Approximate number of items contributed to the Woman's
Building Library by participating U.S. states and territories

State or territory	Number of items
Alabama	35
Arkansas	7
California	7
Colorado	77
Connecticut	213
Delaware	7
District of Columbia	141
Florida	10
Georgia	13
Illinois	508
Indiana	1
Iowa	6
Kansas	5
Kentucky	25
Louisiana	32
Maine	45
Maryland	62
Massachusetts	136
Michigan	33
Minnesota	29
Mississippi	3
Missouri	4
Montana	4
Nebraska	22
New Hampshire	4
New Jersey	392
New York	2,206
North Carolina	27
North Dakota	1
Ohio	106
Oregon	11
Pennsylvania	542
Rhode Island	52
South Carolina	12
Tennessee	15
Texas	33
Utah	5
Vermont	1
Virginia	13
West Virginia	7
Wisconsin	14
Total	**4,866**

Source: Clarke, *List of Books Sent by Home and Foreign Committees.*

headings).[98] Altogether Illinois contributed over five hundred volumes to the Woman's Building Library. Illinois women also produced a volume of statistics about professional women in the state, several thousand copies of which were distributed free. As in the Woman's Building (and in women's clubs across the country), participation by Illinois women in gathering items for the state exhibit facilitated a feeling of community and the development of networks.[99]

The Iowa Board of Lady Managers used Township Clubs and County Societies to raise funds and prepare and collect exhibits. In the fall of 1891, the Ladies Literary Association of Dubuque gave a reception for Mrs. John Bagley, BLM member-at-large from Michigan, who talked about the scope of the women's exhibit. Bagley urged her audience to help make the exposition "the vestibule through which she [woman] can walk triumphant into the twentieth century."[100] In July 1892, the president of the Iowa Board of Lady Managers sent a circular to Iowa women asking for help in putting together an exhibit of "works of superior merit for the gallery of honor" in the Woman's Building. "Our desire is to exhibit . . . all articles which illustrate woman's share in the industrial, educational, artistic, religious and philanthropical activities of Iowa . . . in such a manner as to indicate the progress women have made in all these various departments during the comparatively few years of our state's existence." She then listed the kinds of things they wanted to incorporate, including "copies of all books, pamphlets or newspapers now or heretofore written or edited by Iowa women," and "all books and papers illustrated by Iowa women."[101] Despite their ambitions, however, the Iowa contribution numbered only six titles cataloged in the *List of Books,* including a novel, a musical chart, a translation of the Bible, a German textbook, a record of early Dubuque clubs, and proceedings of the Davenport Academy of Natural Sciences.

On November 4, 1891, Michigan's Board of Lady Managers sent out a circular "To the Women of Michigan." Response was gratifying, Mrs. John Bagley reported to the *Chicago Tribune.* The Michigan Committee "is receiving valuable assistance from women journalists and writers in every line of literature." Michigan contributed thirty-three volumes, roughly half of them works of fiction. Neighboring Indiana produced a volume titled *The Associated Work of the Women of Indiana,* which investigated the condition of women workers in the state, including union workers, although it contributed only one book—Lora S. La Mance's *Beautiful Home Surroundings*—to the Woman's Building Library. Minnesota prepared a typewritten pamphlet titled *Minnesota in Literature: Minneapolis,* as well as gathering more than two dozen works by women of the state.[102]

"Columbian Clubs" formed in Kansas to produce a history of women's work for each county in the state. The Kansas Equal Suffrage Association (KESA) planned a "Woman's Room" in the Kansas Building that would contain a small library of Kansas authors. The April 15, 1893, issue of *Woman's Journal* carried a letter from the KESA librarian appealing to all readers for funds to buy "rare Kansas books." She also identified a number of female Kansas authors who "gave us the sale of their works on a commission." All found their way into the scrapbooks displayed in the Woman's Building Library; none was separately cited in the final bibliography, which listed only a handful of volumes from Kansas. Apparently, the Kansas Building was the primary beneficiary of the KESA's efforts.[103]

Nebraska's building also included a reading room, where the works of nearly a score of female Nebraska authors identified by the Nebraska Woman's Auxiliary Board found places on the shelves.[104] The Woman's Building Library featured twenty-two volumes by Nebraska women, including several treatises by the pioneering chemist Rachel Holloway Lloyd, the first American woman to earn a Ph.D. in chemistry (at the University of Zürich in 1887), and Mary Tremain's scholarly study *Slavery in the District of Columbia* (1892). North Dakota contributed only one volume: Frances Chamberlain Holley's *Once Their Home; or, Our Legacy from the Dahkotahs* (1890).

In May 1892, members of the Connecticut Woman's Board of Managers informed women in the state that their exhibit would contain, among other items, "literature," including "Selections from the Writings of Connecticut Women." They sent notices to all state newspapers that for the library in the Woman's Building "only books of scientific, historical, and literary value will be received." Under Jeannette Lindsley [Mrs. J. G.] Gregory, a Committee on Literature compiled and published five hundred copies of the professionally printed, suede-bound *Selections from the Writings of Connecticut Women*, which identified 103 authors, fifty of whom were short story writers. The committee sent a copy to every state and college library in the country, as well as many public libraries.[105]

In Connecticut, where the Woman's Board of Managers received its "Scriptural tenth" of the $50,000 state allocation, officials acknowledged the stimulus of central BLM planning. Because the response to BLM flyers was so overwhelming, Connecticut decided to limit its collection of authors to those born in the state. (The one exception to this rule was Catharine Beecher, whose birth on Long Island, the Connecticut board argued, was a "mere accident . . . we simply set down among the visitations of Providence, the kind of thing which no amount of regret will alter.") It concentrated on collecting first editions and, wherever possible, autographed copies. Connecticut women also gathered a special collection of "literary curiosities" that included a portrait and diary of Lydia Huntley Sigourney and early editions of her works, a manuscript volume of compositions from Catharine Beecher's school, and "first compositions" of Harriet Beecher Stowe, Fanny Fern, and others. The collection they eventually forwarded to the Woman's Building consisted of more than two hundred books as well as a special display of editions of *Uncle Tom's Cabin* to be showcased in a mahogany cabinet. Among Connecticut's contributions were nearly a hundred volumes of fiction, more than twenty volumes of poetry, and the doctoral thesis of Margaretta Palmer, one of the first women astronomers. In addition to Fern, Sigourney, and Stowe, the literary women represented in the collection included Rose Terry Cooke, Grace Greenwood, Mary Jane Holmes, Louise Chandler Moulton, and Margaret Sidney.[106]

Gregory later recorded humorous anecdotes that surfaced from Connecticut's efforts to assemble a collection. One woman, she said, sent in nearly a hundred handwritten verses on subjects like infant baptism, firemen's duty, and "true religion." She requested that the committee print them into a pamphlet titled "Flowers of Thought" for display in the Woman's Building Library, and have "as many copies forwarded to her address as we could conveniently spare." Another asked which of her many books the Connecticut Committee on Literature wanted for the exhibit. When the committee requested that she make a selection, the author said she could not but would send them all, "provided we would purchase them." The committee declined her offer. A third woman said she had written "a profound and exhaustive treatise on a psychical subject" that was "more adapted to a collection of works written by *men* of deep thought than to a woman's library." The husband of a fourth, who had been queried for materials, responded that his wife had recently died but that he "had a copy of her book in the house, which he would sell to us for two dollars and a half—postage 16 cents." When his second wife found out about the offer, she informed the Connecticut Woman's Board of Managers that she feared sending the volume "might awaken painful associations" for her husband and begged them "not [to] pursue the subject."[107]

New Jersey established its Board of Woman Managers in June 1892 and appointed Margaret Tufts Yardley chair of the Committee on Literature. Yardley promptly launched an effort to collect two copies of every book written by a New Jersey woman, one for the New Jersey Building and the other for the Woman's Building Library. Ultimately, she discovered that although a large number of women authors lived in New Jersey, they published in and identified with New York City. Others had never published books but were regular contributors to magazines and newspapers. To include the latter, Yardley decided to compile a two-volume *New Jersey Scrapbook*. When five hundred copies were published in the spring of 1893, the *New Jersey Scrapbook* contained one article each (sometimes abbreviated) from hundreds of female authors whose work appeared in numerous periodicals.[108] The *New Jersey Scrapbook* was shelved in the Woman's Building Library along with nearly four hundred other volumes by New Jersey women, including nearly 150 works of fiction, twenty-seven volumes of poetry, and the *History of Woman Suffrage* by Elizabeth Cady Stanton, Susan B. Anthony, and Matilda Joslyn Gage.

In his first report, E. C. Hovey, secretary of the Massachusetts Board of World's Fair Managers, complimented Bay State publishers for contributions "to the literature of the country." He made no mention, however, of the works Massachusetts women were gathering for the Woman's Building. Nonetheless, *Woman's Journal* noted that "Mr. Hovey is greatly interested in all the advance which women are making in every avenue of labor open to them." Moreover, he wanted women of the state to drop off items for the Massachusetts exhibit at his office in Boston. All exhibit applications for the Woman's Building would go through the Board of Lady Managers, *Woman's Journal* reported. "With Mrs. Potter Palmer at the head of this work, and Mr. Hovey so fully in sympathy with women's interests, Massachusetts women have a clear field and every prospect of a grand and successful exhibition at Chicago."[109]

In another article *Woman's Journal* described the Massachusetts Woman's Columbian Exposition exhibit: "It is proposed to exhibit by charts, reports, photographs, publications, and illustrations the scientific work of women's organizations and that of women in institutions for both sexes, and of individual women outside of organizations; also of educational or scientific enterprises instigated and supported by women." For its contribution to the Woman's Building Library, Massachusetts sent nearly 140 books, limiting most of its authors to one book. To supplement this selection, the novelist Margaret Deland, who chaired the state's library committee, compiled a list of two thousand books by Massachusetts women to be displayed in the Woman's Building Library.[110] Visitors to the exposition who scanned the shelves of the Massachusetts section would have found many of the authors who later defined the canon of nineteenth-century American women writers, including Louisa May Alcott, Catharine Beecher, Lydia Maria Child, Rose Terry Cooke, Maria Susanna Cummins, Emily Dickinson, Mary E. Wilkins Freeman, Margaret Fuller, Lucretia P. Hale, Sarah J. Hale, Julia Ward Howe, Helen Hunt Jackson, Sarah Orne Jewett, Lucy Larcom, Louise Chandler Moulton, Frances Osgood, Elizabeth Peabody, Elizabeth Stuart Phelps, Catherine Maria Sedgwick, Margaret Sidney, and Harriet Spofford. Although a few earlier women were also represented (for example, Anne Bradstreet, Abigail Adams, and Mercy Otis Warren), for unknown reasons the Massachusetts women's board omitted Mary Rowlandson and Phillis Wheatley. Elsewhere in New England, New Hampshire sent a handful of books, Vermont a single volume of poems. Maine contributed nearly fifty volumes, and Rhode Island prepared a bibliography of the state's literary women to accompany its collection.[111]

The District of Columbia received help from the BLM's Mary Lockwood, who in early January 1892 delivered a lecture in Washington "for the benefit of World's Fair work." With the help of eight stereopticon views, she "traced the progress of the works in arts and manufactures showing that the initial steps were in every case taken by woman from the time when she was first seized with the desire for knowledge, and took the forbidden fruit."[112] The District's contribution to the Woman's Building Library included (among other items) twenty-three volumes of German fiction translated by Mary Joanna Safford, fourteen volumes of fiction by Frances Hodgson Burnett, and three volumes of poetry by Lillian Rozell Messenger (an author also claimed by Arkansas)—including "Columbus; or, It Was Morning," a poem she first publicly read in the Woman's Building on July 4, 1893, before the women's congresses assembled there.

In the spring of 1892 Pennsylvania's World's Fair Commission authorized $50 per month to rent a room in Pittsburgh to "receive and push the women's work." Philadelphia women assisted by collecting statistics on women librarians, curators, and editors, along with books written by Pennsylvania women. A steady supply of information came from a system of Ladies Auxiliaries in sixty-seven counties with a total membership exceeding eleven hundred.[113] Pennsylvania's contribution to the Woman's Building Library consisted of over five hundred volumes, including over one hundred volumes of fiction, thirty-five volumes with the Dewy Decimal category "Christian experience, practice, life," more than thirty volumes of poetry, twenty-eight texts categorized as "Gynecology and other medical specialties," Sarah Wister's *Amusing Scenes of the Revolution* (1789), and four studies by pioneering biochemist Helen Abbott Michael.

Since Missouri allocated no money for displaying women's work, the Woman's World's Fair Association of St. Louis put forty committees to work "devising ways and means to raise funds for this purpose." To generate revenue the association opened a dining room and gave regular dairy luncheons.[114] In the end, however, Missouri contributed only four volumes to the Woman's Building Library. Kentucky's committee identified seventy-five women authors, forty of whose books they placed in their state building; and twenty-five works by these authors they entered in the Woman's Building Library. Texas and Virginia followed the example, placing the works of native daughters in state buildings as well as the Woman's Building Library. Virginia compiled a list of Virginia authors from colonial times, which identified more than 2,300 volumes written by some five hundred women. Texas supplemented its collection with a portfolio showcasing the work of the state's women artists and journalists.

In North Carolina, Lady Managers divided the work of their state into several categories, including "colonial display, art, needle and fancy work, press work, literature, inventions, and statistics." Sallie Southall Cotten of Falkland took responsibility for literature and at her own expense traveled the state to find titles written by Tarheel women, often accompanied by her twenty-year-old son, Bruce. Cotten discovered very few libraries in the state, and no bibliography to help identify North Carolina authors. Despite persistent searching, she came up with only twenty-seven volumes to forward to the Woman's Building Library, seventeen of them novels by Christian Reid (Frances Christine Fisher Tiernan).[115] Georgia contributed a collection of thirteen novels by Elzey Hay (Eliza Frances [Fanny] Andrews), Mary Edwards Bryan, Sarah Barnwell Elliot, and Odessa Strickland Payne, and Alabama's collection of thirty-five items included a volume about Helen Keller as well as seven novels by Augusta Jane Evans. Mississippi contributed two volumes of fiction by Kate Lee Ferguson, together with *The Power*, a publication edited by "Lady students of the Industrial Institute and College in Columbus." Among Louisiana's thirty-two volumes, six were in French.

Some of the mountain states followed suit. In May 1891, Colorado Lady Managers mailed a circular to thousands of the state's women. "We ask from those who are interested suggestions as to the best method of showing to others what we can do, and are doing, as bread-winners and workers in this 'New West.'" In addition to suggestions for the "preparation of meals—doubtless woman's first employment," the project also included journalism and "the making of books." Later, Colorado women proudly announced that "copies of the works of every Colorado author are to be collected in the State building."[116] The Woman's Building Library contained nearly eighty volumes by Colorado women, including fifteen by Helen Hunt Jackson. In Utah (then still a territory), Mormon leader and suffragist Emmeline B. Wells encouraged women to form "Columbian Clubs" and "Queen Isabella Circles." The Utah Territory established a Woman's Department as part of its delegation in the spring of 1892 but in time shifted its responsibilities to a Board of Lady Managers, whose "work of collecting exhibits was pushed with vim and energy." Most of the exhibits ended up in the Utah Building, although the Woman's Building Library included *World's Fair Ecclesiastical History of Utah*, edited by suffragist Sarah Kimball, *Salt Lake City Literary Society Club Book*, two copies of the illustrated multiauthor anthology *Songs and Flowers of the Wasatch*, edited by Emmeline Wells, and a twenty-year run of the prosuffragist newspaper *Woman's Exponent* (1872–1893).[117] Montana's contribution consisted of a volume of juvenile stories and poems by children of the state, two scrapbooks, and *Gathered Leaves*, a "souvenir" volume by Carrie E. Robinson.

On the Pacific coast, Oregon women contributed eleven volumes, including six volumes of history and fiction by Frances Fuller Victor. In California, women affiliated with the San Francisco World's Fair Association prepared a bibliography of California writers to be sold at the state's literary exhibit for twenty-five cents per copy.[118] The novelist and playwright Ella Sterling Cummins (later Mighels) prepared a history titled *The Story of the Files: A Review of Californian Writers and Literature.* Issued by the World's Fair Commission of California, *The Story of the Files* drew extensively on magazines and journals published in the state. Careful to highlight the contributions of women writers, Cummins featured chapters on "The Women of *The Golden Era*" and the magazine writer Olive Harper, who penned travel sketches of "Yo Semite," Egypt, and Turkey. She also included brief profiles of Josephine Clifford, Frances Fuller Victor, and other women of the "Overland School." The volume highlights women's contributions to *The Wasp*, the first color cartoon paper (featuring satirical sketches by Charlotte Perkins [Stetson] Gilman); women of the "Argonaut School"; and female contributors to *The Californian, The Golden Era, The Ingleside,* and *The Wave;* along with sketches about Gertrude Atherton, Kate Douglass Wiggin, and many other writers. *The Story of the Files* further emphasizes the role of women writers with an essay on "Literature as Profession for Women," a chapter on "San Francisco Journalism from a Woman's Point of View," a profile of the Woman's Press Association (which included further commentary on Gilman), and a chapter on "Women Writers of Southern California."[119]

Publicly, Bertha Palmer seemed pleased with progress on collections being generated for the Woman's Building Library by state delegations. "Almost daily letters from the Woman's Board of various states and Territories mention additions to the collections of books by women being made for the library in the Woman's Building," the *World's Columbian Exposition Illustrated* noted in June 1892. With only one exception, Palmer imposed no restrictions on state delegations' collecting practices. In early April 1892, the BLM sent a letter to state delegations suggesting that the library not include any women's translations of books written by men. (Ultimately, however, the collection did include translations of works by male authors.) "In the library will be gathered all the books which women have written," *Harper's Bazar* told readers in August, adding, "The ladies at Chicago bid the ungallant and unsophisticated part of the masculine public to prepare itself for the discovery that, so far from women's book writing confined to fiction in prose and verse, it includes a large portion of works on nearly all the arts and sciences."[120]

Everything seemed to be progressing according to plan. When the exposition hosted an official dedication ceremony on October 21, 1892, a crowd estimated at between 100,000 and 150,000 attended, most gathered in the nineteen-story Manufactures and Liberal Arts Building, at that time the largest in the world. The Chicago Symphony provided music with a five hundred–member orchestra and 5,500-member chorus, while visiting dignitaries—including Vice President Levi P. Morton—gave numerous speeches, which most people could not hear. The road to this day had not been easy. Draining the wetland on which the fairgrounds stood had taken longer than expected, and on many days men and horses worked knee-deep in mud. Moreover, the winter of 1892 had been particularly severe. On several occasions temperatures dropped to twenty degrees below zero, and heavy snows sometimes collapsed the roofs of unfinished buildings.

As Bertha Palmer approached the lectern, "handkerchiefs waved from all parts of the building, and from the chorus stand came the shrill voices of hundreds of school children, joining in the sound of greeting."[121] In a day full of speeches, she had been allocated eight minutes. Palmer made no mention of the Woman's Building Library, but she did set a tone. "The provision of the Act of Congress, that the Board of Lady Managers appoint a jury of woman's peers to pass judgment upon her work," she announced, "adds to the significance of the innovation, for never before was it thought necessary to apply this fundamental principle of justice to our sex." As is implied by the rhetoric of law and justice, Palmer was staking a claim for women's fundamental right to unbiased representation and self-determination in the public sphere. "Even more important than the discovery of Columbus, which we are gathered together to celebrate," she concluded, "is the fact that the General Government has just discovered woman."[122] By October 21, 1892, it was clear—at least in Palmer's mind and in the minds of participating middle- and upper-class white women across the country—that the Woman's Building and its library were to be emblematic of this "discovery."

3

Empire Building

At the time of the October 21, 1892, dedication ceremony, Bertha Palmer knew that the New York delegation was working hard on the Woman's Building Library. She was unaware of its specific goals, however, and could not have foreseen the enormous impact those goals would have on the library that would debut to hundreds of thousands of fairgoers six months later. In fact, New York's contribution to the Woman's Building Library would be especially influential for several reasons. First, the New York Board of Women Managers took the lead in collection development, as well as in furnishing and decorating the library. New York Women Managers successfully organized and coordinated the efforts of prominent women's clubs statewide. New York also distinguished itself by fostering an exhibit representing African American women. And, in addition to the New York Board of Women Managers, another group heavily influenced by New Yorkers—the American Library Association (ALA)—was helping to professionalize the Woman's Building Library. Because of the contributions of these groups—the New York Board, New York clubwomen, and the ALA—no other geographical region or state played so large a role in shaping the design, content, and administration of the Woman's Building Library.

Initially, Empire State women struggled to find direction. In the late spring of 1891, the New York members of the BLM informed Palmer that the state legislature had not yet appropriated funds to construct an exhibit, and asked her advice. "The president of the Board of Lady Managers wrote them a letter from mid-ocean which was stirring as a bugle-call," Nancy Huston Banks reported in the July issue of *World's Columbian Exposition Illustrated.* "Canvass New York," Palmer said, "find out what women are doing and what they want to do."[1] In response, Mary Trautmann, a New York member of the national BLM, spearheaded efforts to plan the contribution of New York women to the exposition. Then, in the spring of 1892, the New York legislature allocated $25,000 for the state's showing at the World's Fair.

In time New York's Board of General Managers appointed a twenty-one-member Board of Women Managers "to assist the representative women of the nation in obtaining for that occasion a full and complete portrayal of the industrial and social conditions of woman and her achievements and capabilities in all the avenues and departments of life." They were to be drawn representationally from New York's eight judicial districts (with five representatives allocated to New York City), given office space in Albany, and required to submit monthly reports. The New York women's board elected Mrs. Erastus Corning as president. On December 1, 1891, Palmer met the New York women in Mary Trautmann's home. "A great deal of enthusiasm was expressed in the work as Mrs. Palmer unfolded it," the *New York Times* reported, "and a number of ladies made short speeches."[2]

By that time New York women had separated themselves from other state delegations by appointing Joan Imogen Howard, an African American woman, to its board. Ostensibly, they "were particularly desirous of giving prominence to the arts and industries of the women of that race," but these New York women may also have been reacting to the BLM's treatment of Lettie Trent, Hallie Q. Brown, Fannie Barrier Williams, and their colleagues earlier in the planning stages. Many of the New York women were proud that their state had been a center of abolitionist activity. Howard was a New York City schoolteacher from an old Boston family integral to the success of the Underground Railroad. Determined to make the most of her opportunity, Howard assumed "entire charge of the collection of exhibits, as well as statistics of this department." To complete her exhibit, she traveled the state and corresponded with hundreds of African American women for nearly a year.[3]

New York's contribution to the Woman's Building Library was unique in another way; it included the work of Candace Wheeler, the designer responsible for the building's interior decor. On March 16, 1892, Palmer thanked Wheeler for agreeing to donate some of her tapestries, embroideries, and rose panels for display in the main gallery of the Woman's Building. In the same letter she asked: "How would it suit you to decorate the library?" Palmer indicated that a 50-by-50-foot room—"one of the best rooms in our building"—was designated for that purpose. Although other names had been suggested as potential decorators, she assured Wheeler, "I will try to reserve it for you if you prefer it."[4]

Palmer had good reasons for choosing Wheeler. A decade earlier, the two had become personally acquainted when Palmer hired Wheeler's firm, Associated Artists, to decorate her mansion. Later, in the midst of the debate over the

separation of women's exhibits at the exposition, Palmer consulted Wheeler, a
successful professional woman whose opinion she respected. Wheeler's reply
was unambiguous. "My present feeling about the Exposition," she wrote, "is
that I should like to have all—and the best that we can do, in the Womans [*sic*]
building." With characteristic determination, she continued, "You know I have
always felt that one great purpose of my work was to prove to women their
ability to make conditions & results which were entirely favorable & I should
like to emphasize the fact of its accomplishment."[5]

Wheeler had already established a reputation as the interior decorator of
some of the most palatial homes in New York City and its environs. Her clients
included Cornelius Vanderbilt II and Mark Twain. As her biographer Amelia
Peck points out, she was "one of the first women to be well known as an interior
decorator, a profession she helped to create." Wheeler's career demonstrated
that women could achieve professionalism within the public sphere by extending skills traditionally performed in the home. As Peck observes, "Wheeler's
most significant accomplishment was that both as an early 'career woman' and
as a designer she became a role model for women at the dawn of the twentieth
century, inspiring them to demand a place in the workforce as the equals of
men."[6] Wheeler was also well connected socially and culturally; her friends
included Mrs. Dean Sage of the New York Board of Women Managers, as well
as many prominent women artists and writers whose work would be featured
in the Woman's Building—Mary Mapes Dodge, Ruth McEnery Stuart, and
Kate Douglas Wiggin, to name a few.

Even aside from her impressive resumé of professional successes, Wheeler
was an excellent fit for the job of decorating the Woman's Building. An advocate of the "New Woman" (a term she embraced as early as 1891), Wheeler
dedicated herself to improving the lives of middle-class women.[7] Although the
enterprise most famously associated with her is Associated Artists, the firm
she cofounded with Louis Tiffany and directed from 1883 onward, Wheeler
also formed two cooperatives—the Society of Decorative Art and the Woman's
Exchange—that allowed women to sell their handicrafts and other homemade
products to the public.[8] Even her design aesthetic—which had been influenced
by the Pre-Raphaelites and the Arts and Crafts Movement—reflected her
feminist commitments. Elevating needlework and textile design to fine arts
helped raise the status of these traditional women's handicrafts while promoting the domestic sphere as a site of creativity, artistry, and economic productivity. On April 28, 1892, the Executive Committee of the BLM recommended
appointing a committee to oversee the design and outfitting of the library in
the Woman's Building, to consist of seven prominent New York women with

Mrs. Dean Sage as chair. It was at this meeting that Wheeler was formally named their first choice as the best person to decorate the library.[9]

Seventeen of the twenty-one members of the New York Board of Women Managers showed up for their first meeting on June 7, 1892. Also in attendance were Susan Gale Cooke, secretary of the BLM (representing Palmer) and BLM member Mary Trautmann. Cooke described how the women of several states had assumed responsibility for furnishing and decorating various parts of the Woman's Building. A day later the New York women's board reviewed the duties assigned to the members of state boards as Palmer and her colleagues had outlined them. They then discussed "with considerable enthusiasm" the feasibility of assuming responsibility for the Woman's Building Library. The New York women approved the recommendation of its Executive Committee and authorized the Committee on the Decoration and Furnishing of the Library to begin work. "It is expected that the Library will be the gem of the entire building," the *Brooklyn Eagle* reported. Later, New York women also decided to create a Bureau of Applied Arts under Wheeler's direction (they anticipated she would be made responsible for decorating the entire building); but they worried they would not have sufficient funds to carry out the work. At the time they believed the library would be located on the first floor of the Woman's Building.[10]

To make their work easier, the Executive Committee also created a local committee of New York City and Brooklyn members (who agreed to meet every other Tuesday) to work directly with Wheeler's Bureau of Applied Arts. The New York/Brooklyn subcommittee subsequently decided to contact the exposition's Fine Arts Department and request that two women artists be named to the department. Unfortunately, they met the same kind of resistance Palmer experienced with the National Commission. Only after considerable pressure did the Fine Arts Department agree to add to its numbers the painter Mary Cassatt and Mary Hallock Foote, a highly respected writer and illustrator best known for her sketches of the Far West.[11]

On July 19 the New York women's board sent a letter to the state's Board of General Managers requesting they be allowed to appropriate $5,000 from the $25,000 allocated for the exposition to furnish and decorate the Woman's Building Library. By that time they had learned that all the space on the building's first floor had already been assigned, and the library would be located on the second floor. On the same day Mrs. Corning, the president of the women's board, noted that the New York State Building had "received many donations of carpets and furniture," and she expressed her hope that "we shall have the same courtesy shown to us." *Woman's Journal* reported that for the Woman's Building

Library "the Associated Artists will supply the tapestried hangings for the walls, and the book-cases and other furniture will be designed by women."[12]

Blanche Bellamy, chair of the Committee on Literary Work, proposed an additional way to generate funds. If her committee could identify the forty best poems by New York women, she said, "they might be collected and then put in such form as might be sold for the benefit of the Library Fund." She reported that her committee had decided to seek the cooperation of several New York women's clubs, gather the work of "Women in the Press," and collect the books for the Woman's Building Library. Bellamy also announced that "the Board had been asked to donate the library, made up of the work of New York State women authors, to the State Library at Albany, after the exposition."[13]

On September 6, 1892, Sage observed that the "new room" on the second floor assigned for a library had "a small room at either end, which would be very desirable for the exhibit of statistics." She indicated that Wheeler had asked Palmer if these two rooms could be used "for this purpose." She also noted that the library's ceiling and furnishings would be "in Venetian style" with panels "divided by gold work," and that "everything was to be in harmony." Sage announced that Wheeler "was to have entire charge of the decoration of the Woman's Building," and explained that Wheeler would soon leave for Chicago "to oversee matters generally."[14] Under Wheeler's management, decoration of the library would thus be coordinated with the rest of the building.

When the New York board met again the next day, Sage reported that the Board of General Managers had approved their $5,000 request for the library committee. She also announced that Associated Artists "would lend all hangings needed for the library and put them up at its own expense, and that Mrs. Dora Wheeler Keith would loan the ceiling, to be put up at the expense of the committee." The daughter of Candace Wheeler, Dora had earned an impressive reputation as a painter, illustrator, and designer.

Bellamy then submitted a report from the Committee on Literary Work. Although this committee had initially planned a collection of works authored by Empire State women, within months it had decided to expand its agenda to compile a three-part exhibit: "First, an historical and chronological collection of all books written by women, native or resident of the State; second, a series of chronicles prepared by and representing every literary club, which had been organized for more than three years; and third, a record of the work done [by women] in the [New York] press and in [New York] periodicals; the entire exhibit to be presented afterwards to the State Library." To assist the committee Bellamy identified three New York women's clubs that had agreed to take on particular responsibilities. The Wednesday Afternoon Club would collect the books, the Sorosis Club began gathering data on seventy-five women's literary clubs, and the Graduates' Association of Buffalo started collecting statistics on women working for and writing in newspapers and magazines of the state.[15] The Graduates' Association also began to solicit samples from women journalists, asking each to submit "the best thing she ever wrote," to be included in a display volume at the exposition, "where a niche is being built for them." "These clubs," Bellamy reported, "while being exhibitors, will thus also become themselves exhibits showing the value of organized labor, and the energy, capacity and loyalty of their members."[16]

Thus, the act of forming textual alliances that was an established practice among local women's clubs would now reach across the state to expand a sense of community and function as a catalyst for assembling the library's collection. Bellamy appealed to all New York clubwomen for assistance in identifying "as many books as possible" in their districts, and she solicited her fellow Women Managers for the names and addresses of all women in their districts who had written for the press or who had been members of women's clubs and classes "for more than three years." When she publicly recognized "the valuable assistance of one of the State Librarians, who has prepared lists of books and publishers and of contributors," she also acknowledged a formal working relationship her committee had developed with the State Library and its director, Melvil Dewey.[17]

At the September 7 meeting, Imogen Howard submitted a progress report. "Calls have been made in New York, Brooklyn, Saratoga and Albany," she relayed, "and written appeals have been sent to other parts of the state." She said she did not expect many exhibits, but she hoped a few already submitted would meet the board's approval. A subsequent New York board report noted that Howard's first efforts focused on statistics: "Lists are being prepared of the different pursuits engaged in by colored women of the benevolent and charitable organizations conducted by them, and of women who are connected with the press, or have ever contributed any literary work to the same." Howard indicated that she would focus particularly on the work of African American female teachers. After hearing Howard's report and concluding that "in making her researches she came upon so much that was interesting outside of New York," the Executive Committee determined she should be released from geographic restrictions and "authorized to extend her efforts to other states," noting that "she, therefore, enlisted the aid of colored editors of newspapers, the teachers in schools all over the country, and others whose positions gave them a knowledge of their people."[18] There is no indication that the Executive Committee consulted with or sought permission from the Board of Lady Managers or its president in allowing Howard to exceed New York's charge. On its own, the New York board decided to address a gap in the Woman's Building and its library resulting from racial prejudices that some of their colleagues from the South would have preferred to perpetuate.

On October 14 Bellamy met with the board of directors of Sorosis to discuss her ideas about gathering data on New York's women's clubs. After a brief discussion, Sorosis appointed a committee to assist Bellamy. Several days later Bellamy and the committee chair met in New York to prepare circulars that Sorosis could use for its work. On October 17 Bellamy met with directors of the Wednesday Afternoon Club to discuss efforts to collect books for the Woman's Building Library, and the directors appointed a committee to carry out the work. Several days later the directors voted to contribute an additional $500 to fund the effort. Within weeks the Wednesday Afternoon Club obtained a room in the Bible House on Third Avenue in New York City and furnished it with donated library furniture to accommodate the books they expected to collect. A member of the club paid the rent; she also paid for the "services of a clerk during a considerable period when a place of deposit and a custodian were needed for the books." In the meantime, Bellamy had hosted the president of the Buffalo Club at her house, and together they outlined the club's responsibilities for collecting newspaper and periodical publications by New York women. Bellamy requested that each club appoint a statistician who would report to her biweekly.[19]

The women's clubs employed a variety of methods for organizing within counties. Some wrote letters to clergymen, others to county supervisors, and they solicited from them the names of prominent women who might be interested in the board's work. As a New York women's board report later noted, "A vigorous correspondence was kept up, advertisements sent out broadcast, private libraries, bookstores and bookstalls ransacked, and every means patience and ingenuity could devise was employed to insure the success of the work." Because many of the works written by Empire State women before 1840 were so rare that no copies could be found in the United States, several had to be obtained from England.[20]

Some of the club circulars included questions designed to identify and locate materials for the library. "Have you on your shelves books which you know to have been written by New York women?" one circular asked. "Have you, in some out-of-the-way corner such of these books as are now out of print and which you would like to give to this library? Do you know of any women in your village, or town, or city, or countryside, who have ever written anything of any kind for the papers or magazines?" Months after sending out their circulars, club members fanned out across the state to search for all kinds of information about New York women, including titles of works by New York women authors, artists, and scientists.[21]

At the October 4 New York board meeting, Wheeler announced that two colleagues would approach Duveen Brothers, the renowned New York dealers in fine art and antiques, "to procure tables, chairs, and chimney pieces, all in Venetian style." Eight days later, the board approved Bellamy's request for an additional $300 to help her committee with its work.[22] At their November 1 meeting Bellamy explained the vetting process the collections of women's contributions to newspapers and periodicals had to go through in order to make it into the library. First, the material was screened by the Buffalo Graduates' Club; second, it was sent to Bellamy and a committee colleague for approval; and third, it was handed to the editors. Bellamy also reported that the New Jersey Board of Woman Managers had asked New York to assist in identifying New Jersey writers having close associations with New York in order to minimize duplication of materials in the Woman's Building Library. On November 10 Bellamy met with representatives of all three clubs "to secure a thorough understanding of the plan of work."[23]

Meanwhile, back in Chicago, the Executive Committee of the BLM was considering issues that would potentially affect work all the state delegations were doing on the Woman's Building Library. At a meeting on October 26, 1892, Oregon's Josephine Allen moved that books for the library "be given rather than loaned, that they may be kept afterwards in a permanent Woman's Library in the City of Chicago." Her motion was seconded, but Mary Cantrill, of Kentucky, offered an amendment to have the books donated to Bertha Palmer, who in turn could present them to the women of Illinois "to form the nucleus of a collection of the work of women brain workers throughout the world." When Palmer revealed that plans were afoot to build a memorial building in Chicago after the fair closed that would house "all the beautiful and artistic works" donated to the exposition, it was moved that "all these books be presented to that building." One BLM member from Illinois cautioned her colleagues that "if the board gave these books to the City of Chicago it voted them out of its own control." Instead, she proposed, "We wish to keep possession of them so that we may place them in this memorial building." All agreed, and Allen's original motion was unanimously amended to reflect the committee's sentiments.[24]

Five days later the Executive Committee took up the matter of staffing and rules. The committee empowered Palmer to appoint a "Librarian for the Woman's Building," and then charged "the committee already appointed" to articulate a set of "rules for the library and the librarian." At the same time, however, the Executive Committee advised the committee in charge of the library to "observe the following rules. . . . In the Library, only books of scientific, historical, and literary value will be received. Magazine and press articles of the women writers of each State and Territory may be bound together and placed in this Library, forming complete and attractive volumes upon the subject matter contained therein." In addition, the Executive Committee also passed a rule that "books, magazines, pamphlets, etc. shall be classified according to subject-matter."[25]

A month later, the library committee drafted four "Rules for the Library in the Woman's Building" and ten "Rules for the Librarian." For the former, Rule 1 said that all books, magazines, and pamphlets would be classified by subject. For the latter, rules required one librarian "to prepare a complete catalogue" of the library's contents, and at least one librarian to be present at all times the library was open in order to give visitors "proper information and assist them to view the Library to the best advantage." And although all librarians must "always act courteously and discreetly," they nonetheless had complete responsibility for the collections' security and for making sure "all rules are strictly obeyed." Throughout these discussions, it was obvious the Executive Committee and its library subcommittee regarded the library's book collection as a unified exhibit to be classified under a single subject system. Within a week the BLM began circulating the rules its subcommittee had drafted to state delegations.[26]

When Blanche Bellamy learned from Mary Trautmann on November 14 that the BLM Executive Committee had decided "that no collective exhibits of books from the various States shall be presented in the Library of the Woman's Building," she immediately drafted a response to Palmer. "When we were asked last June to assist in carrying out the scheme of the national Board of Managers for the Woman's Building," she wrote, "we decided to prepare and to place in the Library a record of the work of the women of the State in literature." Because the BLM had made no objection, she said, New York women began to assemble a (projected) three-thousand-volume library of New York women authors, adding that they had delegated the task to three leading women's clubs, two of which eventually contributed $1,100. She pointed out that in western New York Oneida County clubwomen had identified more than 140 local authors who, like Emily Chubbuck, a composition teacher at Utica Female Academy who wrote under the pen name Fanny Forrester, had published scores of stories and sketches in periodicals such as *Mother's Magazine*.[27]

Bellamy also reported that "experts in the State Library" had developed a preliminary catalog, and an advisory committee "of the best known literary women in the State" was monitoring the quality of the collection. The New York board had sent the preliminary catalog "to every large library and to every publisher in the country and to every author named, asking them to give us books and to help us by noticing any omissions or errors" in order to make the catalog "complete." And, she continued, "to each and every one of this great body of women"—the Sorosis, Buffalo Graduates, and Wednesday Afternoon Clubs, the New York librarians, the advisory Literary Committee, and the New York Board of Women Managers—"we have appealed for a State collection which, after the Exposition, shall be presented to the State Library in the Capitol." Because her colleagues had worked so hard and had assembled such an impressive collection, and because they had contacted publishers, authors, and librarians on the premise that New York would have a separate collection, Bellamy argued, the New York collection had to remain separate. "Unless we are able to do so," she threatened, "we must either at once stop our entire work, or secure the presentation of this exhibit elsewhere than in the Woman's Building." Bellamy concluded by asking Palmer if the BLM would reconsider its decision.[28] Palmer must have realized it was not a request to be considered lightly.

The following day Imogen Howard submitted a progress report to the New York women managers. She indicated that she had made contact with African American women's groups in Philadelphia, Washington, and Boston (but not Chicago), each of which took responsibility for generating statistics on African American women. Initially, Philadelphia had promised to cover the Middle Atlantic states, Boston the New England states, and "the large organization of women in Washington" the states in the South and West. Ultimately, however, the three committees found their task so daunting that they asked to confine their reports to the cities of Philadelphia and Washington and the state of Massachusetts. But Howard was not intimidated by the plan's original scope. She asked for the New York board's approval to send a circular "to all newspapers in the United States devoted to the interests of colored people" requesting them to send her relevant data. She also indicated that in more than a thousand personal letters she had especially appealed to teachers, authors, artists, editors, librarians, missionaries, lawyers, and doctors, and those serving in institutions for the poor, elderly, and orphaned, to identify the "deeds of heroism" that "have characterized the lives of many."[29]

Data she generated on African American women of New York she sent to Anna Roosevelt (mother of eight-year-old Eleanor Roosevelt and the New York board member in charge of statistics); all other statistical data she incorporated into her exhibit. "I have only evenings and Saturdays at my disposal" to work on the proposed plan, she lamented; several days later Sage reported that Howard "was accomplishing a great deal and deserved all the help she could get." Her colleagues on the Board of Women Managers agreed to a motion that "all work of the Afro-American race should be marked, crediting such work to that race."[30] Their action was commendable but, unfortunately, not particularly helpful to Howard. Although New York had determined that Howard's exhibit would address a racial gap in the Woman's Building, they were not prepared to level the playing field through personal sacrifice. The resources available to Howard as a working African American woman contrasted sharply with those available to Bellamy, Wheeler, Corning, and Sage, all of whom benefited from the flexibility, time, and resources their social standing afforded. Their blind spot was not unusual. This pattern of white middle- and upper-class women failing to take practical measures to extend to marginalized groups the advantages they enjoyed was repeated in women's clubs across the country.[31]

Welcome news about progress on Howard's exhibit was overshadowed by another matter. Bellamy reported to the New York women's board that the Literary Committee had just been informed that "a collective exhibit of books by the State of New York would not be received by the National Board [i.e., the BLM], as they intended to unite the exhibits from the different states." To Bellamy and her committee this was unacceptable. A large sum of money had been pledged "for a collective exhibit of books for the library," she objected, "and this could not be used for a united exhibit." She then read the letter of protest she had drafted the previous day, which the board quickly approved and authorized her to send. She also read a letter from Mary Trautmann (a "natural-born speaker," according to one observer), who volunteered to press New York's case personally in Chicago. It was also moved that the board approach the New York Commission immediately "and ask if this exhibit could be made as part of the furnishings of the Library in the New York State Building if it was refused as a collective exhibit for the Woman's Building." After that motion passed, the board approved copyrighting the list of women authors that the Literary Committee had compiled.[32]

When the New York board met in Mary Trautmann's home on December 6 "over fragrant cups of tea beside a sparking fire," Palmer still had not replied to Bellamy's letter of November 14. At the meeting Candace Wheeler announced that Palmer had tentatively approved one of the rooms attached to the Woman's Building Library for statistical displays and exhibits. After Bellamy reported that the work of the Literary Committee "was progressing favorably," the board authorized her to "expend the money that was needed to make this exhibit what she wished it to be." The library, the board determined, was to be New York women's "most important exhibit and the members wished to help it along in every way they could." "Their bright talk flashed to and fro with quip and jest and repartee," Margaret Sangster later reported, "but there was a serious undertone beneath the merriment as they discussed with great earnestness their plan for showing at the World's Fair what the women of New

York State have done in literature."[33] The message was clear: New York would not compromise on a collective library exhibit.

In response to an invitation from the BLM subcommittee in charge of the library "to confer upon the subject of the classification" of its collections, Bellamy traveled to Chicago in mid-December. She met the subcommittee on December 19 and showed no willingness to compromise.[34] After members listened to Bellamy and "heard her scheme for an exhibit," Trautmann later told New York board members, the meeting unexpectedly turned "enthusiastic." Palmer, who was also present, remarked, "I certainly think this ruling will have to be changed, and I will call a special meeting of the Sub-Committee of the Executive Committee to reconsider the matter." But the public characterization of the BLM response glossed over private reaction. Trautmann also told the New York women that Bellamy had "appalled the Committee by the magnitude of [her plan], and the members felt that every other State would be lost if New York made such an exhibit."[35]

Clearly, the subcommittee's enthusiasm and Palmer's willingness to reconsider the original ruling did not indicate that the BLM was willing to yield. This became obvious on December 20, when the subcommittee took up New York's request to reconsider the library rules adopted by the Executive Committee. Again Palmer was present. She offered a resolution to ask Bellamy whether the requirements of the New York board would be met "by providing for distribution in the Library of the Woman's Building the catalogue of the books sent from New York . . . (which catalogue would preserve the entirety of the New York collection), and by allowing the books themselves to be installed under the rules and regulations governing the library." She also proposed that Bellamy be made "head of the library work of the country."[36]

But she went on to suggest that perhaps New York women had "never understood the higher aims" of the Board of Lady Managers in assembling a library. "The interests of women will be better served," she argued, "by the carrying out of the model library idea" that the BLM had in mind.[37] "If the books are classified otherwise than by the approved library classification [she did not mention which one would be used], we depart from our high purpose and it becomes a matter of mere state pride in showing its literary wealth, rather than showing a systematic thoroughly classified and well-filled library of books written by women upon all lines of thought." If more populous states with longer histories, such as New York and Massachusetts, carried out plans for separate exhibits, she reasoned, it would "wipe out the entire West, and place it in a most humiliating position, as the Western States are of such recent growth that their inhabitants are largely natives of the East."

Palmer concluded by arguing that "the classification according to subject matter would obviate painful comparisons, as well as illustrate a more perfect and systematic result." As her remarks suggest, the arrangement of books would substantially influence how visitors interpreted the collection as a whole. The subject classification would highlight the diversity of topics among women writers and draw attention to subjects and genres represented by substantial numbers of titles. In contrast, the state-by-state arrangement would encourage visitors to view the collection through the lens of regional and national identity. In all likelihood, this would mean focusing on geographically determined subsets rather than viewing the collection holistically. It would also invite comparisons between states and countries that had generated very large contributions and those that had contributed only a few titles, or none at all.

But the New York faction was not intimidated. In an undated letter Bellamy undoubtedly sent Mary Trautmann shortly after the Executive Committee meeting, she held her ground: "We beg you to make it perfectly clear to the members of the National Board that it is not only that we are unwilling, but that we are positively unable to enter into their plan," which had been rejected "at once" by all three clubs that were putting the New York exhibit together. Then Bellamy added another wrinkle. "From the outset," she wrote, "I have been in consultation with Mrs. [Candace] Wheeler who thinks that this will be not only a very important but a very beautiful exhibit & who has had no idea that it would not be welcomed as New York's addition to the Woman's Library." Left unsaid was the fact that Palmer and her colleagues were counting on Wheeler to decorate not only the library but the entire building. "Personally, however," Bellamy continued, "I feel most unwilling to *urge* this admission, as I am assured that a fine place will be offered elsewhere & I should wish all the other States to feel particularly satisfied with their arrangement in the library where New York women must be in a sense 'hostesses.'" She concluded the letter decisively: unless New York was allowed a separate exhibit in the Woman's Building Library, "we should withdraw with disappointment and sincere regret."[38]

After Bellamy told the New York board at a meeting on January 10, 1893, that "literary women" around the state were cooperating fully with her committee, she reported on the BLM meeting that she and Trautmann had attended in Chicago. After reading a letter from Palmer imploring the New York women not to insist on a separate state exhibit, Bellamy indicated her willingness to withdraw from the Literary Committee and allow someone else to take over as chair, "who would in all probability carry out the scheme of the National Board of Lady Managers as to the general classified form of the books in the Library of the Woman's Building." But her colleagues would have none of it. "Members of the Executive Committee expressed their opinion that the New York State library of books written by women should go as a whole collection, according to Mrs. Bellamy's first plan, or not be sent to the Woman's Building at all," the meeting minutes record.[39]

The next day the treasurer of the New York board reported expenditures of $5,000 for the Woman's Building Library exhibit, and $2,000 for the Children's Building being erected next to the Woman's Building, in which an entire second-floor wing was being "set aside for New York." Sage read Candace Wheeler's progress report on decorations in the library, including $800 for the installation and removal of Dora Wheeler Keith's ceiling painting, $250 to create a three-foot plaster frieze in Italian Renaissance style, a three-foot wall panel of "richly carved" antique oak donated by Duveen just above the bookcases, and tapestries to be hung between the paneling and the frieze donated by Associated Artists. Bookcases, she said, would be five and one-half feet high, constructed of the same oak paneling and molding as other parts of the room, and made in sections so they could be quickly disassembled and sold at the close of the exposition. Four carved tables and a large stand to display the folios of the Literary Committee would "carry the same ornament" as the bookcases. Doors to the library would contain leaded glass insets, as would three transoms bearing the State of New York coat of arms, the seal of the Board of Lady Managers, and the seal of the New York Board of Women Managers. Associated Artists had also offered the use of several sofas and twelve chairs "in suitable style for this purpose," and several dealers offered to lend "bric-a-brac" and "other articles which will probably complete the furnishing necessary." The total cost, Wheeler estimated, would be $5,350. In discussions that followed, the New York women agreed that because the library was "not to be used as a reading room" and because "thousands of people would pass through it every day," the floor ought to be polished pine rather than carpet.[40]

Next came Bellamy's report. "We propose," she began, "to make the literary contributions of the women of New York a historic, chronologic, comprehensive, and, as far as possible, complete record of one small section of American literature for one hundred years, and to install this record in the Library of the State Capitol at Albany." She also noted that her recent visit to Chicago had convinced her that New York's exhibit would so differ "in its scope and character from that of any other State" that it would distinguish and dignify New York women. She then turned the floor over to Mary Trautmann, who reported her version of events in Chicago. Trautmann indicated she had communicated with members of other state boards of women managers, all of whom, she said, "were perfectly willing that New York should make a collective exhibit and they still have their classified one." She also noted that the BLM subcommittee in charge of monitoring progress on the library was so impressed with Bellamy's work that they offered to make her "the head of the Library work of the country" and conveyed Palmer's desire for a combined exhibit but separate state catalogs. Instead, New York members passed a resolution that "Mrs. Bellamy's original plan of a collective exhibit should not be departed from."[41]

Ultimately, the New York women left Palmer and her colleagues little choice. Without New York's contribution, the library in the Woman's Building would be greatly diminished. The BLM bowed to the inevitable and acquiesced to New York's demands. As Trautmann later reported to her New York colleagues, "New York would be allowed to enter her exhibit, as an exception to the rule, although the committee would rather have her make an exhibit similar to that made by the other States." The *New York Times* celebrated the forthcoming exhibit in a February 19 editorial. "The exhibit will be exhaustive and attractive," it predicted, "and the arrangement of it will facilitate the inspection and study of what has been accomplished in every part of a wide field."[42]

Palmer was not eager to publicize the arrangement, however. To a February 27 letter of inquiry from a Maryland delegate concerning the size of collections from each state, she replied, "In every case the number of books written by the women of each state is sent to us," and, if the collection was too large, "say, in the case of Massachusetts, 500 volumes," the BLM would "suppress some of the publications of the most prolific writers, inserting the titles in the catalogue, but keeping one book only on the shelves." In the event an author's work appeared in several different fields, "she can send one book representing each department of literature in which she has done herself credit."[43] Palmer said nothing about the huge exception to these rules New York had forced.

Despite Trautmann's assurance to the contrary, other state delegations were irritated with New York's power play. For the most part they disguised their sentiments in veiled comments. New Hampshire librarian Caroline Garland later noted, for example, that Massachusetts could "count up more women writers probably than any other State," but instead had decided "that quantity was nothing, that quality was everything, and that nothing but the very best of its kind should be sent, and only one book from an author." As a result, although it had caused "great ire on the part of many Massachusetts women," the Bay State's contribution was "a small collection of picked volumes" when matched against collections from some other state delegations.[44]

With the separate New York exhibit settled, the New York Board of Women Managers turned its attention to other matters. At a February 14 meeting, Candace Wheeler reported that the Haden Company signed a contract to build the bookshelves, and that the carvings from Duveen would have to be purchased because the firm would not loan them.[45] Although she did not say so at the time, Wheeler was having some difficulty with people assigned to help her in Chicago. "All sorts of incompetent women were placed upon my staff as helpers through somebody who had influence," she later revealed. As a result, this was "not entirely a rosy time" for her, although whenever she found herself "absolutely at bay," she "had recourse either to Mrs. Palmer or Mr. [Frank] Millet": "It was like being taken up by some heavenly angel to be carried by Mrs. Palmer across the long distance to the main offices in the only carriage allowed and unquestioned in the park," she recalled, "and so brought into actual touch and equal place with the governing powers!" Wheeler happily admitted she regularly used her access to Palmer to get around the exposition's bureaucracy.[46] Despite her recent clash with other New Yorkers, Palmer obviously harbored no grudge against Wheeler.

At a New York women's board meeting on March 7, Bellamy reported that the Literary Committee had collected 1,728 books, that 200 letters had been written to authors asking for books, that the Wednesday Afternoon Club had 230 women working on the project, and that one Brooklyn committee member had collected more than 200 books by herself. She also reported that a grandniece of novelist Charlotte Ramsay Lennox had offered to send a picture of the author for display in the library (her offer was later accepted), that Sarah B. Cooper had volunteered to send two "elegantly bound volumes" documenting work she had done for kindergartens in New York State, and that the houses of Harper & Brothers and G. P. Putnam's Sons had offered to donate all books they had published by New York women. Finally, she indicated that the Massachusetts and Connecticut Boards of Women Managers had contacted her for "advice and assistance." Massachusetts, she said, even stated, "We owe it to you that New York will be at the head of the Exhibits of Literature; even Massachusetts certainly will take second place." In the spirit of cooperation, Bay State women evidently chose to suppress their irritation with New York. Before the meeting ended, Bellamy asked whether the seal of the Women's Board ought to go in every book in the New York collection and suggested that an "expert librarian be selected to install the books, making the collection topical, and beginning with translations."[47] Whether she was referring to Palmer's forthcoming hire or suggesting that New York engage its own librarian is unclear.

On March 22 Bellamy updated her figures. She told the Executive Committee that two thousand books had been received by the Wednesday Afternoon Club (only forty-six had to be purchased) and that on April 1 the Literary Committee would host a reception in New York City to generate more publicity. One woman had contributed thirty volumes of her translations.[48] "I think we shall all be surprised to find how much there is that is valuable in our collection," she noted. She also announced that several committee members had written fifty letters to obtain one particular book, "and others have worked in much the same manner." Jane Cunningham Croly, a pioneering journalist, founding member of Sorosis, and the first president of the General Federation of Women's Clubs, had nearly finished the bibliography of newspaper and periodical articles written by women. Martha Joanna Lamb agreed to donate her *History of the City of New York,* Clara Stranahan had contributed her *History of French Painting* and "other valuable works," and Julia Ward Howe "had contributed all her books, pointing out that she had lived in New York the first twenty years of her life." Bellamy also announced that the Wednesday Afternoon Club had raised its contribution by $2,000 and that the London Atheneum had been asked to look for New York State women authors in British bookstores.[49]

Finally, Bellamy reported that the Parisian fine-art publisher Goupil & Co. was preparing a catalog of all titles in the Woman's Building Library, but that it would not compile a separate one for New York State. Because the New York State Library needed a separate catalog, however, Bellamy's committee agreed to have one printed as a copyrighted pamphlet and make it available only in the New York Building—perhaps to minimize the resentment their separate exhibit had generated among other state delegations. By that time the New York collection (which was being sent by express) was approaching 2,500 volumes and consisted of children's stories, fiction, poetry, cookbooks, translations, biographies, and periodicals, as well as works on household economics, education, science, travel, history, art, language, and religion. Bellamy also reported that Palmer wanted the books to arrive by April 15 and that bookcases (which had been sent by slower freight) had been provided to accommodate 4,440 volumes, with more available on short notice if necessary. New York board member Florence C. Ives arrived in Chicago on April 5 to supervise the arrangement of materials.

Folios represented a special category within the New York exhibit. Some were compilations; Bellamy's committee selected over three thousand newspaper and magazine articles written by New York authors "under separate heads" (sixty-five of New York's three hundred women's clubs participated in the identification process) and displayed them in thirty-nine typewritten folios. New York women's literary clubs submitted another seventy-five folios "representing every club of prominence and many of the minor associations in the State." Each folio contained a history of the club, its constitution and bylaws, and four "representative papers" read at its meeting. All these folios were bound in russet suede designed by Associated Artists, all carried the Board of New York Women Managers seal on the outside, and all were typewritten by S. Louise Conklin of New York and her assistants "with the utmost care and perfection, in order that [they] might form in a secondary way an exhibit of model type-writing."[50]

By that time Candace Wheeler was putting the finishing touches on the room after months of careful arranging. The large leaded glass window, she said, "gave a softened beauty of lake and sky." The ceiling painting, which her daughter had finished in New York to cover "an expanse of white which was overpowering in emptiness," had been installed by fellow New Yorkers whom Wheeler had brought to Chicago to finish the room. Together "with a wide deep border and a modeled frieze" cast and molded in Chicago, the ceiling painting brought the vast expanse of the upper room "within reasonable distance of the paneled bookcases." Wheeler completed decoration of the room with busts of notable women sculpted by women artists.[51]

At a meeting on May 2, 1893, the New York board's Executive Committee discussed a problem with the African American exhibit Imogen Howard was constructing. Anna Roosevelt reported she had received word from "the colored women in the west" (probably the same Chicago groups which earlier had battled Palmer and her BLM colleagues) that they objected to Howard's work being called "a national exhibit." Hoping to appease them, the New York board decided to call Howard's work "the Afro-American Exhibit collected by Miss J. Imogen Howard of New York" and to take responsibility for deciding which items would be returned if the exhibit proved too large for space assigned it; in addition, Mary Trautmann would take charge of its care and placement in the Woman's Building. The board also approved funds to transport a sculpture of a scene from Longfellow's *Song of Hiawatha* by Edmonia Lewis (owned and loaned by the Boston YMCA) that Howard wanted to include in her exhibit. Eventually, the sculpture found its way into the library.[52]

At the same meeting Bellamy reported that J. Henry Harper of Harper Brothers had promised to publish, under the title "Distaff Series," six small volumes from the thirty-four volumes of periodical pieces. The books were to be placed on sale in the Woman's Building Library.[53] Typesetting, cover design, and printing would all be executed by women workers. Bellamy recommended that the money earned from royalties be turned over to the permanent "Memorial Building" the BLM hoped to construct at the end of the fair. The board also passed a resolution thanking Wheeler and her daughter "for the beautiful work done" in the library.[54]

"We have attempted to make an historic, chronologic collection of all the books ever written by women either residents or natives of the State of New York," Bellamy wrote in the summary piece published after the fair closed. "The oldest book is a novel, 'The Female Quixote,' by Charlotte Ramsay Lennox, who is said to have been the first native-born author in the province of New

York. . . . From this eighteenth century beginning we may trace the evolution
of American fiction through the writers of the sentimental school." She pro-
ceeded to chart this development from Elizabeth Fries Ellet, Emma Catherine
Embury, Susan Pindar, Caroline Cheseboro, Caroline Kirkland, and Grace
Greenwood, "to the novel which portrays the manners of our own day—the
pleasing, graceful stories of Amelia Barr, Grace Litchfield, Mary Hallock Foote;
the society studies of Mrs. Burton Harrison and Mrs. Van Rensselaer Cruger,
and the character studies and sketches of Augusta Larned and Maria Louisa
Pool." She also identified eighty-one volumes of children's serials; "conspicuous among them are those of Mary Mapes Dodge, 'who . . . slid into celebrity
upon the silver skates of "Hans Brinker,"' and who has been long and hon-
orably known as the editor of *St. Nicholas*." In addition, Bellamy highlighted
"'Musical Instruments and Their Homes,' by Mrs. Julia Crosby Brown; a very
complete collection of the works of Miss Catherine [*sic*] Beecher; a 'History
of French Painting,' by Mrs. J. S. T. [Clara] Stranahan, and thirty-one volumes
by Lydia Maria Child." Bellamy also proudly emphasized the significance of
Imogen Howard's role, noting that "one of the few Afro-Americans connected
with the World's Fair, in an official way, . . . volunteered to collect the works of
Mrs. Child as a tribute from the blacks to her noble work in the anti-slavery
cause."[55] New York's literary exhibit would also feature a collection of woman-
authored medical texts contributed by female doctors of the state and an array
of foreign-language books by New York women that included works in Bur-
mese, the Swatow [Shantou] dialect of Chinese, Arabic, Hindustani, German,
and French.[56] By that time, the magnitude of New York's contribution—more
than two thousand of the library's eight thousand volumes—had become evident to every attentive visitor to the Woman's Building Library, thanks to the
separation from the rest of the collection that the New York women had so
persistently demanded.

Besides Blanche Bellamy and the New York Board of Women Managers,
another contingent of New Yorkers had a major impact on the Woman's Building Library. Sometime in the summer of 1891 Bertha Palmer heard that the
American Library Association planned to erect "a model library building"
somewhere on the fairgrounds. To find out more, she contacted BLM member Mary Crease Sears of Massachusetts, where the ALA had incorporated in
1879. On September 9, E. C. Hovey, the secretary of the Massachusetts Board
of World's Fair Managers, wrote that he had just received a note from Sears
about Palmer's inquiry concerning an ALA library at the exposition. Hovey
told Palmer he was sending a copy of his letter to Frank Hill, librarian of the
Newark Free Library in New Jersey and a member of the ALA subcommit-

tee in charge of developing an exhibit at the Chicago World's Fair. "I have no doubt," Hovey said, "that the Board of Managers will hear from him within a day or two."[57]

Shortly thereafter, Palmer learned from Hill that the ALA was applying for exhibitors' space, and that only a fraction of that space would be used for a model public library collection of several thousand volumes. Palmer replied to Hovey a week later that she was "glad to know" that the ALA was "about to apply for space for a building," and asked him to keep her informed of "further developments." To the exposition's director-general, George Davis, she wrote that Hill would soon be applying "for space for a building to contain the [ALA] exhibit" and asked him to "notify me when this application is received as I desire to consult with you before the location is fixed."[58] While Palmer may have been concerned about duplication of efforts, it is more likely that she hoped to benefit the Woman's Building Library by learning about the latest library organization and practices. For several months, however, she made no further effort to contact the ALA.

When books for the Woman's Building Library began arriving during the summer of 1892, Palmer turned her attention to finding a librarian—who, she had determined from the start, would be a woman. In a May 27 letter, W. E. Parker of the Library Bureau of Boston, which at that time managed a placement service for librarians, offered to help. Two weeks later Palmer responded: "Will you kindly give us the names and addresses of the women librarians of whom you speak? We believe that their knowledge of books would be of service to us in collecting the books to be placed in the library of the Woman's Building, and would like to correspond with them in regard to the matter."[59]

On June 24 Palmer broadened her search by addressing a letter to the ALA. "I write to ask if you will be kind enough to give me the name and address of some woman whom you would be willing to recommend for the position of Librarian in the Woman's Building." The Board of Lady Managers required, she said, "someone preeminently fitted to take this place." She requested that the ALA nominate the most qualified candidate, "stating her experience and qualifications and also giving the reasons why you consider her training as superior to that of other librarians who have not been educated in your methods." Perhaps because her letter was addressed to an association without formal headquarters, she did not receive a response. On July 7 she instructed her secretary to inquire of Director-General Davis the name and address of the ALA official working with the exposition.[60]

Frank Hill replied on July 15. He informed Palmer that under the direction of Mary S. Cutler, vice-director of the New York State Library School, the ALA was preparing "an elaborate exhibit next year not only of appliances, but of methods, having in operation a working library of from 3 to 5,000." If the BLM was preparing a library for the Woman's Building, however, he assured her, "our interests will not conflict." As an association, he wrote, the ALA "has no 'royal road' to librarianship, so there is no method which is peculiar to the A.L.A." Each librarian had to solve library problems unique to his or her own situation, "keeping in mind always certain well-defined rules which custom has established." Concerning recommendations for a librarian, he asked Palmer for "your requirements—the work to be done, the time and the hours and the salary. I think I can find someone, but it is essential to know your needs, as a librarian suitable in our case might not do at all in another."[61]

Four days later Palmer contacted Melvil Dewey, ALA president, secretary to the Board of Regents of the University of the State of New York, and director of the New York State Library and New York State Library School.[62] In 1892 Dewey was at the center of a public library movement that was sweeping the country. Andrew Carnegie was just beginning to give away millions of dollars for the construction of new buildings, most of them initiated by local women's clubs and many of them needing trained staff.[63] Dewey's school turned out graduates to fill scores of new positions opening in increasing numbers of pub- lic libraries across the country. The vast majority were females, often referred to as "Dewey's girls." In their new posts, "Dewey's girls" practiced the kind of librarianship Dewey's curriculum taught them in Albany. That curriculum concentrated on two things—how to manage a library efficiently, and the professional expertise (e.g., cataloging and classification, reference, collection development) deemed necessary to help library users get the information they needed. As secretary to the Board of Regents, Dewey was also responsible for managing the state's education exhibit at the exposition. Because New York had focused so much on education, this amounted to one-sixth of the space devoted to education exhibits at the 1893 World's Fair.

By connecting with Dewey, Palmer unknowingly tied the Woman's Building Library even more tightly to New York. In July 1892, however, Palmer was more interested in the people Dewey trained. "I write to ask if you will send me the names of two or three you consider the best librarians in the country," Palmer said. "I beg that you will explain in your letter the advantages that your system of training librarians possesses over other methods."[64] Although no record of Dewey's response exists, Palmer did answer Frank Hill on July 15. She reassured him the library in the Woman's Building would in no way conflict with the exhibit the ALA was planning; but she also told him, "It is impossible to give requirements [for a librarian] at present as our appropriation is in such a doubt- ful state before Congress that we have delayed making the necessary plans for carrying on the work."[65] Perhaps this inability to define requirements for the librarian in the Woman's Building explains why Palmer did not communicate with Hill or Dewey for the next several months.

By the end of January, however, shortly after the BLM acquiesced to the New York delegation's insistence on a separate exhibit, Palmer returned her attention to hiring a librarian. She wrote to Dewey (whom she mistakenly addressed as "Frank") on January 31, "We are anxious to secure, if possible, the very best woman librarian in this country, and feel that your opportunities for knowing the qualifications of women librarians are so much greater than ours that we ask the benefit of your experience." She indicated that the BLM would probably not be able to compensate the librarian for the high-quality work she would undoubtedly provide. She hoped to obtain someone "who could make arrangements to return to her present position after the six month leave of absence" necessary to cover the library while it was open at the exposition.[66]

When Dewey responded on February 4, he mentioned no candidates but did ask about the librarian's duties. In her response two days later, Palmer suggested that the duties were "somewhat indicated in the preliminary rules" she enclosed. She also recognized, however, that "they are subject to alteration upon the installation of the library, at which time we will undoubtedly find that our plans have to be modified very much to meet unexpected conditions." She told Dewey that "it is not the intention to have a reference or circulating library, but merely to have such illustrated, statistical or other books as may attract attention, subject to inspection by visitors." The librarian would be paid between $750 and $1,000 for six months' work; she should "have full knowledge of the authors and their works," and she would also be responsible for the collection's security. "We especially desire to have a woman in charge who understands the modern library movement," she continued, "one that would interest people so that they would go home with the purpose of establishing libraries. One of our main objects is to show that this line of work is especially adapted to the capacity of women, and is a particularly congenial field." She concluded by asking Dewey if the duties suggested in the preliminary rules she enclosed represented a separate line of work from cataloging, for which she expected the library to have immediate need.[67]

Dewey responded on February 15. By this time he probably knew that the New York Board of Women Managers had forced Palmer to abandon a collective exhibit, thus rendering impossible a common classification scheme to organize the Woman's Building Library bibliographically into a unified collection. Almost surely, Dewey would have recommended his own system. But he responded to the situation as he understood it. "It is clear to us," he wrote, "that you need two very different things." The first was a cataloger, and he indicated that one "can be secured at about $100 a month." And depending on the number of volumes the library secured, the cataloger would also need clerical assistants. Cataloging, however, was "a totally different branch of work" from the kind of leadership that "a woman of tact, enthusiasm and wide knowledge of the modern library movement" could do to "stimulate visitors to a new interest in libraries so that when they return from the exposition they will wish to provide their own communities with better library facilities."[68]

Such women already occupied important positions across the nation, Dewey pointed out, and could not spare the six months necessary to staff the Woman's Building Library. Thus he could see "only one practicable way" to address the problem: "to appoint say, six of the leading women librarians of the country carefully selected for their adaptation to this work, each of them to spend two months in Chicago giving half of every day to this work and using the other half in studying the exposition." He thought that opportunities to see the fair would be sufficient to induce these women to request leaves of absence for two months; since most earned about $2,000 per year, they would probably be willing to give half-time service for the two-month period for about $100 per month (for a total of $1,200 for the six librarians). "Your money will go farther this way," Dewey explained, "and you will get such a corps of librarians as it would be impossible to secure otherwise. You will also get a freshness in the work impossible with a single librarian." With characteristic self-assurance, he added: "I have given this much thought, and am confident that this will give you the best results at the least cost." He then offered to furnish the six women, to be drawn from the ALA's membership, "with various documents to be given to visitors, explaining the modern library movement, giving information, etc., and to give you constant help in connection with the general library exhibit which we are making." Dewey obviously hoped his brand of librarianship and the messages it conveyed would be reflected in the kinds of services the Woman's Building Library ultimately offered.

"You will be glad to know that the best library work of the country is being done by women," he concluded, "that many of the most efficient workers and library trustees are women, and that many libraries owe their organization entirely to the energy, enthusiasm and liberal gifts of women." And "in spite of the very great pressure on me this year," he promised "any personal assistance in my power in making this library feature of the Woman's Building one of the conspicuous successes of the fair." He agreed with Palmer that the Woman's Building Library ought to function as a model and stimulus for the establishment of libraries in cities across the country. Palmer quickly warmed to Dewey's recommendation to rotate high-profile professional women to function as guides in the library.

In his correspondence with Palmer, Dewey never mentioned that another Chicago-based group was preparing a second library conference, and that both were at the center of a power struggle within the ALA. His willingness to participate in the organization of the Woman's Building Library may have been motivated in part by the desire to prevent Palmer from connecting too tightly to the other group. In preparation for the 1893 conference, in 1891 the ALA had appointed a committee consisting of Dewey, Florence Woodworth, and Mary S. Cutler (all of the New York State Library), Frank Hill (Dewey's close associate), and Frederick P. Hild of the Chicago Public Library, who was to act as liaison with the local Chicago librarians, including the Chicago Library Club. At the same time, however, William Frederick Poole, director of Chicago's Newberry Library, chaired a World's Congress of Librarians Committee, which functioned as part of the World's Congress Auxiliary, an organization authorized by the exposition's National Commission.

The World's Congress Auxiliary consisted of twenty departments and 225 general divisions, each of which had responsibility to advocate for a series of meetings at the fair. To be held between May 15 and October 28, the meetings would be conducted by a variety of professional groups and were expected to address questions of religion, literature, art, education, social problems, and language.[69] "Not Matter, But Mind" was the auxiliary's official motto, and harmony was its goal. Programs the auxiliary generated would feature presentations, but no comments. On March 25, 1892, Congress made the auxiliary independent of the National Commission. The auxiliary also contained a "Woman's Branch," but because this branch was headed by Ellen Henrotin and Bertha Palmer, its efforts were carefully coordinated with all World's Congress Auxiliary activities slated for the Woman's Building. Not so for librarians. For a long time the two World's Fair library committees ignored each other and operated just below the sight line of the ALA, another sponsoring body more concerned with harmony than conflict.

In late April 1892, an unexpected incident occurred that radically changed the situation and profoundly affected the ALA. It had the effect of tipping the balance of power away from the ALA's old guard—whose mantle of leadership Poole had inherited in the mid-1880s—and toward Dewey and other librarians who sought greater efficiency and systematization in the profession. On April 28, the ALA's president, Klas August Linderfelt (a Poole protégé), was arrested for embezzling funds over a seven-year period from the Milwaukee Public Library, which he directed. By May 10 he had resigned as ALA president.[70] At the annual conference a week later, ALA members decided that Dewey should be president, counting on him to rescue the association from embarrassment and lead it successfully into the Chicago World's Fair.

As a result, Dewey and his allies dominated the ALA's Executive Board and commanded the exposition committee through its chair, Mary S. Cutler, a subordinate whom he often called "one of his special lieutenants." The Linderfelt affair had hurt the old guard, who now had no one but Poole of sufficient stature within the organization to counter the momentum created by the energetic Dewey. The only official link between Poole's Chicago-based World's Congress committee and Cutler's Albany-based committee was Frederick Hild. The ALA's 1892 conference had not reduced the potential for conflict between the two groups, but it did bring about significant changes in the balance of power among competing interests.

Less than two weeks after the conference, and just prior to Palmer's July 19 letter to Dewey inquiring about names of the two or three "best librarians in the country," Dewey's leadership received the first of two challenges from the old guard. Acting on behalf of Poole's committee, Hild requested that Cutler step down as chair of the ALA's exposition committee because, he said, as a woman she would not be as effective as a man. Because Hild suggested Charles Ammi Cutter, director of the Boston Athenaeum and another member of the ALA old guard, as Cutler's replacement, Dewey saw the incident as not so much an issue of gender as one of ALA politics. He immediately issued a circular soliciting the Executive Board, and on June 22 announced the results. "We find ourselves unable with proper regard to the interest of the ALA to consent to the proposed change," he declared. "The decision is clear, strong and unanimous."[71] Hild lost.

A second test came several months later, when Dewey found out that Hild and Poole were planning a World's Congress of Librarians conference as "a rival meeting the week before ALA" that would, he feared, "take the wind out of our sails." Dewey wanted a combined conference, with ALA meetings scheduled in the morning and international Congress meetings in the afternoon or evening. His Executive Board, all of whom shared his ideas about the future of the profession, agreed. "I can't help thinking that if Poole or Hild had been elected [ALA] President," commented Frederick Morgan Crunden, director of the St. Louis Public Library, "there would have been no plan of this kind proposed." Hannah P. James of the Osterhout Free Public Library in Wilkes-Barre, Pennsylvania, shared his criticism. "I am thankful you are at the helm, with a crew that will follow you in the straight path . . . ," she told Dewey. "All the storms we have will be of Poole's own raising—he'll soon find they will not wreck us!"[72]

On September 28, Dewey reported to the Chicago-based World's Congress of Librarians committee that the ALA Executive Board had unanimously agreed that there should not be two separate conferences. He followed his letter with a personal visit in mid-October, and by threatening to write to librarians around the world about the conflict between ALA and the Congress of Librarians he forced Poole and Hild to agree to schedule ALA meetings concurrently with the international congress. The former would meet for six to nine days in single sessions each morning; the latter would meet in the afternoon.[73] Dewey had successfully met both challenges, had moved his own people into place, and was playing every angle he could. The Woman's Building Library was one of those angles.

Bertha Palmer was probably unaware of the ALA's shifting political horizons. Nor had she shown any interest in working through prominent Chicago librarians such as Poole and Hild. When she responded to Dewey's letter of February 15 two weeks later, she told him she would "write definitely" about his plan "within a few days" and asked particularly about the libraries organized by women. "We are most anxious to make a record of their good work in every direction," she said, "and this is a field we had not before considered." She also thanked him for his counsel but wondered whether the BLM might not hire the six ALA women for $1,000 instead of $1,200. "If so," she concluded, "I feel authorized to make that arrangement at once, and would beg you to send me as soon as possible the names of candidates you would propose."[74]

By that time a BLM subcommittee and the Committee on Assignment of Space had agreed on a final set of rules and regulations for the Woman's Building Library. Rule no. 1 had originally determined that "books, magazines, pamphlets, etc. shall be classified according to subject matter," but the New York group's threat to pull its exhibit shifted it to a segregated geographic arrangement. Rule no. 2 allowed authors and translators to be represented "in all branches of literature" by more than one book. Rule no. 3 declared that "there shall be published a special catalogue" of the library's entire book collection prepared by the librarian, "which catalogue shall contain also under the name of the book exhibited a list of all the works by the same author." Rule no. 4 gave the librarian permission to take materials from the shelves or cases "for inspection," but not to allow them "to be handled by the visitors."[75] None of these rules and regulations had been circulated to practicing library professionals for advice before the BLM approved them. Thus, when Dewey and his ALA allies were brought into efforts to organize the library, they inherited a situation over which they would have limited control, and certain rules (such as restricting access to books) that ran counter to newer library practices they advocated.

As spring arrived, Palmer grew more concerned about slow progress on the building. On March 11 she asked when New York would finish decorating the library. "We are getting very uneasy," she said, "because we expected to have an expert cataloguer come the first of April to catalogue and arrange the books. At present there is no part of the work for the library delivered and in place." Several days later Mrs. Dean Sage reassured her that New York would meet its mid-April deadline.[76]

On March 22, Dewey identified for Palmer as "the very best women in the country" three librarians recently elected to the ALA Council, "which like the French Academy represent the most eminent." (Dewey exaggerated the importance of the ALA Council, which as ALA president he was trying to make into an honorary body.) Two of the three women we have already encountered, Mary S. Cutler of the New York State Library School and Hannah P. James of the Osterhout Free Library in Wilkes-Barre; the third was Ellen M. Coe, director of the New York (City) Free Circulating Library. Dewey had hired Cutler as a cataloger in the Columbia College Library in 1884, had taken her with him when he became New York State Librarian in 1889, and a year later made her vice-director of the New York State Library School, which he had transferred from Columbia. Hannah P. James had been recommended by Dewey for her position at the new Osterhout Free Library in 1887 (Dewey spoke at the building dedication), and she regularly guest-lectured at Dewey's library school. Ellen Coe worked with Dewey on a number of cooperative library schemes while Dewey was at Columbia between 1883 and 1888; in the 1880s she also served with him on the ALA Cooperation Committee, which he chaired.[77]

All three women were Dewey allies; all shared his vision of modern library science. None appears to have been contacted in advance for permission to put forward her name. Dewey told Palmer, "After much thought I am sure that your wisest course is to secure if possible these three women as seniors, and with them three or more younger librarians who would accept something smaller as a compensation. If we said $50 a month to these and $37.50 to the others it would make your total expenses $1050 for the six months." Because Dewey was convinced they would "very likely" decline an invitation directly from Palmer, he offered to contact each "in behalf of the association" and point out the "opportunity for public usefulness that will result in their accepting and in their trustees allowing them the necessary two months." Then, "in council," he would also encourage them to select three subordinates.[78]

Dewey's response reflects his obsession to control and his willingness to overreach his authority in quest of a goal he thought in the best interests of the particular brand of librarianship he advocated. No record exists that authorized him to negotiate on the ALA's behalf with the BLM. Nor does any existing record authorize him to negotiate salaries for the women he nominated. Moreover, that he was negotiating from Albany when a committee of librarians that had ties to the exposition already existed in Chicago demonstrates how tightly Dewey wanted to manage all library matters at the fair. And, without notifying Palmer beforehand, Dewey contacted Mary Wright Plummer, director of the Pratt Library School in Brooklyn, about becoming "one of the librarians in the Woman's Building in Chicago" after he learned that Cutler and James could not commit. It would involve "being paid $75 per month for your services," he informed Plummer, "and having part of your day to look at the exposition."[79] Palmer made no objections to Dewey's unilateral initiatives; she seemed happy to delegate authority to him to negotiate for the BLM. She was more concerned about the immediate and pressing need for a cataloger.

On March 23, Palmer cabled Dewey that not only would the Board of Lady Managers "like to receive your nominations . . . for the several skilled librarians who are to rotate in charge of the Library," she also wanted a nomination "for our expert cataloguer." All names had to be sent to the Executive Committee for final approval, she said, and "negotiations should begin immediately in order that the cataloguer may come to Chicago and take charge of the books which are arriving daily." Dewey responded the next day that he had "immediately written strong letters to the ladies concerned" about becoming librarians in the Woman's Building Library. As for the cataloger, he wrote, "you will have to pay at least $100 a month for a good one," and added, "I suppose the length of service will be simply what time is required to get things in proper consideration."[80] Edith Clarke of the Newberry Library, he said several days later, "would be an admirable cataloger. She is one that we should select to serve during the six months,—a perfect lady, college bred, and being right there in Chicago specially adapted to your work, as cataloging is her specialty." He did not tell Palmer that Clarke was one of "Dewey's girls," nor that she had been feeding Dewey information about Poole and his activities as the ALA prepared for the exposition. Because she followed the professional practices Dewey advocated, Dewey simply assumed she would adhere to the cataloging rules he had instituted at the New York State Library.[81]

Clarke wrote Dewey on April 3 that she had just received word from Palmer that he had nominated her to catalog the Woman's Building collection. She was surprised; clearly Dewey had not first sought her permission. She thanked him for the opportunity, but wondered if "they offered me no more than I am getting at the Newberry . . . would it be better for another who needs it more to take it?" She suggested her own assistant as a substitute—"a classical scholar and at home in French and German." Dewey responded two days later. Because he had understood that Clarke planned to leave the Newberry soon, he said, he thought the Woman's Building position would have been "a feather in your cap to be selected for the place." If she was not looking for another job, however, Dewey agreed it might be better to "arrange for one of your assistants so that you can supervise it," or "you might take the place with the right to have most of the work done by your assistant." Either way, he urged, "it will be a credit to the Newberry to have you selected."[82] Days later Clarke decided to accept Palmer's offer. On April 11, Palmer informed her that she had written General Alexander McClurg, president of the Newberry board of trustees, "in regard to your leave of absence."[83]

Dewey was having more difficulty finding three women to serve as "junior librarians." On April 12 he circulated a note titled "The Woman's Library at the World's Fair" to several female librarians to alert them to "the finest opportunity yet offered for enthusiastic workers full of the modern library spirit to interest large numbers of people in library matters." He told recipients he had just received a telegram "from Chicago authorizing me to select librarians for the woman's building during the exposition," and claimed (prematurely) that he had already obtained commitments from Cutler, James, and Coe to serve as "senior librarians." But he still needed "five or six more so that we can have two on duty, each of them taking half a day," and he noted that "the salary will be $75 a month with free admission to the grounds." He asked recipients to respond quickly and indicate whether he needed to write their trustees to obtain permission for leaves of absence. It would be "a great compliment to your library to be thus selected," he said, and he added that for a librarian it was "the highest honor that can be offered to be selected to serve for a month or two in this capacity." To Ellen Coe he was even more forceful. Because he wanted "a New York woman, and just about your size, on duty" when the library opened, he declared, "I want you to be no. 1 in the woman's building."[84]

Coe responded quickly. Although she was honored to be asked, she said, she needed more information: "I do not know what you want me to do, nor how you want me to do it." She also wanted more time, admitting, "All the follies of womanhood have not been driven out of my head by business and I would so like time to have some *pretty clothes* made." Mary Wright Plummer told Dewey she had responsibility for the Pratt Institute's exposition exhibit on alternate days. Thus, she could monitor the Woman's Building Library only on "alternate days instead of half-days." And she was available only in May: "I can't give up my rest-time," she wrote, "which would be in June and July." Theresa West, who had replaced Linderfelt as director of the Milwaukee Public Library, also thanked Dewey for the high honor, but replied that because of the press of work and her need for a vacation, "I dare not undertake it."[85]

Perhaps in response to Coe and others, Dewey drafted a document detailing more specifically what librarians staffing the Woman's Building Library were expected to do: "The librarians should be prepared to explain the functions of the public library as a people's university and as an adjunct to the schools. . . . They should be familiar with the salient points of the latest and best library laws and be able to suggest to those whom they have interested, definite methods for interesting others and for starting libraries in their own localities." All questions for technical information, he noted, should be referred to the ALA exhibit in the U.S. Government Building.[86] The draft was vintage Dewey. It conveyed his vision of the role the public library was to play in late nineteenth-century America and communicated his evangelistic sense of mission. It said nothing about the unique and gender-distinct nature of the collection the librarians would be monitoring.

On April 16 Clarke informed Dewey that her library's trustees still had not approved a leave of absence. In the interim she wondered about the "style and system" of the New York State collection catalog, which she quickly recognized as something different from the rest. "Is yours to come printed, and to be a separate one from ours, or is it to be a card catalog, or is it to be in the shape of ms for the printer, to be combined with ours?" She also told Dewey that "unless it is an absolute necessity to make the sacrifice" she had not yet decided to become the cataloger for the Woman's Building Library, since it would bring her "a less income than the one I am now earning." She had recently visited the Woman's Building, she reported. Decorations were not yet up, and more worrisome, "not a single exhibit is yet in place." In the library, she found only two small boxes of books waiting to be cataloged. "I would be very glad to have the books sent to the Newberry Library, and do the work there," she offered. "It would otherwise have to be done in the midst of a crowd and confusion with not a reference book in the office of the building."[87]

Dewey responded on April 21 that Rhode Island had a "handsomely printed catalog," and that Tiffany's was printing a "fancy catalog" for New York's collection. "I think all you need is a shelf list as an inventory of the stock and a condensed author index of the entire library for people who will wish to know if any one of their names wrote a book. . . . There seems to be no chance for classification or treatment in the ordinary library way," he conjectured. To Dewey, this meant arranging books by subject according to the Decimal Classification (DDC) scheme. Clarke would have to follow the dictates of the library's organizers and shelve the books separately by states and countries. (Had Palmer solicited his help in December, Dewey would have favored her position on overall organization of the library as long as the subject classification she agreed to implement was DDC.) "I have had nothing to do with this," he said. "My interest is in having some of our best librarians there do missionary work in interesting people in the library movement at large." He then encouraged Clarke to press her library's board for a leave of absence on the grounds that it would "increase [her] acquaintance with library people."[88]

In the meantime Dewey struggled with scheduling. Ellen Coe was prepared to begin work on April 20, but because the exhibition was not scheduled to open until May 1 and she could give only a month's service from her date of arrival, Dewey decided to take advantage of Mary Wright Plummer's offer to cover the library on alternate days in May. To Palmer he wrote that Coe's "services are too valuable to waste on simple work when there are no people ready." He asked her if the library would open on May 1 and "if you wish the two people on duty then, or whether you wish to delay a little and thus save their salaries." He also inquired about Edith Clarke's responsibilities. "I presume the books must be kept by states and countries and under each that the works of the same authors must be kept together," he said. Such an arrangement "is not like an ordinary library," he added, noting again that they would need only a shelf list and an author index rather than a full catalog. Of Plummer he inquired on April 21, "How would you like Miss [Elizabeth] Harvey [of the New York State Library] to alternate with you" in May? He also advised her that, if possible, she should schedule her responsibilities at the Pratt exhibit for half rather than alternate days. "I am sure it will tire you much less . . . instead of taking a whole day at sight seeing and then a whole day at work." On April 26 Dewey informed Palmer that Plummer and Harvey (both "Dewey's girls") were ready to staff the library "as soon as you notify us that you wish them to begin."[89]

Existing correspondence indicates that Dewey was determined to place in the Woman's Building Library only women with a high professional profile (and mostly from New York) who shared his views about librarianship. For example, when Mary Titcomb of the Rutland Free Library, in Vermont, inquired about vacancies and included a letter from one of her board members granting her a leave of absence, Dewey responded to the board member that those selected would include only "women who have been very prominent in the national association and its work and who are very familiar with general library interests throughout the country," adding, "However admirable Miss Titcomb's work may have been with you, she has not made herself known outside."[90]

Eventually, the trustees of Clarke's library granted her leave of absence, and on April 25 she met with the BLM Executive Committee for instructions. In response to Palmer's solicitation for "suggestions . . . as to unpacking and installing," Clarke requested that she be allowed to "take the books by boxes up to the Newberry Library . . . and catalogue them there, to use all the record books that we have there." She estimated it would take one person about a month to catalog between 1,000 and 1,500 books, and that it would take five assistants about a month to catalog the entire collection. Palmer also asked Clarke if "the librarian . . . could not assist" her with cataloging. Because "I knew there would be no physical impossibility to having this assistance," Clarke later wrote Dewey, she "said yes." After a motion that Clarke "be instructed to prepare an ideal catalogue" passed, Clarke immediately began cataloging materials on site. This undertaking involved "installing, listing, invoicing, classifying, and cataloging each book, beside interviewing and corresponding with those in charge of each collection, and the gathering from reference books and correspondence statistics concerning each author and incorporating them in the Catalog."[91]

At an Executive Committee meeting on April 28, Mary Eagle (reportedly "the best parliamentarian on the Board") moved that the BLM create a separate Committee on the Library, "to whom shall be referred all differences of opinion about the location of books in the Library." When her colleagues informed her that the Committee on Press and Printing (chaired by Mary Lockwood) "had already done much of the work in connection with the Library," Eagle volunteered to withdraw her motion "if the committee referred to is construed as being the Committee on Library." All agreed, and Palmer declared that "Mrs. Lockwood's committee will be given charge of this work." The next day the BLM hosted an informal ceremony in the midst of chaos to acknowledge the gifts of assembled foreign guests. Candace Wheeler used the occasion to announce that decorating the building's interior would not be finished until May 9.[92]

Although the interior was still unfinished and most of the exhibits not yet set up (the building itself had been substantially completed by mid-March), an audience of fifteen hundred stood in the rotunda on April 30 to sing Julia Ward Howe's "Battle Hymn of the Republic," an abolitionist anthem that the exposition's directors refused to allow in the opening ceremonies on May 1 for fear of alienating the South. The journey to this day had been fraught with politics of all sorts, not least of which was whether to locate all works of art and literature by women in the Woman's Building or to scatter them throughout the exposition grounds. Although some women preferred their work to be displayed in their state buildings, no evidence exists to indicate that any of the authors represented in the Woman's Building Library wanted their works located elsewhere.[93] On April 30 the hallways of the Woman's Building were cleared of boxes, plants, and ornaments so that sweepers and scrubbers could ready them for the fair's grand opening the next day. At that time the library existed as an uncataloged collection of books, some loosely arranged and others still in crates, in a partially decorated room.

4

Grand Opening

The World's Columbian Exposition officially opened on May 1. The morning brought a driving rainstorm, but by noon the skies held only dark clouds. Almost 200,000 people—most dressed in their Sunday best—crowded onto the grounds. Dignitaries arrived by carriage. Bertha Palmer rode with the Duchess of Veragua, whose family were descendants of Columbus himself. Opening ceremonies took place in front of the Administration Building, where President Grover Cleveland and other VIPs followed an agenda carefully laid out for them.[1] After Cleveland gave a brief address, he pressed the key to a 2,000-horsepower engine, and as a large choir sang Handel's "Hallelujah Chorus" in the background, fountains gushed and flags unfurled all over the grounds. "Amid the enthusiastic cheers of the vast multitude, the shrill whistling of the lake craft, and the deep diapason of booming guns, the formalities were complete," the exposition's president reported.[2]

After a luncheon in the Manufactures Building for visiting dignitaries, Palmer led her fellow Lady Managers to the Woman's Building for its own formal opening. BLM officials had issued invitations to five thousand people for the ceremony, which took place inside the main hall. "The main court of the building was packed with men and women long before the hour announced for the commencement of the program," the *Daily Columbian* reported. "Fully 3,000 found seats on the main floor and 4,000 more lined the long galleries in three tiers around three sides of the court."[3] On the dais Palmer sat regally amidst scores of luminaries as the World's Fair chorus sang pieces written by female composers. Palmer had good reason to celebrate that day. Despite the fact that the suffrage debate charged the political atmosphere, Palmer and her BLM colleagues had managed to sidestep the issue by assembling an extensive array of exhibits profiling women's achievements in science, art, and service.

When she was called on to speak, the crowd "found vent in cheers, applause and a fluttering of white handkerchiefs." With carefully worded comments she recounted the political history of the building in which they sat. "We have traveled together a hitherto untrodden path, have been subjected to tedious delays and overshadowed by dark clouds which threatened disaster to our enterprise. We have been obliged to march with peace offerings in our hands lest hostile motives be ascribed to us" she said.[4] Yet despite these difficulties, "our burdens have been greatly lightened . . . by the spontaneous sympathy and aid which have reached us from women in every part of the world, and which have proved an added incentive and inspiration." She said she would not focus her remarks on the benefits of industrialization that were everywhere evident on the fairgrounds, but at the same time she wanted to bring attention to the impact of industrialization on women and children. "Of all existing forms of injustice," she pronounced, "there is none so cruel and inconsistent as is the position in which women are placed with regard to self-maintenance—the calm ignoring of their rights and responsibilities which has gone on for centuries." Even the notion that women ought to stay at home was suspect: "The theory which exists among conservative people, that the sphere of woman is her home . . . tells heavily against her, for manufacturers and producers take advantage of it to disparage her work and obtain her services for a nominal price, thus profiting largely by the . . . helplessness of their victim."

Many, she recognized, romanticized the sanctity of a home where women and children were protected from the evils of an industrialized world run by men. But such views were out of touch with the reality of life for the vast majority of women. "Would that the eyes of these idealists could be thoroughly opened that they might see, not the fortunate few of a favored class, with whom they possibly are in daily contact," she pressed, "but the general status of the labor market throughout the world and the relation to it, of women." Palmer then indicated that the statistics gathered in the Records Rooms would demonstrate that many women had no "natural protectors" and that hundreds of thousands of women were "forced to work shoulder to shoulder with their husbands in order to maintain the family." Applause regularly interrupted her speech.

Represented within the walls of the Woman's Building, Palmer noted, "are the real heroines of life, whose handiwork we are proud to install in the Exposition, because it has been produced in factories, workshops, and studios under the most adverse conditions and with the most sublime patience and endurance." Yet even as she critiqued the conservative view of woman's sphere, she identified domesticity as the pinnacle of women's achievement. She also advocated "the thorough education and training of woman to fit her to meet whatever fate life may bring; not only to prepare her for the factory and workshop, for the professions and arts, but, more important than all else, to prepare her for presiding over the home." Palmer made no specific mention of the library or the authors represented therein as examples of women's labor. At the end of her speech she called for her audience to help her honor the building's architect and the women whose work it displayed. Her final words—"we now dedicate the Woman's Building to an elevated womanhood—knowing that by so doing we shall best serve the cause of humanity"—brought wild applause from the crowd assembled.

But not everyone was happy with the Woman's Building. In private Mary Logan continued to argue that women's exhibits should have been displayed "side by side with the men in accordance with the Resolutions which we passed at our first session." She also wrote Palmer that "the decorations at the ends of the Hall were humiliating to me, and most disappointing in every way."[5] Ellen Henrotin liked Dora Wheeler Keith's work on the library ceiling, but remarked that as a whole the paintings in the Gallery of Honor "seem comparatively inferior to the other exhibits, lacking warmth, color, and depth of tone," and she concluded that "woman has not yet (if the collection of the Woman's building is a faithful representation of her work) mastered the art of painting." *American Architect* was condescending. "The Woman's Building is neither worse nor better than might have been expected. It is just the sort of result that would have been achieved by either boy or girl who had had two or three years' training in an architectural school, and its thinness and poverty of constructive expression declares [sic] it to be the work of one who had never seen his or her 'picture' translated into substance."[6]

Despite minor carping, the Woman's Building quickly became a focal point for women who visited the fair. Parisian fairgoer Madame Léon Grandin reported spending many days in the Woman's Building, "fascinated and never bored." It was, she wrote, "without question, one of the most interesting places of the entire site." In her autobiography, Helen Keller recalled meeting there the Princess Maria Schaovskoy of Russia and "a beautiful Syrian lady." "The Woman's Building is now headquarters for the good-looking and high-class young women of the world," the Chicago *Record* revealed in August. "Within the four white walls you can see more bright, intelligent faces, jaunty summer styles of the sensible kind, and confident but proper demeanor, than you will be able to find anywhere else on a globe which makes a speciality of studying womankind. It seems that every girl who has studied or travelled or who has any special aspirations, gives the Woman's Building a share of her time."[7]

Other journalists also took notice. "Daily crowds of the sex which more than outnumber its opposite . . . filled the Woman's Building," Isabel Bates Winslow told readers of the magazine *Far and Near.* And it was in the Woman's Building, she said, that "by their work, their intelligence, energy and executive ability women have won for themselves first rank among all unprejudiced and discriminating people." For some, the building also provided a site for statements on gender politics. At the "Special Service" window one day, a visitor asked, "Is this the Ladies Building?" "It is the Woman's Building," the employee replied. "Ladies Building," came a sharp retort, as the speaker left the window "with an air of having impressed upon" the attendant "a great lesson." Equally emphatic was an editorial in *Forum* by the journalist Helen Watterson criticizing the building for its emphasis on "material results" rather than women's social relations within the home. "Even the imposing collection of books, written by women and kept with such devotional spirit in the library in the Woman's Building," she complained, emphasized "things temporal" at the expense of "things spiritual." The effect, she maintained, was merely "a humorous one, suggesting as it does, the immodest modesty of a New England spinster, who once set all the volumes written by men in a row on one side of her library, and all those written by women in chaste seclusion on the other." Clearly, the separatism debate continued to ignite strong reactions.[8]

Women's periodicals offered advice on how to negotiate the grounds and often concluded, along with Isabel Bates Winslow, that "the Woman's Building must interest every woman." One journalist offered practical advice on what to pack. "Two dresses are enough, if they are made so that different waists can be worn with them. Two changes of underclothing will take little room, and will be needed." As for hose, "two pair . . . will do, because they can be washed out in your room." Winslow advised that "a woman used to economies may spend a week in Chicago, visit the World's Fair every day, live comfortably and healthfully, and spend less than $20 from the moment of her arrival in the city until she steps aboard her homebound train."[9]

The Woman's Building often left an indelible impression on fair visitors, and those who described the appearance of the library were undeniably impressed by the sight that greeted them. Guests were struck by the palatial repository decorated in greens and blues to echo the hues of Lake Michigan, with accents of red, gold, and brown. They admired the exquisite gilding, ornate moldings, richly adorned Renaissance fireplace, neoclassical frieze, Turkish carpets, intricately carved tables and chairs, and gleaming bookcases filled with seemingly endless rows of books. "So far as possible its collection of books and manuscripts shows what women have done in literature in all times and all lands. The exquisite carving of the bookcases, the handsome wall decorations typical of the arts, science, and literature are all the results of woman's thought and labor," the *Chautauquan* reported. "The bookcases themselves surrounded the room, filled with books, a great army of them beginning with the very earliest utterances of women in print and following down the centuries to the present," Candace Wheeler recalled. "Altogether I was satisfied. I felt that the women of America would not be sorry to be women in the face of all that women had done besides living and fulfilling their recognized duties." Wheeler refrained from remarking on the texts themselves, beyond the impression they made in the aggregate as a spectacular exhibit of women's literary productivity. The power of the scene lay in the grandeur of the room itself and in the cumulative effect of viewing more than eight thousand volumes of women's writings. Highlighting a handful of British authors in this mammoth collection—Harriet Martineau, George Eliot, Frances Burney, Lady Jane Grey, Jane Austen, and Charlotte Brontë—Minneapolis journalist Marian Shaw echoed Wheeler's imperialistic metaphor ("a great army" of books) when she pronounced that the library gave "indisputable evidence of woman's inherent right to occupy the field of literature, since . . . in this department she has 'come, seen and conquered.'" And, like Wheeler, Shaw moves from admiration of the room, to observation of the large number of books, to reflection on women's achievements in print and the strength they implied. In *Samantha at the World's Fair*, Marietta Holley has her fictionalized persona admire the library, "full of objects of beauty and use," as "one of the largest and finest rooms in the house, and every book in it writ by a woman." As she views her own volumes surrounded by thousands of other books written by women, she is filled with pride and "carried a good ways off a-ridin' on Wonder."[10]

Perhaps ironically, the Woman's Building Library maintained its symbolic power in part through the BLM's determination that it should function chiefly as a display, or spectacle—a lavish array of bound volumes, hand-picked and arranged in order to be admired from a distance. By opting to display books explicitly as objects or artifacts in a kind of museum for books rather than highlighting their content as readable texts, the BLM may have set itself at odds with the World's Fair Congress's slogan of "mind over matter" and the ALA's commitment to usability and service. Nevertheless, their decision seems to have heightened the immediate impact of this "other space."

Once the library was open, staff had to be on site, despite the fact that work on the collection's catalog had barely begun. In late April Palmer had written Dewey that the BLM "would like to have Miss Plummer come as soon as possible after May 1," adding, "you will be duly advised when an assistant is needed." When Elizabeth Harvey withdrew as a candidate for a "junior" position, Dewey was forced to look for a replacement. On May 4 he wrote Caroline Garland of the Dover Public Library in New Hampshire and asked her to be ready to go "any day." Garland agreed two days later, but she wondered what her duties were: "I would like to know what you expect of me," she wrote, "where to go for an admission pass to the grounds, and any detail of instruction or advice that you can find it in your heart to bestow."[11] Although she did not yet know it, librarians selected to staff the library were to be issued badges admitting them to any exposition entrance. They also qualified for reduced rates in the Women's Dormitory, located near the fairgrounds. The *Official Directory* noted that the dormitory, which was capable of housing a thousand women per day, was "presided over by refined, motherly women who keep a watchful care over unprotected girls who come singly or in groups." There the librarians mixed "with artists, teachers and self-supporting women from all walks of life."[12]

Four days after opening, Edith Clarke complained to Dewey about the library's condition." "I am in charge of a room in which I am unpacking the books, the floor and furniture are not yet finished, and boxes are everywhere." Her highest priorities, she said, were "to get the catalog finished," label the books "for their place," and put a BLM Woman's Building Library bookplate in each one. She predicted the collection would number over five thousand volumes. Two things worried her: that the "ladies of N.Y. State" had not provided enough bookshelves to accommodate everything they collected, and that the BLM "were anxious that I should catalog 5,000 books in a month & I told them I must have 5 assistants for that." She also reported that Mary Wright Plummer, who had arrived the previous day and was scheduled to spend every other day on site to answer questions about the library, had agreed to fill out slips for the printed catalog while working. But cataloging constituted the real problem, she said. "The trouble with the cataloging is that [only] one person can do the looking up as that must be done by lists which come in the boxes, and which I myself must take up to the Newberry [Library] & fill out the names on."[13]

Dewey responded four days later that Clarke "quite misunderstood" the position of Senior Librarian. "These librarians are not to write slips or have anything to do with the cataloging. The two things are distinct." He said he had specifically told Palmer "to employ you in charge of the cataloging, giving you such assistance as might be needed." Plummer could volunteer to write slips, but it was not part of her job description. Rather, she was "simply to meet the public and answer their questions, explain to them about modern libraries, tell them about the woman's library, and interest them in the library movement in general." Dewey also informed Clarke that Garland was ready to come "the day when she is wanted."[14]

On May 11 Clarke sent Dewey a draft of a document prepared for the BLM Press Committee summarizing her understanding of "The Library in the Woman's Building." "The library . . . is an exhibit, rather than a working library," she stated. "It is intended to be complete, not competitive, and its scope includes all books written by women, especially since 1800." She also noted that because the books were collected by different state and national committees they manifested "a want of evenness and uniformity." Some states and countries sent all books by all authors, some "only their best," some only one book from each author, and some living authors only. Although the BLM intended that the collection "be preserved permanently . . . in the Woman's Memorial Building to be erected at the end of the Fair," the document also noted that "as some collections are gifts, [and] others to be taken back at the end of the Fair," exhibitors had obviously not agreed to a "concerted action." She called attention to the pamphlet and monograph collection ("these cannot, usually, be obtained except through their authors, who have donated them here"), the cabinet of Harriet Beecher Stowe's manuscripts and editions of *Uncle Tom's Cabin,* and tables containing samples of periodicals edited by women.[15]

Clarke confirmed that the arrangement of books on the shelves would be by state and country and that the books were not to be "generally handled or examined." Instead, visitors would consult a classified catalog "showing at a glance on what subject women have been most prolific as writers." An author index would give brief biographical details (such as birth and death dates, degrees obtained, "special line of work in which the person has been engaged") and refer "to pages on which each author's works appear." She added, "The value of such a catalogue prepared from such a representative collection of books will be a permanent one, and should make it worth placing on the shelves of every library in the country, and be a bibliography of women's writings."[16] *The Critic* reported that Clarke was classifying and cataloging the collection "in the most approved methods of the librarians," and further indicated "there will be a card-catalogue of authors, in which the works of each writer will be preceded by an 'information-card' giving a few salient facts in her life." *The Critic* also announced a forthcoming "printed catalogue, which will contain, besides the index of authors, a list of the books classified broadly under the subjects of which they treat. Great care is expended upon this catalogue, and it will therefore be of permanent value to all collectors as a bibliography of the literary work done by women."[17]

Owing to the patriarchal structure of Western society, the cataloging rules librarians had developed over the centuries did not easily accommodate the contents of the Woman's Building Library. For an American library cataloger working in the last decade of the nineteenth century, Clarke wrote, dealing with "Women in literature" was "a thorn in the flesh" because of frequent name changes.[18] How to catalog *Ramona,* whose author (Mrs. Helen Maria Fiske Hunt Jackson) had been twice married? ALA rules required that women be entered under their "own personal names" in library catalogs "instead of their husbands," but to do so would require the well-known author Mrs. Burton Harrison (who autographed her books with that name) to be entered as an unrecognizable "Mrs. Constance Cary Harrison." To be consistent, Clarke rejected a request by Mrs. E. Lindon Bates "that her chosen name be respected," and instead "a cross-reference was ruthlessly made from that form to Mrs. Josephine White Bates, under which guise her works now appear." Other oddities invaded the catalog. "Mrs. Fred Burnaby masquerades under the burden of Mrs. Elizabeth Alice Frances Witshed Burnaby Main, where I hope her readers may have the good luck in finding her," an exasperated Clarke declared.

Practices in non-English speaking countries further complicated matters. Upon marriage, Italian, Swedish, Austrian, and Spanish women often connected their original names with their husbands' surnames. In Slavic countries family names often had masculine and feminine forms. Because of inconsistencies in practices from country to country, Clarke later revealed, on occasion she had to "toss up a penny, enter under one form, refer from the other, and . . . not worry." Some authors changed nationality after marrying (English poet Agnes Mary Frances Robinson had crossed the Channel to become Madame Jacques Darmesteter on her title pages); and Clarke found no consistency "in use of the form of Mrs. in every language." All of these problems, which demonstrate how library practices addressed the female and foreign Other, greatly slowed the task of cataloging the collection. Clarke knew her work would be carefully scrutinized by ALA members in July, and she wanted to get it right.

"I am glad you started right," Dewey wrote on May 15. He reminded Clarke that all books from the New York delegation "come back to this library," since "they were given with that agreement, and many of them belong to us." He added, "You will be there more permanently than the others, and as you are one of our immediate family, I shall rely on you to look after things." He informed Clarke he had scheduled Ellen Coe for June, that Mary Cutler would work from July 15 to August 15 with Ada Alice Jones and Florence Woodworth of the New York State Library as subordinates, and that Hannah P. James and Mary Sargent would cover September.[19]

Garland described what was happening at the library in a May 18 letter to Dewey. "When I first looked about here," she said, "it all seemed so desolate and chaotic that I hardly knew what to do." Although she was greeted cordially by Edith Clarke and the New York women in charge of decorating the library, Garland needed two days just to get "what sailors call the bearings." She told Dewey she had no one around to spell her for a half day, and that if she left her post "the passing multitude go to Miss Clarke's assistants for information and make large drafts on their time and patience." To avoid contact with the public, Garland said, Clarke had actually moved her desk into one of the Record Rooms.[20]

Despite these inconveniences, however, Garland said she was willing to continue, "for I am quite sure it is what you would want done." She observed that "the grade of visitors grows better each day," and although she did not feel she had "accomplished much yet in the missionary line"—most visitors "are interested only in the decorations and furniture"—she did receive questions "of all kinds." Five days later she told Dewey she was willing to stay on "a week or two longer," provided she could use half days to "see some of the beautiful things there are on this great ground." And Garland wondered whether Mary Titcomb—"an old school friend of mine" whose candidacy for a position in the library Dewey had rejected earlier in the month—might substitute for half days to provide her with some relief. (Titcomb had probably already told Garland that Dewey had rejected her.) She also complained about the unseasonable weather, "for sitting all day in these cold rooms requires a cast iron constitution." On May 25 Dewey received a letter from the New York Installation Committee saying that it "would be gratified" if Garland "might be continued" for a few weeks because she "has given so much satisfaction in her work."[21]

Despite Dewey's initial reservations about Titcomb's low ALA profile, staffing needs took priority. Within days Dewey asked Titcomb to go to Chicago as soon as possible and staff the library half days until Ellen Coe arrived at the beginning of June. Although Garland did not say so, the arrangement to share time in May with Mary Wright Plummer, which Dewey thought was in place, had not worked out, first because Plummer felt obligated to give priority to the Pratt Institute exhibit, and second because Bertha Palmer had not yet authorized her to take a position in the library. Because of this situation, Plummer initially arranged with Garland to begin work in June. "If I could do double duty until then," Garland later told Dewey, "she would do double duty after that." But when Dewey named Coe to take over in June, and Garland stayed on to share half days with her, Plummer thought her services were no longer necessary and Titcomb returned home. When Dewey found out about these arrangements, he was annoyed. "I am greatly surprised by a letter from Miss Titcomb . . . I understood that she was to stay through the ALA meeting [in July] when she came on." He asked Garland to clarify arrangements—especially as they related to salaries. "We must be sure there is no misunderstanding," he cautioned. Worried that she had done something "very stupid," Garland responded three days later, "I am quite sure that Miss Titcomb did not understand that you expected her to stay on thru [sic] the A.L.A." She noted she was now sharing days with Coe, who covered the hours from nine to one, while Garland staffed the room from one to five. Regarding finances, she informed Dewey that when she had sent in the requisition for library salaries, "the authorities were surprised at the amount of the bill." They contacted Mary Lockwood, and once she verified the amounts, "the salary bill was sent along to be paid." "Now as I understand it," she concluded, "I am to stay on with Miss Coe till the A.L.A. Is that right?"[22]

Dewey also received updates from Edith Clarke. "We are going to make a permanent card catalog at the World's Fair," she wrote on May 18, "and print from the cards. We will also classify according to D.C.... but arranging under state during the time of the exhibit." Clarke explained that Garland worked "all day every day," in part because Plummer "waits to get explicit orders from Mrs. Palmer direct," but because Palmer was so busy, "it is a difficult matter indeed." She also reported that the clause in the document she had originally drafted and sent to Dewey on May 11 about the New York library ultimately going to Albany after the fair closed had been "ordered . . . struck out" by Palmer, who did not want New York's arrangement copied by other states and countries. "[The BLM] desire to get all they can for the permanent library in the Memorial Building." Clarke also surmised that Palmer wanted to get "authors not yet represented to send their works to this permanent collection." Finally, because the New York collection "has so many volumes that other states have also," duplicates across the collections would increase the number of volumes that would eventually go into the permanent collection.[23]

While "Dewey's girls" struggled with conditions in the library, the fair schedule went forward. At many points this schedule intersected in some way with the library. For example, on May 26 members of the New York Board of Women Managers hosted an informal tea there in conjunction with a ceremony organized by Connecticut women to unveil the bust of Harriet Beecher Stowe sculpted by Anne Whitney. Although a New Englander, not a New Yorker, Stowe was "the dean of American literary women," as Laura E. Richards pronounced in *Art and Handicraft in the Woman's Building.* "The refined coloring and rich carving of the beautiful room was the background," the *Chicago Tribune* reported, "the animated faces of brilliant women assembled to do her honor its most striking feature." Less flatteringly, the *Boston Globe* reported that so many people attended the event that the Woman's Building "resembled a monster beehive." Blanche Bellamy opened the ceremony by recounting the history of the New York collections. She suggested that the occasion called for amending Sir Richard Steele's compliment to Lady Elizabeth Hastings: instead of "to love her is a liberal education," Bellamy proposed "to read her is a liberal education." Bellamy then noted that *The Female Quixote,* by Charlotte Ramsey Lennox, was the oldest book in the collection and pointed to many other Empire State authors. She praised the philanthropy that brought to the library thirty-one volumes by Lydia Maria Child (whose "name is inseparably connected with the anti-slavery movement," as Richards noted in *Art and Handicraft*); and she commended the efforts of Imogen Howard to bring printed materials authored by African American women into the collections. She then relinquished the floor to Candace Wheeler, who, "looking a bit proud," described the history of the library's decoration. (With the prominence given Stowe and Child and its "visual homage" to abolitionist poet Lydia Huntley Sigourney, the room's decor accorded well with Wheeler's own abolitionist roots.)[24]

Next Wheeler introduced Frederick Douglass, "who complimented the ladies on their great achievement and then delivered a stirring address in eulogium" of Stowe. According to a reporter from the Aberdeen (SD) *Daily News*, Douglass posed as Uncle Tom while Isabella Beecher Hooker unveiled the newly crafted bust and presented it as a loan to the BLM for the library.[25]

The bust of Stowe had been paid for by ten-cent contributions from women and schoolchildren in Connecticut. Behind Hooker, who sported "beautiful snowy curls" and gave "a peculiar, petulant toss of the head that is a characteristic of the Beecher family," stood the five-foot case filled with various editions of *Uncle Tom's Cabin*, many of them translations. "After she finished speaking and while the other exercises were going on," one observer recounted, "Mrs. Hooker slipped up to the bust unostentatiously and laid over the white marble a cluster of pinks and ferns." The ceremony concluded with songs written by New York women, including "Rocked in the Cradle of the Deep," "Battle Hymn of the Republic," and "The Legend of the Organ Builder."[26] That Harriet Beecher Stowe merited elevated status was something BLM members from the South suffered in silence, while members from Connecticut, Massachusetts, and New York give every evidence of reading into *Uncle Tom's Cabin* a political message Stowe probably never intended. If the racial and gender politics on display in the room caused discomfort to some in the audience, the press did not notice or chose not to comment.[27]

The following afternoon New York women formally presented their collection of books to the library. With Blanche Bellamy presiding, Candace Wheeler explained the room's decorating scheme. Before the invited guests adjourned for tea and a social hour, they were treated to a performance of "Suwannee River" in "dulcet tones," followed by "The Battle Hymn of the Republic" (according to the *Columbian Woman*'s "Exposition Notes") "recited with thrilling power"—a clear effort to assuage sectional tensions with a careful balance of Northern and Southern sentiment. "The occasion was a veritable 'love feast,'" the *Columbian Woman* reported, "and many and hearty congratulations followed this successful achievement of New York's fair daughters."[28]

Another set of programs that intersected in several ways with the Woman's Building, its library, and its librarians was the World's Congress of Representative Women. Put together by the Woman's Branch of the World's Congress Auxiliary, this event was held at the Art Institute of Chicago May 15–21. During the planning stages, not everyone had agreed on what the focus of the Congress of Representative Women should be. When it came up for discussion in late 1892, Ellen Henrotin argued that no congress ought to focus specifically on the "Woman Question." May Wright Sewall, a member-at-large of the Indiana Board of Commissioners who had been an American delegate to the Congress of Women at the 1889 Paris exposition and who represented members of the National Council of Women and suffragists across the country, wholeheartedly disagreed. By applying constant pressure, Sewall forced Henrotin (and ultimately Palmer) to acquiesce. "This branch is intended to embrace the whole scope of Woman's Work and Progress," a World's Congress Auxiliary circular announced in late 1892, "and is planned to present . . . a more comprehensive and complete portrayal of women's achievements in all departments of civilized life than has hitherto been made. . . . The special object . . . is to show the capabilities of women for more varied employments, greater usefulness and higher happiness than she has hitherto enjoyed."[29]

During the winter and spring of 1893 more than five hundred women "who represented the civilized world" from 24 countries, 35 states and territories, and 126 separate organizations helped prepare the World's Congress of Representative Women. Between May 15 and 21, more than three hundred women—including Frances Willard, Julia Ward Howe, Susan B. Anthony, Anna Howard Shaw, Elizabeth Cady Stanton, and Jane Addams—spoke in one of 147 sessions to a total attendance of 150,000 people, all of whom had the opportunity to respond to these "leading addresses."[30] The goal of the congresses was "not only [to] demonstrate what woman has done in the lines of mental and spiritual work, and in the sunny field of letters," Enid Yandell and Laura Hayes noted in *Three Girls in a Flat;* it was also hoped that "the public discussion of practical subjects by trained thinkers will uplift the masses and open the way to a better understanding of many facts needful to the housekeeper, the educator and the philanthropist."[31]

Sewall made sure that African American women were invited to speak at the congress; two delivered major addresses, four commented on other presentations, and one—Sarah J. Early of the Woman's Christian Temperance Union—was named "Representative Woman of the Year." Frances Harper emphasized gender over race and argued that the United States needed women to "stand foremost among the nations of the earth." Fannie Barrier Williams pushed race to the center of her address on "The Intellectual Progress of the Colored Women of the United States since the Emancipation Proclamation" and castigated the white establishment for its sordid legacy. In brief remarks that followed, Anna Julia Cooper noted that the history of African American women "is full of heroic struggle, a struggle against fearful and overwhelming odds, that often ended in a horrible death, to maintain and protect that which woman holds dearer than life." Philadelphia educator Fannie Jackson Coppin recounted the educational progress African American women had made since emancipation, and Early delivered an address titled "The Organized Efforts of the Colored Women of the South to Improve Their Condition." Hallie Q. Brown lauded Tuskegee's successes and praised African American women for publishing books against unlikely odds. It is not known if any of these representatives toured the Woman's Building Library while attending the fair to check for books by African American women. If they had, they would have found copies of Harper's novel *Iola Leroy; or, Shadows Uplifted* and volumes of her poems, but not Anna Julia Cooper's *Voice of the South*, or Ida B. Wells's *Southern Horrors*, both of which had been published in 1892. Both Cooper (born in North Carolina) and Wells (born in Mississippi) were natives of states represented by BLM members who had pledged less than two years earlier "to cooperate with any person appointed to represent the colored people in this State, in order that the whole exhibit of our State may be brought out." As we saw in chapter 2, Lettie Trent had correctly predicted the outcome of this pledge.[32]

As the congress was being planned, several prominent female librarians had pressed Annie Dewey, Melvil's wife, to accept an invitation to deliver a paper on "Women's Work in Libraries." On May 10 Hannah P. James wrote to Annie, "You know all about the sisterhood." Although some might think it was "unwise [for you] as Mr. Dewey's wife to speak for us," James said, "I think it is most wise. It is through his influence and inspiration that library science has made such rapid progress in these last 16 years, & especially is it entirely due to him that women are taking such prominent places in libraries. No one else would have started the Library School & no one else *could*. So as his wife & helpmeet in the good work it is meet and right for you to speak for us." For her efforts, James received a mild rebuke from Melvil seven days later. "Mrs. Dewey is visiting friends in Sandusky and Chicago and was to be at the meetings as a spectator," he wrote. "I did not mean at all that she was to be your representative." Plummer and Garland were fully capable of delivering an address, Dewey argued, but "rather than have anything go by default" his wife "would stand up for the profession. But," he added, "she did not go with that at all in mind."[33]

For unknown reasons, the subject of "Women's Work in Libraries" did not become part of the Congress of Representative Women programs.[34] Perhaps congress officials balked at the suggestion that a wife should tell one of their audiences how much her husband's contributions served a female-dominated profession. Nor did it enter into the published proceedings of the smaller Congress of Women, held in the Woman's Building. In fact, only a few of the papers ultimately published in the collection Mary Eagle edited even mentioned women and libraries. In a talk titled "The Novel as the Educator of the Imagination," May Rogers spoke about the library as an agency of culture. She noted that in the public library of her hometown (Dubuque, Iowa), fiction accounted for 78 percent of circulation; in Chicago's public library it accounted for 62 percent, in Boston's 80 percent. For her, however, libraries were not a subject of analysis; they merely provided convenient statistical data proving her point about the popularity of fiction (a point that may have implicitly justified the large proportion of novels in the Woman's Building Library). In her talk on "The Legal Condition of Women in 1492–1892," Mary A. Greene, a lawyer from Providence, Rhode Island, included a section on "Professions and Occupations Open to Women" that mentioned law, medicine, the clergy, journalism, art, and commerce, but said nothing about librarianship.[35]

Perhaps it was the absence of discussion of women and libraries at the congresses that prompted Adelaide Hasse of the Los Angeles Public Library to vent irritation with her peers in the July 15 issue of *Woman's Journal.* "With every State provided with laws for the formation of libraries within its boundaries, there is room for an army of missionaries in this line, and the American girl who has a well-balanced education is as certain of success in this vocation as in most that she undertakes," Hasse wrote. The best cataloging was now being done by women, she argued, and she lamented "the mediaeval notion" that women could not manage a library. She soundly criticized her professional peers for not contesting that presumption. "Librarianship is a distinct calling," she concluded, "and if women hope to rise in it they must acquaint themselves as familiarly as men have done with these important details of the work."[36] Although her message was clear to the readers of *Woman's Journal,* it had not been articulated at the congresses themselves.

Nor was it expressed at the World Congress Auxiliary's "Congress on Literature" held July 10–12, which did host a session titled "Congress of Libraries" on the final day. At that session six women presented papers on a variety of topics, including C.A. Catell of the New York City YMCA Library, on "YMCA Libraries as a Special Type of Library"; Jesse Allen, of the Omaha Public Library, on "The Library as a Teacher of Literature"; Tessa Kelso, of the Los Angeles Public Library, on "Some Economic Features of a Library"; Caroline M. Hewins, of the Hartford Public Library in Connecticut, on "The Pictorial Resources of a Small Library"; and M. S. R. James of the People's Palace Library in London, on "The People's Palace and Its Library." Although Giulia Sacconi-Ricci of the Marcellian Library in Florence, Italy, could not attend, her paper, "Observations on the Various Forms of Catalogs in Modern Libraries; with Special Reference to a System of Mechanical Binding," was read for her. All spoke mostly about librarianship; they said almost nothing about gender. Discussion following the papers led to a consensus that "post-graduate courses should be instituted in all the large universities for the benefit of students who desire to prepare themselves for the profession of librarian."[37]

By that time the Woman's Building Library had been open for more than two months, during which it had functioned as a physical space for a variety of purposes. One female visitor used its comfortable furniture to breastfeed her baby. Comments by other visitors demonstrate that its exhibits were differently appropriated. "Yesterday my attention was directed in the Library to an interesting exhibit," the editor of *Woman's Tribune* noted in her July 7 "World's Fair Letter." "Autograph letters and portraits of noted women are placed under glass on a revolving stand. It would be impossible to give a complete list of letters in the collection, but among them were one or two from George Eliot, George Sand, and from Queen Elizabeth to Mary Queen of Scots, Elizabeth Barrett Browning, Lucretia Mott and Lydia Maria Child &c." She marveled "that sight-seers should spend so much time in admiring laces and needlework rather than study this collection which gives an insight into the character of these good women."[38]

The librarians staffing the library also reported visitors' reactions. "Why have a library of women's books?" was a standard question people asked when entering the exhibit, Edith Clarke recounted. "Why not let them take their place side by side with the men, and be judged equally with them?" In her own mind, Clarke told the Chicago Library Club after the fair closed, the reason was obvious and could be summed up in another question: "Why not?" The Wisconsin Historical Society collected materials written by Wisconsin inhabitants, schools and colleges acquired works written by alumni, and many men regularly collected books addressing their hobbies. Most of the library's visitors, Clarke noted, came from "small towns and country districts," and most (male and female) had seen women occupied only in "housekeeping and the rearing of children." Once they entered the library, however, many were "amazed when they are brought face to face with the achievements of the same abilities when brought into competition with men in art, literature, science, or business," and often they remarked, "Why, I did not think there were so many books in the world written by women." Clarke also reported that Thomas Wentworth Higginson had spent a couple of hours there, and because he was so impressed with the "remarkable library of women's writings," offered to donate his own sixteen-hundred-volume collection of women's works if the proposed permanent Woman's Library materialized.[39]

Numerous other testimonies echoed Clarke's experience. Caroline Garland later reported that one woman, "attended by a sedate colored servant," delivered her book in person. "[It] is the story of my life," she explained, adding that the book had "changed the legislation of 32 states." As a young woman she had been committed to a "mad-house" by her husband in order to take possession of her property, but "after three years' confinement she escaped, found friends, wrote books, and then made successful applications to the States for better legislation in regard to the insane." This book joined two other exposés by the same author—Elizabeth Parsons Ware Packard—on the shelves of the Woman's Building Library.[40]

Many newly published women authors also visited the library. "They were as a rule hopeful," Garland observed, "and entirely free from the vice of modesty." She recalled one who gave her a book she had written. "You'll read it, won't you?" When Garland responded "If I have time," the author snatched it out of her hand, exclaiming, "I won't leave it if you don't promise to read it!" Garland confessed that "the librarian's desire to increase the size of the library got the better of truthfulness," and she promised the author she would read it. Garland also recalled a visit from Virginia Smith Jones, who donated a two-volume set of *Illustrations of the Nests and Eggs of Birds of Ohio* (valued at $375), which she had worked on "with eight years of untiring industry." When Garland asked, "How did you ever have the patience to complete it?" Jones responded, "I did it in memory of my daughter. She had just begun the work when she died. So for her sake I made it as perfect as possible."[41]

Not all shared the kind of middle-class values the Woman's Building made manifest. "Were these pictures all painted by women?" a "severe lady" asked in early May. "I'll warrant you they didn't have families to look after or they'd never have found the time." Upon observing an opera cloak made of prairie chicken feathers, she remarked tartly, "the woman might have found better use of her time." After she had toured the building, including the library, she pronounced, "These things will do for rich people, but if you're poor you'd just better not see them at all."[42]

Although the library was drawing substantial numbers of visitors, there was a constant need for adjustments to unexpected circumstances. At a June 20 meeting of the New York Board of Women Managers, Mrs. Dean Sage reported that the mantelpiece obscured the library's entrance from public view, and that bringing visitors through the Records Rooms was not working well. As a result, she said, "many people were kept from seeing it." Several suggested placards directing visitors to the library, but Sage recommended instead that the mantelpiece be raised so people could enter directly from the hallway. This work was completed by the time the ALA met there on July 21.

Blanche Bellamy also noted that several people had complained about the inscription above the door, which read "The Library of the Woman's Building Contributed by the State of New York." After a brief discussion the New York women's Executive Committee "decided that it should continue to remain as it now reads."[43]

At its August 8, 1893, meeting, New York's Executive Committee heard a report about the theft of a gold chain, earrings, and broach from Imogen Howard's exhibit, and that as a result a special guard had been detailed for the room and security increased throughout the building. The committee also discussed sale of Distaff Séries books in booths at building entrances, which it recommended be reduced to clear inventory before the exposition closed. Finally, it agreed that when the exhibits were being packed after the fair closed, the chair of the Installation Committee would be authorized to employ extra guards to increase security.[44]

In her July 21 report to the BLM Executive Committee, Mary Lockwood, chair of the Press Committee, reported that Edith Clarke had continued to supervise the cataloging; although her task was complicated by not knowing how large the final collection would be, she nonetheless closely monitored the process of receiving and unpacking the books, preparing lists of all items, placing a bookplate in each and locating them on the shelves, and cataloging and classifying the entire collection. Careful records were essential, Lockwood noted, in order "to prove a case against any which may be claimed later to have been sent, and yet which has never been added to the library." Clarke was also compiling a list of books to be returned to their owners at the end of the fair. In her report Lockwood thanked Clarke for her services but noted that because she needed to return to her regular job at the Newberry it was essential that the BLM appoint a permanent librarian. "This seems to be absolutely necessary to avoid confusion at the end of the Fair."[45]

Because Clarke wanted the library catalog to reflect the profession's latest rules, its construction took longer and cost more than Palmer had initially anticipated, despite forewarnings by Dewey and Clarke. When, toward the fair's end Palmer pressed Lockwood to complete the project quickly, Lockwood tried to buy more time by arguing that Isabellans and suffragists would heavily criticize an uncataloged library. Clarke, Lockwood said, wanted to complete a catalog that "would be purchased extensively by libraries," adding that she knew "the disappointment it will be to Miss Clarke to leave the work in such an unfinished state which will result in really no credit to her, a work which she has made every effort to make as near-perfect as possible." But Palmer was unsympathetic, and on September 15 Lockwood was forced to stop the cataloging project for lack of funds. In the few weeks remaining to her Clarke performed abbreviated cataloging (author/title) on remaining titles so that all were at least included in the public catalog.[46]

Concerned about finances, Lockwood asked Dewey at the end of July not to appoint any more librarians. She noted that Clarke had hired two assistants shortly after beginning work and later two additional "inexperienced" helpers who worked from nine to five daily. After more than three months, however, they still had not completed cataloging and classifying the collection. A month later Dewey wrote Palmer that he had committed only to Mary Sargent for September, and had given permission to have Elizabeth Clarke take over the job of cataloging and classifying from her sister, Edith, since Elizabeth "offers to take the entire day at $80 a month, thus reducing expenses nearly half, if that is important."[47]

When Mary Loomis reported to Dewey on October 21 that she and Mary Davis had been on the job since October 2, Dewey responded that "after November 1 [when the exposition was scheduled to close] Miss Clarke's sister will attend to anything finally left so it will be unnecessary to stay beyond the limits of the month unless they should ask you." Some confusion also arose when Ada Alice Jones asked Palmer why her salary had been delayed. In response, Palmer noted that Dewey "had never sent to the Board the necessary bills, showing the date and period of time which each assistant served." She told Jones she had written Dewey, and as soon as he sent her the information she "will see that vouchers are made out and sent to the Treasury." To an accountant in the World's Fair Administration Building, she wrote, "Will you please ask Mr. Dewey for a statement in regard to the girls who served, and the time of service of each?" On November 11 Mary Lockwood sent Palmer a final report on the librarians and catalogers.[48]

The Board of Lady Managers hosted its last major meeting of the fair on October 28. In the Assembly Room, women spoke for a variety of organizations that represented multiple political, social, and cultural perspectives. After Palmer delivered her greetings, Susan B. Anthony spoke for the National American Woman Suffrage Association. In the forty-five years since a small group of women first demanded the right of suffrage, she said, the issue had become central to women's concerns. Representatives of the Woman's Christian Temperance Union followed. They praised the organization they represented for "belt[ing] the earth with its white ribbon and [doing] its work not alone in the cause of temperance, but social purity."[49]

Following a paper that summarized events at the Woman's Building since the exposition's opening day, representatives of many women's groups bade the fair goodbye. The spokeswoman for the General Federation of Women's Clubs (GFWC) said that "in leaving to women the control of the heart" man "left to her the destiny of nations, for so long as woman rules the home she rules the world." Recognizing this, she continued, the GFWC "has drawn its membership from the home. Of the American home, its beauty and its love, we would make the federation a symbol." Other speakers represented the International Board of Women, the Ladies Catholic Benevolent Association, the YMCA, the King's Daughters, the Daughters of the American Revolution, the Women's Industrial and Educational Union, and the Grand Army of the Republic Women's Relief Corps. May Wright Sewall spoke for the million-member National Council of Women, and reminded her audience of the council's efforts on behalf of two pending federal bills, one to ensure women workers equal pay, the other to secure uniform marriage and divorce laws throughout the nation. Other women spoke for the Women's Press Club, the Home and Foreign Missionary Society of the Episcopal Church, the South End Flower Mission, the Girl's Friendly Society, the Non-Partisan WCTU, Eastern Star, *Women's Work*, the Philanthropic Organization of Oregon, the Emma Willard Association, the Shut-in Society, the Protective American Society of Authors, the Keeley Rescue Cure, and the Loyal Women of America, among many others. Every one of the points of view—and most of the people and organizations featured on this day—were amply represented in the Woman's Building's exhibits and in the printed materials collected for its library. Many of the booths were staffed by members who, like the women representing the National American Woman Suffrage Association, were to "receive visitors, answer questions, distribute literature, and arrange for subscriptions" to relevant periodicals.

With the Woman's Building Library in full swing, its distinctiveness as a cultural institution became evident. Although not a working library in any conventional sense of the term, it functioned simultaneously as a workplace for resident librarians, a "port of call" for World's Fair visitors, and a meeting place for organizations and individuals alike. As such, it operated as a "contact zone," where "geographically and historically separated groups establish ongoing relations." As James Clifford points out, "contact zones are constituted through reciprocal movements of people, not just of objects, messages, commodities, and money."[50] Over the course of the fair's six-month run, the library brought together tens of thousands, perhaps even hundreds of thousands of people in just this kind of dynamic exchange, even as it served as a catalyst for disseminating a wide range of women's texts, modeled the homelike atmosphere Candace Wheeler created that was emulated in thousands of new public libraries run largely by women for the next hundred years, and provided a platform for the preservation and publicizing of women's print culture at the end of the nineteenth century.

Yet contact zones also function like "frontiers," where "a center and a periphery are assumed: the center a point of gathering, the periphery an area of discovery." As a center and a gathering point, the Woman's Building Library greatly amplified and expanded a sense of community bound mostly by gender for the countless people who visited it. And at the periphery, the books lining the walls constituted a seemingly endless "area of discovery." The next three chapters explore the library's textual "periphery" to reveal what these late nineteenth-century women considered most important to collect, to display, and for future generations to preserve. These chapters illustrate how, as Clifford emphasizes, "centers become borders crossed by objects and makers."[51]

5

"To Read Her Is a Liberal Education"

"The successful bringing together of human bodies was as nothing in comparison with the marshaling of thought forces, and the main power of material profit which had made the whole great drama possible sank into insignificance in sight of what it had evoked." So writes Candace Wheeler in her autobiography, *Yesterdays in a Busy Life* (1918). The Columbian Exposition, Wheeler explains, "might have been one merely of the commercial activities, but it was far more than that." While the material products of business and technological progress received great fanfare, the congresses, which represented "the most advanced knowledge in all the various fields of science, morality, and religion," brought about, in Wheeler's assessment, "a focusing of the immaterial forces of progress." To Wheeler, the relationship between matter and mind was not one of simple opposition. Instead, she describes a dialectic of tangible and intangible forces: "I could almost see the real and spiritual at work together in this great theater of preparation," she recalls of the Woman's Building, "where material fingers were spinning the inexhaustible thoughts of the mind into material which could be made a part of life itself."[1]

Like the exposition itself in Wheeler's account, the texts collected in the Woman's Building Library represent a synthesis of ideas, objects, and makers. This chapter presents a multilayered analysis of the library that aims to illuminate the collection as a whole, by identifying key Columbian texts and bringing into focus the currents of thought they embody. Content analysis, based on Dewey Decimal Classification (DDC), allows us to outline in broad strokes the subjects and genres that defined the collection. At the same time, a survey of selected novels written by exposition "insiders" on both sides of the suffrage debate illustrates themes and approaches reflected in scores of the library's volumes. And throughout, sustained attention to the gendered discourses of duty, vocation, and progress reveals a range of responses to crucial issues such as work, education, and marriage. Through these interlocking modes of analysis, we draw out some of the prevalent "thought forces" that circulated through the Woman's Building Library and investigate pertinent questions these texts implicitly ask: How can women progress? What does progress look like? What gains are to be made? What, if anything, might be lost?

To some degree, all libraries bear marks of the preferences, assumptions, and goals of those who developed them. Often these traces are most easily discerned in aspects of the collection that are in some way exceptional, unusual, or distinctive. In the Woman's Building Library, these distinguishing features derive not only from individual collectors and organizers such as Bertha Palmer and Blanche Bellamy, who left their stamp on the collection, but also from the "collective collector"—the intermeshed network of institutions that worked together to assemble and display the materials. As Candy Gunther Brown points out, "In theory, the [Woman's Building Library] was designed as a repository of the sum total of women's achievements as published authors. In practice, for every volume included in the library someone made a decision to send the text to a state affiliate of the fair's Board of Lady Managers [BLM], who agreed upon its appropriateness for the collection."[2] These state affiliates, their international counterparts, the extensive network of local women's clubs they tapped into, and the BLM's library committee all helped shape the collection and give it its distinctive character.

One notable feature of the Woman's Building Library is the presence of texts that owe their existence to the building's creation. The international appeal to submit writing by women resulted in a host of books conceived and produced especially for the occasion—in essence, a Columbian genre. This category of texts includes scrapbooks, club histories, cookbooks, literary miscellanies, literary history, women's history, drama, poetry, and even novels. Many of these texts were compiled by Lady Managers or their associates—volumes such as Candace Wheeler's *Columbia's Emblem, Indian Corn*, Margaret Tufts Yardley's *New Jersey Scrap-book of Women Writers*, E. D. Deland's *Scrap-book of Articles from Periodicals*, Mrs. J. G. Gregory's *Selections from the Writings of Connecticut Women*, and *The Story of the Files: A Review of California Writers and Literature*, by Ella Sterling Cummins (later Mighels). Some emanated from "Columbian Clubs" specially organized for the exposition. Others, like the Distaff Series volumes, had the financial backing and imprimatur of a major commercial publisher. In her introduction to the series, Blanche Bellamy explained that it comprised "representative work of the women of the State of New York in periodical literature," with a "woman of eminent success in each department" serving as volume editor for each of the "conspicuous divisions" of literature: "Poetry, Fiction,

History, Art, Biography, Translation, Literary Criticism, and the like."[3] Although she does not mention it, the series also included volumes devoted to current social issues. With its emphasis on women's education, pedagogy, charity, social reform (including essays on the antislavery movement, African Americans' experience, Native American education, tenement management, and criminal reform), decorative art, literary history, and fiction (in particular, regional, sentimental, and morally uplifting stories), the six Distaff volumes bear unmistakable evidence of the interests and tastes of the BLM and the New York Board of Women Managers, the federation of women's clubs, and other constituents of this "collective collector."[4] Products of "a gala day of effervescing 'Columbian' literature," according to the *New York Times,* they also echo larger trends in the writing exhibited in the Woman's Building and in nineteenth-century culture more broadly, even as they reflect the unique circumstances, characteristic flavor, and overall design of the Woman's Building Library.

The unusual and distinctive circumstances of the library's creation are evident, too, in the numerous volumes by women who played a vital role in the building's administration or who contributed in other ways to exposition events. In many cases, the women who helped plan, organize, or otherwise facilitate the fair's exhibits, publications, programs, and congresses were established authors with books or articles in general circulation. In such cases, their involvement in the Columbian Exposition very likely helped secure their works shelf-space.[5] Even though writing was not their primary professional activity, a number of Lady Managers, particularly those involved in the various literary and library committees on national and state boards, were published authors with books on display, as were many speakers in the Congress of Women and the World's Congress of Representative Women. There was "dear, persistent Susan Anthony," for example, "whose whole life was spent in the spirit of 'seventy-six,'" Candace Wheeler noted. Wheeler recalled "pacing the outside corridor of the Woman's Building with her one afternoon after one of the congress meetings," and being "so taken possession of by this spirit in her that the outside and inside crowds seemed all to be a part of one brooding spirit of right in the world and of love in the world." Also among the speakers were well-known reformers, scientists, ministers, poets, and novelists, including Julia Ward Howe, who "seldom spoke," according to Wheeler, but "when she did, people listened," and the popular novelist E. D. E. N. Southworth, who gave a paper in the form of a novelette titled "'Between Two Fires'—Publisher and Plagiarist" in connection with the American Protective Society of Authors.[6] And the World's Congress of Representative Women included a raft of conference committees as well as foreign and domestic advisory boards that boasted both established and rising literary stars. Among dozens of women serving on the Home Advisory Council, for example, were Charlotte Perkins Stetson (Gilman), Julia Ward Howe, Elizabeth Stuart Phelps Ward, Mary E. Wilkins (Freeman), Frances E. W. Harper, Kate Douglas Wiggin, and Sara J. Lippincott (Grace Greenwood), who delivered a cautionary address at the congress exposing the financial chicanery of her various publishers.[7] Several journalists covering the fair authored or edited volumes placed in the library as well—for example, Kate Field, editor of *Kate Field's Washington* and World's Fair correspondent for the *Chicago Herald;* Marian Shaw, reporter for the Fargo *Argus* and author of three novels in the library, including two unrecovered serials and a school story; and Teresa Dean, reporter for Chicago's *Inter Ocean* and the author of *How to Be Beautiful: Nature Unmasked* (1889).[8] Given the large number of women writers directly involved with the fair in some capacity (as board members, speakers, journalists, exhibitors, club representatives, advisors, and so forth), it is not surprising the interests of these women would be well represented in the Woman's Building Library, not only through their own writings, but also through the publications of women who influenced and inspired them. Taken together, these contributions to the library, amounting to at least 436 separate works by 150 writers in the American portion alone, reveal how individuals closely involved with the exposition helped shape the content of the overall collection, both directly and indirectly.[9]

Publications of these World's Fair "insiders" offer considerable insight into "the Columbian Woman"—a useful abstraction that embodies the values and ideals associated with the vision of women's progress the Columbian Exposition celebrated. Although these women may not have been "typical," their writing—especially their fiction—fuses the representative and the exceptional in illuminating ways. Their publications are representative because they reveal a remarkable degree of consonance and consistency with the collection as a whole, reflecting topics and concerns that recur many times over in the Woman's Building Library. They are exceptional because they often clarify, complicate, or intensify concerns and preoccupations adumbrated by their contemporaries and more faintly sounded in other texts in the library. In sum, the Columbian literature possesses a strong affinity with mainstream late nineteenth-century American women's culture, although its perspective tends to be more pointed, and often more progressive. While concentrating on matters of broad interest to contemporary readers, the numerous books these women authored heightened the library's reformist content and lent it something of a progressive slant, although these authors often disagreed on what constituted "progress" and how it was to be achieved.

The Columbian literature considered in this chapter casts light in two directions: it shines in on the literary community that helped shape the Woman's

Building Library, and it radiates out to the cultural history of women in the late nineteenth century. The myriad publications of these women imbued the library with a distinctly "Columbian" ethos manifested both in the self-consciously up-to-date topics, ideas, interests, and ideals their individual works conveyed and in their mingled praise and critique of fin-de-siècle society. An analysis of a cluster of novels by Columbian Women suggests that, like the White City itself, their fiction attempts to fashion what Alan Trachtenberg describes as a "truer vision of the real," a heterotopia of words that aspires to "correct" the troubled, disorderly, sometimes brutal society of late nineteenth-century America.[10]

Closely linked to the New Woman (in fact, at least three Columbian Women writers had already embraced the terminology of "new womanhood" by 1893), the Columbian Woman represents a range of interpretations of women's role in society and other social issues, rather than a fixed set of beliefs.[11] As earlier chapters indicate, the women who took part in the organization of the Woman's Building Library and the activities that occurred there held varying, sometimes conflicting, views, although they shared a sense of pride in women's accomplishments, a positive conviction that women would continue to advance in society, and an unwavering commitment to women's role as a force for the greater social good.[12] This commitment found varied expression in their writings, giving rise to an entire genre that could appropriately be termed—after the title of a Distaff Series volume—"the literature of philanthropy." Moreover, like Candace Wheeler, many shared a belief in "the reforming power of beauty."[13] For these women, the Woman's Building Library was not merely a physical exhibit, or a spectacle to be taken in passively, and the volumes in it were not simply to be admired from afar. Columbian Women writers took an active role in shaping the collection's content; as a result, the library reflected their interests, embodied their ideas, and expressed their creativity, while giving concrete form to the expressed conviction that (as one Columbian Woman put it) "thought-power moves the world."[14]

Accounting for some 2,200 volumes or approximately 45 percent of the American titles, the largest general category of books in the American portion of the library (as defined by DDC class) was "Literature."[15] The fact that many Columbian Women wrote fiction, poetry, and other forms of literature is one indication of the extent to which their published works "track" patterns and trends in the Woman's Building Library in particular and nineteenth-century women's writing in general.[16] In addition, that these women often composed fiction and poetry alongside works of art, music, religion, home economics, medicine, and a host of other topics, not only suggests that the fair's literary and congress committees looked to creative writers as a pool of potential authorities on a wide range of subjects, it also demonstrates that many women active in reform movements and professional careers wrote imaginative literature as well, often in tandem with nonfiction works. Indeed, in their view, literature— like women's clubs, political tracts, courses of study, newspapers, magazines, petitions, and church auxiliaries—constituted a potentially effective medium of social reform. And, typically, their creative writing reflects precisely the social problems and concerns they addressed through other avenues.

While American poetry in English accounted for nearly four hundred identified volumes (about 8 percent of U.S. texts), American fiction in English, represented by more than fourteen hundred volumes, dwarfs even that substantial number.[17] And, consistent with the general popularity of novels, this was a genre many Columbian Women writers embraced. For the most part, Columbian Women's novels descend from the large class of fiction Jane Tompkins discusses in *Sensational Designs*—fiction that "articulat[es] and propos[es] solutions for the problems that shape a particular historical moment."[18] This was a literary tradition developed by women writers and reformers who identified the home as their locus of influence and sought to bring the highest ideals of woman's sphere to bear on the world at large. In many cases, late nineteenth-century novelist-reformers upheld this time-honored belief in the sanctity of women's domestic role while actively engaging in timely reform efforts targeting a wide range of social ills beyond the domestic sphere. In a chapter titled "Novel-Reading" in *How to Win: A Book for Girls* (1886), Frances Willard expresses the view that novel writing is "the most unproductive of all industries" unless it be invested with "some high, heroic, moral aim." Similarly, one of the central characters in Elizabeth Boynton Harbert's novel *Amore* (1892) faults novels that lack a "soul-satisfying philosophy." In her opinion, "the power of a book is not so much in its plot or artistic construction, as in the spirit of the writer." Elizabeth Cady Stanton goes further in recommending fiction as a vehicle for change, as well as a moral force, in her preface to Helen H. Gardener's *Pray You, Sir, Whose Daughter?* (1892). Citing the impact of *Uncle Tom's Cabin*, Stanton argues that "the wrongs of society can be more deeply impressed on a large class of readers in the form of fiction than by essays, sermons, or the facts of science." As a lecturer for the Woman's Christian Temperance Union put it, fiction is "too powerful a weapon to be left in careless hands."[19]

In using fiction to address complex social problems, these novelist-reformers participated in a sweeping and influential literary movement in nineteenth-century America. Enlisting fiction as an agent of social change was one way for late nineteenth-century women to build what the novelist, poet, and reformer Frances Harper described as "stately temples of thought and action," or, in the words of Bertha Palmer's opening-day address, to dedicate themselves "to an elevated womanhood" in order to "best serve the cause of humanity."[20] The specific causes Columbian Women writers addressed in their fiction ran the gamut from women's rights, children's rights, and temperance to care for the mentally ill, racial justice, and workers' rights.[21] Many Columbian Women sought to reform literature itself, for they recognized the capacity of fiction not only to reflect reality but to create it. As a female doctor in Lillie Devereux Blake's novel *Fettered for Life* explains, "Just so long as all our literature is pervaded with the thought that women are inferior, so long will our sex be held in a low estimate."[22] Often the aims of these novelists coincide with those of early and midcentury writers like Sedgwick, Stowe, and Child; however, the novels of these fin-de-siècle writer-reformers—often analytical, sometimes ironic, and occasionally acerbic—are decidedly postsentimental in ideology and technique.[23]

While many have faulted reform literature, "problem novels," and protest literature for privileging didacticism over aesthetics, critics of the day often recognized in the best fiction of this type a synthesis of the didactic and the aesthetic that challenged the status quo.[24] The novelist and social reformer Celia Parker Woolley addressed this matter head-on in an 1893 letter to the *Dial*, asking, "Is our coming literature to be chiefly a medium of instruction of moral impulse and inspiration, or of mere aesthetic or intellectual enjoyment? Is it to be dominated most by the living instincts of those who write and those who read, or by the so-called art-spirit? What is the true proportion between this art-spirit and a more didactic purpose? In a word, how real and strong and vital are we willing our literature should become?" As Lee Schweninger notes, Woolley answers this question with reference to Hamlin Garland—whom she characterizes as "profoundly stirred by those new ideals which demand a larger thought and life-content in literature, which would make it the servant of humanity's most pressing needs, using it to stimulate thought, elevate social conditions and standards, sweeten and ennoble life all round"—and Helen H. Gardener, "a still more marked example" of "that class of writers who care more about life than about theories of the art which seeks to express and represent life."[25] In enlisting their fiction to fill the role of "servant of humanity's most pressing needs," many of the novelist-reformers represented in the Woman's Building Library joined Woolley in holding their fiction to higher ethical standards and aspiring to greater humanitarian heights than the "art-spirit" alone could attain.[26] Yet even as these novels register a profound engagement with social questions and the problems confronting middle-class (and sometimes working-class) women, they also reveal the great extent to which Columbian women's fiction was embedded in the broader print culture reflected by the library's many volumes of nonfiction.

Although it represents only one of many facets of the overall collection, and is almost impossible to isolate as a subject, theme, or approach, domesticity was nearly ubiquitous in the Woman's Building Library. Many of the more than 260 American books assigned to the DDC class "Useful Arts" are devoted to domestic topics. More than eighty of these fall under the subject heading "Food and Drink," and nearly thirty additional volumes of the U.S. contribution addressed temperance. And, of course, many novels in the collection can be considered domestic fiction. Indeed, thirty-one of the forty-seven authors Nina Baym identifies in her bibliography of women's fiction between 1820 and 1870 are represented in the library.[27] Many of the library's texts show women moving outside traditional roles while maintaining strong ties to the domestic sphere. Domesticity is exalted, but these books show that American women in the late nineteenth century could be "domestic" while traveling abroad, or laboring in the workforce, or even performing on the lecture circuit. More than a few contributors sought to extend women's role into such traditionally male professional havens as law (Myra Bradwell, for example) and medicine.[28] Rather than confining domesticity (and the women who practiced it) to the home, the Woman's Building Library shows women extending the ideals of domesticity into the outside world.

Next to "Literature," the largest DDC class in the library was "Geography and History" (accounting for about 11 percent of U.S. titles). The large number of titles in this class is chiefly owing to an abundance of biographies (more than 160 U.S. volumes), bolstered by a substantial number of books about the United States (at least sixty), plus nearly fifty identified volumes on geography and travel in North America and an additional thirty-two American volumes on geography and travel in Europe. This result is consistent with current research on the reading interests and creative contributions of nineteenth-century women. Nina Baym has drawn attention to a substantial body of historical writing by antebellum women, and in her recent study of public art at the Columbian Exposition, Wanda M. Corn reveals how women artists who contributed to the fair used public art as a medium to reconceptualize the narrative of history.[29] The diaries of American women of the period, Susan K. Harris observes, manifested "an intense interest in biographies of heroic women." Between 1820 and 1850, Scott Casper reports, "the number of 'female biographies,' lives of women subjects, increased exponentially."[30] Alison Booth's research into group biographies of women reveals that 1893 was a peak year—with many of these volumes "generated by the occasion" of the World's Columbian Exposition. "The multibiographical collaborations that flurried in the early 1890s figure the middle-class woman as the heroine of the progress of the races," Booth notes, "while these volumes pit each state and region against the other in boasting of their women."[31] As well as displaying numerous biographical compilations of the kind Booth describes, the library featured many volumes of eulogistic memoir, along with biographies of famous literary and historical figures representing a range of periods, nationalities, and fields of distinction. Biographical subjects represented in the library include St. Theresa of Avila, Martin Luther, Sir Philip Sidney, Shakespeare, Anne Bradstreet, Mary and Martha Washington, Mary Shelley, Margaret Fuller, Louis Agassiz, LaFayette, Queen Victoria, Charles Sumner, Robert E. Lee, Ulysses S. Grant, William Tecumseh Sherman, Emma Lazarus, Helen Keller, Frédéric Chopin, and Victor Hugo, along with abolitionists Harriet Tubman, Sarah and Angelina Grimké, Isaac T. Hopper, and James and Lucretia Mott. Eliza Allen Starr contributed her biography of Queen Isabella, which she dedicated to fellow members of the Queen Isabella Association.

The contributions of Columbian Women writers mirror these historical and biographical trends, with titles such as Frances Willard's *Nineteen Beautiful Years* (1864), a personal memoir of Willard's deceased sister, and Mary Florence Taney's *Kentucky Pioneer Women: Columbian Poems and Prose Sketches* (1893), which adopts a woman-centered approach to history in its biographical sketches of fifteen women she identifies as "types of Pioneer Women . . . who established homes, founded families, introduced refinement and culture, and made civilization and sound morals permanent occupants of our State."[32] Similarly, in the historical novel *Lang Syne; or, The Ward of Mount Vernon: A Tale of the Revolutionary Era* (1889), Mary Stuart Smith incorporates a substantial biographical appendix, in which she acknowledges the difficulty of gleaning information "from diverse and obscure sources" and argues, "The historian must indeed be superficial, who . . . ignores its domestic relations, as an important factor in the great sum whose mysteries he is endeavoring to solve."[33] In identifying the value of women's social history, Smith—like Columbian Woman writer Alice Morse Earle and the prolific Elizabeth Fries Ellet, both well-represented in the Woman's Building Library—articulates a significant revision of historiography and anticipates feminist approaches to history that would be widely accepted a century later. In a *Columbian Woman* article titled "Daughters of the Revolution" (1893), DAR founding member Flora Adams Darling enlists this approach to advance an idealized vision of womanhood in the interests of the larger body politic: "Let us teach our children the history of our country from woman's point of view," she urges, "and the republic will be secure." A more radical intervention, the three-volume *History of Woman Suffrage* (1881–86), by Susan B. Anthony, Elizabeth Cady Stanton, and Matilda Joslyn Gage, wrote women directly into the narrative of American political history as key actors as well as constituents.[34]

Even as she formulates a revisionist theory of history, Smith, in her novel *Lang Syne,* recognizes that most women will primarily read her "Tale of the Revolutionary Era" for credible role models, rather than to learn about the nation's past. Her appendix of notable women concludes with an appeal that readers "set forth anew to emulate their sturdy virtues."[35] Rather than "promoting a single ideology of gender roles and expectations," Casper points out, nineteenth-century women's biographies "suggested visions of women's realm ranging from the most constricted 'woman's sphere' to an expansive Christian womanhood with the power to reform society." Like the biographies Casper surveys, Columbian Women's novels present a wide variety of admirable female characters that do not always conform to the essentialized, idealized, unitary "type" of the singular nineteenth-century "Woman." Sometimes the fiction offers models of appropriate and "improving" reading that includes biographies of admirable women. In Annie Nathan Meyer's *Helen Brent, M.D.,* for example, the heroine habitually "refreshe[s] herself with the biography of some great woman. She would take down some volume from her shelf and enjoy a peaceful reading of the career of Dorothea Dix, or Mary Somerville, or Margaret Fuller; of some woman that had nobly lived up to some definite purpose, some great life work." Reading such biographies helps restore the protagonist's "damaged faith in womanhood. It was like breathing the fresh air of the fields after the heavy atmosphere of the crowded parlor." As Casper's research reveals, "biographers, critics, and readers alike believed that biography had power: the power to shape individuals' lives and character and to help define America's national character."[36]

Another category of books credited with the power to shape character and define groups, "Religion" is the DDC class that accounts for the largest number of titles in the Woman's Building Library after "Literature" and "History": more than 450 American items, or just under 10 percent of the U.S. contribution. The vast majority of books in this category fall under the headings "Christian experience, practice, and life" (more than 160 items identified) and "Devotional literature" (90 items identified). Many volumes in the library (including hundreds of works of fiction, many of them for young readers) bear the imprint of religious institutions: Presbyterian Board of Publication (233 volumes identified); American Tract Society (49 volumes); American Sunday-School Union (27 volumes); American Baptist Publication Society (18 volumes); Lutheran Board of Publication (16 volumes); Congregational Sunday-School and Publishing Society (11 volumes); Lutheran Publication Society (9 volumes); Presbyterian Publication Committee (8 volumes); Friends' Book Association (6 volumes), and many others. Here, too, the library's makeup reflects a larger trend in contemporary American print culture. As Susan Griffin stresses, religion was "a topic that pervaded virtually every genre of women's (and for that matter men's) writing" in the nineteenth century. Robert H. Abzug similarly emphasizes this breadth, noting that reformers of the period "made religious sense of society, economy, race, politics, gender, and physiology." This perspective is reflected across the board in the Woman's Building Library.[37]

Not surprisingly, Columbian Women writers—some of whom were (or would become) ordained ministers—contributed a significant number of books exploring spirituality and religion. Their contributions reflect a range of Christian denominations and a variety of rhetorical approaches, from mainstream evangelical tracts to treatises on the new Christian Science. Several Columbian Women writers took up various branches of church history, and a few even explored non-Christian faiths.[38] Several of the volumes on church history addressed gender as well: for example, Lucy Rider Meyer's *Deaconesses: Biblical, Early Church, European, American* (1889) and Eva Munson Smith's musicological compilation *Woman in Sacred Song* (1885). Although some of the Columbian Women's contributions reflect conservative views on women's role with respect to organized religion, others were shaped by what Beverly Zink-Sawyer identifies as an "unyielding belief in the political *and* ecclesiastical equality of women." For these women, as Zink-Sawyer suggests, suffrage was "a religious crusade." Congress speaker Antoinette Brown Blackwell, whose 1853 ordination was an event "unprecedented in the United States—or anywhere in Christendom, as best as scholars can discern," authored six volumes included in the library: *The Physical Basis of Immortality* (1876), *The Philosophy of Individuality; or, The One and the Many* (1893), three scientific texts, and a local color novel (*The Island Neighbors* [1871]).[39] Blackwell's volumes were joined by [Phebe?] Hanaford's *Shall Women Vote in Church Matters?* (n.d.)[40] and Frances Willard's *Woman in the Pulpit* (1888), as well as several volumes by agnostics or freethinkers, such as Matilda Joslyn Gage and Helen H. Gardener, whose *Men, Women, and Gods and Other Lectures* (1885) criticized attitudes toward women expressed in the Bible. Although not directly involved in the Columbian Exposition (unlike Gardener and Willard), Gage was also an influential figure: she helped draft the "Declaration of Rights" read at the Centennial Exposition and coauthored the *History of Woman Suffrage* with Susan B. Anthony and Elizabeth Cady Stanton. In *Woman, Church, and State* (1893) she argued that for nearly two millennia Christian civilization had systematically oppressed women through the linked patriarchies of civil and ecclesiastical institutions. An ambitious and incisive historical analysis, Gage's book was also extremely controversial, inciting Anthony Comstock, the well-known anti-vice crusader, to threaten legal action against schools that allowed it to circulate.[41]

Many works of fiction in the Woman's Building Library reflect both the contemporary popularity of devotional literature and the intersection between religious freedom and women's rights. One subgenre, in particular, brings into sharp focus the active engagement with questions of religion shown by women like Blackwell, Hanaford, Willard, Gardener, and Gage. Among Columbian Women's contributions are several "theological novels," specimens of a literary mode that peaked in the 1880s, including Elizabeth Stuart Phelps Ward's *Beyond the Gates* (1883), the sequel to her wildly popular *The Gates Ajar; or, Our Loved Ones in Heaven* (1889), and Kate Gannett Wells's *Two Modern Women* (1890). These are novels that, in Lee Schweninger's summation, reflect an "overriding concern with the religious questions of the day"; in such novels "the romantic relationship represents in microcosm the culture generally."[42] While promoting what Candy Gunther Brown terms a culture of "domestic piety," many of these novels simultaneously critique that culture's patriarchal institutional foundations.[43]

As Schweninger points out, Celia Parker Woolley's first novel, *Rachel Armstrong; or, Love and Theology* (1887), typifies "the late nineteenth-century wave of popular theological fiction that tells the story of religion and the minister's place in an increasingly secular and rationalistic society."[44] Addressing the conflict between Calvinism and the new liberalism, *Love and Theology* (as the novel was later called) reflects American women's struggles with religious concerns during the late nineteenth century. Woolley's career resonates with many facets of Columbian Women's writing. Ordained a Unitarian minister in 1894, she became a prominent figure in the Chicago women's club movement and an important advocate of human rights and racial justice. Founder and president of the Chicago Political Equality League, founder of the League of Religious Fellowship (formed in response to the 1893 World's Parliament of Religions), and founder, director, and resident of the Frederick Douglass Center (a settlement house for African Americans established in Chicago's "Black Belt" in 1904), Woolley was a "literary activist" of the first order. Schweninger characterizes her as "exemplary of her historical moment"—a woman who "typified her class, sex, and generation in several ways" even as she "stands out as somewhat unique among her contemporaries" in extending her commitment to equal rights and opportunities to African Americans and other oppressed groups.[45] Woolley wrote the introduction to a history of the Chicago Woman's Club (she was its president from 1888 to 1890), a thousand copies of which were printed for distribution at the exposition. She also delivered an address on Margaret Fuller at the Congress of Women. "In her stories and novels," Schweninger notes, "Woolley problematized the conventional attitudes toward gender differences.

. . . [S]he recognizes some sexual biological differences but concurrently argues that many of the differences are social or cultural as opposed to biological."[46]

Love and Theology, which went into a fifth printing in its first year, is the story of Arthur Forbes and his fiancée, Rachel Armstrong, "both moral enthusiasts, with that vein of fervent religious faith which marks the devotee." Rachel, the favorite daughter of a narrow-minded Calvinist preacher, has a "grave and reflective disposition" that "yield[s] readily to [her father's] severe methods of training." As a result, "the belief that life is a discipline whose chief end lies in the extinguishment of all the natural instincts and affections was one that she had imbibed along with her early reading-lessons." Although reared in the same church and aspiring to a career in the ministry, Arthur experiences a period of doubt and soul-searching during his religious training that leads him to reject Calvinism "as so many dead and useless dogmas." He no longer "accept[s] the Bible as literal truth," finding such fundamentalism antiquated. Although formerly the couple had been of one mind and one heart, Arthur's crisis of faith alienates him from Rachel, who regards the church as the seat of "militant authority and power." Rachel breaks off their engagement. "How can a woman promise a wife's honor and obedience to one whom she believes pledged to the support of the worst principles?" she asks in a letter. In addition to engaging contemporary debates over religious orthodoxy, Woolley's novel contemplates the relationship of education and social class to religious institutions, as Arthur wonders whether modern liberalism speaks only to the cultured few and not to the masses. A period of time spent among rough and uncultured people in the West allows him to see how class need not be a barrier to truth.[47]

Eventually, Rachel and Arthur reconcile, although the two do not recover the perfect mutual understanding that characterized their beliefs before Arthur's conversion. Instead, Arthur suggests their convictions may complement one another. The two marry, but Rachel is "not that active sharer of his labors that many ministers' wives are." Although "she has dropped many of the old beliefs, she has never come to share the more radical convictions of her husband, remaining in that twilight land of faith, midway between the rejection of the old and the acceptance of the new." At the close of the novel, Woolley leaves her heroine's conflict unresolved. Adrift amidst "the wreck of the faith and hopes once hers," Rachel salvages "two or three main truths which . . . she clings to," resolves to "do her duty, and, leaning her heart on One stronger, waits."[48]

Although Woolley was progressive and even, in some respects, radical, her heroine is reluctant to change, a doleful and unlikely pupil of her husband's liberal teachings. Possibly Woolley's decision to characterize Rachel as a stern Puritan daughter with a narrow view of woman's idealized nature was calcu-

lated to appeal to mainstream readers for whom a more progressive heroine
might have seemed unsympathetic. Yet Woolley provides a foil in the character
of Hester Forbes, Arthur's sister. In contrast to Rachel, the "strong-minded"
Hester belongs to the suffrage society and is a former medical student, political
pamphleteer, "contributor to a few periodicals, most of them devoted to reform,"
and "speaker at the conventions and public gatherings, which she frequently
left home to attend." Having raised Arthur, Hester has "the knowledge, forced
upon her, of the unjust discrimination of the laws against women." She rejects
notions of ideal womanhood "engendered in false sentiment and a romantic
sense of duty."[49] Through Hester, Woolley questions the prevailing belief in the
separate natures of men and women and, without denying the importance of
sentiment and duty, acknowledges these may be sadly misguided. In the contrasting characterizations of Rachel and Hester, Woolley's treatment of gender
foreshadows the kinds of debates that surfaced at the Columbian Exposition
over the representation and responsibilities of women.

Occupation, vocation, a yearning for something to *do* in life—the publications of Columbian Women continually return to the relationship between
duty to others and fulfillment of one's own ideals, goals, and talents. *"Keep to
your specialty,"* advises Frances Willard in *How to Win*, "to the doing of the
thing that you accomplish with most of satisfaction to yourself, and most of
benefit to those about you."[50] Many books in the Woman's Building Library
offer instruction in traditional domestic arts, including cookbooks and housekeeping guides by a number of Columbian Women: Jane Cunningham Croly,
Helen Stuart Campbell, Frances E. Owens, Mary J. Lincoln, Sara Tyson Rorer,
Juliet Corson, Lavinia Hargis, Mary Foote Henderson, Emily Huntington,
Agnes Bailey Ormsbee, and Eunice White Beecher. Others, however, draw
attention to opportunities denied women, to their wasted talents, unrealized
potential, frustrated hopes, and the detrimental effects of limiting the educational and professional avenues open to them. Education is often their point of
entry into the larger debate on women's sphere; it is also a topic that reverber-
ates throughout nineteenth-century women's writing.[51]

Like religion, education was a popular subject at the World's Columbian
Exposition. *The Columbian Woman* touted the fair as "a world's training-school,"
and Melvil Dewey maintained that "for any child over twelve a month at the
Fair was greater than a year at school." Many Columbian Women spoke about
education at the World's Fair congresses; it was also a goal they pursued in
their own lives, cultivated as a site of reform, and explored through their creative writing. The Woman's Building Library included works by educational
theorists and reformers such as Elizabeth Palmer Peabody, Emma Willard,
Louisa Pollock, Esther Baker Steele, and Columbian Women writers Sarah

Brown Ingersoll Cooper, Anna C. Brackett, Kate Douglas Wiggin, Helen Ekin
Starrett, and Laura Parsons Stone Hopkins. It also housed many Columbian
Women's juvenile texts designed for pedagogical use: for example, *Open Sesame!
Poetry and Prose for School-Days* (1891), edited by Blanche Bellamy and Maud
Wilder Goodwin, *Poetry for Home and School* (1876), edited by Anna C. Brack-
ett and Ida M. Elliott, *Attractive Truths in Lesson and Story* (1889) by Alice May
Scudder, *Boys and Girls in Biology* (1875) by Sarah Hackett Stevenson, and *Real
Fairy Folks: Explorations in the World of Atoms* (1887) by Lucy Rider Meyer. Sev-
eral Columbian Women's novels address education, including Woolley's *A Girl
Graduate* (1889), which takes this topic as its primary theme.[52]

In *A Girl Graduate,* Woolley writes of Maggie Dean, a recent high school
graduate in the midwestern town of Litchfield. Although a star orator, smart
and well-liked, Maggie finds that after finishing school she has no direction, no
pressing plans. Instead, "a hundred contradictory plans and ambitions filled her
mind." She is restless, "unwilling to spend her days in a round of empty cares.
She could not be always arranging her room or making over her dresses." Consequently, Maggie's real education begins after graduation, when she confronts
the limited expectations and opportunities granted her. In the process of rising above these limitations, she disappoints an earnest suitor, walks a fine line
between friendship and flirtation with a less honorable young man, and rebuffs
the undesired advances of two other men—a married minister old enough to
be her father, whose attentions to her are altogether repellant, and an even older
judge, who hopes his high status in the town will reconcile her to a "mercenary
marriage." Rather than acquiescing, Maggie spends "hours in profound study,"
determined to "work . . . study . . . improve herself in a hundred ways . . . be
discreet and dignified . . . [and] learn to say sharp things to people."[53]

Woolley writes, "Maggie had no special theories on the sphere of woman,
and no ambition to solve any knotty problems or point an example. Her young
activities only demanded some kind of natural outlet." Following the example
of her older sister, Maggie overcomes her "girlish dread of being considered
'literary' and 'strong-minded,' terms of opprobrious meaning in a community
like Litchfield." Eventually, she befriends Miss Graham, an "independent"
and somewhat bohemian "spinster" who presides over a liberal reading and
discussion group known as the Emerson Club. (As the narrator informs us—
possibly with a veiled allusion to Woolley's own project in *Love and Theology*—
"through the insidious paths of literature [Miss Graham] tried to lead [the
young people's] minds away from a decrepit theology.") Maggie encounters
many stumbling blocks over the course of this bildungsroman—including her
mother's grave illness, her father's crippling on-the-job injury, a social humili-

ation, employment discrimination, and sexual harassment. Contending with these hardships, she gains independence, maturity, and self-respect.[54]

In her study of female readers in nineteenth-century America, Susan K. Harris observes that throughout the diaries of these readers, "there is a sense that knowledge is power, definition; a chance to 'BE SOMEBODY.'"[55] In *A Girl Graduate* this desire to define and empower oneself through education inspires Maggie. She takes a teaching job, rather than becoming a clerk or telegraph operator, two other lines of work open to her. As a teacher, Maggie makes efforts to introduce new pedagogical methods rather than simply going "on in the same old way the rest did,—singing the capitals, and repeating the multiplication table backwards." Like other Columbian Women writers, Woolley examines the links among occupation, usefulness, and duty. As a teacher, Maggie becomes "absorbed in her work, and pleasantly convinced of her own growing usefulness in it." When a struggling (and apparently incompetent) widowed mother is deemed in greater need of gainful employment, however, Maggie loses her teaching post and accepts family duties closer to home. In the end, she becomes engaged to a deserving young man.[56]

Building on the research of Nancy Cott, Cathy Davidson, Mary Kelley, and others, Harris points out that "women's desire for better educations is another hallmark of this community [of readers]."[57] In *A Girl Graduate*, Woolley explores this desire by contrasting Maggie's limited opportunities as a working-class girl with those of her affluent friend Laura. Shortly before the novel's publication, Woolley summed up its dominant theme as the "social life and aspirations of a beautiful young girl, daughter of a working man[,] who has been educated beyond the sphere in which she was born."[58] Through Maggie, the novel reflects on the intersection of class and gender in the matrix of educational and employment opportunities. To Maggie, Laura represents "certain social lines and distinctions she proudly believed herself able to overcome." Over the course of the novel, Maggie discovers, however, that these divisions are more difficult to bridge than she anticipated, and the opportunity to pursue higher education proves a barrier that separates the two girls. While Maggie must stay close to home, Laura's family sends her back East, where she spends two years at a women's college—an experience that transforms her life. As a result of her college education, Laura decides to study medicine rather than marrying a fortune-seeking cousin, and glimpses "a life of useful womanhood stretched before her."[59] By continually stressing usefulness and service to others, Woolley emphasizes that women who seek education and employment outside marriage are not indulging in a selfish pursuit. Far from shirking their duty, they are fulfilling it in more expansive and rewarding ways.

Marriage is such a pervasive topic in the Woman's Building Library that it is impossible to isolate and quantify all the texts that address it. Many novels in the collection feature conventional marriage plots, such as those found in *Beechwood* (1873) and *Self* (1881) by Rebecca Ruter Springer, wife of the Illinois congressman who introduced the amendment that brought the Board of Lady Managers into existence.[60] Just as telling, however, are the host of novels whose titles register concern with ways in which marriage can be degraded or threatened (examples are *A Mad Marriage* by "Cousin May Carleton," Minnie L. Armstrong's *Illma; or, Which Was Wife,* Mary Clemmer's *His Two Wives,* Mrs. Clara Collins's *Rented a Husband,* Irene W. Hartt's *Another Man's Wife,* Margaret Lee's *The Missing Marriage Certificate,* Harriet Lewis's *Two Husbands,* Laura Jean Libbey's *A Forbidden Marriage, Pretty Freda's Lovers; or, Married by Mistake, We Parted at the Altar,* and *All for Love of a Fair Face; or, A Broken Betrothal,* Annie Bliss McConnell's *Half Married,* Euphemia Johnson Richmond's *Zoa Rodman; or, The Broken Engagement,* Marie A. Walsh's *His Wife or His Widow: Wife of Two Husbands,* and Mrs. R. S. Williams's *Another Man's Bride*). Even *Three Girls in a Flat,* the novelistic memoir by Enid Yandell and Laura Hayes, incorporates the theme of bigamy, as the authors recount the plight of Tessa, a young single mother who finds employment as a nude model for Yandell, a sculptor who worked on decorations for the Woman's Building.[61] A number of texts address the topic of divorce, notably Madeleine Vinton Dahlgren's *Divorced* (1887), Margaret Lee's *Divorce* (1882), Millicent Mack's novel *The Leland Hall Mystery* (1892), which dramatizes anguish and tragedy brought on by a second marriage, and Woolley's *Roger Hunt* (1892), which considers the topic of divorce, as well as bigamy, in the context of a failing marriage. Far fewer in number but no less noteworthy are texts by women known for their "sex radicalism." Mary Gove Nichols's *Experience in Water-Cure* (1849) was in the library, although her controversial "free love" novel *Mary Lyndon* (1855) was absent. Also represented in the library were Victoria Woodhull (Martin), author of *The Origin, Tendencies and Principles of Government* (1871), and Lois Waisbrooker, whose *From Generation to Regeneration: Three Pamphlets on the Occult Forces of Sex* (1890) might have raised eyebrows (had it not been encased behind glass) with its argument for women's sexual freedom. The library also included Sapphic novels by Maria Louise Pool, such as *Roweny in Boston* (1892) and its sequel, *Mrs. Keats Bradford* (1892), in which the protagonist's attraction to another woman appears to be an impediment to her marriage.[62]

Among Columbian Women novelists, Lillie Devereux Blake exemplifies the critical trend of questioning marriage, exposing its abuses, and exploring alternatives. Blake was not only reformist, according to her biographer and editor Grace Farrell, but "radical," and "revolutionary." The author of *Southwold*

(1859) and *Fettered for Life; or, Lord and Master: A Story of To-Day* (1874)—both housed in the Woman's Building Library—and "one of the important missing links of women's literary tradition," Blake spoke (rather aptly, as it turns out) on "Our Forgotten Foremothers" at the Congress of Women. *Woman's Place To-day* (1883), a popular collection of Blake's public lectures, was also included in the library's New York section, and her tract *Woman's Rights Fables* could be purchased for ten cents per hundred at the exhibit of the National American Woman's Suffrage Association (NAWSA) in the Woman's Building's Organizations Room, where visitors could also sign a petition for suffrage.[63]

Born in 1833 in Raleigh, North Carolina, and descended on both sides from Puritan divine Jonathan Edwards, Blake was raised in Connecticut, settled briefly in St. Louis following her first marriage, and later moved to New York City. After her husband committed suicide, Blake supported herself by writing hundreds of stories and essays for popular periodicals. She also served twice as a Washington-based Civil War correspondent and later became a columnist for the prosuffrage *Woman's Journal*. Following her second marriage, Blake became a key player in the suffrage movement. A woman with a "sparkling platform presence" and stylish gentility, she served as president of the New York State Woman Suffrage Association, the Civic and Political Equality Union of New York City, and the National Legislative League, which she founded. She achieved such prominence that Elizabeth Cady Stanton (with whom she collaborated on *The Woman's Bible*) supported her as successor to the NAWSA presidency. (She did not have the support of Susan B. Anthony, however, and was passed over for political reasons.) Along with Annie Nathan Meyer, Blake was instrumental in establishing Barnard College.[64]

Firm in her belief that "people share a common nature but are trained in gender roles," Blake used her fiction to dramatize the tension between marriage and women's professional fulfillment.[65] *Fettered for Life* is an ambitious social novel with an extensive cast of characters and intersecting plot lines, which Blake uses to expose ways in which social, political, and economic inequality allows women—young and old, rich and poor—to be victimized by unscrupulous men. One of her characters aspires to a law career but is coerced instead into marriage with a controlling man who enjoys reducing her to a state of helpless dependence. Blake explores other facets of the issue of women's right to work through a range of female characters who struggle to support themselves in poorly paid jobs—the only ones they are permitted to hold. As one character attests, "I have seen that women are shut out from every means of earning a living that is really remunerative, crowded into certain narrow walks, which, in consequence, are so thronged that the poor creatures are forced to work for the merest pittance."[66]

At the same time, *Fettered for Life* exposes the brutality of the drunkard husband, the venality of politicians, the potentially fatal consequences of sexual harassment and domestic violence (or "conjugal discipline," as the title of one chapter terms it), and the injustice of taxing female property owners but denying them the right to vote. Counterbalancing the throng of women with tragic lives, the narrative presents three women's success stories: those of Laura Stanley, a young woman trying to make her way as an artist; Frank Heywood, a woman who disguises herself as a man in order to pursue a career in journalism; and Mrs. D'Arcy, doctor, widow, and mentor of Laura and Frank. Mrs. D'Arcy, who embodies the voice of optimism and perseverance in the novel, encourages Laura to take an active role in advancing women's education: "Once women were not educated, were not admitted to any professions, were not considered capable of attending to any business; now their education has much improved, though it is not yet what it should be," she tells Laura. "Two great professions are open to them, medicine and journalism, not with equal chances it is true, but still they can obtain admittance where once all doors were closed, and the time is surely drawing near, when the last barrier shall be removed and the civil and political equality of women shall be acknowledged. Every one of us can do something to help on that time; you can yourself do much."[67]

Fettered for Life is not as hopeful as Mrs. D'Arcy's appeal might suggest, however. Opposing the inspiring story of her happy marriage and successful medical career are stories of women like Rhoda Dayton and Maggie, both country girls who seek an honest living and honorable life in New York City, only to be seduced and abandoned by ruthless men of power and influence. The consequences for these women are disease, suffering, and death, and Blake inspires pity and even admiration for them: though victimized, they are virtuous and heroic. Maggie retains her innocence and charm, while Rhoda represents an innovation in the seduction narrative tradition by exercising agency as valiant protector in a crisis. Blake illustrates through her characters that, for unmarried women, "virtue" and "purity" are not synonymous with virginity, and that women can retain their character and self-respect even in degrading circumstances. Through its representation of strong female characters struggling to support themselves and shape their own lives in the harsh surroundings of New York City, Blake's work, like Woolley's, gave women readers new ways to think about themselves, their world, and their rights as human beings.

Flanking the Woman's Building Library on either side stood the two Record Rooms through which visitors could gain access to the literary exhibit. While the north Record Room was largely dedicated to musical manuscripts, the south Record Room housed vast quantities of statistics concerning women's work, in the United States and abroad, displayed in charts, graphs, and bound volumes. It was here that Imogen Howard's compilation of data on African American women could be found, gathered into a book and displayed on a "table bookcase." Bertha Palmer reported, "Our Record Rooms were visited by statisticians and educators." In her view, the "initiative taken at the Columbian Exposition" would undoubtedly prompt "governmental study and investigation" into "the part which woman plays in the social and political economy of every nation." According to Jeanne M. Weimann, "these statistics caused a great stir at the Fair."[68]

For many authors in the Woman's Building Library, too, women's work and its relation to social class was a matter of concentrated "study and investigation." Among more than two hundred U.S. texts assigned to the DDC class "Sociology" (the fifth largest class in the American section), more than thirty specifically addressed the role of women, and many of these focused on women's work. "During the last third of the nineteenth century," Grace Farrell observes, "writing about women and work constituted one way of entering the intense social debate over the changing status of women."[69] In addition to novels like *A Girl Graduate* and *Fettered for Life,* the Woman's Building Library contained many nonfiction volumes that addressed women's work, including practical guides to employment, such as Virginia Penny's *500 Employments Adapted to Women, Married or Single* (1868), Marion Edmonds Roe's *How Six Girls Made Money; or, Occupations for Women* (1887), an article by Dr. Sarah Linton Phelps on "Woman in Scientific and Professional Work" (date unknown), and Martha Louise Rayne's *What Can a Woman Do; or, Her Position in the Business and Literary World* (1883), along with specialized manuals on beekeeping, silk farming, and other commercial pursuits. Other texts, such as Helen Stuart Campbell's *Prisoners of Poverty: Women Wage-Workers, Their Trades, and Their Lives* (1887) and *Woman's Work in America* (1891), edited by Annie Nathan Meyer, presented research into the conditions of women's labor. A few texts advanced progressive and even radical pro-labor critiques: for example, *Labor and Finance Revolution* (1880) by Louise M. Heath and B. S. Heath, *The Origin, Tendencies, and Principles of Government* (1871), by Victoria Woodhull (listed in Edith Clarke's bibliography as Mrs. V. W. Martin), which includes her "Papers on Labor and Capital," *A New Monetary System, the Only Means of Securing the Respective Rights of Labor and Property and of Protecting the Public from Financial Revulsions* (1861), written by political economist Edward Kellogg and edited by his daughter Mary Kellogg Putnam, and Josephine Shaw Lowell's pamphlet *On the Relations of Employer and Employed* (1885). The library contained at least a few works by working-class women, such as *A New England Girlhood* (1889), by Lucy Larcom, and *The Trojan Sketch Book* (1846), a miscellany of writings from

Troy, New York, edited by Abba A. Goddard and containing her story "Legend of the Poestenkill." As young women both Larcom and Goddard worked in the mills of Lowell, Massachusetts. Working-class perspectives could be found, too, in a volume of sketches compiled by the New Century Guild of Working Women and in *Thoughts of Busy Girls* (1892), a compilation of essays written by members of New York's Thirty-Eighth Street Working Girls' Society and edited by Grace Hoadley Dodge.[70]

Yet despite all the interest in improving the lives of working women, the library's contents suggest that concern for female laborers sometimes masked anxieties middle- and upper-class women harbored about the working class. Perhaps nowhere is the combination of expressed interest and tacit anxiety more evident than in contributions several Columbian Women novelists made to the debate over women and work in fin-de-siècle America. In the remainder of this chapter we examine fiction by Columbian Women writers Margaret Deland, Annie Nathan Meyer, and Caroline Corbin. The publications of these women reveal something of the diversity of their political views even as they uncover a common foundation in shared assumptions about social class and its bearing on women's rights.

As noted earlier, late nineteenth-century American women writers embraced an impressive range of social reform movements, from women's rights, to workers' rights, to temperance, racial justice, and the rights of children. Deland, Meyer, and Corbin—like Woolley and Blake—are, in some respects, typical of a period in which the novel was often enlisted in the service of social bet-terment. All three advocated forms of social change reflected in many other volumes in the Woman's Building Library—most prominently, ecclesiastic reform (Deland), education reform (Meyer), and reform of the laws protecting women (Corbin). As advocates of reform they followed diverging paths, yet one common cause united them even as it set them apart from many other women writers of the period (including Woolley and Blake): all three opposed universal suffrage. Read alongside the contributions of suffragists such as Celia Parker Woolley and Lillie Devereux Blake (as well as Susan B. Anthony, Eliza-beth Cady Stanton, Marietta Holley, Mary Livermore, and Myra Bradwell), works by women opposed to suffrage reveal the complexity of contemporary attitudes regarding women's place in a rapidly changing society. Like many other Columbian Women writers, Deland, Meyer, and Corbin were white, middle-class "progressive conservatives" whose forward-looking positions on specific gender-related reforms conflicted with a more conservative stance on social class.

As opponents of universal suffrage, Deland, Meyer, and Corbin aligned themselves with elite women Thomas J. Jablonsky calls "conservative activists" who were paradoxically "the unwitting imitators of their own opposition."[71] An analysis of three novels by Deland, Meyer, and Corbin points up inherent tensions in their position—a position the BLM largely shared. In the conflict expressed between women's duty (seen as a social responsibility) and vocation (or individual calling), all three novels hint at submerged anxieties about shifting class structures and political ideologies.

Margaret Deland, chair of the Library Committee of the Massachusetts Board of Women Managers, was one of the more successful turn-of-the-century American fiction writers, her popularity peaking with such New Woman novels as *The Awakening of Helena Richie* (1906), *The Iron Woman* (1911), and *The Rising Tide* (1916). She is "our leading woman novelist," Maud Howe Elliott wrote in her essay on the Woman's Building Library for *Art and Handicraft in the Woman's Building*.[72] Raised in Pittsburgh, Deland married at twenty-three. When she remained childless for several years, she devoted herself to assisting unwed mothers by taking them and their infants into her own home and helping them find gainful employment. As a result of this experience, Deland became an advocate for sex education and birth control. She opposed universal suffrage, however, believing that "unqualified" female suffrage (like unqualified male suffrage) would be detrimental to the nation. Her books in the Woman's Building Library included an early collection of poetry (*The Old Garden and Other Verses* [1886]), a volume of regional fiction (*The Story of a Child in Old Chester* [1892]), and her first two novels (*John Ward, Preacher* [1888] and *Sidney* [1890]), both of which weighed in on contemporary theological and humanitarian debates.

"Because she was neither arch conservative nor radical reformer," Diana Reep notes, Deland's "fiction more nearly reflects the intelligent middle-class American of her time." This mainstream quality did not prevent Deland from becoming a controversial figure. Reep writes that her first novel, *John Ward, Preacher,* "attacked traditional religious ideas of hell and damnation and brought vehement criticism by the clergy."[73] Set in the sleepy Pennsylvania village of Ashurst and the nearby lumber town of Lockhaven, the novel is peopled with characters who espouse conflicting religious views. The cast includes the Calvinist John Ward, his bride Helen Jeffrey, who has Unitarian leanings, and Helen's uncle, Archibald Howe, an Episcopal rector who occupies a middle ground. Firmly convinced of the orthodox Calvinist doctrines of election, predestination, damnation, and hell, Ward believes he must save Helen from eternal punishment by converting her to his beliefs. Helen is equally convinced these doctrines are antithetical to the existence of a just and loving God. Just as John is determined to save his wife's soul, Helen, neither bound by tradition nor controlled by patriarchal authority, yearns to free her husband from the "hideous shadow of Calvinism."[74]

"I'm a sinner," she tells Ward, "we're all miserable sinners . . . and perhaps we all sin in original ways; but I don't believe in original sin." Her religious convictions follow from her own instinctive sense of justice, goodness, and reason. For Helen, "love of good was really love of God. . . . Heaven meant righteousness, and hell an absence from what was best and truest." Deland (like Woolley in *Love and Theology*) thus presents a seemingly insoluble conflict between two good, earnest people, each thoroughly convinced of a particular idea of truth and each wholeheartedly committed to a sense of duty that follows from it. A foil to both characters, the conventional, well-meaning Howe clings to a "text-book spirituality," preferring to "be content with what light he had" rather than confronting "those doubts which may lead to despair, or to a wider and unflinching gaze into the mysteries of light." Although he is a kindly and affectionate uncle, Howe reproves his niece for "meddling" with theological questions, finding something "unpleasant . . . in seeing a little mind struggle with ideas." He also worries that "the search for truth" will "teach her to think" and "push her into positive unbelief."[75]

In her autobiography, Deland comments on the theological debate at the novel's center and recalls how it alarmed, and even alienated, members of her conservative family. Deland had been brought up in the Dutch Reformed tradition and accepted its Calvinist teachings, but her marriage to a New Englander "born into the rarefied atmosphere of Transcendentalism" brought her into contact with a compelling anti-Calvinist influence. Her father, she wrote, "was greatly displeased at the impropriety of a young female of his family writing a book on religious dogma!" She recalls her bewilderment when her uncle, the recently retired president of Rutgers University and "the spiritual hierarch of the [family] connection," strongly approved of her protagonist's character: "Uncle William, a gentle old saint, incapable of sending a puppy to hell-fire for a day—let alone a human being to the same fate for eternity—declared that he wished there were more John Wards in the churches! The deduction I had hoped might be made from the book was that all such good but misguided men had better be weeded out of the churches." Her more immediate family felt, however, that the character of John Ward was a libel on the ministry. Her father, Deland believed, refused to read the book.[76]

John Ward, Preacher examines the tensions between duty to self and duty to others, the danger of stubbornly adhering to a false conviction, and the conflicting demands of moral responsibility. To John Ward, converting his wife is his Christian duty, just as it is his duty to come to the aid of a drunken woman in the street when others spurn her. Yet as Deland makes clear, "duty," commonly understood, threatens to tyrannize over women, who, by tradition and law, are duty-bound to obey their husbands. It would be "better a thousand times," Reverend Howe tells his daughter, for Helen to "settle down to look after her household and cook her husband's dinner, and be a good child," rather than worrying her husband with her unconventional religious beliefs. Confronting Helen directly, he urges, "It is the wife's place to yield . . . you must give in." This popular sentiment is echoed by Mrs. Dale, a neighbor. Citing the authority of St. Paul, she insists, "A woman should be in subjection to her own husband." Later, scandalized by the separation of John and Helen, Mrs. Dale reiterates the point to her husband: "It is this new-fangled talk of woman's rights that has done all this. What need has Helen of opinions of her own? A woman ought to be guided by her husband in everything!"[77]

Deland emphasizes that even people with good intentions can cling dutifully to wrong principles. In the novel's first chapter, John Ward makes a telling remark concerning the Civil War: "I have always sympathized with a mistaken idea of duty," he admits, "and I am sure that many Southerners felt they were only doing their duty in fighting for secession and the perpetuation of slavery." John argues that if Southerners believed the Bible permitted slavery, then it was their duty to fight for an institution they considered sacred, even if it went against their own judgment and inclination. Helen takes the opposing view, arguing that "if one did think the Bible taught something to which one's conscience or one's reason could not assent . . . there could be only one thing to do,—give up the Bible!"[78] By implication, John is like the rebel South, blindly devoted to a false idea of duty. His sincerity may be admirable, but it does not make natural depravity true, any more than the Bible justified slavery and secession or the epistles of St. Paul made it right for husbands to tyrannize over their wives.

True to her belief in divine goodness, righteousness, and justice, Helen refuses to submit to what she considers a misguided principle. Finding herself at an impasse, she leaves her husband and returns to her childhood home. After John becomes ill and dies suddenly, she "search[es] for her place in the world," yearning to fulfill some useful office, to help others, and to make a difference. Mindful of the poverty and suffering among John's former congregation, she has a vague notion of returning to her husband's parish in working-class Lockhaven. Soon, however, she turns instead to her elderly uncle, whose need for her assistance "save[s] her life from hardness."[79] But the contrast Deland sets up between the genteel villagers and the unenlightened and intemperate urban population is telling, as is Helen's decision to attend to her uncle rather than the working-class poor. Ultimately, the novel's interests lie in shoring up traditional middle-class domesticity, even at the expense of women's independence, as personal vocation and social betterment take a subordinate role to familial duty.

The tension between duty and vocation also informs Annie Nathan Meyer's *Helen Brent, M.D.* (1892). One of more than a dozen Jewish women identified in the American section of the Woman's Building Library, the twenty-six-year-old Meyer served as chair of the Women's Congress Committee on Literature, presiding over a group of literary women that included Mary Hartwell Catherwood, Caroline Kirkland, and Jane Cunningham Croly, among others. "While all the other subdivisions of the Congress represented large organizations such as the W.C.T.U., the Suffragists, the White Ribboners, etc.," Meyer wrote in her autobiography, "the function of our committee was simply to secure well-known literary figures who would speak on various topics of interest." Proud of her egalitarianism, Meyer adds, "We were also the only committee to invite men to help."[80]

Born in New York City to Sephardic parents who traced their American roots to the Revolutionary War, Meyer was a cousin of the poet Emma Lazarus (author of two titles in the library). She enrolled in Columbia's collegiate course for women in 1885, married Alfred Meyer, a physician, a year later and, with his encouragement, left Columbia to pursue her studies independently. Shortly after her wedding, Meyer (following a suggestion from Melvil Dewey) circulated a petition among prominent New Yorkers to establish a college for women and wrote an article on the topic for the *Nation*. Her efforts succeeded; Barnard College opened in September 1889 as the women's branch of Columbia University. Meyer remained actively involved with Barnard for the rest of her life, although she also pursued other women's issues along with her writing career. In the years after the Columbian Exposition, Meyer published plays, short stories, memoirs, and an additional novel. Like Woolley, she fought racial discrimination and the systematic oppression of African Americans. "Meyer's faith in American institutions and the promise of American life," Lynn D. Gordon notes, "led her to work with the National Association for the Advancement of Colored People, to donate books on black history and culture to Hunter College, to sponsor Barnard's first black student, Zora Neale Hurston, and to write and produce a play opposing racial prejudice."[81] For this play, *Black Souls* (1932), which, Meyer believed, "showed up . . . nakedly what lay behind the persecution of the Negro," Meyer paid the noted African American poet and critic James Weldon Johnson a consulting fee "to go through the play with a fine-toothed comb for any expression that was not completely in character."[82] As editor of *Woman's Work in America*, Meyer brought together eighteen essays, totaling nearly five hundred pages, surveying a range of professional outlets for women, including law, the ministry, medicine, education, and philanthropy (though not librarianship). As Meyer well knew, and as the organizers of the Woman's Building took pains to demonstrate, men were not the only breadwinners.[83]

In the early twentieth century Meyer was "looked upon as the most forceful of the Antis," her autobiography speculates. "Perhaps it seems odd," she admits, "that one who fought so hard for higher education for women should have been against giving them the vote." Like Deland, Meyer came to oppose women's suffrage on the grounds that education was a necessary prerequisite for the ballot. "We called the ballot in no sense a right but a responsibility and an obligation," she explains. Moreover, she reports that she "was disgusted by the fantastic claims that were made as to the results that were certain to happen" if women were allowed to vote. "It would do away with prostitutes, with children killed in the streets, with graft in politics, with liquor, with war!" Gordon notes that "the shift in feminist ideology from gender equality to the notion of women's morally superior status offended Meyer." "From an early age I had little belief in the superior chastity of women," Meyer states in her autobiography. "I believed they hated to kick over the traces . . . because the punishment for such misconduct was swift and merciless. But that women were really any more spiritual, any 'better' than men at heart, never seemed convincing to me. I always held that the strictness with which the 'double standard' was maintained, sufficed to explain the somewhat shopworn halo that clung to women." In 1904 she voiced these opinions in a *North American Review* article titled "Woman's Assumption of Sex Superiority" (later reprinted as a pamphlet); she also participated actively in the New York State Association Opposed to the Extension of Woman Suffrage.[84]

As Susan K. Harris observes, evidence from letters and diaries suggests that "nineteenth-century women readers shared an interest in, and admiration for, outstanding women, that they desired an education that would give them what they conceived of as power in the world of ideas, and that they were intensely attracted to fictional heroines who determined to develop themselves professionally—as in *Aurora Leigh*—or who learned, painfully, emotional self-sufficiency."[85] In *Helen Brent, M.D.*, Meyer combines the themes of professional development and the struggle to achieve emotional self-sufficiency in the character of her protagonist. The novel was inspired in part by the careers of Elizabeth and Emily Blackwell, among the first women in the United States to earn M.D. degrees, founders of the New York Infirmary for Women and Children, and coauthors of *Medicine as a Profession for Women* (1860). (The Blackwells were also sisters-in-law of Columbian Woman writer Antoinette Brown Blackwell.) Three volumes by the Blackwells joined works by many other women doctors in the Woman's Building Library, including Columbian Women Anna M. Fullerton, Mary Putnam Jacobi, Mary Amanda Dixon Jones, Lucy Rider Meyer, and Anna Howard Shaw.[86] Of approximately one hundred U.S. texts assigned to the DDC class "Natural Science," nearly half were devoted to "Gynecology and other medical specialties."

Helen Brent, M.D. is about a young woman who has dedicated her life to the medical profession, surmounting tremendous obstacles and enduring relentless resistance from the male establishment. Trained in Europe because she lacks access to medical schools in the United States, Helen later helps found a women's medical college in New York. At the college's dedication ceremony, she cautions her audience that the duties of a professional life need not replace duties traditionally entrusted to women. "In assuming these new duties and responsibilities," she argues, women "need not cast aside any of the great responsibilities which she has inherited from the past ages." Assuming the stance of New Woman (and echoing the title of Dr. Anna M. Fullerton's article "The New Womanhood," published the same year), she explains: "The new womanhood is a development, an enriching of the old womanhood—not, in any sense, a narrowing down, nor a dwarfing of our noblest conceptions. It means growth in every direction." In essence, she encourages women to accept double duty as they take on new responsibilities in the professional world while preserving their role within the domestic sphere. The message is calculated to allay fears that meals will be left uncooked, babies unfed, and furniture undusted if women pursue professional opportunities outside the home. As Meyer slyly reveals in her autobiography, "I had a shrewd theory that to put any radical scheme across, it must be done in the most conservative manner possible."[87]

Meyer makes the radical suggestion in *Helen Brent, M.D.* that, rather than "absorb[ing] themselves entirely in being household utilities and domestic animals," women would be better off saving themselves for more worthwhile and satisfying pursuits. Housework "starve[s] the mind and soul," Helen laments; it is a "slow, miserable death-in-life." But if women were "to go out and earn a living, at least there would be some *living* to it." She tells her protégée, "Most women work for the happiness of others when they set about their philanthropic work. You may be surprised when I tell you that my chief aim in working is to make all women find themselves." In reversing the conventional altruism tentatively advanced by Deland, however, Helen betrays a hint of the author's intellectual elitism. "What we must work for is the recognition of the true dignity of the individual," she insists. "The rights of the individual genius must be recognized everywhere in man or woman, but they are not."[88]

In the end, *Helen Brent, M.D.* is as much about marriage as education and work; it is concerned with the conflicts between marriage and career, and the ways they might intersect if society were less determined to make them mutually exclusive for women. As Meyer later summarized, it is "the story of a woman who refused to give up her career for marriage" and "had for its theme the tragedy of the choice."[89] Subtitled "A Social Study," *Helen Brent, M.D.* belongs to an important class of novels in the Woman's Building Library that turn the traditional marriage plot on its head. Rather than tracing the course of a successful courtship and wrapping up with "A Shower of Rice," as does Woolley's *A Girl Graduate,* these novels might begin with marriage and show its aftermath or unraveling (as in Deland's *John Ward, Preacher*), or trace the course of seduction and its consequences rather than the path to the altar (as in Woolley's *Roger Hunt*), or, as in *Helen Brent, M.D.,* turn on a broken engagement rather than a happy betrothal.

In Meyer's novel, Helen's hard-earned professional satisfaction is tempered by the fact that she has recently broken off her engagement to a man unable to comprehend her commitment to a career. Before their separation, Helen had tried to explain the importance of pursuing her profession: when honor, duty, and virtue are conquered by passion or sacrificed to a man's overbearing will, she maintains, the woman loses self-respect and the respect of others: "To accept from a woman the sacrifice of her professional life is almost as dangerous to future happiness as to accept from her the sacrifice of her honor. . . . [If I am to sink my whole existence into being your wife, I shall feel degraded. I shall feel as much so as if I had lost the respect of the world. It would mean to me the victory of passion over reason, of my inclinations over my sense of duty. . . . [T]o give this all up for you, is to make myself fall utterly in my eyes." With their emphasis on passion, degradation, and downfall, Helen's words recall the conventional language of popular seduction narratives. Pondering this plea, Helen's fiancé imagines her capitulation and speculates on its consequences: "Suppose she yielded to him, what would the future have in store for them both? Would they be able to crush those terrible moments which would be sure to follow, moments when everyday life would interpose with thoughts of life's earnest duties, of duties forgotten, of powers wasted? There could be nothing but final misery to them, unless marriage could mean between them a long life of sympathetic friendship, of self-respect; a union with the consciousness of duty performed."[90]

Addressing "this great problem of marriage," *Helen Brent, M.D.* radically redeploys the cherished nineteenth-century signifier "duty" while completely revising the signified. Meyer refutes the culturally (and biblically) sanctioned formula of husband = head and wife = heart, challenging the notion of separate spheres and the idealized, "essential," morally superior nature of "Woman." To Helen, her profession is "a mission, a duty to perform," and the notion that woman's true sphere is the home is as unreasonable as the idea that "to attain the sphere of a husband, a father" is "the only true and real life for any noble man." She tells her incredulous fiancé, "I think you have just as much right to ask me to give up my profession as I have to ask you to give up yours." Men, she realizes, "must be educated to allow greater liberty of thought and action in their wives, to seek in them companionship in marriage, to seek sympathetic co-operation, not merely physical gratification, nor the mere oiling of the household machinery." Ultimately, she concludes, "Marriage becomes purified and ennobled just so far as the higher claims of soul and mind enter into it."[91]

Helen Brent, M.D. argues that the institution of marriage falls far short of this ideal. Although Helen succeeds spectacularly in her career, her life seems incomplete, and she feels "a fierce longing that her whole nature could rise and expand, grow as it was intended it should grow—full, proportioned, equable, beautifully rich in all the blessings of life; not warped, thwarted, stunted, as she could not but realize it was." The fate of the man to whom she was engaged is far worse, however, and in the events that befall him it is hard not to detect a vindictive pleasure along with the insinuation that uncultivated females lack sound morals. Harold Skidmore, the man who would deny Helen her vocation, marries a frivolous "Priestess of the Beautiful," a "Goddess of Ease and Luxury." When he habitually neglects his wife in order to advance his career, his wife becomes the mistress of a notorious roué. His life in ruins, Harold writes Helen an abject letter acknowledging his mistakes and predicts, "Not now, not now, but some day there will come knocking at your gates a broken Harold, as a suppliant will he come, hat off, eyes lowered, kneeling in the dust." That Meyer concludes the novel with this pathetic image points to the drastic reversal needed to rectify male-female relationships.[92]

Caroline Fairfield Corbin's *Rebecca; or, A Woman's Secret* (1868) offers a different twist of the conventional seduction plot. The novel charts the heroine's life after she has been seduced into a fake marriage, abandoned, "sold" to another man, and nearly forced into prostitution, and has borne a child, given the baby up, and finally begun her life afresh in a village where her past is unknown. Despite her misfortunes Rebecca (like Lillie Devereux Blake's minor characters) is untainted in character and, in Corbin's terms, "womanliness," a point the novel staunchly buttresses with the rhetoric of True Womanhood. "Women, as a general thing, have more power of endurance than men," Corbin writes. They "will actually live through more physical suffering, and come out less reduced in the end, because they have deeper faith, and patience, and courage, and love."[93] As much as Meyer was repelled by claims of the superior nature of women, Corbin resoundingly defends the conventional ideology of gender difference.

Although sympathetic to the suffrage movement at the time of *Rebecca*'s publication (she dedicated the novel to John Stuart Mill "for his noble efforts in behalf of the enfranchisement of Woman"), Corbin later became a dedicat[ed] antisuffragist. Unlike Deland and Meyer, her antisuffragism was grounded not in gender-blind class prejudice that would deny the vote to socially, economically, and educationally disadvantaged men as well as women. Instead, Corbin, who spoke on "The Higher Womanhood" at the Congress of Women, was thoroughly committed to the notion of separate spheres and the idea that to "Woman" is entrusted "marriage and motherhood and the control of the moral and spiritual destinies of the race." For Corbin, women's power was indirect; she advised that "nature, by making man the bond-slave of his passions, has put the lever in the hands of woman by which she may control him"; she counseled, "Few women understand at the outset, that in marrying, they have simply captured a wild animal, and staked their chances for future happiness on their capacity to tame him." Paradoxically, Corbin's rhetoric is rife with terms suggesting power, control, and hierarchy as she wrests the diction of patriarchal authority into the service of female superiority: "Heaven's supreme excellences centre around and find their best earthly expression in the ideal woman and her work," she exults, and "to this high office the duty of man is subordinate."[94]

Lengthy and wide-ranging, *Rebecca* takes on temperance, sexual harassment, abortion, infant mortality, women's health, education, employment, oppression within the home, the inadequacy of laws for the protection of women, and prostitution—a topic Corbin researched extensively in her campaign for "social purity."[95] But underlying the novel the seeds of another political concern begin to germinate. In an 1888 "open letter" to Frances Willard, Corbin linked her antisuffragism to an awareness that "mischievous teachings were coming in thick and fast; . . . false ideals were luring women from the natural and holy ministries of the home, and promoting a coarse and selfish individualism." Corbin traced these pernicious trends to socialism, "of which," she wrote, "suffrage is a vital and integral part." In her study of the antisuffrage movement, *Women Against Women,* Jane Jerome Camhi observes, "Corbin feared that if the natural relationship of the sexes was so perverted as to provide for equal labor and equal pay for men and women, and equal political rights, 'What guarantee have we that its demand for equal purity would not quickly degenerate to the Socialistic standard of equal license?'" As president of the Illinois Association Opposed to Woman Suffrage (which she founded in 1897), Corbin "issue[d] numerous bulletins designed primarily to warn the public against the ubiquitous threat of socialism." "If any single theme characterized the association," Camhi notes, "it was the need to forestall the advent of socialism by impeding the progress of woman suffrage."[96]

Corbin's near-obsession with woman's sexual and spiritual purity in *Rebecca* clearly anticipates this anxiety about the perceived threat to women posed by egalitarianism and equal rights. At the same time, however, the question of "equal license" hints at an underlying uncertainty about woman's "higher" nature that belies Corbin's relentless trumpeting of True Womanhood and essential gender difference. Contrary to the tenets of True Womanhood, Corbin's political rhetoric, which predicted that in a socialist system "both men and women shall . . . be absolved from all domestic obligations," seems to position domesticity as an external imposition, rather than an innate and inalienable component of female identity.[97] A similar contradiction underlies the biographical statement accompanying the printed text of Corbin's Women's Congress address. According to this statement, "In her early years Mrs. Corbin advocated Woman's Suffrage, but deeper study and experience convinced her that the doctrine implied a low materialistic idea of the value and destiny of women, and she has in recent years written many pamphlets in opposition to the political rights of women."[98] Implicit in the statement is the fear that suffrage would somehow realize and fatally unleash this "low materialistic idea" of women's "value and destiny."

In her speech to the World's Congress of Representative Women, Frances Harper contrasted the role men played in the history of the New World with the role women were poised to fulfill on the cusp of a new era: "Not the opportunity of discovering new worlds," she declared, "but that of filling this old world with fairer and higher aims than the greed of gold and the lust of power, is hers. Through weary, wasting years men have destroyed, dashed in pieces, and overthrown, but to-day we stand on the threshold of woman's era, and woman's work is grandly constructive." Clearly, not all the women who contributed to the Woman's Building or the World's Congresses shared Harper's optimism. Fears about social change—the political enfranchisement of the uneducated for Deland and Meyer, and the threat of unregulated equal-opportunity licentiousness for Corbin—simmer beneath the surface of these three antisuffragists' novels. Submerging these fears, all three novels foreground the conflict between personal vocation and duty to others as they attempt to establish a secure footing for their protagonists on the shifting ground of late nineteenth-century gender and class relations. In stark counterpoint to prosuffrage writers like Celia Parker Woolley and Lillie Devereux Blake, antisuffragists, as Jablonsky notes, "saw the female franchise as a threat to the United States and to their own lives as women."[99] For these authors, conventional conflicts between duty and vocation help to define women's role in society while masking deeper anxieties about immigration and social class, gender identity and cultural caste—anxieties that remain largely unacknowledged and wholly unresolved in the novels discussed here.

Viewing her books in the Woman's Building Library, Marietta Holley's popular homespun protagonist Samantha reflects on the role of literature in society: "As I stood and looked at them books I got carried a good ways off a ridin' on Wonder—a-wonderin' whether them books had done any good in the world. . . . I'd wanted 'em to, I wanted 'em to like a dog. Sometimes I'd felt real riz up a-thinkin' they had, and then agin I've felt dubersome. But I knew they had gin great enjoyment."[100] Holley was best known as a humorist, yet in her fiction she took on Indian rights, suffrage, temperance, dress reform, and other current social and political issues. In a similar vein, much of the fiction in the Woman's Building Library reveals a profound desire to give readers "great enjoyment" while enlisting literature as a means to "do good in the world," often by addressing multiple areas of social reform.[101] In the context of the Woman's Building Library, reform novels like those by suffragists Holley, Woolley, and Blake, and antisuffragists Deland, Meyer, and Corbin demonstrate the ways in which Columbian Women's fiction not only emerges from a "vertical," diachronic tradition of women writers (beginning with the "thin, long line" Frances Willard described), but is also deeply embedded in the "horizontal," synchronic fabric of nineteenth-century culture, "connected," in heterotopic fashion, "with all the space that surrounds it."[102] As Farrell points out, Blake's *Fettered for Life,* for example, is actually *about* reform movements, weaving together "abolitionist, temperance, and women's rights issues with the plight of urban working women (especially poor women) and problems of women's personal freedom . . . ; issues of women in the workforce, their housing arrangements and their limited vocational options; the various forms of sexual harassment to which they were subjected; their educational options; and the push for reform in matters of property rights and marriage and even of female attire and exercise." Caroline Corbin acknowledges a comparable degree of social complexity in the preface to *Rebecca,* explaining, "Many themes have been simply touched, which would require volumes for their elaboration"[103] As part of the Woman's Building Library, Corbin's novel—like those of other Columbian Women writers—was surrounded by, and connected to, thousands of volumes that answered that end.

6

Ghosts and Shadows

A library, wrote Annie Nathan Meyer, "may be a place overflowing with dynamic energy as up and doing as a modern business office."[1] The description accords well with the story of the Woman's Building Library, with its panoply of committees, efficient staff of industrious librarians working on deadline, and the busy tide of fairgoers flowing continually across its orderly, well-lighted expanse. The "dynamic energy" of the Board of Lady Managers (BLM) and affiliated state boards pervades the record of the library's development, while the correspondence of "Dewey's girls" reflects the up-to-date professionalism of their cataloging and management.

Writing over half a century after the doors of the Woman's Building closed forever, Meyer offered a second image that is equally—though not as obviously—apt: alternatively, she wrote, a library "may be a place of ghosts and shadows."[2] Meyer's spectral imagery evokes the library as an inhospitable site, hushed and somber, a vacant repository of shrouded forms and indistinct outlines. Despite its facade of optimism, gaiety, energy, and enthusiasm, the Woman's Building Library was also a place of omissions, gaps, silence, and obscurity. Its official narrative of limitless progress and unitary, idealized womanhood eclipses counternarratives that reflect experiences of oppression, which the fair masked through "a dream scenario" and reinforced through exclusionary policies. The Woman's Building belonged to what Rosemarie K. Bank describes as "the 'White City' (with full racial inflection) of a power elite, simulating for a mass audience its own sense of beauty, control, hierarchy, and self-secured success."[3] To their credit, Candace Wheeler (who "grew up in a mental atmosphere strongly tinctured with abolitionism") and the New York Board of Women Managers created a library space in which the work of race reformers such as Stowe and Child appeared prominent.[4] In addition, the room made a subtle but important visual statement by incorporating artwork that honored the nation's multiracial heritage.

Yet in many respects, the contents of the library recapitulate the racial politics of the BLM in particular and the Columbian Exposition in general, where, Hazel Carby argues, the exclusion of African Americans "embodied the definitive failure of the hopes of emancipation and reconstruction and inaugurated an age that was to be dominated by 'the problem of the color line.'"[5] Indeed, the legacy of genocide, slavery, "removal" and forced assimilation, institutionalized discrimination, and cultural erasure haunts this archive in manifold ways. In this chapter we survey the Woman's Building Library from the perspective of race, uncovering a complex response to the way individual lives as well as the nation's history were shaped by ideologies of European supremacy and entitlement.

Among the library's fourteen hundred works of American fiction was an anonymously published novel titled *Towards the Gulf: A Romance of Louisiana* (1887). A few weeks after its original publication, Lafcadio Hearn, reporting for the *New Orleans Times-Democrat*, revealed that *Towards the Gulf* was the work of Mrs. Alice Morris Buckner, daughter of Colonel E. W. Morris, former sheriff of Warren County, and the widow of Captain Richard L. Buckner, a New Orleans cotton merchant and "soldier of the Confederacy." The recent death of her husband had exacerbated a "financial crisis" that prompted Mrs. Buckner to write the novel, which was "founded on fact," in the hope of earning money to support her five children. Writing in the mid-twentieth century, the folklorist John Q. Anderson provided additional details of Buckner's life. "Born Mississippi Morris on Bending Willow Plantation, Madison Parish," he writes, "Mrs. Buckner was the daughter of Mrs. Minerva Morris." "Missie" and her sisters Virginia, Louisiana ("Lou"), and Missouri ("Zou") were neighbors of Kate Stone, whose journal of the years 1861–1868 Anderson edited and published.[6] At the time of the novel's release Hearn praised Buckner's novel as "a work of art,—a literary masterpiece,—a story of astonishing power and pathos;—which contains no social untruths, offends no social prejudices, and champions no hypotheses"; he called it "the most powerful story that any Southern writer, without exception, has yet produced."[7] William Dean Howells commended the novel as "intensely touching" and "pathetic," with "an abundance of local color."[8] Notwithstanding the cachet of a largely positive notice from Howells in *Harper's Monthly*, however, Buckner has been all but lost to twenty-first-century readers. Her erasure is not unusual: Buckner's obscurity is emblematic of the way many writers represented in the Woman's Building Library "disappeared," leaving only ghostly traces through which contemporary scholars may recover them.[9]

Aside from its relevance to the vanishing of women writers from prefeminist literary histories, Buckner's novel is pertinent in other respects to the idea of the Woman's Building Library as "a place of ghosts and shadows." A novel that "manifests many of the period's anxieties about race mixture," *Towards the Gulf* tells the story of John Morant, scion of an old Louisiana family whose plantation flourished until devastated by the Civil War.[10] Morant's fortunes seem to rebound when he weds a beautiful and wealthy young woman, the daughter of an English widower. The woman's mother, who had been raised by a prominent Southern family, educated abroad, and married to an Englishman, named her Alabama, after her native state, and she has come to be known as Bamma. Although Morant loves his wife, a whispered suspicion that Bamma is of mixed Anglo-Saxon and African descent throws him nearly into despair. Establishing the setting and context for this story of miscegenation through the depiction of Creole women who live near the Morant mansion—some "dark, rich colored, merry," others "pallid and sad-eyed"—the narrator cautions that if one "comment[ed] on their strange dark beauty, there came instantly the chill shadow of reproach, the shadow of race distinction in the frown which silenced discussion." Later in the novel, when Morant brings his bride to his ancestral home, Bamma feels a powerful sense of dread from the "forbidding," "aristocratic" establishment that seems to warn her to "pass on."[11]

As we saw in chapter 2, African American women's efforts to be represented in the Woman's Building met with similarly forbidding attempts to censure and silence them. As with the refusal of the General Federation of Women's Clubs (GFWC) to accept African Americans, the result was that "what could have been a moment of gender solidarity became instead a women's movement divided along the lines of race."[12] Evidently "the chill shadow of reproach, the shadow of race distinction in the frown which silenced discussion" was as conspicuous in the BLM as it was in the racially stratified society of Buckner's French Quarter. Like the personified Morant mansion in *Towards the Gulf*, most of the exhibits in the Woman's Building—New York's African American exhibit being the notable exception—cautioned African American women to "pass on."

The paucity of texts by nonwhites in the library reflects socioeconomic conditions that afforded women of color extremely limited opportunities to write and publish books. "One needs both leisure and money to make a successful book," Frances Harper observes in her novel *Iola Leroy*.[13] Neither the BLM nor the GFWC, with their exclusionary practices and white, Protestant, middle-class biases, did much to mitigate the situation, or to heighten the visibility of the few texts in the collection authored by African Americans. From the earliest BLM discussions, representation of marginalized groups—initially, women—had engendered controversy. To some women, the very idea of creating a separate exhibit solely for women threatened to isolate them and trivialize their accomplishments. For others, the prospect of an entire building devoted to high-profile displays of women's work better served their interests by drawing attention to their achievements, giving them control over their representation, and providing a physical meeting place as well as a social and ideological nexus for millions of women who converged on the fairgrounds. Although the latter group prevailed, the BLM refused to apply the same reasoning to support separate exhibits for women of color, despite the insistence of a prominent group of African American women that "under the present arrangement and classification of exhibits, it would be impossible for visitors to the Exposition to know and distinguish the exhibits and handwork of the colored women from those of the Anglo-Saxons." Because of this, they argued, "the honor, fame and credit for all meritorious exhibits, though made by some of our race, would not be duly given us."[14] As a result of the BLM's refusal to cooperate with them, any works in the library written, edited, illustrated, or translated by African American women were merged with the collection as a whole.

The BLM's policy of treating all races "equally" and singling out none reflected a persistent process of denial and negation through which women writers marginalized by race became virtually indistinguishable to the multitudes who passed through the library. It was a process complicit with the exposition's unofficial message, which, in Robert W. Rydell's formulation, stressed that "not only the national, but also the international, body politic needed much racial purification before the dream of perfection could be realized." As Toni Morrison argues in *Playing in the Dark*, "the act of enforcing racelessness in literary discourse is itself a racial act."[15]

Questions surrounding race and ethnicity in the Woman's Building Library are compelling. How well *were* women writers from marginalized groups represented in the library? Which of their texts were displayed there? How did publications by white women reinforce, elaborate, diminish, or subvert contributions by these writers? What kind of story did the library tell about itself, women's writing, and women's experience, more broadly—including the experiences of racial and ethnic Others? How might the context of the World's Columbian Exposition have inflected the presentation of and responses to texts by nonwhite women? As a physical embodiment of American women's literary history, how does this "Columbian" library reflect on what Morrison describes as "the silence of four hundred years"? Finally, what does it reveal about "the impact," as Morrison writes, "of notions of racial hierarchy, racial exclusion, and racial vulnerability and availability on nonblacks who held, resisted, explored, or altered those notions"?[16] Our efforts to identify women writers of color in the Woman's Building Library, to characterize their contributions, and to situate them in the library's larger context suggest that writing by—and sometimes about—members of groups marginalized by race or ethnicity offered an important "counter-site" to the prevailing discourse in the Woman's Building, despite the fact that their writing was conspicuous neither in the physical display of the library nor in the surviving bibliographical records.[17]

Given the erasure of race in the overall presentation of the library's texts, a different interpretive strategy is required to disclose the impact of race in, and on, the collection as a whole. By reading the Woman's Building Library as "a place of ghosts and shadows," one can begin to see it as a site of "cultural haunting," to borrow Kathleen Brogan's phrase, in which silences, gaps, and "absent presences" reveal the contours of this "other space" in literary and cultural history. Writing of the trope of haunting in American literature of the 1980s and early 1990s, Brogan explains that "the ghost gives body to memory, while reminding us that remembering is not a simple or even a safe act." Brogan's analysis points to the recurring image of "partially obliterated records . . . the family papers mildewed and faded, stories left without endings or explanations, crucial words that resist translation." Like these incomplete archives, unfinished narratives, and utterances lost in translation, "the ghost's elusiveness conveys a past not easily accessible."[18] With Buckner's deeply ambivalent "Romance of Louisiana" as a paradigm, in this chapter we attempt to trace the legacies of race in the Woman's Building Library through a parallel journey into "a past not easily accessible." The library was an institution with its own "partially obliterated records," undeciphered texts, and the ghostly "absent presences" of texts that should have been there, but were not. Our investigation follows the lead of Bamma Morant, who comes face to face with the specter of slavery and in "essaying to trace the tessellated shadows below, . . . reached a region of more fantastic shadows above."[19]

For the first half of the fair's six-month run, the place of honor on the wall over the library's fireplace was left blank. The portrait destined for the spot—a copy of *Pocahontas* by an unidentified English painter working from Simon de Passes's 1616 engraving—had successfully made the journey from England to Chicago. For reasons that remain obscure, however, it was left in storage and the mistake not rectified until the end of July.[20] The specific use of this site had been the subject of discussion among BLM members before the fair opened. At a meeting on September 7, 1892, one member had suggested hanging a portrait over the mantelpiece. In response, Dora Wheeler Keith offered to loan a portrait she had painted of James Russell Lowell. Clara Harrison Stranahan objected, however, and moved the picture "be that of a woman, and that the matter be given over to the Art Committee to decide." The motion carried.[21] A month later, Stranahan recommended a portrait of the late Emma Willard. A pioneering educator and advocate of women's higher education, Willard seemed an excellent choice. But the Fine Arts Committee thought otherwise; it recommended the portrait of Pocahontas, specially commissioned for the Columbian Exposition by Henry S. Wellcome, a wealthy patron of the arts. Bertha Palmer approved.[22] As a visual icon, Pocahontas was undoubtedly more recognizable than Emma Willard; more important, perhaps, her image resonated with the themes of female fortitude, independence, progress, and American cultural identity that reverberated throughout the Woman's Building.

Images of Native Americans were utilized extensively in and around the exposition in everything from the iconography of fair decorations and emblems to the staged Indian villages along the Midway Plaisance. In the seemingly endless paeans to Christopher Columbus and the European discovery of America, Native Americans' images often served as allegorical figures symbolizing the New World. Just as frequently, however, they were proffered to the public as "primitive" and "savage" foils to modern "civilization," a rhetorical move that yoked the idea of American progress to white domination.[23] In addition to highly popular "life groups" displayed by the fair's Department of Ethnology and Archaeology in the Anthropological Building alongside "exhibits referring to the development of the white race in America," the U.S. Bureau of Indian Affairs had "constructed its own attempt to evade the 'savage past'": "a schoolhouse/residence on the fairgrounds," Rosemarie Bank notes, "with both mounted displays and a rotating cadre of Indian students studying, making handicrafts, singing songs for visitors, and the like." At the same time, Bank adds, a large number of Native Americans "labored in show capacities" at the exposition and "were vocal, as well as visible, in shaping the performances fairgoers saw."[24] Presented in this way, the juxtaposition of indigenous and invading peoples served to valorize Euro-American conquest and validate the notion of society's evolutionary advancement along rigid, racially determined lines. Indeed, as Rydell has shown, the Midway, "officially classified under the auspices of the exposition's Department of Ethnology," was "hailed as a 'great object lesson' in anthropology" that "provided visitors with ethnological sanction for the American view of the nonwhite world as barbaric and child-like." In her Women's Congress speech, Caroline Corbin offered her audience precisely this lesson. "Go with me to the Midway Plaisance and look at the Samoan houses, the village of the South Sea Islanders, the huts of the Esquimaux and Laplander," she urged, "and then stand with me in the Court of Honor, amid all its sublime and unearthly beauty . . . ; measure, if you can, . . . the progress, the achievement which humanity has made from the Midway to where we stand."

As Rydell stresses, "The fair did not merely reflect American racial attitudes, it grounded them on ethnological bedrock."[25]

Exhibits like these ensured that by the time visitors passed through the Woman's Building Library, they had already run a gamut of scenes, images, and messages reinforcing European—and especially Anglo-American—supremacy. Although by no means free from such exploitative portrayals of non-Western cultures, the presentation of the "primitive" in the Woman's Building (including "Woman's Work in Savagery" and a Navajo weaver working her loom in the "Indian Alcove") is more complex. As Erik Trump has argued, conservative and progressive women shared "a common interest in primitive women, expressing itself either in praise for the quality and importance of her domestic work (especially her handicrafts), or in envy for her perceived position of relative equality to men within primitive societies." As Trump concludes, "both positions go some distance in undermining the standard interpretation of the Fair's racist anthropological exhibits, and the feminist position further gives us a significant exception to the assessment that the fair presented a conservative image of women."[26]

Like Trump's analysis, the precarious career of Wellcome's *Pocahontas* highlights the ambiguous representation of race in the Woman's Building Library. Locked away in storage, the painting was neglected, hidden from view, and forgotten. Upon discovery, it was prominently displayed, but it clearly advanced a European rather than an Algonquian perspective. The portrait depicts an assimilated and Europeanized Pocahontas attired in high Renaissance fashion, complete with hat, cape, and Shakespearean ruff setting off a light complexion framed by brown hair.[27] As a contemporary description notes, "This portrait of Pocahontas was painted from life after she was converted to Christianity and became Mrs. Rolfe."[28] As in the case of *Pocahontas,* the portrayal of non-whites in the library was complicated and, quite frequently, compromised by the Anglo-American culture through which it was mediated.

And yet other voices were not completely absent. As we saw in chapter 4, Frances Harper, Fannie Barrier Williams, Sarah J. Early, and Hallie Q. Brown presented papers at the World's Congress of Representative Women (held at the Art Institute of Chicago, rather than in the White City), and Anna Julia Cooper and Fannie Jackson Coppin served as discussants. Williams also gave a speech at the World's Parliament of Religions. Like Simon Pokagon, a Potawatomi who spoke out publicly at the fair's Chicago Day (October 9, 1893) against the treatment of Indians,[29] and Ida B. Wells, who created her own "display" by compiling and publicly distributing (in person, in the Haiti pavilion, where Frederick Douglass presided as Haiti's commissioner to the exposition) the pamphlet *The Reason Why the Colored American Is Not in the World's Colum-*

bian Exposition—ironically subtitled "The Afro-American's Contribution to Columbian Literature"—these women resisted efforts to silence them. In the Woman's Building Library, the contributions of women writers of color presented vital counternarratives to what Jill Bergman, in characterizing the GFWC, describes as "a site of confluence for the rhetorics of progress and Americanness" that "constructed the New Woman as representative of a specifically white national identity."[30]

In an article on W. E. B. Du Bois and the African American exhibit at the 1900 Exposition Universelle in Paris, Rebecka Rutledge Fisher comments on the "dual nature" of exhibiting cultural artifacts at such venues. According to Fisher, Du Bois's exhibit, which included more than two hundred books by African American authors, "articulate[d] at once a metaphoric African American 'presence' in the modern context as well as a metonymic African American 'absence' in modern social discourses." Expanding on this paradoxical absence-in-presence, Fisher carefully explicates the ways the Paris exposition "reinforced . . . a narrow, nationalistic insistence upon the metaphysics of race and society that sought to, but did not quite succeed at leaving them voiceless in the matrix of western discourses."[31] Kathleen Brogan, in her analysis of "cultural haunting," remarks on a similarly paradoxical linking of absence and presence in ethnic literature, a duality often expressed symbolically through the "presence" of a ghost:

> All ethnic reconstruction is predicated on the inevitable absence of cultural origins. . . . The curious dual force of the ghost who makes present what is absent powerfully shapes the American story of cultural haunting. As both presence and absence, the ghost stands as an emblem of historical loss as well as a vehicle of historical recovery. It offers writers who take as their subject the survival and transformation of ethnic cultures, who recognize disconnection even as they assert continuity, a particularly rich metaphor for the complexities of cultural transmission.[32]

In *Towards the Gulf* the contention of "dual voices" for recovery or suppression echoes the double nature of a cultural legacy that is "passed on" (that is, transmitted as well as repudiated). Similarly, in their analyses of the "dual nature" or "dual force" of racial representation these critics explicate conflicting versions of history, whether personal, national, or cultural. At the same time, they explore the spectral paradox of an invisible presence (e.g., the cultural invisibility of racial and ethnic Others) and a conspicuous absence that can be understood, as James C. Davis suggests, as "industrial-commercial-publicity's reproduction of the classical public sphere's founding logic of exclusion, that is, as a constitutive absence."[33] Excavating the representation of nonwhite women in the Woman's Building Library necessitates reading beyond the partially obliterated historical record, analyzing exclusions as well as inclusions, in order to seek out the "ghosts and shadows" amidst the enduring artifacts and carefully preserved texts. Like Buckner, who contrives an elaborate verbal tissue that knits together "the past" and "the passed," we must recognize that the historical record not only illuminates the past insofar as it transmits, or "passes on," but also obfuscates whatever it denies, or "passes" on.[34]

Only three years after the Wounded Knee massacre, the Columbian Exposition occurred at a nadir in the historically vexed relations between the United States government and Native American peoples. For many white Americans, Wounded Knee signaled the eradication of the Indian from the American frontier, and hence the removal of the most significant obstacle to white settlement in the vast and valuable territories of the West. Frederick Jackson Turner's famous Columbian Exposition address, in which he theorized about the closing of the frontier in a "performance" (Bank notes) that "simultaneously affirm[ed] and negate[ed] constructs of the native and the American enacted [at the fair],"[35] reflects the recent appropriation and "filling in" of what had been, until quite recently, Indian lands.

Even as Turner's landmark address proclaimed the end of the frontier, and by extension, the hegemony of Euro-American settlement, the Midway's "Congress of Races" invited fairgoers to observe, in pseudo-scientific fashion, representative ethnic "types." Reconstructed Indian villages from California, Arizona, and Nevada dotted the Midway, which also featured an Esquimaux Village and a village of Chilcat Indians, both transported from Alaska. In addition, the Ethnological Congress assembled, in a bizarre "conflation of real and faux," an Alaskan Village, a Cliff Dwellers Exhibit, and a Village of Penobscot Indians, all designed to display the habitations of "uncivilized peoples."[36] According to Davis, both the "absence" of nonwhites in the White City and their "presence . . . on the Midway served . . . to establish and confirm white supremacist thinking."[37] At the same time, however, this polarity may have prompted some fairgoers to question the consequences, if not the premises, of such thinking. In her poem "The Captive of the White City," for example, Ina Coolbrith reflected on the appearance of the Dakota chief Rain-in-the-Face (alleged to have killed Custer at the Battle of Little Big Horn) as a "captive" under guard in the cabin in which Sitting Bull and his son were killed:

> *Why is the captive here?*
> *Is the hour of the Lord so near*
> *When slayer and slain shall meet*
> *In the place of the Judgment seat*

For the word of the last decree?
Ah, what is that word to be?
For the beautiful City stands
On the Red Man's wrested lands,
The home of a fated race;
And a ghostly shadow falls
Over the trophied walls
Of the House of the Unhewn Tree,
In the pleasant Midway Place.
There is blood on the broken door,
There is blood on the broken floor,
Blood on your bronzëd hands,
O Rain-in-the Face![38]

Just outside the exposition grounds, not far from Sitting Bull's cabin, visitors to the fair could also attend Buffalo Bill's phenomenally popular Wild West Show, where an estimated six million attendees witnessed the reenactment of Indian attacks on a wagon train, a pioneer settlement, and the Deadwood mail coach in a frenzied spectacle of staged racial homicide. It was a "performative display," Bank remarks, "one simultaneous showing of the simulation that had, by 1893, become the history of the 'native' and the 'American.'"[39] According to Rydell, Wild Bill's Congress of Rough Riders "captured and put into effect" the idea that "Indians were . . . apocalyptic threats to the values embodied in the White City who had to be tamed." Nor were these popular Cowboy-and-Indian stereotypes confined to the more raucous entertainments of the Midway and its environs.[40] Inside the White City, near the Mining Building on the east bank of the lagoon, stood Alexander Proctor's statue of an Indian (modeled on Chief Red Cloud, who participated in Buffalo Bill's show), a companion piece to his statue of the Cowboy, symmetrically situated between Choral Hall and the Transportation Building on the lagoon's western edge. In the fair's "heterotopic play of imaged and real," Bank observes, "science, culture, entertainment, and history moved freely through sites at once false and true, each offering its own view of the work and culture of the 'real' America and Americans."[41]

The Woman's Building featured a number of positive appreciations of indigenous cultures, side by side with the kinds of stereotyped racist presentations examined by Davis, Rydell, Bank, and others. According to Enid Yandell and Laura Hayes, the building's archaeological exhibit was intended to "show woman as the inventor of the industrial arts and the first maker of the home."[42] Consistent with this aim, in the Model Kitchen fairgoers could order "Zuni Indian dishes made with corn" from recipes provided by an anthropologist, Frank Hamilton Cushing. In the sales rooms visitors could purchase exquisite

nested baskets made by Attakapas women of Southern Louisiana—identified by
BLM member Nancy Huston Banks as a nearly extinct tribe—and on a nearby
landing, blankets made by Navajo women formed "a gorgeous canopy and wall
drapery."[43] And the World's Congress of Representative Women included a
full evening program devoted to the Women's National Indian Association: the
session featured singing by students from the Indian School of Albuquerque,
New Mexico, and an address, titled "From the Indian's Point of View," given by
Captain Chauncey Yellow Robe (Sioux) of the Carlisle Indian School. In the
Woman's Building Library, however, visitors would probably have looked in
vain for writing by Native Americans.[44]

Sarah Winnemucca Hopkins's *Life Among the Paiutes* (1883) and Sophia
Alice Callahan's *Wynema: A Child of the Forest* (1891)—the latter considered
the first novel by a Native American woman—were absent from the Woman's
Building Library. Not only were these books rare, but neither Nevada nor
Indian Territory—both thinly settled areas of the West—submitted any books
to the library.[45] The library's subject index may have helped visitors identify
volumes containing Native American subject matter, but these books would
invariably have been written by white authors. Even when the content is of
Native American origin, that content is mediated through a white author-
interpreter. In the library's books, as in its art (with one exception, discussed
later in this chapter), Native Americans were portrayed by whites who recast
them in their own image (as in the portrait of Pocahontas), classified them as
"savages" or childlike innocents to be "civilized" through radical reacculturation, or idealized them as domestic primitives.[46]

Images of Native Americans appeared within the library in a surprising
number of texts representing a wide range of periods, genres, and perspectives.
In surveying these images, a striking feature is the extent to which discrete
genres are inhabited by differing forms of, and responses to, racial prejudice.
Even within a single genre, however, the texts register varying assumptions and
attitudes about race and ethnicity. Two captivity narratives illustrate this range.
*A Narrative of the Captivity of Mrs. Johnson, Containing an Account of Her Suffer-
ing, during Four Years with the Indians and the French* (1796) is one of the earliest
American texts in the Woman's Building Library.[47] In it, Susannah Willard
Johnson points out that the country had "so long been exposed to Indian wars,
that recitals of exploits and sufferings, of escapes and deliverances have become
both numerous and trite." Despite the sense that she is telling a familiar tale,
however, Johnson challenges readerly expectations by interrupting her narrative periodically to comment on the humanity, civility, sagacity, and patience of
her captors. Although her account relies on stock tropes used to vilify Indian
foes, Johnson appeals to "those who have profited by refinement and education

. . . to abate part of the prejudice, which prompts them to look with an eye of censure on this untutored race."[48]

In contrast to Johnson's effort to mitigate the prejudices of sophisticated readers, Margaret (Kent) Hosmer's *The Child Captives: A True Tale of Life Among the Indians of the West* (1870) offers naive readers an education in racism. *The Child Captives* repackages the popular form of the captivity narrative for a late nineteenth-century audience of juvenile readers. Published by the Presbyterian Board of Publication (which issued more books in the Woman's Building Library than any other publisher), *The Child Captives* disseminated anti-Indian propaganda in the interests of promoting Christianity and proclaiming the "goodness and superiority" of "the white people as a nation."[49] Although the young protagonist initially pictures Indians "in a very heroic light," he is soon disillusioned. As a visitor to Fort Laramie and, later, as a captive, Philip comes to fear "contamination" from his exposure to Indian customs. Hosmer informs her young readers that Indians are lazy, wasteful, dirty, foolish, and reckless people whose "untutored natures developed into uncouth and brutal habits and ideas, like the growth of vile weeds."[50] In *The Child Captives,* Hosmer paints the presence of Indians as a threat to the security of an American nation the text explicitly constructs (and unwittingly deconstructs) as both Christian and white.[51]

Another of Hosmer's five books in the Woman's Building Library (all published by the Presbyterian Board of Publication), *Chumbo's Hut; or, The Laguna School* (1879) is, in differing ways, both more blatant and more subtle in its message of white supremacy and entitlement. A variation on the school story with a protagonist modeled on the popular figure of the "good bad boy," *Chumbo's Hut* revolves around a multiethnic school near the Presidio in San Francisco. The school is attended by the "dark-faced, mischievous" sons of "idle Spanish fishermen" who live in tule huts; the children of Irish laborers "far too ready to drink and fight and set a bad example to the rising generation"; and the sons of "men of wealth" who live in "beautiful suburban villas." The central character, James, befriends and defends an impoverished Indian named Chumbo; this puts him at odds with the other boys and contributes to his reputation as a troublemaker. Hosmer's Chumbo is a degraded, pathetic figure, subjected to ridicule and persecution.[52]

Chumbo's Hut ostensibly teaches children to be kind to the unfortunate. A more forceful lesson unfolds at the end of the novel, however, when Chumbo repays James's kindness by rewarding the boy with a long-lost deed to an original Spanish land grant. With shocking guilelessness, Hosmer's text thus rehearses and legitimizes a cultural script that had been playing out in far less pacific ways for hundreds of years. The young readers who encountered this script in *Chumbo's Hut* would have seen the appropriation of Spanish titles and the usurping of Indian claims seamlessly combined in a plotline that confers on the Anglo-American male the ownership of Western land while casting the disparaged Spanish and the displaced Indian as willing and even grateful partners in the transaction. At the conclusion of the story, "poor" Chumbo conveniently dies, while Hosmer, in a final gesture of absolution, reassures her readers that "having constituted James his heir, [Chumbo's] mind seemed at peace."[53]

Although sometimes critical of U.S. government policy and more attuned to the cultural double-standard that defined Indian-white relations, historical works, such as Frances Chamberlain Holley's *Once Their Home; or, Our Legacy from the Dahkotahs* (1890) and Rose N. Yawger's *The Indian and the Pioneer* (1893), and frontier memoirs such as Mrs. John H. Kinzie's *Wau-bun: The "Early Day" in the North-west* (1856) cast additional shadows.[54] Combining elements of both genres, Elizabeth Bacon Custer's historical memoir *"Boots and Saddles"; or, Life in Dakota with General Custer* (1885) and its sequel, *Following the Guidon* (1890), evoke life in Custer's military camps. In these reminiscences, Elizabeth Bacon Custer, who became a close friend and associate of Candace Wheeler's, describes, for an Eastern audience, Indian villages, buffalo hunts, military marches, everyday army life, battles, Indian prisoners, and "friendly Indians" who received monthly salary rations for leading the regiment to Native American homes.[55] Her recounting of the Battle of the Washita is almost cinematic: "All the marching scenes, hunting experiences, the quips and quirks of the camp-fire, the jokes of the officers at each other's expense, the hardships of the winter, the strange and interesting scouts, are as familiar to me as oft-told tales come to be, and . . . the whole scene spreads out before me as the modern diorama unrolls from its cylinder the events that are past." Against the artifice of this diorama-like backdrop, however, Custer projects a raw, understated sequence of harrowing images: "woman-like," she confides, "the cry of the Indian baby, the capture of a white woman, the storm that drenched our brave men, are all fresher in my memory, and come to my pen more readily, than the actual charging and fighting." Cutting back and forth between excerpts from her late husband's official report and her own impressionistic narrative, Custer punctuates her wartime documentary with heartrending vignettes: a grueling march, Indian women and children who fought like warriors, dirges sung by Cheyenne women "believing their own last hour had come," and the slaughter of eight hundred "mute and helpless" ponies, a task that took three companies an hour and a half to complete.[56]

Images of indigenous peoples also populated historical novels such as Catharine Maria Sedgwick's *Hope Leslie; or, Early Times in the Massachusetts*

(1827) (set during and after the Pequot War in seventeenth-century Massachusetts) and Helen Hunt Jackson's late nineteenth-century romance of California
Indians, *Ramona* (1884). These texts insist on the presence of Native Americans
in the nation's history and recast the Indian from the hackneyed villain of the
captivity narrative into more sympathetic (and sentimental) roles. Both *Hope
Leslie* and *Ramona* bent the conventions of sentimental fiction to address contemporary moral and political issues. In *Hope Leslie,* as Karen Woods Weierman argues, Sedgwick indirectly reflects on the Cherokee removal, "a topic of
great national moment just as Sedgwick was composing her text," and "presents
an alternative history to the traditional Puritan accounts of the victories of
God's new chosen people over the 'savages' of New England."[57] *Ramona*, which
Annie Nathan Meyer paired with *Uncle Tom's Cabin* as one of "two great stories
that immortalized the wrongs of two great races," dramatizes the struggle of
Mission Indians to survive the rapid influx of Anglo-Americans into Southern California.[58] These texts reenvision the past while directing attention to
the ongoing impact of historical relations on current social issues. They also
vigorously reject the kinds of racial politics at work in the anthropological and
spectacular displays of Native Americans at the Columbian Exposition as well
as in late nineteenth-century public policy.

Volumes of ethnographic verse both reinforced and criticized the romantic
narrative of the vanishing race. Mary Gardiner Horsford's *Indian Legends and
Other Poems* (1855), published the same year as Longfellow's *Song of Hiawatha*,
appropriates Native American myths and legends, including a Dakota mother
who steers her canoe, with herself and children inside it, over St. Anthony Falls,
on the Upper Mississippi River, in tacit compliance with the cultural project
of Manifest Destiny. Conventional in form and sentimental in ethos, Horsford's volume repeats familiar stereotypes, both horrific and romantic, of what
she terms "that race / Who were destined to vanish before the Paleface."[59] A
more progressive example of Indian-inspired poetry is *The Story of Chief Joseph*
(1881), by Martha Perry Lowe, in which the speaker provides a "poetic version
of Chief Joseph's narrative," interspersed with photographs, with the hope of
"excit[ing] sympathy and justice for the Red Man." In her verse, Lowe exposes
the inherent hypocrisy of the reservation system, asking "If 'twas true . . . / That
white men should go where they may / And red men in one place must stay,"
and pleads, "Give us back our lands! / Give us freedom, give us law, / And there
shall be no war."[60]

The Woman's Building Library included one biography of a Native American noteworthy for portraying its subject as a unique historical subject esteemed
for her deeds, rather than simply as an anthropological specimen or exemplar
of the race. *The Life and Times of Kateri Tekakwitha: The Lily of the Mohawks,*

1656–1680 (1891), by Ellen H. Walworth, tells the story of an orphaned daughter
of a Christian Algonquin and an Iroquois chief. Kateri (Catherine) Tekakwitha
embraced Catholicism in 1667 when Jesuit missionaries arrived at her Mohawk
village. Eight years later, when the village was visited by Father James de Lam-
berville, she was indoctrinated in Catholic theology, baptized, and renamed. As
a Christian Indian, Tekakwitha became the victim of persecution in her village,
where many Mohawks rejected the Jesuits and their mission of conversion. As
a result, she moved to the French mission of St. Francis Xavier (Kahnawake)
near Montreal, where she devoted herself to a life of prayer, penance, and chastity. Following her early death (apparently a result of self-mortification), her
grave became a destination for pilgrims, including "Christianized Indians, poor
French farmers, and even the colonial elite," many of whom attributed miracu-
lous cures to her influence and intercessions.[61] A "literary invention" that is both
"modern and essentially secular," Allan Greer observes, Walworth's telling of
Tekakwitha's story advances the "campaign to provide the Catholic Church of
the United States with a symbol in the form of an Indian maiden from another
century that could anchor this 'foreign' religion in American soil."[62]

The daughter of a founding member of the Daughters of the American
Revolution, "Nelly" Walworth, Greer writes, "attacked her subject as a historian,
gathering together seventeenth-century sources and ransacking the archaeological and ethnographic literature for background information."[63] The effort
to research indigenous cultures rigorously according to contemporary academic
methodologies is also reflected in several anthropological texts in the Woman's
Building Library. Erminnie Adele Pratt Smith's *Myths of the Iroquois* (1883) is
a scholarly study that first appeared in the second annual report of the Smithsonian Institution's Bureau of Ethnology. According to J. W. Powell, director
of the Bureau of Ethnology, the volume is "an authoritative rendering of some
of the Iroquoian myths, both in their letter and spirit." Her research, based on
linguistic analysis, was facilitated by "prolonged residence among the Iroquois
tribes, into one of which, the Tuscarora, she was adopted." Although *Myths of
the Iroquois* aims to present the indigenous oral tradition without "blunder or
perversion," free from the "disposition to poetize" the material "or color [it]
with European sentiment" (according to the Powell's introduction) it is nevertheless steeped in the assumptions of social evolutionary theory that informed
the anthropological displays in the Midway and the White City alike.[64]

The Religious Life of the Zuni Child (1885) and *Tusayan Legends of the Snake
and Flute People* (1892), both by Matilda Coxe Stevenson, are still considered
landmark ethnographic texts. Along with Frank Hamilton Cushing and her
husband, the geologist and ethnologist James Stevenson, Matilda Coxe Stevenson participated in the first expedition of the U.S. government's newly created

Bureau of Ethnology. She helped assemble materials for the Columbian Exposition's anthropological exhibits, served as one of the award judges for the fair's Department of American Ethnology, served on the Science and Philosophy Committee of the World's Congress of Representative Women, and delivered a talk titled "The Zuni Scalp Ceremonial" at the Congress of Women. She was also "one of the first American women to receive full-time employment in the pursuit of science."[65] Despite the ethnocentrism that undergirded ethnology as a discipline, Stevenson, according to her most recent biographer, "contributed to a better understanding of Pueblo cultures and helped to undermine prevailing racist stereotypes by showing that Indians were rational human beings with rich traditions and valid religions."[66]

Matilda Coxe Stevenson and Frank Cushing became the two leading authorities on the Zuni Pueblo tribe, and their ethnographic research undoubtedly influenced another text in the Woman's Building Library: *The Song of the Ancient People* (1893), by Edna Dean Proctor. This poem, which carries the imprimatur of the Hemenway Southwestern Archaeological Expedition, boasts a scholarly introduction and notes by the historian John Fiske, aquatints by the noted painter Julian Scott, and additional commentary provided by Cushing, and it incorporates Zuni language, beliefs, and social practices.[67] Proctor's interest in Native American culture also informs her ode "Columbia's Emblem," which she recited during the formal opening of the World's Congress of Representative Women.[68]

Missionary and boarding school accounts like Harriet S. Caswell's *Our Life Among the Iroquois Indians* (1892) and Juliet McNair Wright's *Among the Alaskans* (1883) offered ostensibly sympathetic views of Native Americans and sometimes criticized the U.S. government's Indian policies, but their assimilationist perspectives are clearly in opposition to the indigenous cultures they describe. Some of these texts passively observe what their authors regard as the inevitable disappearance of Native American people, while others take a more active role in the eradication of Native cultures. In *Alaska: Its Southern Coast and the Sitkan Archipelago* (1885), travel writer Eliza Ruhamah Scidmore describes her visits to mines, where the work was mainly done by Native Americans and a few Chinese men; the mission school at Fort Wrangell, where "the little Indian girls" were "combed, cleaned, and marshaled in stiff rows to recite, sing, and go through calisthenic exercises"; and "the young mining town and future metropolis" of Juneau, where Native Alaskans had been so devastated by consumption, smallpox, "black measles and other diseases" that Scidmore predicts that "another fifty years may see these tribes extinct."[69] With less forthrightness, Marianna Burgess's *Stiya: A Carlisle Indian Girl at Home* (1891) attempts to show the value of radical reacculturation by tracing the experiences of a fictional Southwest Indian girl returning home after five years at the Carlisle Indian School in Pennsylvania. As a teacher and administrator at Carlisle, Burgess (writing under the pseudonym "Embe," derived from her initials, M.B.) appropriates the photograph of one Carlisle student and the first name of another in order to lend an air of authenticity to a fabricated first-person coming-home story in which Burgess's Pueblo persona is made to recoil from the customs of her tribe and parrot the official boarding-school ideology. The novelist and critic Leslie Marmon Silko, whose great-grandmother and great-aunt were alumnae of the Carlisle Indian School, suggests that Burgess "projected all of her own fears and prejudices toward Pueblo life into her Stiya character." "Robbing the image, voice, and identity of Indian girls," Amelia V. Katanski argues in her study of Indian boarding-school literature, "Burgess sought to extend the boarding school's disciplinary power to the reservations, to enact a pedagogy of oppression that would reproduce the Carlisle curriculum through 'an Indian girl's own story.'"[70] A novel masquerading as a memoir, in which a white teacher plays ventriloquist to fictionalized Indian pupils, *Stiya* exposes the perils of the racial politics embraced by many progressive reformers at the time of the Columbian Exposition.

The library also contained polemical texts such as *An Appeal for the Indians* (1868), by Lydia Maria Child, and *A Century of Dishonor: A Sketch of the United States Government's Dealings with Some of the Indian Tribes* (1881), by Helen Hunt Jackson. Two of the articles contained in the Distaff Series volume *The Literature of Philanthropy* present first-person accounts of women who taught school and conducted other charitable work on Western reservations. In "The Indian," Columbian Woman writer Amelia Stone Quinton, of the Women's National Indian Association (WNIA), explains the steps involved in "civilizing a savage people": "to teach Indians to make and properly keep comfortable homes; to teach them domestic work and arts; to prepare food and make clothing; to care for the sick and for children; to respect work and to become self-supporting; to influence and to help them to learn the English language; and above all, to teach them the truths of the gospel, and to seek their conversion to practical Christianity."[71] Quinton's mission was to "Americanize" indigenous peoples (their only hope of survival, she believed): as Katanski points out, "a century ago, even those who claimed to be 'pro-Indian' in the debates over how to solve 'the Indian problem' held the goal of eventually obliterating tribal culture and identity." Yet Quinton's organization also sought to oust corrupt and incompetent agents working for the Bureau of Indian Affairs and to reform the government's administration of reservations, which the WNIA sharply criticized.[72] The first petition of the WNIA, which relied on Quinton's research, requested the President and Congress to "prevent the encroachments of white settlers upon Indian Territory, and to guard the Indians in the enjoyment of all the rights which have been guaranteed to them on the faith of the nation."[73]

Elaine Goodale Eastman, best known today as the wife of the Dakota writer, reformer, and physician Charles Eastman (Ohiyesa), offers a similar critique of the United States' official relations with indigenous tribes in "The Indian—A Woman among the Indians." A former teacher at the Hampton Institute, Eastman had witnessed the 1890 massacre at Wounded Knee, where she served as a nurse. As Robin Jones comments, Eastman "attempt[ed] a more active engagement with tribes" than did many of her fellow educators and activists: "She spoke Dakota, dressed and lived similarly to her companions while in their company, and attempted to record the lifestyle of the Native American." Writing with affection sometimes mixed with condescension toward her Indian pupils and associates, Eastman concludes her paper with the observation that her "nine years of work among the Indians" have given her "a better opinion of their capacity and a worse opinion of the system under which, and the men by whom, they are managed, than a majority of people entertain."[74] Like Quinton, Eastman deplores the blunders and misdeeds of Indian agents and argues that women could achieve far greater success in encouraging and preparing Indians to become assimilated into American society.

Citing the destruction of the great Mixtec and Maya libraries of preconquest Mexico by Spaniards who "feared the political and spiritual power of books authored by the indigenous people," Leslie Marmon Silko writes, "Books have been the focus of the struggle for the control of the Americas from the start." Whether participating in what Herman Melville termed "the metaphysics of Indian hating" or what Lori D. Ginzburg characterizes as a "benevolent empire," the captivity narratives, children's books, histories, missionary accounts, anthropological studies, essays, novels, and poems of Native American life surveyed here bring into focus the "ongoing struggle for the Americas," in which books, as Silko points out, "were and still are weapons." They also embody some of the "ghosts and shadows" of the Woman's Building Library.[75] The "absent presence" of Native American voices haunts the archive, while the shadows of prejudice and oppression obscure the limited prospect these texts afford of American Indian history and life.

In the fourth chapter of *Towards the Gulf,* John Morant, "sallie[s] forth" in a meditative mood for a stroll through the French Quarter, leaving behind "the gay shops" where buyers "chattered and bargained over the counters . . . , past all evidence of active, busy life, into the solemn stillness of the streets where the old houses . . . hugged the gloom" of lengthening shadows. Absorbed in a "state of pleasant exaltation" as his thoughts turn to love, prosperity, and his beloved

Bamma, he is startled by "a low growl" emanating from "a small, low shop, whose air of wretchedness and decay harmonized with the strange assortment of articles displayed in the one dirty window." It is a taxidermist's shop, and the growl has come from "a fine young tiger" imprisoned in a small cage. When the Creole shop-owner emerges from the shadows, he explains that the tiger was given him as an object to stuff. As John leaves the shop, the man detains him, determined to show him "som'ting strange." Leading the way to a courtyard, he then presents "a slender, graceful white bird" in a "large, handsome cage"—a "freak," according to the shop-owner, a "white black bird" who "has no mate." "Nature," he laments, "is mo' strong 'han we. Po' lill' bird! He kin nevver fin' his own feather."[76]

The bird holds a strange fascination for John Morant; later, after the history of Bamma's mixed parentage has reached his ear, he has a dream in which the creature is transformed into the image of his wife. The white blackbird is an obvious symbol of miscegenation, with its hints of social isolation, imprisonment, ostracization, and death. Yet in the symbolism of the novel, it is more than that, serving also to link cages, captivity, commerce, and the negotiation of price with slavery, the mixing of races, and the plight of the white black woman. As with Bamma's father, who upon marrying a Southern heiress "settled down in England to enjoy his American possessions," the trope of the white black-bird binds together the condition of women and the institution of slavery. As the narrator elsewhere makes even more explicit, "Since the world began, men's hearts have responded to the pitiableness of woman's condition, the slavery of it appealing to them as all bondage appeals."[77]

The link between gender and race, the oppression of women and the oppression of the racial Other, takes countless and sometimes unexpected forms in the Woman's Building, not least in the African American collection Imogen Howard assembled. Consisting of "a varied collection of articles, chiefly the handiwork of colored women with a few interesting loans," most of the exhibit was displayed in a case the BLM furnished in a room just off the main gallery. As the New York delegation later reported, Howard's work (including the statistics displayed separately in the south Records Room) demonstrated that "those colored women who had done the most to show their capabilities" were "teachers, authors, artists, doctors, designers, musicians, nurses (trained), engravers, missionaries, lawyers, inventors, clerks, librarians, bookkeepers, editors, etc." Her efforts also represented "the only collection ever made of the literature of New York colored women," the New York Times reported. "It shows that they have written books, and it contains stories, biographies, poems, and sonnets."[78]

In addition to acquiring books and handicrafts, Howard managed to borrow from the Boston YMCA a sculpture known as *The Wooing of Hiawatha* by Edmonia Lewis, an expatriate American sculptor of African and Ojibwa ancestry. This small marble statue of Minnehaha and her father was displayed in the Woman's Building Library.[79] Lewis, who was mentored by Lydia Maria Child, was well known in the post–Civil War period. Her best-known piece, the large sculpture *The Death of Cleopatra,* had attracted a great deal of attention at the 1876 Centennial Exhibition, where it was the only work by an African American woman displayed in the fair's Memorial Hall. Although Lewis had drifted into obscurity by 1893, three African American authors connected to the Columbian Exposition made explicit reference to her in works published during, shortly before, or just after the fair. Anna Julia Cooper, in *A Voice from the South* (1892), praises "the colored sculptress" for her contributions to the world's culture, and in *The Reason Why the Colored American Is Not in the World's Columbian Exposition* (1893), the African American author and educator Irvine Garland Penn holds her up as an example of the race's "native talent" and progress in the field of art. Hallie Q. Brown, in her comments at the World's Congress of Representative Women, commended Lewis's work, noting particularly her "Hagar in the Wilderness" and "a life-size statue of Phillis Wheatley." Although Lewis's sculpture may have received little fanfare amidst the plethora of artworks and artifacts elsewhere in the Woman's Building, Cooper, Penn, Brown, and other World's Fair visitors attuned to matters of race would certainly have taken note of its presence in the building's library.[80]

The Wooing of Hiawatha (also called *The Old Indian Arrowmaker and His Daughter*) echoes domestic and sentimental themes found in many texts in the Woman's Building Library. As an idealized representation by an African American and Ojibwa woman of an Anglo-American man's popular portrayal of fictional Native American figures loosely based on a European epic (chiseled, no less, in pure white marble), the sculpture—like the library's portrait of Pocahontas—also reflects the profound complexity of racial representation within the library. As with Buckner's white blackbird, the absence of color in Lewis's classically sculpted marblework draws attention to both the meaning of color (including whiteness) and the significance of its absence.[81]

Although the Woman's Building Library contained works by five identified African American authors, the omissions far outnumber the inclusions. Among the library's many "absent presences" are Phillis Wheatley, Sojourner Truth, Harriet Jacobs, Mary Ann Shadd, Lucy Delaney, Josephine Heard, and Hannah Carson—all authors featured at the 1900 Paris Exposition.[82] Elizabeth Keckley's *Behind the Scenes* (1868) was also absent. And, although the library contained many collective biographies of inspiring women, *The Heroines of African Methodism* (1891), compiled by Susie I. Lankford Shorter—identified as "the first 'woman of African descent' to compile a 'collective biography of Afro-American women'"—was absent too, as were a number of other life narratives and several novels: Harriet Wilson's *Our Nig* (1859), Amelia Johnson's *Clarence and Corinne* (1890), and Emma Dunham Kelley's *Megda* (1891).[83]

Like Native American figures in the Woman's Building Library, representations of African Americans often appear in texts by white authors. During the antebellum period, the Civil War, and Reconstruction, white authors' perspectives on race typically bifurcated into antislavery and proslavery texts in which racial representation is filtered through oppositional viewpoints. On the proslavery side, texts such as Lillian Foster's *Wayside Glimpses, North and South* (1860) propagate negative stereotypes while promoting the "peculiar institution" as benevolent and needful. Antislavery texts appear more prevalent in the library, however (unsurprisingly, as Northern states contributed more volumes than Southern states). Abolitionist arguments by Catherine Beecher and Lydia Maria Child could be found in the New York collection, as could Mary L. Booth's translation of Augustin Cochin's *Results of Emancipation*—although Sarah and Angelina Grimké are notably absent from South Carolina's contribution.[84] Both Illinois and Michigan contributed volumes of *A Woman's Life-Work* (1881), by Laura S. Haviland, a subscription book that bears a testimonial by John Greenleaf Whittier and recounts the author's experiences working on the Underground Railroad, teaching fugitive slaves, and assisting in freedmen's aid and relief work; New York contributed *My Story of the War* (1887) by Columbian Woman writer Mary A. Livermore; Pennsylvania contributed Anna Davis Hallowell's *James and Lucretia Mott: Life and Letters* (1884). The library also contained abolitionist children's books, such as J. Elizabeth Jones's *The Young Abolitionists: Conversations on Slavery* (1848), abolitionist poetry, such as some of the verse in Tacy Townsend Purvis's *Hagar the Singing Maiden, with Other Stories and Rhymes* (1881), and abolitionist fiction. Although *Uncle Tom's Cabin* was the most conspicuous specimen of this genre, observant fairgoers might also have noticed Mary Peabody Mann's posthumously published *Juanita: A Romance of Real Life in Cuba Fifty Years Ago* (1887) and Frances Hammond Pratt's *La Belle Zoa; or, The Insurrection of Hayti* (1854). And, along with an array of Southern Civil War novels, such as Augusta Jane Evans's *Macaria* (1864), the library included antislavery Civil War fiction emanating from opposite sides of the North-South divide and defying the norms of their respective regions. Elizabeth Bryant Johnson's *Christmas in Kentucky, 1862* (1892) illustrates a wealthy plantation owner reading his slaves the Emancipation Proclamation and liberating them before the proclamation officially took effect on January 1, 1863; and *What Answer?* (1868), a controversial novel by Anna E. Dickinson, who served on the Home Advisory Council of the World's Congress of Representative Women, exposes Northern racism through its portrayal of an interracial marriage, its depiction of social segregation in New York, and its description of the New York City Draft Riots of 1863. Hailed by Harriet Beecher Stowe as "one of those books which belong to the class of *deeds* not *words*," *What Answer?* carries the debate over racial equality into postwar American fiction.[85]

Two other novels warrant notice for their polarized firsthand portrayals of social conditions in the New South. Annie Jefferson Holland's *The Refugees: A Sequel to "Uncle Tom's Cabin"* (1892), a self-published volume that formed part of the Texas collection, appropriates several of Stowe's most cherished characters (including Uncle Tom, Aunt Chloe, St. Clare, and Topsy) to promote a regressive racist agenda. The "refugees" of the title are white plantation owners fleeing war-torn Louisiana and attempting to reestablish themselves in the Lone Star State. Fanning the flames of hatred, fear, self-pity, and resentment, Holland's novel presents a postwar Texas in which privileged whites struggle to overcome unfamiliar hardships while former slaves, cast by Holland as lazy, ignorant, and prone to vice, are rewarded with lucrative business ventures and political offices. With a vicious twist of Stowe's narrative, *The Refugees* portrays the New South as a dangerous, topsy-turvy world on the brink of catastrophe.[86]

A horrific counterpoint to Holland's self-indulgent travesty, the anonymously published *Other Fools and Their Doings; or, Life among the Freedmen* (1880) traces the events leading up to and including a racially motivated massacre. Signed simply "By One Who Has Seen It," the novel has been attributed to temperance lecturer and suffragist Harriet Newell Kneeland Goff, and, indeed, the name "Goff" appears next to the book's short title in Edith Clarke's *List of Books*. Goff, who served on the Moral and Social Reform conference committee of the World's Congress of Representative Women, set her novel in the town of Baconsville, a thinly disguised version of Hamburg, South Carolina The novel closely parallels the history of the Hamburg Massacre of July 8, 1876; Goff also named several of her characters after the real people involved and echoed dialogue recorded in the official testimony gathered by federal agents. *Other Fools and Their Doings* anatomizes the conflict between freedmen serving on the local militia and a mob of white men seeking to regain political and social control through violence and terror. In the novel, as in the real-life massacre, hundreds of armed white men participated in the execution of six African American men after they were captured and surrounded in a "dead ring." Although Goff's narrative reflects the kind of Romantic racialism evident in other nineteenth-century texts by white authors (including *Uncle*

Tom's Cabin) it also challenges widespread assumptions about race and racism. After reporting how the murderers and conspirators involved in the massacre not only escaped prosecution but rose to political power, Goff remarks, "Such is the justice, and such the tender mercies, to which have been consigned the emancipated slaves of the Southern States, and these and similar experiences have caused the 'Exodus' of the freedmen to the great north-west." Addressing the reader point-blank, the novel concludes, "With such fearful odds, can the reader wonder at their seeming timidity?"[87]

Goff's contemporary biography identifies her as "the first woman ever placed upon a nominating committee to name candidates for the presidency and vice-presidency of the United States." Her entry in Frances Willard and Mary A. Livermore's *A Woman of the Century* further records, "To her presence and influence was due the incorporation of woman's suffrage into the platform of the party at that time." The biographical sketch details how a brush with death revealed to her "new views of human relations and enforced isolations," prompting her to dedicate time and effort to those in need, "preferring those least heeded by others." Yet the sketch also carefully preserves the anonymity of *Other Fools and Their Doings,* noting only that her (unnamed) second book was issued in six editions in its first year. Based on the number of reprintings, it appears that Goff's novel played a role in making Northern readers aware of the Southern reign of terror. Its inclusion in the Woman's Building Library helps fill the gap left by excluded texts like Ida B. Wells's *Southern Horrors* while helping to ensure that neither the victims nor the crime would be forgotten.[88]

A few white authors composed biographies and even "autobiographies" of African Americans, blurring the line between white biographer and black subject. Sarah Hopkins Bradford's *Harriet: The Moses of Her People* (1886) is a revised edition of an earlier book (titled simply *Harriet Tubman*) that Bradford wrote in order to help Tubman save her home from a mortgage lender. In her preface Bradford explains that Tubman, whom she calls her "heroic friend," related the incidents to her personally and encouraged her to publish this updated edition. In *The Kidnapped and the Ransomed: Being the Personal Recollections of Peter Still and His Wife "Vina" after Forty Years of Slavery* (1856), the author, Kate E. R. Pickard, identifies herself as a teacher who became acquainted with Peter Still when he found employment at her school. Still, she explains, was kidnapped from his childhood home in New Jersey, held in slavery for more than forty years in Kentucky and Alabama, and at the time of the book's publication was attempting to earn money to purchase the freedom of his wife and children. A third volume in the library, *Autobiography of a Female Slave* (1857), by Mattie Griffith, "a conscience-ridden Kentucky slaveholder who rebelled against the slave system," collapses racial and generic boundaries: written by a white female abolitionist "passing" as a slave-narrator, *Autobiography of a Female Slave* (like Marianna Burgess's *Stiya*) is a novel masquerading as personal narrative.[89]

Another African American life story, *Memoirs of Elleanor Eldridge* (1838), is nearly as complicated in its representation of racial identity and cultural heritage as Lewis's *Wooing of Hiawatha*. A free woman of mixed African and Narragansett ancestry, Eldridge was the subject of a biographical sketch by Frances Harriet Green (McDougall), a white Rhode Island reformer. Like Sarah Hopkins Bradford's biography of Harriet Tubman, *Memoirs of Elleanor Eldridge* was a fundraising effort. Eldridge's home had been sold fraudulently; Green, in recounting the complicated chain of events that included the theft of Eldridge's property and her repurchase of it at an inflated price, exposes these transactions as a scam concocted by white men to take advantage of an innocent African American woman. In *Elleanor's Second Book* (1839), Green sandwiches an abridgement of the original *Memoirs* between a frame narrative in which Green and four friends agree to help "Ellen" by producing a new book containing four short stories purportedly composed for the volume by these four fictive friends. The frame also incorporates Ellen's account of her success in selling the earlier *Memoirs* in Boston, New York, Philadelphia, Providence, Newport, and other northeastern locales. By integrating Eldridge's booksell-ing report with the *Memoirs* and enacting in this sequel the story of its own creation and dissemination, *Elleanor's Second Book* inscribes an illiterate African American woman into the book's own history and hence into the History of the Book. In doing so, *Elleanor's Second Book* helps reveal how the economies of authorship, publishing, and bookselling impinge on the construction of racial and gender identities.[90]

Not all African American contributions to the Woman's Building Library foreground race, however. Henrietta Cordelia Ray, a highly educated poet of mixed African American and Native American heritage, chose to assume what Amina Gautier describes as "racial blindness" in order to celebrate abstract uni-versal themes in her collection *Sonnets* (1893).[91] The volume contains a dozen poems that address subjects such as "Aspiration" and "Self-Mastery" as well as sonnets in praise of Milton, Shakespeare, Raphael, and Beethoven. In her choice of classic forms and conventional themes, Ray embraces an aesthetic shared by many of her contemporaries in the library, including Edmonia Lewis and a host of late nineteenth-century women poets. As Angela Sorby argues, the "genteel idealist" poets in the library (including Ray) "echoed the aesthetic principles of the Woman's Building and the White City."[92]

The library contained one other volume of Cordelia Ray's work: a biography Ray coauthored with her sister Florence. *Sketch of the Life of Rev. Charles B. Ray* (1887) is an honorific volume devoted to their father, a pastor and the editor of *Colored American* magazine. As a eulogistic biography with an emphasis on the subject's spiritual vocation, *Sketch of the Life of Rev. Charles B. Ray* mirrors several dominant trends in the Woman's Building Library. Similarly, Julia A. J. Foote's spiritual autobiography, *A Brand Plucked from the Fire* (1879), shares with many of the library's other texts a dual focus on religion and reform.[93] Foote, an African Methodist Episcopal evangelist who refused to yield to her husband's demand that she refrain from proselytizing, became firmly committed to preaching the Gospel. In addition to recounting her early life, marriage, and the "indignities" she suffered "on account of color," *A Brand Plucked from the Fire* touches on controversial subjects of keen interest to Columbian Women, including her excommunication for preaching as a woman.[94]

In the African American exhibit assembled by Imogen Howard, Cordelia and Florence Ray's *Sketch of the Life of Rev. Charles B. Ray* and Cordelia Ray's *Sonnets* joined *Aunt Lindy: A Story Founded on Real Life* (1893) by Victoria Earle (Matthews), a New York journalist, fiction writer, educator, and reformer.[95] Both in Earle's text and in the accompanying illustrations by Mary L. Payne, *Aunt Lindy* offers a powerful corrective to the stereotype of the Southern mammy propagated in the performances of "Aunt Jemima," which were staged by the Quaker Oats Company in the nearby Food Building. It also reclaims the figure of African American womanhood from texts by white authors in the Woman's Building Library such as *Afro-American Folk Lore as Told 'Round Cabin Fires on the Sea Islands of South Carolina* (1892), by the suffragist, socialist, and Columbian Woman writer Abbie Holmes Christensen; M. Agnes Thompson's *Metairie, and Other Old Aunt Tilda of New Orleans Sketches* (1892); and, most significant perhaps, *Aunt Pokey's Son,* by Orra Langhorne, a prominent suffragist and prolific contributor to the Hampton Institute's newspaper, *The Southern Workman*.[96] Langhorne's short story, subtitled "A Story of the New South," tells of the friendship between an old African American woman (Pocahontas, nicknamed Aunt Pokey) and the ailing woman who once owned her. In her preface Langhorne writes nostalgically of the "kindly relations" that existed between the races under slavery and expresses hope that "the two races can meet as friends in the changed conditions that have come to both." *Aunt Pokey's Son* "work[s] out this idea" by having Aunt Pokey's well-educated son give up a professorship at a Richmond institution in order to manage the plantation of his former owner.[97] In *Aunt Lindy,* a story that could easily have been a response to Langhorne's well-meaning but insidious and facile invention, Earle presents a dramatic tale of suffering and retribution that frankly acknowledges the human desire for vengeance while revealing "a mystic vein running through humanity" that opens the way to redemption.[98]

Set in Fort Valley, Georgia, where Earle was born into slavery, *Aunt Lindy* inverts stereotypes by characterizing a kindly white doctor as having a "great heart and gentle, childlike manner" while portraying the title character as a "tall, ancient-looking Negro dame" famed for her skill as a nurse. Aunt Lindy suffers secretly for the children taken from her in slavery, hiding her grief from "an unsympathizing generation." After a devastating fire ignited at the Cotton Exchange destroys half the town, Lindy's former master, an unidentified silver-haired stranger, is brought to her for healing. When she recognizes the old man, Lindy is transfigured by a "bitter hatred" that mirrors the destructive force of the "fire-fiend": Consumed by this "quick, vengeful flame," Lindy contemplates with "demoniac gleams of exultation" and "a dozen wicked impulses" the possibility of murdering the man who sold her children and (the story implies) coerced her into an illicit relationship. (The delirious man's murmuring "Lindy, Lindy, don't tell Miss Cynthia" hints at this abuse.) Just as she is poised to "spring . . . with clutching fingers extended," the sounds of rejoicing from a nearby prayer-meeting thwart her fury. Prayer, forgiveness, reconciliation, and the return of Lindy's son—a reunion Lindy's old master facilitates—follow in the wake of this incident. The "great Refiner's fire," Earle writes, has "burned away" the dross and left the gold. Within the context of the books represented in the Woman's Building Library, *Aunt Lindy* is striking for its realistic contemporary setting and unsentimental (though still "mystical") treatment of a racially charged conflict. The story also addresses the intergenerational impact of slavery.[99]

All three of the texts featured in Imogen Howard's African American Exhibit—*Aunt Lindy*, Cordelia Ray's *Sonnets*, and the Ray sisters' *Sketch of the Life of Rev. Charles B. Ray*—were also shelved among the New York books in the Woman's Building Library, where they blended in with thousands of other volumes. In the adjacent New Jersey section, the work of a little-known African American poet—Hetty (Esther) Saunders—would have been even less visible to the library's visitors. Buried within Margaret Tufts Yardley's *New Jersey Scrap Book of Women Writers*, an anthology of periodical writing published by the New Jersey women's board "to represent the many writers who are not bookmakers at the World's Columbian Exposition," two poems are identified as "verses composed and dictated by Hetty Saunders, an ancient colored woman, long a servant in a Salem County family." The prefatory note goes on to explain that although Saunders dictated many other poems as well, "these were selected as being distinctly typical of the old African servant of the past."[100] Saunders composed the first poem, "The Hill of Age," to honor a friend who died at the age of 109. The second, "Peace and Quiet," speaks of moving back to her employers' home from the private cottage Saunders built on her own hard-earned land. Beginning with a sense of dread at leaving her solitary home in the African American community, the poem concludes with mingled gratitude and regret for the tranquility she must soon relinquish.[101] Although Saunders's name does not appear in the *List of Books*, her presence in *The New Jersey Scrap Book of Women Writers* shows that not only did New Jersey's literary committee make a concerted effort to include this all but unknown African American poet; they also made a deliberate editorial decision to highlight race in the presentation of Saunders's work.

With four volumes on display, the most conspicuous African American writer in the Woman's Building Library was Frances Ellen Watkins Harper, author of *Moses: A Story of the Nile* (1869), *Sketches of Southern Life* (1872), and *Iola Leroy; or, Shadows Uplifted* (1892). (All three volumes appeared in Pennsylvania's collection, while a second copy of *Iola Leroy* formed one-fourth of New Hampshire's showing in the library.) A former teacher, abolitionist, and Underground Railroad operative, Harper was a well-known reformer whose activism extended to equal rights, anti-lynching, educational and employment opportunities for African Americans, temperance, and suffrage. She participated in several predominantly white organizations, including the Woman's Christian Temperance Union (WCTU) and the American Woman's Suffrage Association, both of which had strong ties to the BLM.

Harper was the only African American author in the Woman's Building Library to play a part in the official proceedings of the fair. As such, she was the only Columbian Woman writer of color. "Woman's Political Future," her address before the World's Congress of Representative Women, advocated women's suffrage and endorsed a national education bill to promote literacy, underscored women's spirituality and "aristocracy of character," and deplored the fact that even the most "ignorant and brutal" of men could vote while deserving women could not. In the latter half of her speech, Harper shifted attention to racial violence and inequality, remarking that "political life in our country has plowed in muddy channels, and needs the infusion of clearer and cleaner waters." She concluded by calling on the women of America to "create a healthy public sentiment; to demand justice, simple justice, as the right of every race; to brand with everlasting infamy the lawlessness and brutal cowardice that lynches, burns, and tortures your own countrymen."[102]

In *Moses: A Story of the Nile*, a forty-page narrative poem in blank verse, Harper recounts the biblical story of the Jews' deliverance from slavery to create an allegory of African American history with both spiritual and political dimensions.[103] *Sketches of Southern Life* is a collection of verse and prose that takes its name from the volume's foremost piece: a first-person narrative poem told from the perspective of Chloe Fleet, known as Aunt Chloe. The poem consists of several distinct parts—a preamble, in which Chloe's two sons are sold to pay off their master's debts; "The Deliverance," which tells of the Civil War, emancipation, and the vote (including the defrauding of newly enfranchised voters); "Aunt Chloe's Politics," which stresses the importance of "voting clean"; "Learning to Read"; "Church Building"; and "The Reunion," in which Chloe is reunited with her children. "Sketches of Southern Life" represents a dramatic retelling of recent Southern history in which former slaves have a voice and "women radicals" play a crucial (though indirect) political role through their adamant defense of the vote.[104] Something of a miscellany, the volume also includes "The Jewish Grandfather's Story" (a first-person verse narrative of Old Testament history), an allegorical tale called "Shalmanezer, Prince of Cosman," and a cluster of short poems with Christian and temperance themes. Yet Aunt Chloe's narrative is clearly the collection's keynote, and the progress it describes from slavery to freedom is echoed in the imagery of later poems that figure poverty, vice, and addiction as other forms of thralldom. Its title evoking the late nineteenth-century fascination with local color, *Sketches of Southern Life* also stakes a claim for the African American experience as a legitimate province of southern literary regionalism.

One of the earliest novels by a black woman, Harper's *Iola Leroy* is a historical romance set during and just after the Civil War. In it, Harper rejects the expedient of passing along with the convention of the tragic mulatta; instead, she reinvents the racially mixed protagonist as a strong, independent heroine who proudly claims her African American heritage. Like other Columbian Women writers, Harper regarded fiction as a potentially powerful medium for social change, and *Iola Leroy* reflects her vision of literature and reform. As Hazel Carby points out, Harper viewed this novel as a "cultural intervention" akin to her political lectures, speeches, and articles; she even incorporated into chapters 26 and 30 passages from her articles and lectures, including the address she gave before the World's Congress of Representative Women. Similarly, chapter 30, "Friends in Council," reenacts a symposium on "the welfare of the race" that models the kind of intellectual exchange carried out at the World's Congress meetings.

Confronting current racial tensions, like Earle in *Aunt Lindy* (along with Buckner, Dickinson, and Goff), Harper refuses to consign racial oppression to the antebellum past. Unlike *Towards the Gulf*, however, where the "impassive" maid, a "white-souled negress," "allows" Bamma "to pass," and where "passing" gives way to "silence and dulness," Harper's "nearly white characters," as Gautier observes, "align themselves with the African American race . . . on terms of equality, with no desire to be part of the blue-vein society or to presume superiority." "In order to usher itself into the new Gilded Age," Gautier concludes, "America must 'pass' as a cohesive nation."[105] As in *Towards the Gulf*, Harper uses imagery of shadows to represent the "penalties" of race prejudice and the oppressive power of whites who consider theirs to be "the master race." In contrast to *Towards the Gulf*, however, where shadows lengthen and the prospect dims, *Iola Leroy* (aptly subtitled *Shadows Uplifted*) offers a hopeful counternarrative in which "shadows bear the promise / Of a brighter coming day."[106]

Two-thirds of the way into *Towards the Gulf*, we find Bamma Morant, somber and dejected in the snug library of her husband's New Orleans mansion. During a visit to the old family plantation, John Morant had begun to piece together the evidence of his wife's racial heritage: a string of beads exhumed from an ancient Indian burial mound that matches beads given to Bamma as a small child, and a mouldering portrait of a long-dead slaveholder—Bamma's grandfather—discovered in the library of an abandoned plantation. When John restores the forgotten portrait to its place over the library's mantelpiece, an "inexplicable likeness" perplexes him, and "the eyes seemed to follow him . . . the familiar smile haunted him."[107] Now, Bamma, too, finds herself haunted by an inexplicable burden:

> Almost imperceptibly there had grown upon her a sense of mystery in their relation to each other. Every available feminine charm against unknowable trouble, her brightest smiles, her tenderest caresses, were futile to banish it. It settled down upon the household like an unbidden guest, determined to make the most of an unwarranted intrusion. It rested in the beautiful drawing-room, even when they were filled with as light-hearted material as ever gathered together to drive away care. It sat down beside Bamma when she ate and drank. It took its place prominently in the cosey library.
> Yes, there was not a shadow of doubt that the library was its favorite haunt. It was there that it gathered force and thence diffused itself.

In this passage, the menacing "it," the ghostlike "guest" that "haunts" the library of John Morant, represents "the sense of mystery" that comes between husband and wife as a result of "still, small, cruel voices of hereditary prepossessions and prejudices"—voices that grow "sharper and more ferocious with every struggle to repress them." Lacking knowledge of the "taint" in her blood, Bamma is confused and depressed by "the shadow of the change that had come upon him," and "tears rose in [her] eyes as she thought how pleasant a place the library might be and was not."[108] Bamma's melancholy reflection poignantly recalls Annie Nathan Meyer's observation that "a library . . . may be a place of ghosts and shadows."

That the library is the "favorite haunt" of the menacing spirit of racism in *Towards the Gulf* is ironic, but fitting. The library is a repository of ideas, but it is also a conduit for their circulation: "It was there that it gathered force and thence diffused itself." Not coincidentally, Morant's library houses an array of volumes devoted to the emerging science of ethnology: "Quatrefages on the Negro Races, Gobineau on the Inequality of Races, Riboût on Heredity, Périer on Ethnical Crossings, Knox on Race, and others"—volumes that (like the Columbian Exposition's ethnological exhibits and Midway entertainments) insidiously propagated notions of white supremacy in the persuasive guise of scientific thought. No wonder that, as Bamma's attention turns to these books— books which her husband pores over "with contracted brow and contracted heart"—"something of the darkness which was closing around her certainly emanated from the sombre bindings and rustling leaves."[109] As Buckner conceives them, books, in this context, function like a contagion; Morant's library is a site of contamination, where the germs of a cultural pestilence incubate and infect the susceptible. Ultimately, this novel suggests, ideological transmission is a potentially fatal exchange.[110]

The last image Buckner presents of John Morant's library occurs near the end of the novel, after Bamma has committed suicide, her child has incurred a fatal accident, and the Creole shop-owner and his wife have emigrated to France. Morant, whom Howells, in his review, describes as having "an ineffaceable stain in his thought," is relieved that the couple have left New Orleans, since he is convinced they recognized in his wife a "type." Nevertheless, Buckner writes, he has "a constant memento" of the shop-owners "in the white blackbird, that freak of nature which occupies a place upon his library mantle-piece instead of the contemplated raven above the chamber door, as it serves much the same purpose of arousing similar but more subdued elements of sorrow and despair."[111] The allusion to Edgar Allan Poe's gothic masterpiece is telling in light of the persistent engagement of American Gothic writers with the nation's heritage of racial conflict.[112] But the bird presiding over the library is apt for other reasons as well. In the context of the Woman's Building Library, the white blackbird is as appropriate a monument to the library as "a place of ghosts and shadows" as is the bust of Stowe to the library as a bustling, "up and doing" place of business.

In *Towards the Gulf,* a text "haunted" by images of specters and spirits, Bamma's hereditary memories of the slave-yard, the old French Quarter Creole shop, and the plantation owner's city mansion—"mutilated memories" that "stirred from their hiding places in the dimmest corners of her mind"—stand in for cultural memories possessed by all in a nation darkened by the legacy of slavery.[113] As Brogan notes, "Stories of cultural haunting . . . explor[e] the hidden passageways not only of the individual psyche, but also of a people's historical consciousness." For this reason, she concludes, "Ghosts . . . figure prominently wherever people must reconceive a fragmented, partially obliterated history, looking to a newly imagined past to redefine themselves for the future."[114] Reading the Woman's Building Library as "a place of ghosts and shadows" reveals the extent to which American women writers in the late nineteenth century reimagined the nation's past either by "passing on" or choosing to "pass" on their own "fragmented, partially obliterated histories."

7

"I Will Write for the People"

In 1886, a year prior to the publication of Alice Morris Buckner's *Towards the Gulf*, the Boston firm of Roberts Brothers brought out *Atalanta in the South*, "a Romance" (as it was subtitled) that contains striking thematic parallels to Buckner's "Romance of Louisiana." Written by Maud Howe Elliott—Columbian Woman writer, editor of *Art and Handicraft in the Woman's Building*, and painter of frescoes in the mansion owned by Bertha and Potter Palmer—*Atalanta in the South* centers on the patrician society of economically depressed, racially divided New Orleans in the post–Civil War era.

Like *Towards the Gulf*, *Atalanta in the South* reveals the tragic consequences of interracial love in a society that forbids it by dramatizing the relationship between an upper-class white man of French extraction and a young woman who possesses "one burning drop of negro blood."[1] In each novel, the girl's ancestry is concealed and she is raised in Europe as an aristocratic young lady. Like Bamma Morant, the equally white-skinned Therese Caseneuve attempts to avert what she perceives as the fatal consequences of racial mixing in the segregated South. And, as in *Towards the Gulf* and many other novels of the American South, the emplotment of the lovers' story within the larger "plot" of Southern history reveals, with oppressive irony, that slavery is a curse to both races. As in Buckner's romance, the sins of the forefather—in both novels a wealthy planter who fathers the child of a slave—are visited on his descendents.

Atalanta in the South and *Towards the Gulf* both register a preoccupation with social taxonomies that was pervasive in late nineteenth-century America. They also reflect the era's widespread anxiety about the crossing or collapsing of social hierarchies, including those marked by gender, race, and class. The novels respond differently to what each one presents as a crisis of racial mixing (Bamma commits suicide, while Therese, like Harper's Iola Leroy, forsakes the white society into which she was born); yet both respond to a society in flux by exposing the fault lines of social division.[2] The precise coordinates of those fault lines vary. Although both texts are laced with the language of racial and ethnic "types," in *Atalanta in the South* the social boundaries of caste loom larger than the biological consequences of racial mixing and what was termed "reversion of type."[3] Both novels, however, offer prospects of reconciliation and redemption that hint of regional and national cohesion. Both novels present the reader with scenes of horrific devastation (a flood of the Mississippi in *Towards the Gulf,* a plague in *Atalanta of the South*) that serve symbolic ends: through the extremity of hardship and suffering, social divisions are (at least temporarily) rendered inconsequential. If only fleetingly, these stories offer glimpses of a world in which "all barriers of caste were swept away," and humanity is united and redeemed through suffering, as saint and sinner, fugitive and aristocrat become like "brother[s] and sisters to one another in blood."[4]

In *Towards the Gulf,* Buckner draws parallels between the artificial barriers of society kept in place by laws and traditions that separate the races and the levees that restrain the mighty Mississippi in its inexorable race to the Gulf of Mexico. This device is doubly significant, for the image actually contains its own opposite: the "gulf" evokes both an unbridged chasm that separates the races in the segregated society Buckner portrays and a common reservoir, defined by the surrounding land, into which the races unavoidably meet and mix.[5] The ambiguity of the image reflects profound ambivalence toward rigid hierarchies of types, classes, and castes during what Hazel Carby calls "the era of the separation of the races."[6] Navigating first the shelves of the Woman's Building Library and then the fictional landscapes of its regionalist writers, in this chapter we consider various manifestations of regionalism in the library, paying particular attention to the way authors, books, people, and places become typed, classed, and ranked in place-based taxonomies. An examination of the classification and representation of stories, places, and people reveals multiple ways in which this library—as a physical repository as well as a collection of texts—reproduced and revised prevailing ideologies, even as it made space for alternative narratives of regional, national, and transnational identities. Here, as in the previous two chapters, the library as a physical space with its own internal organizational logic points to relevant strategies for reading the kinds of texts displayed there.

The late nineteenth-century affinity for systems of categorization founded on types was one response to a rapidly changing society. "References to 'types' frequently appear in periodicals of the 1890s," Susan Harris Smith and Melanie Dawson observe, "emphasizing continued and often conflicting efforts to define identities and confirm prejudices about where and how individuals fit into society." As Smith and Dawson note, the "language of 'types,'" which "combines ideas of class with ideas about patriotism, upward mobility, and cultural skills, . . . could be deployed to create the illusion of stable hierarchies."[7] Concentrating on gender, Martha Banta argues that between the 1870s and 1910s "a canon of types remained prominently in view," and Americans "were tutored to see objects and persons in the form of [these] generalized types." As Banta writes, "The categories they pictorialized acted to contain change; at the same time, these elected types revealed the fact that mutations and alterations of meaning were taking place."[8]

The Columbian Exposition catered to, gratified, and sometimes problematized this cultural enthusiasm for totalizing systems and essentialized "types." In his analysis of colonialism, Orientalism, and "the modern representational order exemplified by the world exhibition," Timothy Mitchell argues that the 1889 exposition held in Paris "was a place where the artificial, the model, and the plan were employed to generate an unprecedented effect of order and certainty."[9] Mitchell's insight transfers easily to Chicago, where organizers sought to wrest control and impose order via the meticulously engineered artifice of the White City. The Woman's Building Library reflects many of the classifying tendencies at work in the fair as a whole; yet in its decentralized development, unconventional physical arrangement, eclecticism, and wide-ranging, regionally identified content, the library simultaneously manifests and engages the tensions and contradictions Banta finds emblematic of the era itself. "Unity within multiplicity was the cultural aim," she observes, "but the cultural fact was multiplicity without unity."[10]

Writing of the Columbian Exposition, Henry Adams famously remarked that "Chicago was the first expression of American thought as a unity."[11] Even as the fair expressed cultural unity, however, it also gave voice to a chorus of regional disparities. This counterpoint between national and regional identities appears—to point to just a few examples—in the large showing of dedicated state buildings (many of which replicated locally distinctive historical structures), in the legion of state boards that rallied to the exposition's call, and in the sometimes jarring undercurrent of North–South and East–West divisions that rippled through the proceedings of the fair's Board of Lady Managers (BLM). The composition of the Woman's Building Library also reflects a dialogue between nation and region, illustrating the extent to which the nation defined itself as a union of diverse regions. Its librarians may have resisted the geographical organization implemented in response to the mandate of the New York State women managers; but the collections separately gathered and contributed by forty states and territories and the District of Columbia indicate that the women who wrote and collected the texts generally embraced

cultural regionalism. Long after the library's dispersal, its regional foundations endure in Edith Clarke's geographically arranged shelf-list, a document
that reflects the ways American women constructed their literary identities
through their sense of region even as they constructed their regional identities
through their writing.

It is significant that the library's unifying taxonomy was geography: nationalism within the global context (books organized by country) and regionalism
within the national, or American, context.[12] As we pointed out in chapter 5,
national and regional histories and volumes of travel (both domestic and international) were among the most abundant categories of books in the American
section of the library. Authors wrote of their experiences in Cuba, Mexico,
South America, Africa, the South Pacific, China, Japan, Burma, India, Thai-
land, Russia, and Siberia, as well as elsewhere in Europe and North America,
and their fiction spans the globe, from the Kimberley diamond fields of South
Africa to Algeria and Australia.[13] Sometimes fictionalized foreign settings
become stages on which the authors play out complex problems closer to
home. For Mary Peabody Mann and Frances Hammond Pratt, for example,
Caribbean settings enabled them to expose the inhumanity of slavery outside
the context of North American sectionalism.[14] Animal rights activist Caroline Earle White, who represented the Anti-Vivisection Society on the Home
Advisory Council of the World's Congress of Representative Women, also used
a faraway location to address matters of race. In her novel *Love in the Tropics*
(1890) a British castaway falls in love with a young woman of the South Pacific.
Reminiscent of Melville's *Typee* (but lacking Melville's artistry), White's novel
urges on her readers "the certain truth, that as warm a heart, as noble a nature,
and as bright an intellect may be found under a yellow, a brown, or a black skin
as under a white one."[15] Like the library's numerous travel narratives, the many
volumes of fiction with foreign settings present a wide field on which American women writers could explore imperialism, identity, and the intersections of
race and place from a range of vantage points, from the culturally conservative
to the broadly humanitarian.

Cutting across multiple genres, regional American texts were even more
abundant and more diverse in the perspectives and conflicts they explored.
Not only did the library reflect the once-definitive North–South sectionalism,
as is evidenced in numerous volumes pertaining to the Civil War (including
memoirs, poems, novels, abolitionist texts, histories, and plantation stories), it
also contained many volumes of fiction by literary regionalists from all over
the country: canonical figures such as Harriet Beecher Stowe, Sarah Orne
Jewett, Mary Wilkins Freeman, Rose Terry Cooke, Alice Cary, Caroline Kirkland, Mary Noailles Murfree, Ruth McEnery Stuart, Grace Elizabeth King,

and Mary Hallock Foote, but also many more noncanonical writers, including Columbian Women Margaret Deland, Mary Hartwell Catherwood, Antoinette Brown Blackwell, Elizabeth C. Wright, Lillie Buffum Chace Wyman, and Maud Howe Elliott.[16]

In many ways, regionalism in the Woman's Building Library looks different from regionalism in literature anthologies used in college classrooms. Although regionalist texts abounded, many of them bear little resemblance to the sketches and short stories by the canonical figures who have come to represent American literary regionalism. A majority of canonical regionalist texts emanate from New England and the Deep South, written (conventional wisdom holds) for a metropolitan audience in the Northeast intrigued by local color. The library's regionalist texts are all over the map, however, not only in the locations they represent, but in their places of publication and the audiences they address.[17] Moreover, canonical regionalism tends to consist of short stories, tales, and sketches; some scholars even argue that late nineteenth-century regionalism is defined, in part, by the distinctiveness of these genres.[18] In the library, however, regionalism takes the form of novels, novellas, and cycles of poems, as well as short fiction. Finally, rather than being set in a recent past that evokes nostalgia for a vanishing way of life (a quality of much canonical regionalism that critics have emphasized), many of the library's regional texts are set in the remote past (regional historical novels), and many others address contemporary social problems through a distinctly regional lens (regional reform novels).[19] Like the library itself, regionalism could thus be a channel for certain kinds of progressive activism as easily as it could be called upon to safeguard traditional values and accommodate conservative viewpoints. And if, at times, the combined agendas of regionalism and "progress" seem to clash, the resulting tensions often arise from the regionalist project of representing not only distinct and clearly delimited landscapes but, in addition, an eclectic and sometimes uneasy mix of the typical and atypical people who dwell there.

The ramifications of the library's geographical organization far exceed the purely literary context, however; for according to this taxonomy, in which "place" is the most visible heuristic blueprint, region becomes key to interpretation. *Every* text in the library was, in effect, indexed geographically (based on the author's affiliation), assigned a physical place according to its national, state, or territorial designation, and grouped with its peers in a glass-covered bookcase emblazoned with the name of its state, territory, or country. And for Americans living in an era when differences in cultural geography often seemed threatening, regionalism could be enlisted as a healthy antidote to the sectionalism that had divided, and nearly destroyed, the nation. The New York women may have forced these geographical divisions by insisting that their books be displayed separately; but in the end the overall arrangement of the library performed valuable cultural work by highlighting regionalism (safe, unifying, creative) in an era still laboring under the legacy of sectionalism (dangerous, divisive, destructive). The arrangement may also have helped to depoliticize the library by ensuring that books on controversial topics would be safely distributed, scattered according to authors' states and surnames, rather than clustered into potentially eye-catching blocks. Arranged by Dewey number, for example, a block of eight abolitionist texts would have been flanked on the left by a three-year run of *The Revolution,* together with another suffragist periodical (*The National Citizen and Ballot Box,* edited by Matilda Joslyn Gage), and the multivolume *History of Woman Suffrage,* and, on the right, by half a dozen volumes on women in the workforce, followed by books dealing with labor, socialism, the executive power in the United States, and divorce. As a result of this diffusion of materials, contentious issues, including those of suffrage, slavery, and labor, would not stand out so conspicuously among the myriad subject areas women writers had addressed.

In "Rewriting the Museum's Fictions: Taxonomies, Stories, and Readers," Sharon Macdonald and Roger Silverstone examine the relationships among collecting, classification, display, and interpretation within the context of the modern museum. "Collecting must, of course, take place within some system of classification," they point out. These systems of classification influence categories of display, which, in turn, guide visitors' interpretations of objects in an exhibit, enabling them to make sense of the collection as a whole. But systems of classification are, inevitably, subject to historical change. Charting a late nineteenth-century transition ushered in by the 1851 Great Exhibition in London's Crystal Palace—an important precursor of the Columbian Exhibition—Macdonald and Silverstone observe that "early museum collections were motivated primarily by the rare and exotic"; as a result, "the key feature of the objects they collected was their singularity, and it was in this that that 'special magic of museums'—authenticity—lay." In contrast, the Great Exhibition "was concerned with objects as signs of progress, and thus 'the latest' developments became collectable." "Objects selected in this way" claimed authenticity "not through their specificity but as icons, as representatives of classes." An important consequence of this shift was a new emphasis on "taxonomic modes of display" that help visitors make sense of groupings of objects by projecting a "fictional coherence." More recently—in the late twentieth century—yet another shift has occurred: a move toward modes of display grounded in narrative. In this scenario, "the visitor, the viewer, the reader" interprets objects and texts in light of "his or her own socially defined experiences and interests, which provide both the context of, and the control for, the meanings which

emerge and become significant in the interaction between body and text."
"'Stories' and 'messages,' rather than taxonomies . . . are the museums' new fictions," Macdonald and Silverstone conclude, "as the visitor . . . is more and
more inscribed in the text as active, as a contributor to, if not a creator of, his or
her own experience of the museum."[20]

These observations provide insight into the methods of classification, display,
and interpretation operating within the Woman's Building Library. As we saw
in earlier chapters, its organizational rubric was a matter of earnest contention.
New York's separatism provoked strong reactions on both sides, just as gender
separation remained a flashpoint not only within the Board of Lady Managers
but for some visitors. Indeed, the library's taxonomy necessarily influenced the
way visitors interpreted what they saw there. Had the BLM implemented their
original plan of organizing books according to subject matter, visitors would
have made sense of the collection in a very different way from the one promoted by the geographical organizational scheme. Left to their own devices,
Edith Clarke and her team of Dewey-approved protégées would have arranged
the books by Dewey Decimal Classification—the most up-to-date classification system of modern librarianship. Compelled to adhere to a model insisted
on by the New York faction, librarians had instead grouped the material first
by state and country and then, for the most part, alphabetically by author. The
original plan would have lent the overall collection an epistemological coherence meticulously engineered to mirror the sum total of human knowledge and
creativity; the latter method projected a "fictional coherence" derived instead
from the uneven and often ambiguous terrain defined by geopolitical borders.

In her essay on the library in *Art and Handicraft in the Woman's Building*,
Maud Howe Elliott makes this distinction explicit when she describes the
library's catalog and then the impression made by the books on the shelves:
"The catalogue is so arranged that a very cursory examination will show the
subjects with which women writers have chiefly dealt." (Although she doesn't
mention it, the subject classification would have made the overwhelming dominance of American fiction even more conspicuous.) A survey of the library's
bookcases prompts quite different observations. Because "arrangement of the
shelves shows the number of books sent by the different States and countries,"
Elliott remarks, "at a glance, the visitor may see that Belgium is well represented, and that France, Germany, and Great Britain lead among the foreign
collections; that New Hampshire has given itself very little trouble, and New
York a great deal." Of course, Elliott does not point out the salient feature of
New Hampshire's tiny collection: that one fourth of it was African American
literature.[21] As we saw in chapter 6, that feature was rendered "invisible" by the
colorblind classification system implemented in the library and the decision

not to profile African American women's texts with special displays such as those devoted to Harriet Beecher Stowe and Lydia Maria Child.

As organizational taxonomy, interpretive rubric, and basis of a particular kind of "fictional coherence," regionalism posed several challenges. First, the collection exhibited a distinct "want of evenness" in its development, as librarian Edith Clarke observed, as a result of its diffuse, regionalist origins. Second, the state-by-state divisions did not correspond neatly with the ways Americans tend to think about the nation's regions: states may comprise multiple regions, and regions often cross state lines, but states and regions are never precisely coterminous. Third, the movement of writers from place to place often resulted in more than one state claiming a particular author, a fact that frequently led to duplicate texts in the library. By the same token, this ambiguity undoubtedly resulted in oversights and omissions. Then, too, a single author might be claimed by one state but associated with quite a different region in the minds of readers, based on the kinds of texts she wrote. (Mary Hallock Foote, for example, wrote popular sketches of Colorado and California, yet these regionalist texts appear under the heading "New York," which was Foote's birthplace.) Finally, a single text might contain multiple regional affiliations. As Judith Fetterley and Marjorie Pryse observe in *Writing Out of Place: Regionalism, Women, and American Literary Culture*, "regionalist texts seem designed to create a crisis for the category of region."[22]

Elliott's *Atalanta in the South* is a case in point. In this "Romance of the South," Elliott subordinates her melodramatic tale of interracial romance to another plotline: a love story centering on Margaret Ruysdale, an artist and a daughter of New England, and Robert Feuardent, white half-brother of Therese Caseneuve. Like New Orleans itself, the racial theme becomes part of the backdrop, a wash of local color over what is essentially a female *Künstlerroman*. By depicting New Englanders on an extended visit to Louisiana, where they become well acquainted with members of New Orleans society and catalyze a North–South reunion-through-marriage plot (a popular trope in post–Civil War fiction), Elliott's novel metonymically enacts interregional relations (and relationships) and explores how the people of one region understand the people of another in light of cultural differences within a shared national heritage.[23]

The complicated regionalist mélange of *Atalanta in the South* is hardly surprising when one considers the author's identity. Youngest daughter of Julia Ward Howe and Samuel Gridley Howe, husband of British sculptor John Elliott, Boston society woman, and associate of many artists and writers at home and abroad, Maud Howe Elliott was a woman of cosmopolitan experience. Written by a Massachusetts-born author who was living in Chicago at the time of the fair, set in New Orleans (and dedicated to the author's friends in that city), peopled with characters who represent their respective genders, regions, and ethnicities, poised between the past of the Civil War and the future of manifest destiny, and weaving together local and national themes, *Atalanta in the South* stands out as a prime example of a kind of fiction which the term "regionalism" only imperfectly describes.

In this novel Elliott's white characters traverse geographical regions but scarcely venture to cross the boundaries that separate races and ethnicities in the social hierarchy of late nineteenth-century America. The novel incorporates the ethnically diverse characters of Southern regionalist fiction (including African Americans, Native Americans, Chinese, Spaniards, and French Creoles) as types and enlists them as supporting characters in service to a national narrative in which "over-hot" Southern whites and Northerners "in whose veins flowed the pure cool blood of the Puritans" may be amalgamated into a more perfect, racially exclusive nationality.[24] In their ability to cross regions, Elliott's white characters possess a freedom of geographical movement that her nonwhite characters either lack entirely or are forced to undertake. And although the novel's narrative voice bemoans the socioeconomic hierarchy that enables the commercial progress of the (white) nation to advance through the subordination, displacement, and exploitation of nonwhites, the novel's stance is one of resigned acceptance. "Railroads must be built, rivers must be spanned, mountains must be tunnelled for the march of commerce," Elliott writes, "and for these things, which the American covets but cannot achieve, the despised Mongolian is imported, and treated as the African never was, execrated and scoffed at by a nation which owes no little of its prosperity to-day to his tireless, uncomplaining industry."[25] The eclectic regionalism of *Atalanta in the South* easily absorbs the culturally and racially diverse population of South Louisiana, but its cosmopolitan and class-bound detachment from the region and people it describes seems to bolster rather than dismantle the social barriers the novel appears to critique.[26]

In contrast to the complicated "interregionalism" of *Atalanta in the South*, Elizabeth Holbrook's *Old 'Kaskia Days* is "intraregional" in authorship, publication, and intended audience. Published in Chicago by an Illinois writer, *Old 'Kaskia Days* is dedicated to, and addresses itself to, the women of Illinois' Exposition Board. The subject of Holbrook's narrative is the old French colony of Kaskaskia, or Notre Dame de Cascasquias, which became the first state capital of Illinois. Holbrook explicitly links the project of the World's Fair with the desire to recover and celebrate the regional, colonial past. "A thought that had lain dormant for years was called into activity when one of your number . . . came to us and organized our county," she informs the Illinois Woman's Exposition Board. "In the development of the Colonial exhibit from Old Kaskaskia, a study of the rich field of village tradition and history caused this thought to take the form of the present work."[27] Holbrook's reference to the Colonial exhibit at the World's Columbian Exposition is key. On the eve of this international and very modern world's fair, Holbrook finds inspiration and value in reconnecting contemporary midwestern society to its premodern, communal foundations and "village tradition."

Visually, *Old 'Kaskia Days* presents itself as a narrative museum, in which interpolated photographs depicting sites and artifacts of the historic village simultaneously resurrect and eulogize the colonial past. The buildings depicted are dilapidated, many with broken windows, fallen bricks, open rooftops; the photographs document all that is left of Old Kaskaskia. In contrast to the static, frozen images of the illustrations, however, the narrative describes a society in flux. Holbrook's village, depicted on the eve of statehood, teems with people of diverse nationalities and races—"mostly French, numbers of English, also Americans, and some Irish," but also Illinois Indians, Rocky Mountain Indians, and African American slaves. Yet the novel clearly differentiates between European and non-European peoples in the types of characters Holbrook creates. While the French, English, and Americans tend to be individuated, the novel's nonwhite figures appear as conventional ethnic types—"crooning" slaves, "grotesque" Rocky Mountain Indians (contrasted with Kaskaskia's Indians, who have been taught "the arts of the white man"), "black Rose," a "mammy" figure who speaks in a Southern dialect, and Sciakape, a classic Pocahontas figure. As in *Atalanta in the South,* these stock characters clearly establish the limits of the novel's regional representation, even as chilling tales of frontier warfare and the massacre of slaves and their owner at a nearby mill seem to threaten those limits with graphic reminders of the colony's human cost.

Counterpoised to the pictorializing of static objects and fixed character types, Holbrook's portrait of a region linked geographically, historically, and culturally to other places and peoples reflects the fluidity of the colonial frontier. The book's title page delineates Kaskaskia's colonial and postcolonial pedigree from its settlement by Jesuits in 1680 to Illinois statehood; but Holbrook's project is not to project an imaginary arc of continuous progress from which to extrapolate the rise of the modern American state. Instead, she highlights the continuing impact of the frontier on the community's social and economic development. "We are yet upon the frontier," a Frenchman tells an American in the novel. Kaskaskia's cultural roots, "drawing sustenance along the lines of connection sent out to France, to Canada, to New Orleans, and to the Rocky Mountains," like the Kaskaskia and Mississippi Rivers, serve as vital channels for trade. The waterways also serve as images of mobility, connectedness, and flux. In Holbrook's river scenes, the constraints on her static African and

Indian types seem to loosen as she positions these figures farther downstream from Kaskaskia's colonial center: slaves load flatboats at the settlement's dock and a pirogue carrying slaves makes its way upstream, but downriver Indians in canoes trap fish, while on a high bluff a wigwam affords its occupants a forty-mile prospect in both directions. At the end of the river, a New Orleans fête illustrates the provisional erosion of Holbrook's sharply differentiated ranks: on the city's crowded esplanade, a "throng" resolves itself into a "moving mass of French, Spaniards, Indians, mulattoes and negroes [that] surged back and forth, according to the interest taken in especial sights."[28]

A recurring motif in *Old 'Kaskia Days* is the passing of the old ways in "the quiet, sleepy village of these old-time French," and the imminent change that looms with the extension of the United States into the Old Northwest: "The country is in a transition state," one character remarks, and another senses that "a more active spirit is approaching." Like Frederick Jackson Turner in his Columbian Exposition address, Holbrook's characters associate Americanness with qualities forged on the frontier. "These Americans are infusing new life and spirit into the territory," a Frenchman reflects. The heroine's father observes that Americans "reproach us and say that we have little ambition or enterprise in our nature, but we make valiant soldiers, never quailing in the bloodiest carnage." Reflecting on "scenes that had transpired on that historical spot," he "turn[s] his eyes in the direction of the Indian lodges" and thinks of others who have been "crowded out." It is inevitable," he concludes. "They are already at our heels. Is [the American] destined to supplant the 'Illinois French'?" The novel's vision of displacement and Anglo-American dominance is tinged with regret. By linking the Illinois French to this "remnant" of Indian lodges, and juxtaposing the "brave," "gentle," "eloquent," and "pious" Jesuit fathers with the aggressive, almost predatory Americans, the novel intimates that the colonizer will become the colonized, the assimilators of the past will, in turn, be assimilated when statehood is achieved and "pioneers of all classes [enter] the new state."[29]

Like *Towards the Gulf*, *Old 'Kaskia Days* draws on the geographical and historical impact of floodwater, with its powerful archetypal connotations, to signal dramatic cultural change. The novel, which hinges on thwarted love, border warfare, and an innocent man's murder trial, concludes with the rising river that destroyed Kaskaskia in 1844. Holbrook foreshadows the catastrophe in her preface: "It is with sadness that we hear the cry from the handful of inhabitants left in the village: 'Old 'Kaskia is doomed.' The hungry rivers are eating the soil that has been pressed by the feet of the red man, by the Jesuit missionaries, the commandants of the French forts, by the 'Long Knife' Virginians, by the brave-hearted pioneers who pushed the frontier beyond them, by noble and disinterested statesmen, by the patriotic Lafayette." The novel culminates with the image of destruction and erasure anticipated in the preface: "When the waters subside, there are entire streets upon which are left only the tall chimneys to mark the place where homes had once existed. A new era has set in—one of decay, and a gradual disappearance of the villagers. Never again will be the glory of the 'Old 'Kaskia Days.'"[30] The imagery of the flood's destruction at once naturalizes and finalizes the successive cultural displacements the novel recites.

Holbrook's text is an elegy to a lost village, lost cultural ties, and a vanished way of life. But the novel's regionalist perspective is distinctly situated within a national context, and the text clearly attempts to consolidate the interests of the two. As Holbrook notes, "Not alone to the people of Illinois should this spot be of vital interest, for along the ancient trails leading to this center great cities have arisen, and thousands of homes established, throughout other commonwealths."[31] Refusing to consign the regional to the margins and history to the past, *Old 'Kaskia Days* calls for a reorientation of history in which the periphery blazes the trail to new centers. Part novella, part history, and part photo essay, *Old 'Kaskia Days* exploits the flexible boundaries of genres to explore the permeable categories of regional identity.

If *Old 'Kaskia Days* uses the geographical fact of a historical flood to evoke the fluidity of the frontier, *The Heroine of '49: A Story of the Pacific Coast,* by Mary P. Sawtelle, employs the economic value of western land to "ground" an impassioned double-edged protest against the commodification of women's bodies and the parallel theft of Native American land. Published in San Francisco and contributed by the Oregon women's board, this regionalist reform novel, in which allegorically named Dickensian villains mingle with real-life historical figures, blends history, satire, romance, and politics in a peculiar hybrid form.

The Heroine of '49 depicts the lives of Oregon's first white settlers in order to expose the gender and racial inequity originating in the past and persisting in the authorial present. In the novel's preface, Sawtelle, a physician, bluntly states her desire to disabuse readers of the commonly held belief that girls mature faster than boys, a conviction then used to justify marriages of convenience to child brides. (In this respect, Sawtelle echoes reformers such as Matilda Joslyn Gage, Helen H. Gardener, and BLM member Rebecca Felton who sought humane age-of-consent laws to protect girls.) Sawtelle's scope broadens significantly, however, taking in the injustices of the Indian wars, dispossession of tribal lands, the reservation system, domestic violence, divorce, homesteading laws that reduced women's bodies to a form of currency, and laws that placed children of divorce with abusive fathers while depriving mothers of children, property, income, and social standing. Angrily chastising lawmakers for failing to protect women and children, Sawtelle directs considerable invective at the

U.S. government for violating treaties, refusing to pay Indians for their land, and failing to compensate American citizens who served in the Indian wars. The government wronged both sides, she argues, in its zeal to annex land. The result, according to one reviewer, was a book that, while "striking" and "real," is "not pleasant reading."[32]

The Heroine of '49 anticipates Turner's major claim that "the true point of view in the history of this nation is not the Atlantic coast, it is the Great West."[33] The novel's heroine, Jean, in an article on homesteading on the Pacific Coast, reflects, "What a pity our forefathers had not planted their feet on Pacific soil instead of on Plymouth Rock." Addressing a western readership, Sawtelle writes that Jean "contrasted our climate with theirs on the bleak Atlantic side, and told [her audience] they would never have to put earth on the sunny side of a rock to grow a hill of corn, as they do in New Hampshire and Vermont, if they lived in California."[34] As Jean journeys from coast to coast to speak her piece in the nation's capital, Sawtelle pieces together a regional text that positions the interests of women and children ahead of commercial gain and inscribes a western woman's point of view into the national narrative of emigration and progress.

Throughout the novel, Sawtelle, like Turner, calls attention to the influence of the frontier in fostering such personal characteristics as toughness and determination and promoting such "American" qualities as egalitarianism and individualism. Sawtelle introduces a twist, however, by emphasizing gender equality and community as well, while locating the strongest of these western—and by extension "American"—values in her female characters. Although Jean initially endures her husband's brutality, in Sawtelle's text the West is a place where women can realize their potential and receive their due. After four years at Oregon's own Willamette University, where Jean "led in every study" she undertook, Sawtelle pointedly sums up the result of her intellectual endeavors in terms of gender: "She is a woman at last." Later, when Jean hopes to matriculate in the university's new department of medicine, the trustees agree to enroll her: "They, with their big, common-sense, Pacific Coast brains, said they did not know why women should not learn medicine as well as their a b c's." In an impassioned expression of gratitude to her adopted western land, Jean declares, "I love it for its just and equal laws, for its recognition of the claims of women."[35]

Even as Sawtelle's narrative revels in the freedom and openness of the West, however, images of confinement, immobility, and racial segregation illustrate the enforced barricades that demarcate the novel's social and physical geographies. Although Sawtelle differentiates a few Umpqua characters, her Indians are nevertheless static "types": Noble Savages, they are childlike, untamed, and essentially good, although categorically inferior to whites. Jean is passionate in their defense, insisting that "the Indian character in its native wildness is grand, until stung to revenge by the villainies of the whites"; and during the Rogue River War, she is the only settler who opts to stay in her own cabin rather than sheltering in the fort for safety. There, she remains with "her babes" and the protection of "one negro servant, a watch-dog, and half a dozen guns," while others are "forted-up" behind a twenty-foot log wall set in a surrounding trench. Juxtaposed against the temporary "horror of the fort life," Sawtelle conjures a second image of forced confinement that follows from a treaty Jean (naively, but in good faith) encourages the Indians to sign: "The government then sent teams, and removed the Indians, with all their household accouterments, to the reservation—dogs, ponies, guns, everything—one hundred and fifty miles away. When they started, they made the valleys ring with the same funeral chant that they make over the dead." Memorializing "that last howl that the Indians ever made in that Umpqua Valley," Sawtelle writes, "The march was terrible to them, leaving the homes that had been theirs through all time that their stories or memories could retain. Another, stronger—a white—race had dispossessed them."[36]

Yet for all its professed regret and concern for Indians, the larger arc of the novel is avidly pro-emigration; and, indeed, the copy of *The Heroine of '49* displayed in the Woman's Building Library carried an advertisement announcing that in Whatcom County, Washington, "there remains untaken considerable first-class public land which can be obtained for government price."[37] Although Jean declares herself "a marauder and foreigner in their country," and her "deep sympathy for them move[s] her to tears," her boosterism for her adopted region results in reduced railway fares implemented to swell the stream of migration to the Pacific Northwest. Superseding the images of confinement associated with the fort and the reservation, the railway, as in *Atalanta of the South*, serves as a vehicle of demographic shifts that ultimately will reinforce and perpetuate a racial hierarchy the novel vocally laments but tacitly endorses.[38]

The styles and structures of the three texts discussed here—*Atalanta in the South, Old 'Kaskia Days*, and *The Heroine of '49*—vary significantly, yet all three develop distinctly regionalist perspectives. Moreover, all three contend (not always successfully) with boundaries and divisions imposed by geographical features, political borders, social codes, and generic conventions. And, while all three narratives are rooted in specific regional landscapes, the fluidity of culture across time and the movement of people through space reveal the limits of the categories constructed to contain them. Finally, all three texts gesture toward the topic of immigration. The topic is rendered distant in *Atalanta* through the nimbus of romance, displaced onto a remote post in *'Kaskia,* and merely intimated in *Heroine* by the analogous trajectory of emigration across the Great Divide. Taken together, however, these texts suggest that in an era marked by sharp increases in immigration as well as emigration, regionalism provided potentially flexible, potentially adaptable ways of thinking about "fixed" social categories in the midst of cultural and demographic flux.[39]

In the Woman's Building Library as a whole, as in the texts discussed in this chapter, immigration is mostly submerged, nearly hidden beneath masses of texts that seem similarly distanced from the waves of immigrants that transformed the nation's cultural landscape. It would have taken keen eyes to spot amidst two thousand books in the New York collection Esther Jerman Baldwin's *Must the Chinese Go? An Examination of the Chinese Question* (1886). In this seventy-page pamphlet Baldwin accuses U.S. lawmakers of "knowingly and willfully, allowing for years the most constant, systematic persecution of the Chinese in our land, in defiance of treaty, law, and justice" and of passing anti-Chinese laws "at the bidding of the lowest, wickedest, most brutal, of our population." Further, she argues, "Anti-Chinese laws, and those who enacted them, are largely responsible for massacres and other outrages that have made so black a page in our national history the last few years."[40] Baldwin's rhetoric is powerful, her message urgent. With its direct appeal for political action, *Must the Chinese Go?* provides a crucial context for regionalist texts such as *Atalanta in the South* and *Wines and Vines of California* (1889), a "treatise on the ethics of wine drinking" in which BLM member Frona Eunice Wait presents as picturesque the picking of grapes by "a small army of Chinamen, garbed in their quaint many shirted costume."[41]

Documenting an analogous but underemphasized movement in which Anglo-Americans are the true "foreigners," several of the library's texts portray Spanish-speaking regions of the American West in which long-established Hispanic communities descend from a colonial past that predates Anglo-American emigration. In addition to Jackson's well-known novel *Ramona,* for example, Evelyn Raymond's juvenile novel *Monica, the Mesa Maiden* (1892) blurs the lines between immigration and emigration, foreign and domestic, nation and region, in its depiction of Mexican culture in Southern California (complete with Spanish vocabulary). In contrast, in Mary Harriott Norris's *Fräulein Minna; or, Life in a North American German Family* (1873), German immigrant life provides a means for the Anglo-American heroine to practice the German she learned in college and "Germanize" herself to advance her goal of studying music and literature in Germany. And, while many texts feature immigrant figures as servants, in Harriet Newell Kneeland Goff's *Other Fools and Their Doings* a German-Jewish South Carolinian risks his life in an effort to protect African Americans from a murderous mob.

Perhaps the text that best synthesizes these disparate strands—regionalism, emigration, immigration, and class—is the novel *Two Modern Women,* by Kate Gannett Wells, an antisuffragist who represented the National Alliance of Unitarian and Other Liberal Christian Women at the World's Congress of Representative Women. In this quintessential Columbian Women's text, Wells explores the intersecting lives of a young woman ordained as a Unitarian minister and the working-class daughter of a radical German labor organizer.[42] The novel's intertwined plotlines take us from an island off the coast of New England to the urban Northeast and, later, to a small Dakota town. The contrasts arising from these shifting settings create a tension that drives the narrative forward. As one young man in the novel says: "I don't care anything about the ism [meaning anarchism]; I only know that week after week I rebel when I come to this island and feel its beauty sinking down upon me and deadening all my earnestness . . . and I want to go into the city, where the air is stifling, and men and women are cursing and babies are dying and money is plenty and bread is wanting."[43] Engaging immigration, theological debates, the woman's movement, labor, and left-wing politics, *Two Modern Women* is a novel of ideas in the guise of a compelling family drama.

As in other regional texts surveyed in this chapter, Wells's novel is preoccupied with strained social barriers and the forces that breach them. In *Two Modern Women* the crisis is a shipwreck in which all but the steerage passengers are boarded onto lifeboats. In the midst of this catastrophe, in which class and caste are ruthlessly separated rather than united, Wells's affluent protagonists come to the aid of a helpless immigrant family. In Wells's scenario, where destructive forces in nature are compounded by human injustice, grace comes through individual sympathy, initiative, and sacrifice. Wells, as Mary M. Huth observes, was a moderate who supported most women's rights (though not suffrage) but feared social disruption. Her working-class protagonist similarly rejects radicalism and looks to "gradual improvement in the laws, upon increasing refinement and enlightenment of feeling, and upon the spontaneous unfolding of noble individualities to work out a social order. Liberty and sympathy were her antidotes for force or special legislation, as applied to classes of people."[44]

Complementing these works of fiction, a small number of nonfiction texts address immigrants more directly. These include an array of German-language publications, such as the newspaper *Texas Deutsche Zeitung* and *Das "Weisse Haus" Kochbuch* (1891), a translation of a popular cookbook and homemakers' guide first published in 1887, Florence Atkinson's *Economía é Higiene Doméstica de Appleton,* published in New York for Spanish-speakers, and a few publications authored by Jewish women for, or about, groups of immigrants, such as Simha Peixotto's scriptural texts designed "for the use of Hebrew children" and *The Poems of Emma Lazarus,* containing "The New Colossus," which ten years later would be chiseled on the pedestal of the Statue of Liberty to extend a "world-wide welcome" to the "huddled masses" arriving from other lands. In contrast to the abundance of regionalist fiction, these texts are barely discernible in the library, yet they too adumbrate seismic shifts in the ways Americans have imagined location, relocation, and resulting forms of community.

At the end of *The Heroine of '49* Sawtelle's protagonist is persuaded by Henry Ward Beecher to "use a pen and the press" to reach millions with her pleas for land reform and the rights of women. Recognizing the power of print as a means of advocacy, she resolves: "I will write for the people."[45] As the readings in this chapter suggest, the wide-ranging, loosely connected forms of regionalism in the Woman's Building Library reflect a parallel desire to "write for the people," with the dual implications of informing the people and giving them a voice. At the same time, the many varieties of regionalism housed in the library reveal—like the library itself—definitional tensions between "the people" and the individuals, groups, and undifferentiated masses that constitute the human aspect of regional—and national—identities.

Shelved amid the two thousand volumes in the library's New York section, a slim volume titled *Columbia's Emblem, Indian Corn: A Garland of Tributes in Prose and Verse* likely drew little attention from the passing multitudes. An eclectic anthology of photographs, poems, and prose excerpts, *Columbia's Emblem* was, as Mary W. Blanchard notes, Candace Wheeler's bid for a new national symbol. The book "contested the values of the fair," Blanchard writes, "by promoting a simple native plant, Indian corn, as our national emblem" and aimed "to redefine citizenship in terms congenial to the Aesthetic Movement." For Wheeler, as Blanchard contends, the Columbian Exposition afforded a chance to "re-write the myth of the West" from a feminist perspective that emphasized sustenance, traditional craftsmanship, and peace. "In a new and obliquely subversive manner," she concludes, "Wheeler integrated female Indian values into America's political dialogue just as she revised public icons to incorporate a domestic 'feminine' aesthetic."[46] In a less direct way, Wheeler's autobiography, *Yesterdays in a Busy Life,* retrospectively critiques the Eurocentrism, racism, and materialism the White City promoted. In a chapter devoted to the exposition, Wheeler tells of her work on the Woman's Building, the finished result of its completed, decorated halls (as well as its library), the World's Fair congresses, and, most vividly, the experience of walking through the exhibit halls amidst legions of visitors from all over the world.

In his Columbian Exposition address, Turner likened the frontier to "the outer edge of the wave," one manifestation of "the fluidity of American life." In a sense, as we argued in the previous chapter, the World's Fair was constructed as a frontier as well, "the meeting point between savagery and civilization," between Midway and White City.[47] "The White City depicted the millennial advancement of white civilization," Gail Bederman notes, "while the Midway Plaisance, in contrast, presented the undeveloped barbarism of uncivilized, dark races."[48] In Robert W. Rydell's terms, the White City was "a Utopian construct built upon racist assumptions," while on the other side of the boundary, the Midway portrayed "the tiers of mankind," in which "every race had its own permanent racial position," and all were "neatly categorized into the niches of a racial hierarchy."[49]

If on some levels—textual as well as organizational—the Woman's Building Library resisted the kinds of inflexible taxonomies reflected in the exposition's official constructs, as we have shown in earlier chapters, so, to an extent, did the flood of humanity that poured through its gates. In contrast to the fixed categories of the fair's organizational rubrics, the experience of "the people" amidst "the fluidity of American life"—"the stream of incident flowing through the six months of its existence," as John Coleman Adams wrote in 1896—worked against the relentless drive to codify and compartmentalize, to erect barriers and defend the resulting lines of division. Writing of the organizational bodies responsible for creating the official version of the "dream city," Bederman states, "Men and women of color . . . were not marginal but absent from the White City." Without question, this was largely true; yet "the human procession marching and countermarching in its avenues" tells a different story.[50]

In *Yesterdays in a Busy Life*, published twenty-five years after the fair, Candace Wheeler reflects on the strangely disorienting experience of seeing so many people of color not only within Midway exhibits but also among the crowds of the White City, where "there were so many beautiful things and so many beautiful human beings to look at!" "Among the most impressive," she recalled, were Native Americans, "whom one met in little companies everywhere. . . . [T]hese silent, well-bred beings walked together up and down the streets, or sat together in the assemblies, with an air of individual superiority." The ethnographically compartmentalized Midway and the universalizing spirit of the congresses evoke contrasting responses. For Wheeler, the Midway was "that place of wonder where all nations were gathered together—from the Mohammedan merchant with his rugs and brasses to the savage Africans of savage jungles, or the stillest and most bewildered Eskimos, all living their own lives." Opposed to these stereotyped images of commercialism, exoticized display, and social isolation, the congresses brought together "the wisdom of the wisest from all lands."[51]

Most impressive for Wheeler were the religious congresses, which made possible "actual communication with so many widely differing religious forms of belief, every one accepted by a large part of the world." In Wheeler's experience, "seeing the Greek bishops, and the English and American bishops, and Mohammedans and Buddhists walking and conversing together along the corridor of one of the great buildings—was like going up on a mountain-top." In sharp contrast to the "Puritan" indoctrination she had received as a child ("one faith, one right, one Church"), she concludes, "I saw that religion, the aspiration of the soul, was a common instead of a restricted heritage." Wheeler supposed that her experience "was that of thousands who were brought under the influence of the widening thought of the world congresses."[52] And, in the fair's exhibit halls, too, Wheeler encountered people of many races and cultures: "Brown people and black people and red people swarmed through our great halls, until those who were white looked simply faded-out human beings beside them," she marvels. "Indeed, I came to see that white is not a color in skin any more than in textiles, and if it had not quality, it had no value even for humanity. I saw that color in skin had a certain advantage in strength and warmth as a means of beauty."[53]

Wheeler's sense of having arrived at a new conception of value, a new aesthetic, and formulating a heightened understanding not only of "color in skin" but also of whiteness as a human characteristic lacking in "quality" and devoid of "value" is remarkable. In the context of a world's fair in which "whiteness" was reified while members of ethnic minorities were relentlessly degraded and systematically excluded, Wheeler's altered perspective marks a moment of epiphany as she observes individuals of other races not as "Types of the Midway" (as guidebooks hawked) but as human beings and fellow visitors equal in dignity within the fair's bastion of whiteness. As a "Puritan" child of the early nineteenth century, Wheeler had learned to associate personal beauty with sinfulness, guilt, even death. In her autobiography she recalls how as a young child, upon overhearing her mother describe her as "a pretty thing," she had wonderingly contrasted her own pink-cheeked reflection with the faces she had considered most beautiful: those of dead children awaiting burial, seemingly refined by their ethereal pallor and beatified in death. "I liked the little face I saw [in the glass], but it was not beautiful like the small white faces we were sometimes taken to see when a neighbor's child had died and was laid, like a precious thing, in a satin-lined coffin," she writes. "I wished I could be white and beautiful as they were, and thought their tiny frost-white hands, with fingers folded into one another, the prettiest things I had ever seen. I used to smooth back the blood in my own small pink fingers and fold them together to make them look like theirs."[54]

Tracing her life's journey from a provincial Puritan childhood to the Columbian Exposition, where the Woman's Building Library was her crowning achievement, Wheeler's autobiography thus moves between two opposing images of beauty—the whiteness of death and the color of life. In doing so, the text implicitly contrasts the Puritanical construction of physical comeliness as sinful with the Aestheticist equation of beauty with goodness. Wheeler, as Blanchard notes, regarded color as a both a "unifier" and "a uniquely American instinct." ("This colorgift belongs to us as a people," she wrote.) It was with regard to decorative arts, not race, that she praised "the national instinct for color"; yet her response to the "swarm" of people of all complexions at the Columbian Exposition—"all the outlandish people, and all the beautiful people"—blurs the boundaries between these categories and suggests that in a social sense, too, the "colorgift" constitutes a potentially unifying force.[55] Ostensibly, perhaps, her response is only "skin deep." Yet given the thoroughness with which she integrated aesthetic values with a progressive social vision, her reflections verge on profound revelation. As James Clifford remarks in "Museums as Contact Zones," "Even encounters that are ethnocentric—which they all are to some degree—can produce reflection and cultural critique."[56]

"Through the simple expedient of demonizing and reifying the range of color on a palette, American Africanism makes it possible to say and not say, to inscribe and erase, to escape and engage, to act out and act on, to historicize and render timeless," writes Toni Morrison in *Playing in the Dark*. "It provides a way of contemplating chaos and civilization, desire and fear, and a mechanism for testing the problems and blessings of freedom."[57] For Wheeler, expanding "the range of color on a palette" seems to enable a radically different "way of contemplating chaos and civilization"—a way that sees through the elaborate devices erected to contain social differences and scaffold the straining, artificial barriers between classes, races, and ethnicities threatened alike by the "flood" of humanity, with its "waves" of immigration, and the twofold "gulf" of segregation and racial mixing. This is hardly surprising, given Wheeler's cultural politics. In questioning the value of "whiteness," her reminiscence, like the regionalist narratives of Elliott, Holbrook, Sawtelle, and many other women represented in the Woman's Building Library, confronts the "vast contending forces" that continually work to erode and dismantle unstable social divisions.[58]

As the analysis in this chapter suggests, in practice (if not in theory) regionalism, paradoxically, tended to work against the White City's reliance on social and spatial categorization with its strict definitions of inside and outside, center and margins, inclusion and exclusion. Regionalism offered some writers a means of engaging with social types and taxonomies in ways that at least implicitly acknowledged their flexibility and fluidity. In Morrison's terms, its "palette" of possibilities provided "a mechanism for testing the problems and blessings of freedom." For library visitors, too, the regionalist mode of display may have facilitated the kind of open response Macdonald and Silverstone anticipate in "Rewriting the Museum's Fictions" in connection with the "undermining of categories" and "the loosening of constraints" on traditional "collection-based" exhibits."[59] Inadvertently perhaps, rather than by administrative design, the Woman's Building Library opened itself up to alternative interpretations rather than promoting a single grand narrative. Defined by regions, shaped by difference, and filled with stories that rewrite the fictions of the past, the library invited visitors from all over the country and all over the world to inscribe its expansive, diverse, variegated collection with a "fictional" coherence of their own construction.

Epilogue

The World's Columbian Exposition officially ended on October 30, 1893, but the celebratory potential for closing ceremonies was significantly dampened by the assassination of Chicago's mayor, Carter H. Harrison, two days earlier.[1] During its six-month run, the fair clocked 27 million admissions. Although it was international in scope, a focused emphasis on American agriculture, industry, technology, and the arts (both popular and high) functioned on a grand scale as a rite of passage demonstrating that the United States had come of age. The fair itself exemplified a new urban-industrial order that thrived on corporate capitalism and mass consumption. It also occasioned a growing sense of nationalism, made manifest in the establishment of Columbus Day and the adoption of the Pledge of Allegiance.

When the fair closed, no one could argue that women had not been an important component of its success. They had accounted for half the clerical work (25,000 stenographers, typists, and press), managed half the exhibits, decorated many of the buildings with frescoes and statuary, and staffed resting rooms and nurseries for children. They managed a mending booth where fairgoers could have clothing repaired, a "remedies" booth where they could go for minor ills, and an information booth where an attendant could direct them to the cheapest luncheon on the grounds or a place to check their coats for the day. Twenty-five women served as guides "to escort the more timid and unknowing lady viewers about the Exposition." And in the middle of all this, the Woman's Building had functioned as one of twelve major buildings at the fair.[2]

With a nod to an idealized communal past, Candace Wheeler summarized her feelings about the Woman's Building in an 1895 article for *Architectural Record*. "The overwhelming value of the arts in sisterhood," she wrote, "has probably never since the centuries of the antique world been so fully demonstrated." Reports of other buildings showed that although women were well represented throughout the fair (for example, 19 percent of exhibits in the Transportation Building were by women, 25 percent in Fisheries, and 46 percent in Horticulture), when they met overt sexual discrimination anywhere on the grounds they found in the Woman's Building additional opportunities to display their work.[3] Mrs. Whiting S. Clark, an Iowa delegate on the Board of Lady Managers (BLM), said that a letter she received from women of her state who had attended the fair "show[s] that the recognition" accorded women's work in the Woman's Building "has been the greatest possible advantage." Because they "amply proved what they can do when banded together," Alice Freeman Palmer announced, "women may now the more easily cease to treat themselves as a peculiar people. Henceforth they are human beings." The official *History of the World's Fair* concluded, "It will be a long time before such an aggregation of woman's work, as may now be seen in the Woman's Building, can be gathered from all parts of the world again." Marietta Holley's Samantha declares as she approaches the fairgrounds for the first time, "I will go first to the place my proud heart has dwelt on ever sence the Fair wuz opened—I will go first to the Woman's Buildin'."[4]

And female fairgoers took the fair home with them in many ways. Hundreds (perhaps thousands) pasted fair mementoes into their scrapbooks; some constructed scrapbooks devoted solely to their World's Fair visit. Others appropriated the Exposition for political reasons. Members of the Equal Rights Association of Massilon, Ohio, who had attended the exposition spent part of their September 1893 monthly meeting reading from works they knew were housed in the Woman's Building Library.[5] As a physical entity, the library reminded all who entered that thousands of women had written many thousands of books and articles to inform and entertain countless people over the centuries since Columbus came to the New World. Its collection—and the shelf-list that documented it—established a baseline for the future study of women and women's writing.

Still, not everyone was impressed. On her second day at the fair, R. S. Dix visited the Woman's Building. "Ninety-nine out of every hundred" who viewed the exhibits, she declared, would conclude that women were best at needlework: "We've known this since the time of Eve." Dix thought it "unfortunate that the really creditable work exhibited there (notably the Library)" was "so placed that they are noticed largely because they are in competition with masses of at least indifferent work."[6] Women of color, immigrants, and the lower socioeconomic classes had even less reason to be effusive, since conditions unique to their circumstances had not received much attention. The Woman's Building did not visibly participate in Colored People's Day, August 25, when exposition officials provided two thousand free watermelons to boost attendance. The Woman's

Building and its library may have helped advance women's suffrage and other feminist causes in the United States, but these benefits applied unevenly across the demographic spectrum. For white middle- and upper-class women, the fair manifested an increased freedom, validated their progress, and documented their contributions throughout history. For most others it was nearly silent.

While new organizations such as the National Council of Jewish Women and the Congress of Mothers traced their origins to discussions held in Chicago in the summer of 1893, some other organizations formed because they had not been asked to participate in Woman's Building activities. In part because they were given such a chilly reception by the BLM, several African American women began a national newspaper in 1895 titled *Woman's Era* and organized the National Association of Colored Women the following year.

As the fair wound down, Mary Lockwood's Press Committee issued its final report on the library. Total costs, it noted, were $2,822.38, and almost half of that sum ($1,391) was for labor necessary to catalog the collection. All U.S. books had been cataloged except the New York collection (which had come to the fair already cataloged), and all foreign books had been cataloged except the collections from Germany, Holland, Belgium, and Norway.[7] All together, Edith Clarke and her associates cataloged four thousand volumes at the rate of 23 cents per volume (much less than the 35 cents per volume cataloging services usually cost). The results of the work, "besides the satisfaction of the thousands of visitors," were evident in a card catalog of authors "now on exhibition, containing between 8,000 and 9,000 cards, and comprising 19 different languages. This is to be the permanent catalog of the Woman's Library, to go with it to the quarters in the Woman's Memorial Building."[8]

The BLM had agreed at a July 31 meeting "to establish a fund for the purpose of erecting a permanent memorial building" in Chicago ("a monument to women as a factor in all development," Sallie Cotten wrote in her diary), into which the library collection would be placed. The BLM had already raised $30,000 from the sale of commemorative coins, to which Bertha Palmer added her $9,000 salary as the board's president. In August, *Woman's Journal* noted that the "forthcoming catalogue" of the library collection would constitute a "bibliography of women's writings." Within weeks newspapers began reporting the BLM's intention to create a permanent library. On October 27, the BLM Executive Committee resolved to appoint Mary Lockwood a committee of one "to take charge of the books in this Library" and return those that had been requested by their lenders. The resolution was adopted.[9]

On October 26 a committee of the New York Board of Women Managers met in Chicago to plan how best to repack and ship New York's exhibits. At a later meeting it was noted that "before the packers were allowed to touch them they were carefully listed and checked off by our secretary." By October 31 the print collections had been boxed and shipped; by November 5 the last of the exhibits had been delivered to the express company that would transport them home.[10] At a meeting on November 17, the Executive Committee of the New York board approved compensation of $105 for the items stolen from Imogen Howard's exhibit, agreed to sell the leaded glass in the library to Candace Wheeler, and authorized Blanche Bellamy to invite Empire State women who were instrumental in building New York's collection "to visit the State Library . . . and see installed there the exhibit of books which had come from the library of the Woman's Building."[11]

In mid-November Palmer began thanking international committees for their efforts; she especially thanked those committees that had donated their collections for a library in a permanent building still to be constructed. To the president of the Swedish Women's Committee, who had recently donated her country's collection, Palmer wrote, "This valuable collection will be given due prominence in the Library of the Permanent Building, and will be an evidence of the union between us and our sisters in your far distant country, who are doing such an honor to their sex."[12]

Palmer also kept a close eye on awards, about which she was particularly sensitive. Section 6 of the enabling legislation for the exposition, which authorized the BLM, extended to it what one of its leaflets called "the great and unusual privilege of appointing members of each jury to award prizes for articles into which women's work enter."[13] Although the BLM had adopted a resolution on October 19, 1892, to have the exhibits on display at the Woman's Building reviewed by the awards juries, the exposition's commissioners did not initially consider that the Woman's Building would contain exhibits. After October 1892, however, the BLM acquired hundreds of exhibits by women—especially from foreign countries—for which no space elsewhere on the grounds could be found. But the commissioners resisted placing women on committees to judge awards, which had $700,000 to distribute to winning exhibits.[14]

Not until April 5, 1893 (and only after much prompting), did exposition commissioners recognize the Woman's Building "as one of the exhibit buildings of the Exposition," thus qualifying it for juried awards. In addition, the commissioners agreed to empower the BLM to appoint members to sit on the juries that would vote on prizes for women's exhibits, but to maintain close control of money allocated to juries they insisted that their numbers "shall be in proportion of such exhibits." Commissioners then reserved the right to determine "said number." Palmer protested loudly and, ultimately, successfully. On July 1 the *Daily Columbian* noted that the commission had "practically ceded everything the Board of Lady Managers have asked in regard to women judges."[15]

"Mrs. Palmer has shown her usual sagacity in freeing her board from the unnecessary surveillance of a national committee," the *Chicago Herald* reported. "Hitherto all expenses of the woman's board relating to awards have had to be approved by the chairman of the Committee on Awards, John Boyd Thacher, who never approved women judges at all, and who has been churlish from the beginning toward those appointed under that provision of the law." The *Herald* accused Thacher of attempting "to get a considerable slice of the woman's proportion of the appropriation applied on the expenses of his own office," but pointed out that Palmer successfully defeated his efforts.[16]

Palmer's victory for the BLM had its drawbacks, however. In July and August, 1893, several BLM members launched a lengthy and rancorous public debate over who should sit on juries and how awards should be determined. After observing the first dispute on July 21, Sallie Cotten fretted, "I hope we will not disgrace womanhood in our debates." Three weeks later she noted in her diary: "I do not think the cause of women have been materially advanced by this session, although we have appointed women jurors to act jointly with men, to do the same work and receive the same compensation. This is a great work and marks an era in women's progress." She worried, however, that the "petty personal differences forced upon [the BLM]—have really had a tendency to lower our standing as a body of advanced intelligent women working honestly for a specified object."[17] Not until the BLM approved the request of Virginia Meredith, chair of the Committee on Awards, to dismiss the committee's secretary did the dispute end.

By that time Meredith had asked Melvil Dewey for the names of "two women who would be competent to act as judges of the Library and kindred exhibits in the Columbian Exposition." Dewey recommended Ellen Coe, Mary S. Cutler, Mary W. Plummer, Hannah P. James, Theresa West of the Milwaukee Public Library, and J. S. R. James of the People's Palace Library in London. But Cutler was "too closely connected with me," he said, and although Plummer, as director of the Pratt Library School, was "specially fitted for this work," he ultimately concluded that "if you want only two you can not do better than the English and the American Miss James."[18]

Shortly after the fair closed, Palmer began a campaign to award medals to Woman's Building artists and exhibitors. She was especially concerned about the library. To Susan Gale Cooke she wrote, "I should like a medal to go to the member of the Committee in every country who collected and sent to us the books from its women." She indicated she had placed Janet Jennings of Washington, D.C., in charge, and that she had authorized Jennings to open any boxes to examine the collections. "The Librarian, of course, must care for them during and repack them after this examination."[19]

But as the Committee on Awards began informing her about its decisions, Palmer complained that it was not judging the library "in a very satisfactory way." At first she objected to Thacher's decisions, which she said were "not in accordance" with her understanding. That Thacher wanted to award a medal to Italy for its collection seemed to Palmer "a burlesque" and an insult to Alice Howard Cady, who had done all the work. She also wanted a "separate award for the statistics which were shown in the Record Rooms adjoining the Library." And Palmer was irritated that the Awards Committee had overlooked the contributions of Michigan and Maine, and those of Countess Superunda, head of Spain's committee, who was personally responsible for one of the four collections of books Spain sent to the library. Since the other three received awards, Palmer said, it would be a "marked discourtesy" not to acknowledge her, "as it was at her instigation and under her authority that the other collections were made."[20]

On June 18, 1894, Palmer detailed her concerns to Jennings. "In some instances individual books have received awards"—which Palmer did not want—"and in other cases the award has been given to collections"—which she did want. She told Jennings she had been informed that the library should merit "fifteen or twenty [awards] for the collection." ("I rather fancy that would cover the collections," she wrote, "but in case it does not, I want to boldly demand all that are necessary without any attention to this limitation.") She also said the BLM Executive Committee was counting on Jennings to submit a report it could take to the national commission to justify them.[21]

By the end of July, Palmer was satisfied with the Awards Committee's final decisions, which eventually extended to over fifteen hundred women exhibitors who had displayed their work in the Woman's Building and across the exposition grounds. The African American exhibit received an award; the New York delegation won an award for its decoration of the library; Dora Wheeler Keith won a separate award for her ceiling painting. On April 26, 1894, Virginia Meredith told Dewey that the ALA would receive a Diploma of Honorable Mention for its efforts on the library's behalf.[22]

On January 1, 1894, the Chicago Park Board assumed responsibility for the grounds and opened them to the public. Exactly one week later, a fire destroyed the Music Hall and several adjacent buildings. Six months later a much bigger fire consumed the Machinery, Administration, Mines and Mining, Agriculture, Manufactures, and Electricity buildings. Decorative ornaments from the Woman's Building, which had been stored in the Electricity Building, went up in flames. Except for the Fine Arts Building (which the city converted into the Field Columbian Museum with a substantial grant from Marshall Field), the remaining structures were razed or relocated by the spring of 1896.

Candace Wheeler submitted her final report for the Committee on the Decoration and Furnishing of the Library to the New York board on January 17, 1894. The committee had been allocated $5,000 but had spent $5,300.87. This sum was reduced by a rebate from sales of $916, which brought it below the original appropriation. The New York Executive Committee then moved to have its collection located in "a permanent place" in the State Library. It also requested that the state purchase Dora Wheeler Keith's ceiling painting for $2,500 and display it in the State Library with the collection.

The committee then asked Imogen Howard to report on the African American exhibit. "As I am not chairman of a standing committee," she demurred, "I did not expect to be called upon." She said she regretted not having sufficient time to assemble a complete display but felt rewarded for her efforts. Although she did not say so, the exhibit she had constructed represented the largest exhibit any African American managed to display at the fair. Speaking of the women who had contributed to the exhibit, she said, "It was an education to me, truly, being a member of that race, that even with the small amount of means at their command, they were trying hard to build themselves." She especially commended the black women of the South, who labored under trying circumstances. "One case in point which would be looked upon as being unique," she mentioned, "was that of a colored woman who had become a doctor of dental surgery." In its final report, the board commended her for accomplishing "her several tasks as only a woman with remarkable energy and executive ability could." The New York Board of General Managers called Howard's exhibit "one of the most interesting and instructive exhibits of the fair," noting that it illustrated "the results of the education of the women of the Afro-American race."[23]

On March 10 Palmer asked Ellen Coe to "write a little report of the library for publication." She wanted a "short sketch giving your idea of the collection," especially paying attention to "points of excellence, and different subjects upon which women have written well and authoritatively." She said she had heard from others that Coe had given "very interesting" talks to visitors during June, and she wondered whether Coe would not structure her report "in the same style as these talks." Coe accepted Palmer's invitation, and Palmer asked her to complete her report "by the time the History Committee meets May 8th." If Coe ever completed the report, no copy has been found. On May 4, Palmer met with Clarke to tell her "to begin the compilation" of the library catalog.[24] Eventually, Clarke issued a printed bibliography arranged by state and country, and alphabetically by author's surname within each group. Each entry contained only the author's last name and an abbreviated title. It was better than nothing, but it must have been a disappointment to Clarke and other women who had worked so hard to document the authors and works represented in the collection.[25]

The Executive Committee of the New York board met for the last time in Albany on May 22, 1894. At that meeting Blanche Bellamy announced that she had formed a permanent committee to "continue the work of obtaining books published each year by the women authors of the State." The committee also read a letter from Mary Trautmann about the plaster frieze in the Woman's Building Library. Several BLM members, Trautmann reported, wanted pieces of the frieze "as mementos." The Executive Committee agreed and gave "permission to the National Board to make such use of the frieze as it desires." The Executive Committee also resolved to visit the State Library after the meeting concluded, inspect the women's collections, and request that records generated by the New York Board be made part of the permanent exhibit.[26]

Six days later the BLM's Executive Committee approved a resolution by Mary Lockwood to make application to Chicago's Newberry Library for a room to house the collection that remained until the BLM could find permanent quarters. One member said that the Field Museum had initially offered a room but later had to withdraw the offer because the museum needed the space itself. With no other possibilities to consider, the committee voted in favor of Lockwood's motion.[27]

Hopes for a permanent Woman's Memorial Building and library never materialized—despite the existence of a fund for the purpose and promises from Bertha and Potter Palmer to contribute $200,000 to its construction. New York and New Jersey withdrew their collections from the Woman's Building Library shortly after the exposition closed. As we have seen, the former would go to the State Library in Albany, where it became "the nucleus of a permanent and growing exhibit of the literary activity of New York women . . . separated from the rest of the library as a distinct section." Because the State Library allocated no funds for the collection, growth came only through donation.[28] The collection was destroyed in the fire that swept through the State Library in 1911. Some other states had also planned to take their book collections back after the fair to donate to state historical societies and other repositories.[29]

The four thousand volumes that remained in Chicago after the exposition closed began a peripatetic existence. They were initially stored at the Newberry (the Woman's Building was gradually demolished over a two-and-a-half-year period), and shortly thereafter moved to the Chicago Public Library, where they remained until 1933, when the Chicago Public Library mounted an exhibit of two thousand titles from the Woman's Building Library for the International Conclave of Women Writers held in the city. Northwestern University Library director Theodore Koch then acquired this collection, renamed it the

Biblioteca Femina, and solicited the Chicago Public Library for the remaining World's Fair books. When Koch died in 1941, all of the Biblioteca Femina books were incorporated into Northwestern University Library collections.[30] Sometime between 1894 and 1941, the card catalog Edith Clarke and her colleagues worked so hard to complete disappeared. Most likely the cards had been removed from the catalog case (which was probably put to use elsewhere), and the cards themselves discarded as the collection moved from one site to another.

In 1895 the city of Atlanta hosted the Cotton States and International Exposition, which also contained a Woman's Building. It was one of seven fairs sponsored by various cities in the South between 1881 and 1907 to stimulate a moribund regional economy. The 150-by-128-foot two-story structure had a small library in a room just off a central rotunda on the second floor. Like its predecessor in Chicago, it displayed "many photographs of prominent women writers," and recreated a homelike atmosphere by installing "the handsomest and latest style of library draperies in leather and panels of the same for decoration." Unlike its predecessor, however, the Atlanta facility sought to "exhibit a model library in actual working order." And although it boasted a collection of female authors "from every State and some of the foreign countries," the volumes included numbered just over six hundred. The library was intended to "show to the world the Progress women have made in every branch of literature." Visitors were invited to consult "the complete catalogue of books, illustrated with photos of many familiar and favorite writers."[31]

The Atlanta exposition also hosted a "Negro Department," put together by African Americans from the South to demonstrate progress since emancipation. According to Irvine Garland Penn, who was named the head of the Negro Department, African Americans seized the opportunity provided by the exposition's invitation as "our opportunity to again seek what we wanted at Chicago." (As one of the contributors to *The Reason Why the Colored American Is Not in the Columbian Exposition,* Penn spoke from experience.) The 25,000-square-foot building, which "next to the Woman's Department . . . was the most sought after by visitors," housed scores of exhibits arranged by state. Most reflected pride in the kind of skilled labor Booker T. Washington advocated. It was here that Washington delivered his famous "Atlanta Compromise" speech. Although there was no separate library to demonstrate a "thin, long line" of African American authors linking the past to the present, many institutions of higher education, including Fisk University, Claflin University, the Hampton Institute, Morgan College, Spelman Seminary, and Clark College, featured "literary departments." The Tuskegee Institute exhibited items constructed on its campus, including "furniture of all sorts for bedroom, library, parlor, and kitchen."[32]

A number of expositions followed in the early twentieth century, including the 1900 Exposition Universelle in Paris, which included the American Negro Exhibit, for which Daniel Murray of the Library of Congress compiled the 271-item *Preliminary List of Books and Pamphlets by Negro Authors.* The object of Murray's effort was "to secure a copy of every book and pamphlet in existence, by a Negro Author."[33] Buffalo, New York, hosted a Pan-American Exposition in 1901 designed to encourage trade between the United States and Latin America. Today it is remembered mostly as the event at which President William McKinley was shot. St. Louis was much more successful with its 1904 Louisiana Purchase International Exposition, which covered nearly twice the acreage of the Columbian Exposition and drew 20 million visitors. The St. Louis fair included a Woman's Building, but the facility was used only for social activities and administrative offices. Following other efforts in cities like San Francisco (1915) and Philadelphia (1926), Chicago tried again in 1933, in part to celebrate its centennial. At none of these exhibitions, however, did women play as prominent a role as they had in 1893. World's fairs between 1876 and 1915 did reflect a shift from gender segregation to integration, however, and from identification of women as a group to women as individuals. The Woman's Building Library at the Columbian Exposition played a significant role in that shift. By pursuing a separatist strategy, the Board of Lady Managers made a number of achievements possible for the advancement of women. By the end of the twentieth century, however, world's fairs had lost their popularity to other kinds of heterotopias—especially sporting events and theme parks.[34]

At the final ceremony closing the Woman's Building on October 31, 1893, Bertha Palmer highlighted the evanescent, fairy-tale quality of the Columbian Exposition. "When our palace in the White City shall have vanished like a dream, when grass and flowers cover the beautiful spot where it now stands," she said, "its memory and influence will still remain with those who have been brought together within its walls."[35] As a heterotopia, or "other space," the Columbian Exposition bore a complex relationship to the real world of 1893—and that complexity must be addressed in any thoughtful reading of the fair's meaning and impact. Further complicating historical analysis of the fair's exhibits is the large number of individual people and components contributing to them. But if the contrarieties of the heterotopia, on one hand, and the multiplicity of viewpoints, on the other, preclude simple conclusions, they also highlight the intensity of the experience for fair visitors and the extensiveness of the experiences represented there. Both contributed to the lasting significance of the World's Columbian Exposition generally, and the Woman's Building Library specifically. Without doubt, the library demonstrated the kind of "expansion of the range of things that can happen in museums and museum-like settings" that James Clifford associates with contact zones.[36]

Like its predecessor in 1876, the Woman's Building showed women to be active contributors in all their endeavors and united the suffragists and domestic reformers under one roof. The Columbian Exposition was marked by a desire to construct a closer balance between women's private and public lives, and at the same time to profile contributions women were making in the public sphere. As a result, the BLM used the 1893 congresses to focus on social work, child care, teaching, and home economics, all considered professional endeavors well within women's sphere but conducted in public. (Ironically, women as librarians received scant attention.) Having separate space in which to cultivate this balance also fostered gender solidarity and an enlarged sense of womanhood, and facilitated on a very large scale the kind of female institution building and networking that women's clubs across the country had undertaken in the late nineteenth century.[37] The library constituted a record of a public sphere, manifesting an increased democracy for some women, newly included, but at the same time silently imposing boundaries outside of which others continued to reside. Yet despite obvious class, race, and nativist biases, women who visited the Woman's Building probably came away with an enhanced sense of achievement and inclusion in the public sphere.

The Woman's Building Library contributed to that sense of accomplishment and belonging. As a collection produced by women and judged by "a jury of woman's peers," the library presents a richly detailed cameo of the culture of print constructed, in large part, by participants in the late nineteenth-century women's club movement (a movement Estelle Freedman calls "one of the largest manifestations of 'social feminism' at the time").[38] Clubwomen had invested enormously in an ideology of literacy that promised to improve life for women materially and emotionally, and the library constituted a foundational footing for that ideology. In addition, it demonstrated historically the "textual alliances" clubwomen in the 1890s experienced personally.[39]

The intense emotional and intellectual connection fostered by the social nature of reading that clubwomen had experienced at home was easily transferred to the Woman's Building Library, even though the BLM did not grant visitors permission to pull volumes from the shelves and leaf through the pages. The library's mere existence allowed women to revisit familiar experiences and project them across the miles and through the ages. Many visitors to the library undoubtedly sensed an imagined community that the titles lining the bookshelves facilitated, one bound to some extent by time and geography but to an even greater extent by gender. Equally important, the library represented an unprecedented landmark in the charting of women's literature as a vital cultural enterprise. Although the range and diversity of texts and authors represented precluded any universalizing summation of its contents, the library, in true heterotopic fashion, contained visual and textual elements that critiqued the Columbian Exposition's dominant vision of advancing industrial modernism. At the same time, the celebration of women's important role in international print culture, together with an anticanonical inclusiveness that validated the work of thousands of little-known women writers, conveyed a powerful message to the women who visited the library. Surveying the contents of its shelves, these women could join Marietta Holley in declaring, with mingled wonder, humility, and pride, "Right here I see my own books."[40]

Abbreviations

The following abbreviations are used for archival sources cited frequently in the notes.

BLM Papers   World's Columbian Exposition, Board of Lady Managers Records. Archives and Manuscripts Department, Chicago History Museum.

BWM Papers   New York Board of Women Managers Executive Committee Papers. In World's Columbian Exposition, Board of Lady Managers Records. Archives and Manuscripts Department, Chicago History Museum.

Dewey Papers   Melvil Dewey Papers. Rare Books and Manuscripts Collection, Columbia University.

Logan Papers   John Alexander Logan Family Papers. Manuscripts Division, Library of Congress.

Notes

Introduction

1. Elaine Showalter, *A Jury of Her Peers: American Women Writers from Anne Bradstreet to Annie Proulx* (New York: Knopf, 2009), xiv.

2. Margaret J. M. Ezell, *Writing Women's Literary History* (Baltimore: Johns Hopkins University Press, 1993), 164.

3. "American Publishers' Exhibits at the World's Fair," *Critic*, July 1, 1893, 7–10. According to a report of the Board of Lady Managers, 50 percent of the "new works" on display in the Houghton Mifflin exhibit were by Massachusetts women. Mary Lockwood, undated report, box 8, vol. 23, BLM Papers.

4. Moses P. Handy, *The Official Directory of the World's Columbian Exposition, May 1st to October 30th, 1893* (Chicago: W. B. Conkey, 1893), 181.

5. Boys generally identified "fighting books" as the most exciting, girls "stories and poetry." Young adults who responded named George Eliot's *The Mill on the Floss* as their favorite. Jeanne Madeline Weimann, *The Fair Women: The Story of the Woman's Building, World's Columbian Exposition, Chicago, 1893* (Chicago: Academy Chicago, 1981), 344–45; Tudor Jenks, *The Century World's Fair Book for Boys and Girls* (New York: Century, [1893], 102–3.

6. *World's Columbian Exposition Illustrated*, November 1892, 234.

7. Bates quoted in Weimann, *Fair Women*, 345. From the sale of souvenirs, the Children's Building eventually turned a profit of $17,715 for the Board of Lady Managers. See Weimann, *Fair Women*, 352. On children's literature in the Woman's Building Library, see Anne Lundin, "Little Pilgrim's Progress: Literary Horizons for Children's Literature," *Libraries & Culture* 41.1 (Winter 2006): 133–52.

8. Information taken from Caroline Garland, "Some of the Libraries at the Exposition," *Library Journal* 18 (August 1893): 284–88. See also Weimann, *Fair Women*, 354.

9. Aside from one chapter of Weimann's *Fair Women* and a special volume of essays in *Libraries & Culture* (41.1), the library of the Woman's Building—the first international, comprehensive collection of women's texts ever attempted—has, until now, largely escaped scrutiny. Bernice E. Gallagher's comprehensive *Illinois Women Novelists in the Nineteenth Century: An Analysis and Annotated Bibliography* (Urbana: University of Illinois Press, 1994) isolates Illinois's contribution to the Woman's Building Library, as documented in the *Official Catalogue of the Illinois Woman's Exposition Board*. A few literary historians have studied

the relationship between the dominant themes of world's fairs and the themes addressed in American literature of the period. See Gwen Young Benson, "The Façade and the Reality: World's Fairs Celebrate Progress and Unity While American Novelists Reveal Social Disparity and Individual Isolation" (Ph.D. diss., Oklahoma State University, 1997); and Joseph Claude Murphy, "Exposing the Modern: World's Fairs and American Literary Culture, 1853–1907" (Ph.D. diss., University of Pennsylvania, 1997).

10. Estelle Freedman, "Separatism as Strategy: Female Institution Building and American Feminism, 1870–1930," *Feminist Studies* 5.3 (1979): 513–14. "The achievements of feminism at the turn of the century," Freedman observes, "came less through gaining access to male domains of politics and the professions than in the tangible form of building separate female institutions" (514). Drawing on the views of Elizabeth Cady Stanton and Susan B. Anthony, Freedman identifies 1870 to 1930 as a "transition period" between the separate-spheres ideology of the earlier nineteenth century and the era of the "New Woman": "It was an era of separate female organization and institution building, the result on the one hand, of the negative push of discrimination in the public, male sphere, and on the other hand, of the positive attraction of the female world of close, personal relationships and domestic institutional structures" (517).

11. Mary Newbury Adams, "Mothers of Literature," in *The Columbian Woman*, ed. Mrs. Rollin A. Edgerton (Chicago, 1893), 8. On antimodernism as an important cultural context, see T. J. Jackson Lears, *No Place of Grace: Antimodernism and the Transformation of American Culture, 1880–1920* (1982; repr., Chicago: University of Chicago Press, 1994).

12. Michel Foucault, "Texts/Contexts: Of Other Spaces," trans. Jay Miskowiec, in *Grasping the World: The Idea of the Museum*, ed. Donald Preziosi and Claire Farago (Aldershot, England: Ashgate, 2004), 374. This essay is also available in *Diacritics* 16.1 (Spring 1986): 22–27.

13. All quotations in this paragraph are from Foucault, "Texts/Contexts," 376–78, except "all women's writing from everywhere and every time," from Weimann, *Fair Women*, 355.

14. Alan Trachtenberg, *The Incorporation of America: Culture and Society in the Gilded Age* (New York: Hill and Wang, 1982), 231.

15. Candace Wheeler, *Yesterdays in a Busy Life* (New York: Harper and Brothers, 1918), 347. For more on Wheeler see chapter 1. On the White City as an "ideal city" purged of "the blot and failure of modern civilization," see John Coleman Adams, "What a Great City Might Be—A Lesson from the White City," in *The American 1890s: A Cultural Reader*, ed. Susan Harris Smith and Melanie Dawson (Durham, N.C.: Duke University Press, 2000), 389–96.

16. James Clifford, "Museums as Contact Zones," in *Representing the Nation: A Reader: Histories, Heritage and Museums*, ed. David Boswell and Jessica Evans (London: Routledge, 1999), 439, 438, 551. Implicitly opposed to the museum as heterotopia, Clifford argues that "it is inadequate to portray museums as collections of universal culture, repositories of uncontested value, sites of progress, discovery and the accumulation of human, scientific, or national patrimonies" (451). On contact zones see also Mary Louise Pratt, *Imperial Eyes: Travel Writing and Transculturation* (London: Routledge, 1992).

17. To advance future research, we have published online the database of U.S. works that we used to analyze the contents of the Woman's Building Library at Rutgers University, (http://1893.rutgers.edu). A second database, containing the foreign titles in the library, is currently under construction through ePublications@Marquette (http://epublications .marquette.edu).

1. By Invitation Only

1. Meredith to "American Library Association, Exhibitor in the Columbian Exposition," June 23, 1893; Dewey to Meredith, June 26, 1893, box 3, Dewey Papers.

2. Candace Wheeler, *Principles of Home Decoration, with Practical Examples* (New York: Doubleday, Page, 1903), 199–200.

3. Candace Wheeler, *Yesterdays in a Busy Life* (New York: Harper and Brothers, 1918), 344–45.

4. Maud Howe Elliott, ed., *Art and Handicraft in the Woman's Building of the World's Columbian Exposition, Chicago, 1893* (Paris: Goupil, 1893), 39.

5. Quoted in Jeanne Madeline Weimann, *The Fair Women: The Story of the Woman's Building, World's Columbian Exposition, Chicago, 1893* (Chicago: Academy Chicago, 1981), 357, 371. See also "Woman's Work in the Fine Arts," *Art Amateur*, June 1893, 10.

6. Ellen M. Henrotin, "An Outsider's View of the Women's Exhibit," *Cosmopolitan* 15 (September 1893): 561; "Editor's Outlook: The Queens of the World's Fair," *Chautauquan* 17.4 (July 1893): 474. Cooke and *New York Times* comments quoted in Weimann, *Fair Women*, 373.

7. "World's Fair Letter," *Woman's Tribune* 10 (November 4, 1893), 188. The autograph collection was loaned by Mr. and Mrs. John Boyd Thacher of Albany, New York.

8. Wheeler, *Yesterdays in a Busy Life*, 346. The library is described in detail in "Is a Pretty Room," *Chicago Daily Tribune*, April 26, 1893. See also Amelia Peck and Carol Irish, *Candace Wheeler: The Art and Enterprise of American Design, 1875–1900* (New York: Metropolitan Museum of Art, 2001), 69, 214, 235–38. On Sigourney, see Angela Sorby, "Symmetrical Womanhood: Poetry in the Woman's Building Library," *Libraries & Culture* 41.1 (Winter 2006): 7–9. According to the report of the New York Women Managers, "the ceiling recalled that of some old Venetian palace in richness of color and style of composition, although the subject belonged to and was kept strictly in its place as a part of a great public library." Florence C. Ives, "Report of the Board of Women Managers," in *Report of the Board of General Managers of the Exhibit of the State of New York at the World's Columbian Exposition* (Albany: James B. Lyon, 1894), 170.

9. Connecticut official quoted in Weimann, *Fair Women*, 363–64. See Barbara Hochman, "*Uncle Tom's Cabin* at the World's Columbian Exposition," *Libraries & Culture* 41.1 (Winter 2006): 82–108, for an analysis of the Stowe exhibit.

10. Wheeler, *Yesterdays in a Busy Life*, 346; "Sana," "Woman's Triumph: The Ladies' Exhibit at the World's Fair," *Manitoba Morning Free Press*, June 26, 1893; Frances Willard, "Woman's Department of the World's Fair," in *The World's Fair: Being a Pictorial History of the Columbian Exposition*, ed. William E. Cameron (Chicago: Columbia History Company, 1893), 467; R. A. Felton, "Report of Committee on the Assignment of Space," n.d., box 8, vol. 23, BLM Papers. See also Caroline Garland, "Some of the Libraries at the Exposition," *Library Journal* 18 (August 1893): 284.

11. The comment on the "hootchy-kootchy" is from "World's Fair Yesterday," *Chicago Herald*, August 4, 1893. The journalist Kate Field responded more favorably to Little Egypt, whose performance presented Field with an opportunity to denounce the use of corsets, which rendered such abdominal "gymnastics" impossible. See Gary Scharnhorst, *Kate Field: The Many Lives of a Nineteenth-Century American Journalist* (Syracuse, N.Y.: Syracuse University Press, 2008), 220–21.

12. J. A. Mitchell, "Types and People at the Fair," in Francis Davis Millet et al., *Some*

Artists at the Fair (New York: C. Scribner's Sons, 1893), 53–54; see also David F. Burg, *Chicago's White City of 1893* (Lexington: University Press of Kentucky, 1976), 109–13; Rossiter Johnson, *A History of the World's Columbian Exposition Held in Chicago in 1893*, 4 vols. (New York: D. Appleton, 1897–1898), 1:343–45.

13. Although the City Beautiful movement, characterized by municipal art, civic improvement, and outdoor art, did not gain its name until 1898, it was inspired in part by the White City. See Jon A. Peterson, "The City Beautiful Movement: Forgotten Origins and Lost Meanings," *Journal of Urban History* 2.4 (August 1976): 415–34. For a discussion of the contrast between the White City and Chicago ("the Black City"), see Clinton Keeler, "The White City and the Black City: The Dream of a Civilization," *American Quarterly* 2.2 (Summer 1950): 112–17.

14. Michel Foucault, "Texts/Contexts: Of Other Spaces," trans. Jay Miskowiec, in *Grasping the World: The Idea of the Museum*, ed. Donald Preziosi and Claire J. Farago (Aldershot, England: Ashgate, 2004), 378. For more on heterotopias, see the introduction to this volume.

15. Christopher Robert Reed, *"All the World Is Here!" The Black Presence in the White City* (Bloomington: Indiana University Press, 2000), xxv; "Days for Southrons," *Chicago Herald*, August 5, 1893.

16. "Exposition Notes," in *The Columbian Woman*, ed. Mrs. Rollin A. Edgerton (Chicago, 1893), 21; William T. Stead, "My First Visit to America," *Review of Reviews* 9 (April 1894): 415.

17. The quotation is from Foucault, "Texts/Contexts," 374.

18. "The French Floricultural Exhibit," in Benjamin Cummings Truman, *History of the World's Fair: Being a Complete Description of the World's Columbian Exposition from Its Inception* (Chicago: Mammoth, 1893), 303–5; Madame Léon Grandin, *A Parisienne in Chicago: Impressions of the World's Columbian Exposition*, trans. Mary Beth Raycraft (Urbana: University of Illinois Press, 2010), 131; Marietta Holley, *Samantha at the World's Fair* (New York: Funk and Wagnalls, 1893), 252. On the placement of the Woman's Building, see also Andrew E. Wood, "Managing the Lady Managers: The Shaping of Heterotopian Spaces in the Chicago Exposition's Woman's Building," *Southern Communication Journal* 69.4 (Summer 2004): 294–95.

19. Enid Yandell and Laura Hayes, *Three Girls in a Flat* (Chicago: Knight, Leonard, 1892), 66; "World's Fair Buildings," *American Architect* 38 (November 5, 1892): 86. Rideout's rooftop sculptures represented "The Three Virtues," "Enlightenment," and "The Spirit of Civilization." As Weimann observes, "The Columbian Exposition itself represented a kind of final outburst of allegorical statuary. The female figure stood everywhere, representing Faith, Virtue, Freedom, the State, and all its Endeavours" (*Fair Women*, 284).

20. Kate Field, "Woman at the Fair," *Chicago Daily Tribune*, November 12, 1893.

21. Palmer quoted in Reed Badger, *The Great American Fair: The World's Columbian Exposition and American Culture* (Chicago: Nelson Hall, 1979), 121. Palmer may also have been alluding to the much less positive experience of the Woman's Pavilion of the 1876 Centennial Exhibition held in Philadelphia (see chapter 2). See Weimann, *Fair Women*, 4.

22. Palmer quoted in Weimann, *Fair Women*, 278; Virginia Meredith, "I: The Work of the Board of Lady Managers," *Review of Reviews* 7 (May 1893): 418. Worker quoted in Weimann, *Fair Women*, 263.

23. Elliott, *Art and Handicraft in the Woman's Building*, 25; Candace Wheeler, "A Dream City," *Harper's New Monthly Magazine*, May 1893, 836. *Harper's Bazar* quoted in Weimann, *Fair Women*, 267.

24. Clarence C. Buel, "Preliminary Glimpses of the Fair," *Century Magazine,* February 1893, 616–17.

25. Quoted in Julian Ralph, "Woman's Triumph at the Exposition," *Harper's Bazar,* August 27, 1893, 162–63. Similarly, Henry Van Brunt felt that the building's "delicacy," smaller size, "finer scale," and "sentiment" of "graceful timidity or gentleness" both "differentiate[d] it from its colossal neighbors, and reveal[ed] the sex of its author." Henry Van Brunt, "Architecture at the World's Columbian Exposition—IV," *Century Magazine* 22 (September 1892): 729. For additional interpretations, see Mary Pepchinski, "Woman's Buildings at European and American World's Fairs, 1893–1939," in *Gendering the Fair: Histories of Women and Gender at World's Fairs,* ed. TJ Boisseau and Abigail M. Markwyn (Urbana: University of Illinois Press, 2010), 187–93, 196, 198–99, 202.

26. Information on the interior of the Woman's Building taken from an undated report of the Board of Lady Managers, vol. 8, BLM Papers. See also Garland, "Some of the Libraries at the Exposition," 284; Charlene Gallo Garfinkle, "Women at Work: The Design and Decoration of the Woman's Building at the 1893 World's Columbian Exposition: Architecture, Exterior Sculpture, Stained Glass, and Interior Murals" (Ph.D. diss., University of California–Santa Barbara, 1996), 253–67; and Wanda M. Corn, *Women Building History: Public Art at the 1893 Columbian Exposition* (Berkeley: University of California Press, 2011), 113–48, 158–60.

27. Of her mural, MacMonnies explained: "The women indicate with the completest possible simplicity the bearer of burdens, the toilers of the earth, the servants of man, and more than this, being without ambition, contented with their lot" (quoted in Weimann, *Fair Women,* 206–7).

28. Quoted in Weimann, *Fair Women,* 200–201. See also Mrs. M. P. Handy, "The Women of the World's Fair City," *Munsey's Magazine,* March 1893, 178; Burg, *Chicago's White City,* 164–65. See also Wood, "Managing the Lady Managers," 295–96.

29. Enid Yandell and Laura Hayes, *Three Girls in a Flat* (Chicago: Knight, Leonard, 1893), dedication page. Although the title page lists only Yandell and Hayes as authors, the *List of Books Sent by Home and Foreign Committees to the Library of the Woman's Building, World's Columbian Exposition, Chicago, 1893,* compiled by Edith E. Clarke (Chicago, 1894), includes Loughborough as well.

30. Katharine Pearson Woods, "Books Old and New," *Far and Near* 4 (October 1893): 253; Blanche Bellamy, "New York Literary Exhibit,' in Elliott, *Art and Handicraft in the Woman's Building,* 115–19; Weimann, *Fair Women,* 393–404. See also Gayle Gullett, "Our Great Opportunity: Organized Women Advance Women's Work at the World's Columbian Exposition of 1893," *Illinois Historical Journal* 87 (Winter 1994): 270; "Work of the New York Women at the Columbian Exposition," *Harper's Bazar,* May 20, 1893, 398.

31. Stuart C. Wade, *Rand, McNally & Co.'s Handbook of the World's Columbian Exposition, with Special Descriptive Articles by Mrs. Potter Palmer, the Countess of Aberdeen, Mrs. Schuyler Van Rensselaer* (Chicago: Rand, McNally, 1893), 159. For an insightful overview and analysis of the linked ideologies of imperialism and New Womanhood at the World's Columbian Exposition, see T. J. Boisseau, "White Queens at the Chicago World's Fair, 1893: New Womanhood in the Service of Class, Race, and Nation," *Gender & History* 12.1 (April 2000): 33–81.

32. Several decades later the Association of Collegiate Alumnae merged with the Southern Association of College Women to become the American Association of University Women.

33. Willard, "Woman's Department of the World's Fair," 464.

34. Anne Ruggles Gere, *Intimate Practices: Literacy and Cultural Work in U.S. Women's Clubs, 1880–1920* (Urbana: University of Illinois Press, 1997), 8.

35. Gullett, "'Our Great Opportunity,'" 267.

36. For a "List of Organizations Granted Space in the Woman's Building," see Julia Ward Howe, "Associations of Women," in Elliott, *Art and Handicraft in the Woman's Building*, 156–57.

37. "Still Talks Wildly: Charlotte Smith Harangues the Waverley Hall Crowd," *Daily Inter Ocean*, April 18, 1892.

38. Meredith, "I: The Work of the Board of Lady Managers," 418; see also Weimann, *Fair Women*, 229–32; Nancy Huston Banks, "Woman's Marvelous Achievement," in Henry Davenport Northrop, *The World's Fair as Seen in One Hundred Days* (Philadelphia: National Publishing, 1893), 641; Willard, "Woman's Department of the World's Fair," 460, 464; and Horace H. Morgan, *The Historical World's Columbian Exposition and Guide to Chicago and St. Louis, the Carnival City of the World* (St. Louis: Pacific Publishing, 1892), 71–74. On the second-floor boutiques, see Grandin, *A Parisienne in Chicago*, 129.

39. "Proceedings of the Annual American Library Association Conference, 1893," *Library Journal* 18 (suppl.): 1–96.

40. Ibid., 67, 250–57. For the opinion Dewey expressed privately see, for example, Dewey to Edith Clarke, April 21, 1893, box 3, Dewey Papers.

41. Quoted in Burg, *Chicago's White City of 1893*, 247.

42. "Proceedings," 68.

43. Mrs. M. P. Handy, "The Women of the World's Fair City," 610.

44. "Proceedings," 67–68.

45. Mary Lockwood, "Report of the Press Committee to Board of Lady Managers Executive Committee," July 21, 1893, box 8, vol. 23, BLM Papers. See also Amey Starkweather, "Assignment of Space in Woman's Building," n.d., in section titled "Classification," box 10, vol. 30, BLM Papers.

46. In her "History of Milwaukee Public Library" (prepared for the *Columbian History of Education in Wisconsin* [1893] but also published separately as a pamphlet), Theresa West contrasts "the old library," which, like a cistern, "collects and preserves, and from which, given a certain amount of determination, one may draw water for use," and "the ideal library of today," which "is a true fountain, which pours its waters freely out into the sunlight, flashing an invitation to whosoever will to come" ([3]). Ironically, this slender pamphlet could have been found (though not easily) in the collection of the Woman's Building Library. A copy of the pamphlet is held by the Wisconsin Historical Society.

47. Although some studies have reported that the Woman's Building Library was arranged by subject, archival sources and contemporary reports emphasize the collection's geographical arrangement.

48. West, "History of Milwaukee Public Library," [3].

49. Among the thirteen categories identified, religion merited 4 percent, useful arts 5 percent, travel 8 percent, biography 12 percent, literature 13 percent, history 14 percent, and fiction 15 percent.

50. Katherine L. Sharp, "The A.L.A. Library Exhibit at the World's Fair," *Library Journal* 18 (August 1893): 280–84, quotation on 280. For the story of this model library, see Wayne A. Wiegand, "Catalog of 'A.L.A.' Library (1893): Origins of a Genre," in *For the Good of the Order: Essays in Honor of Edward G. Holley*, ed. Delmus E. Williams et al. (Greenwich,

Conn.: JAI Press, 1994), 237–54. After the fair, the U.S. Bureau of Education published a bibliography of this model library as *Catalog of "A.L.A." Library: 5000 Volumes for a Popular Library Selected by the American Library Association and Shown at the World's Columbian Exposition* (Washington: U.S. Bureau of Education; Government Printing Office, 1893) and distributed free copies to any public library requesting them. Thereafter it became a staple collection guide in the public library movement accelerated by Andrew Carnegie's philanthropy.

51. See Wayne A. Wiegand, *Main Street Public Library: Community Places and Reading Spaces in the Rural Heartland, 1867–1956* (Iowa City: University of Iowa Press, 2011).

52. Caroline Garland, "Some of the Libraries at the Exposition," *Library Journal* 18 (August 1893): 284. Dewey discusses librarians' objections to the Woman's Building Library in Dewey to Clarke, April 21, 1893, box 3, Dewey Papers.

53. The quoted phrase is from a speech given by BLM member Mary Logan (untitled speech, box 50, Logan Papers).

2. Planning and Developing the Collection

1. Deirdre C. Stam, "Women's Libraries," in *International Dictionary of Library Histories*, vol. 1, ed. David H. Stam (Chicago: Fitzroy Dearborn, 2001), 175–79.

2. Ibid.

3. Mildred K. Abraham, "The Library of Lady Jean Skipwith: A Book Collection from the Age of Jefferson," *Virginia Magazine of Biography and History* 91 (1981): 296–347.

4. Higginson quoted in "Books on Woman: Col. Higginson's Gift to the Boston Public Library," *Boston Daily Advertiser,* February 17, 1896; see also Horace G. Wadlin, *The Public Library of the City of Boston: A History* (Boston: Boston Public Library, 1911), 154. Boston Public Library continued to develop the Galatea Collection, which now comprises more than 4,000 volumes plus Higginson's Emily Dickinson manuscripts.

5. United States Centennial Commission, *International Exhibition, 1876: Official Catalogue,* Part III (Philadelphia: Centennial Catalogue Company, 1876), 79; "Woman's Pavilion," *Centennial Eagle,* August 8, 1876, 108–10.

6. Jeanne Madeline Weimann, *The Fair Women: The Story of the Woman's Building, World's Columbian Exposition, Chicago, 1893* (Chicago: Academy Chicago, 1981), 2–4, quotations on 4. For more complete accounts of the Centennial, see Thomas Bentley, *The Illustrated History of the Centennial Exhibition* (New York: John Filner, 1876); John D. Bergamini, *The Hundredth Year: The United States in 1876* (New York: Putnam, 1976); Edward C. Bruce, *The Century: Its Fruits and Its Festival* (Philadelphia: J. B. Lippincott, 1877); Philip T. Sandhurst, *The Great Centennial Exposition Critically Described and Illustrated* (Philadelphia: P. W. Ziegler, 1876); and J. S. Ingram, *The Centennial Exposition* (Philadelphia: Hubbard Bros., 1876).

7. United States Centennial Commission, *International Exhibition, 1876: Official Catalogue,* Part III, 79.

8. See Juliana Tutt, "'No Taxation without Representation' in the American Woman Suffrage Movement," *Stanford Law Review* 62.5 (May 1, 2010): 1473–1512.

9. "Not Exhibited at the Centennial," *Woman's Journal,* November 18, 1876, 372. See also "Our Centennial Exhibit," *Woman's Journal,* December 16, 1876, 404. In her description of the Woman's Pavilion, which (unlike the others on the grounds) was "barren of all exterior decoration," Mary Livermore did not even mention an exhibit of books written by women.

See Mary A. Livermore, *What Shall We Do With Our Daughters?* (Boston: Lea and Shepard, 1883), 86–91. Unfortunately, the authors were not able to locate a complete bibliography of the library in the 1876 Woman's Pavilion.

10. Ann Ruggles Gere, *Intimate Practices: Literacy and Cultural Work in U.S. Women's Clubs, 1880–1920* (Urbana: University of Illinois Press, 1997), 34–35. See also Benedict Anderson, *Imagined Communities: Reflections on the Origin and Spread of Nationalism* (London: Verso, 1983); Barbara Sicherman, *Well-Read Lives: How Books Inspired a Generation of American Women* (Chapel Hill: University of North Carolina Press, 2010); and Theodora Penny Martin, *The Sound of Our Own Voices: Women's Study Clubs, 1860–1910* (Boston: Beacon, 1987). For an example of how women's clubs shared booklists, see "The Price List of Books for a Club Library," *Far and Near* 4 (March 1893): 98–99. For an analysis of female African American literary clubs, see Elizabeth McHenry, *Forgotten Readers: Recovering the Lost History of African American Literary Societies* (Durham: Duke University Press, 2002).

11. Erik Larson, *The Devil in the White City: Murder, Magic, and Madness at the Fair That Changed America* (New York: Random House/Crown, 2003), 23–26, 30, 84.

12. Robert W. Rydell, introduction to Ida B. Wells, ed., *The Reason Why the Colored American Is Not in the World's Columbian Exposition: The Afro-American's Contribution to Columbian Literature* (1893), ed. Rydell (Urbana: University of Illinois Press, 1999), xi; David F. Burg, *Chicago's White City of 1893* (Lexington: University Press of Kentucky, 1976), 28; Robert Muccigrosso, *Celebrating the New World: Chicago's Columbian Exposition of 1893* (Chicago: Ivan R. Dee, 1993), 21; Reid Badger, *The Great American Fair: The World's Columbian Exposition and American Culture* (Chicago: N. Hall, 1979), 48–49, 51; Marie Thérèse Bentzon [Marie Thérèse de Solms Blanc], *The Condition of Woman in the United States: A Traveler's Notes* (Boston: Roberts Brothers, 1895), 55.

13. James P. Holland, "Chicago and the World's Fair," *Chautauquan* 17 (May 1893): 137.

14. Weimann, *Fair Women*, 26.

15. Ibid., 32–33.

16. "Isabella Corner," *Woman's Tribune*, January 17, 1891, 21.

17. Ibid.

18. Quoted in Weimann, *Fair Women*, 31.

19. Quoted ibid., 33. See also Julian Ralph, "Woman's Triumph at the Exposition," *Harper's Bazar*, August 27, 1893, 698.

20. Quoted in Weimann, *Fair Women*, 36.

21. Antoinette Van Hoesen, "Woman's Department in the Columbian Exposition," *Chautauquan* 13 (July 1891): 518–20; Weimann, *Fair Women*, 36, 74.

22. Moses P. Handy, *The Official Directory of the World's Columbian Exposition, May 1st to October 30th, 1893* (Chicago: W. B. Conkey, 1893), 161, 177; Frances E. Willard, "Woman's Department of the World's Fair," in *The World's Fair: Being a Pictorial History of the Columbian Exposition*, ed. William E. Cameron (Philadelphia: National Publishing, 1893), 448; Henry Davenport Northrop, *The World's Fair as Seen in One Hundred Days* (Philadelphia: National Publishing, 1893), 175.

23. Quoted in Weimann, *Fair Women*, 21.

24. Ibid., 47.

25. Rebecca Latimer Felton, *Country Life in Georgia in the Days of My Youth* (Atlanta: Index Printing Company, 1919), 110–11. A letter written by Felton indicates that she strongly believed Southern women had been deliberately slighted and "despised" during

the BLM's organizing stage. See Weimann, *Fair Women,* 85. Recognizing the ill feelings, Hooker informed Palmer that her failure to include Southern women in the BLM's Executive Committee was a "calamitous" mistake (Weimann, *Fair Women,* 95). The comment on Hooker's "piquant remarks" can be found on Enid Yandell and Laura Hayes, *Three Girls in a Flat* (Chicago: Knight, Leonard, 1892), 59.

26. Handy, *Official Directory,* 182.

27. Palmer quoted in Northrop, *World's Fair as Seen in One Hundred Days,* 177. The full text of Palmer's speech can also be found in *Address and Reports of Mrs. Potter Palmer, President of the Board of Lady Managers, World's Columbian Exposition* (Chicago: Rand, McNally, 1894), 5–7. Description of Logan taken from Yandell and Hayes, *Three Girls in a Flat,* 34, 59.

28. Badger, *Great American Fair,* 122; Weimann, *Fair Women,* 12.

29. Weimann, *Fair Women,* 12; Muccigrosso, *Celebrating the New World,* 25.

30. Yandell and Hayes, *Three Girls in a Flat,* 108–9.

31. See Handy, *Official Directory,* 182; Florence Adkinson, "Bertha Honore Palmer," *Woman's Journal,* April 29, 1893, 129.

32. Mary Beedy, letter to the editor (dated October 26, 1891), *Woman's Journal,* November 7, 1891, 358.

33. On Palmer's club activities and labor sympathies, see Weimann, *Fair Women,* 13–19.

34. "Editorial Notes," *Woman's Journal,* February 7, 1891, 41; Willard, "Woman's Department of the World's Fair," 450. See also Weimann, *Fair Women,* 279.

35. Weimann, *Fair Women,* 141. In March 1893 George Davis, the fair's director-general, declared that the Woman's Department "should be equal in status, scope and features to all others." Rossiter Johnson, *A History of the World's Columbian Exposition Held in Chicago in 1893,* 4 vols. (New York: D. Appleton, 1897–1898), 1:201–2; see also Burg, *White City,* 164.

36. Quoted in Weimann, *Fair Women,* 55–56.

37. Grace Farrell, afterword to *Fettered for Life; or, Lord and Master: A Story of To-Day,* by Lillie Devereux Blake (1874; New York: Feminist Press at City University of New York, 1996), 392; Grace Farrell, *Lillie Devereux Blake: Retracing a Life Erased* (Amherst: University of Massachusetts Press, 2002), 27. Farrell elaborates, "Because it was based on the notion that there was an essential woman whose nature could be well defined, the rhetoric of nineteenth-century discussions of women usually called for the singular form: woman suffrage, the woman's movement or the woman movement, the nature of woman, the woman question, the social condition of woman" (afterword to *Fettered for Life,* 422n16). See also Barbara Welter, *Dimity Convictions: The American Woman in the Nineteenth Century* (Athens: Ohio University Press, 1976), for a discussion of the "complete acceptance of radically different natures depending on sex" (78).

38. Farrell, afterword to *Fettered for Life,* 390–91.

39. "Don't Want Separation: The Women Don't Want a Separate Exhibit at the Fair," *Omaha World Herald,* November 23, 1890.

40. Estelle Freedman, "Separatism as Strategy: Female Institution Building and American Feminism, 1870–1930," *Feminist Studies* 5.3 (Autumn 1979): 515.

41. Margaret Deland, "The Change in the Feminine Ideal," *Atlantic Monthly* 105 (March 1910): 298, quoted in Diana C. Reep, *Margaret Deland* (Boston: Twayne, 1985), 14.

42. Weimann, *Fair Women,* 56; Minutes, First Session, Second Day, November 21, 1890, Misc. boxes, BLM Papers. See also Johnson, *History of the World's Columbian Exposition,* 1:141.

43. See *World's Columbian Exposition Illustrated*, March 1891, 91. This same page (which carried the February 3 circular) also carried a circular from the fair's construction chief, Daniel Burnham, dated February 2, soliciting designs for the Woman's Building. In his specifications, Burnham made no mention of a library as part of the building's interior needs. See also Johnson, *History of the World's Columbian Exposition*, 1:202; "An Unusual Opportunity for Women Architects," *Woman's Journal*, February 21, 1891, 63.

44. "World's Fair Notes," *Woman's Journal*, March 19, 1891, 91.

45. Quoted in Florence Adkinson, "Bertha Honore Palmer," *Woman's Journal*, April 29, 1893, 129. See also "World's Fair Notes," *Woman's Journal*, March 19, 1891, 91.

46. The first quotation is from Willard, "Woman's Department of the World's Fair," 451; the second is from Nancy Huston Banks, in Henry Davenport Northrop, *The World's Fair as Seen in One Hundred Days* (Philadelphia: National Publishing, 1893), 635. See also "Naming the Ladies," *Atlanta Constitution*, March 29, 1891.

47. All quotations from Weimann, *Fair Women*, 279–80, 393. "No sentimental sympathy for women will permit the admission of second-rate articles," Palmer later told readers of the *American Journal of Politics*, "for the highest standard is to be strictly maintained." Mrs. Potter Palmer, "Woman's Part in the Columbian Exposition," *American Journal of Politics* 1 (August 1892): 127. See also Mary Kavanaugh Oldham Eagle, introduction to *The Congress of Women Held in the Woman's Building, World's Columbian Exposition, Chicago, U.S.A., 1893* (Chicago: W. B. Conkey, 1894).

48. *Chicago News*, April 4, 1891 ("Almost autocratic power"); *Woman's Tribune*, April 11, 1891, 113.

49. See Christopher Robert Reed, *"All the World Is Here!" The Black Presence in the White City* (Bloomington: Indiana University Press, 2000), chap. 1.

50. BLM Executive Board Minutes, April 20, 1891, vol. 2, BLM Papers. At the April 20th meeting, Mary Logan indicated she "had been appealed to many times" by Chicago's African American women, and had assured Mrs. Trent that her group "might consider they had a friend in her." See Trent to Logan, March 25, 1891, box 10, Logan Papers. The quote from "a Southern Lady Manager" is taken from *Chicago Times*, November 26, 1890. See also Reed, *"All the World Is Here,"* chap. 1.

51. Quoted in Ferdinand Barnett, "The Reason Why," in Wells, *The Reason Why the Colored American Is Not in the World's Columbian Exposition*, 69.

52. Ann Massa, "Black Women in the 'White City,'" *Journal of American Studies* 8 (1974): 322–23, quotation ("so soaked in Southern paternalism") on 323; "World's Fair Doings," *Woman's Journal*, September 5, 1891, 267 ("that there should be no discrimination upon the score of race"). See also Weimann, *Fair Women*, 103–5, 111.

53. Palmer to Anderson, December 17, 1891, Bertha Honoré Palmer Papers, Archives and Manuscripts Department, Chicago History Museum. See also Palmer to Logan, October 10, 1891, ibid.

54. Palmer to Logan, October 11, 1891, box 10, Logan Papers. In the end, Palmer defeated the Isabellans. On September 2, 1891, after a public and rather ugly challenge to her authority, Palmer replaced Phoebe Couzins as the BLM's secretary with Susan Gale Cooke of Tennessee. See Weimann, *Fair Women*, chap. 5.

55. For an example of one of these statements, see Palmer to Felton, October 13, 1891, box 50, Logan Papers. Copy of circular dated October 14, 1891, box 10, Logan Papers.

56. Paul to Logan, October 15, 1891, box 10, Logan Papers. The Virginia representa-

tive was Katherine S. G. Paul; according to Weimann, "Mrs. Paul, a correspondent for the Associated Press, had worked for co-operation with black women of Virginia: she had organized special committees, and sent out circulars and personal letters soliciting black exhibits" (*Fair Women*, 110).

57. Paul to Logan, October 15, 1891; Edgerton to Logan, October 17, 1891; Olmstead to Logan, October 14, 1891; and Trent to Logan, November 4, 1891, all in box 10, Logan Papers. Of the Lady Managers, Trent believed that only five—Phoebe Couzins, Mary Lockwood, Mary Logan, Helen Brayton, and Isabella Hooker—truly supported the African American cause (Weimann, *Fair Women*, 110).

58. "The Appeal to the Representative Negro Women of the United States," *Boston Courant*, October 24, 1891, quoted in Massa, "Black Women in the 'White City,'" 326.

59. Massa, "Black Women in the 'White City,'" 328.

60. "World's Fair Doings," *Woman's Journal*, December, 19, 1891, 410.

61. Barnett, "Reason Why," 71–72.

62. *Halligan's Illustrated World's Fair* 3 (May 1892): 147.

63. "World's Fair Notes," *Woman's Journal*, January 14, 1893, 9. See also Reed, *"All the World Is Here,"* 29–30. See also Elliott M. Rudwick and August Meier, "Black Man in the 'White City': Negroes and the Columbian Exposition, 1893," *Phylon* 26.4 (1965): 355–56. These events are also described in Temple Bryonny Tsenes-Hills, "I Am the Utterance of My Name: Black Victorian Feminist Discourse and Intellectual Enterprise at the Columbian Exposition, 1893" (Ph.D. diss., Loyola University Chicago, 2004), 192–97.

64. Barnett, "The Reason Why," 69; Massa, "Black Women in the 'White City,'" 336.

65. Some BLM members from the South were apparently suspicious of Palmer. "These were the states that endured the shock of the civil war, bound by ties of the strongest nature, blood, suffering, and death, and yet Mrs. Palmer has not noticed a single one," Georgia's Rebecca Felton complained to Mary Logan in March 1891. "I was so anxious that this should be a Peace Congress of Women—*genuine*—but we are despised for some reason." Felton to Logan, March 30, 1891, box 10, Logan Papers.

66. Banks, "Woman's Marvelous Achievement," 633. See also Weimann, *Fair Women*, 147–48.

67. Hayden, who was born in Chile, was the first woman to complete MIT's four-year architecture program. For her thesis, she designed a Renaissance fine arts museum. See Weimann, *Fair Women*, 145–46.

68. Nancy Huston Banks, "Work of Lady Managers," in *World's Columbian Exposition Illustrated*, May 1891, 10; "Women and the World's Fair," *World's Columbian Exposition Illustrated*, June 1891, 12; "Plan of the Women's Building," *World's Columbian Exposition Illustrated*, August–September 1891, 15.

69. Weimann, *Fair Women*, 150. See also Weimann, *Fair Women*, 151–54; BLM Executive Minutes, April 28, 1891, vol. 2, BLM Papers; and Antoinette Van Hoesen, "Woman's Department in the Columbian Exposition," *Chautauquan* 13 (July 1891): 518–20. Descriptions of the building published in Chicago newspapers that summer make no mention of a library; see "Work That Mrs. Palmer Is Doing," *Chicago Daily Tribune*, July 25, 1891, and "An Envoy at the Fair," *Chicago Daily Tribune*, July 26, 1891. In its November issue, *World's Columbian Exposition Illustrated* still had the library located on the first floor, but a diagram of the second floor identified "Ladies Parlors" on either side of a gallery, including the one side that eventually was occupied by the library. See *World's Columbian Exposition Illus-*

trated, November 1891, 16. *An Historical World's Columbian Exposition and Chicago Guide,* put together for dedication ceremonies in 1892, identifies the library on a first-floor room opposite the main front.

70. Minutes, Board of Lady Managers, September 9, 1891, Misc. boxes, BLM Papers.

71. See also *Official Directory, World's Columbian Exposition,* 1047; "American Women's Work," *Los Angeles Times,* September 27, 1891.

72. "American Women's Work," *Los Angeles Times,* September 27, 1891.

73. Quoted in *Connecticut at the World's Fair: Report of the Commissioners from Connecticut of the Columbian Exhibition of 1893 at Chicago; Also Report of the Work of the Board of Lady Managers of Connecticut* (Hartford: Case, Lockwood, and Brainard, 1898), 210. See also Johnson, *History of the World's Columbian Exposition,* 1:209–12. In *Three Girls in a Flat,* Yandell and Hayes claim "that in many instances the [male] legislators acknowledged that their attention had first been brought to the World's Fair through the efforts" of state women responding to the BLM's September circular (56). For reports of meetings and plans of delegations from individual states and the District of Columbia, see "This City and the Fair," *Washington Post,* November 22, 1891; "Appeal to Virginia Women," *Chicago Daily Tribune,* December 18, 1891; "Georgia's Exhibit," *Atlanta Constitution,* January 21, 1892; and "Ladies Annex," *Los Angeles Times,* December 1, 1891. The latter reported that California women hoped California wood and wood carving would be used "for the bookcases in the library."

74. Logan's speech is in box 50, Logan Papers. See also World's Fair Notes," *Woman's Journal,* January 9, 1892, 9. For an example of one state delegation soliciting in-state residents, see "A Request for Material for the Woman's Building," *Los Angeles Times,* February 28, 1892.

75. Palmer to Ward, March 19, 1892; Palmer to William Jackson, March 19, 1892; both in box 4, vol. 13, BLM Papers. See also "World's Fair Notes," *Woman's Journal,* April 30, 1892, 139.

76. The first two quotations are from "Announcement," *Woman's Tribune,* April 30, 1892, 133; the third is from a note about Palmer's trip to New York in "World's Fair Notes," *Woman's Journal,* April 16, 1892, 123.

77. Palmer to Drake, June 9, 1892, box 4, vol. 13, BLM Papers. For sample letters to publishers, see Palmer to Houghton, Mifflin & Co., April 4, 1892, and Palmer to J. B. Lippincott Co., April 4, 1892, both in box 4, vol. 13, BLM Papers.

78. Palmer to Beriah Wilkins, March 28, 1892, box 4, vol. 12, BLM Papers; and Palmer to J. I. Imbrie, April 20, 1892, box 4, vol. 13, BLM Papers.

79. Palmer quoted in Northrop, *World's Fair as Seen in One Hundred Days,* vii.

80. Willard, "Woman's Department of the World's Fair," 449, 450. See also Mary E. Beedy's letter to the editor (dated October 26, 1891), *Woman's Journal,* November 7, 1891, 358; and "Foreign Exhibits by Women," *Chicago Daily Tribune,* October 29, 1892. Chicago newspapers regularly carried stories listing items donated from European royalty for the Woman's Building. See, for example, "Siam Is Interested," *Chicago Daily Tribune,* October 1, 1892; "Work of the Women," *Chicago Daily Tribune,* April 23, 1892 and May 21, 1892; and "Writings by Women," July 9, 1892.

81. Weimann, *Fair Women,* 107; and Willard, "Woman's Department at the World's Fair," 457.

82. Untitled article, *World's Columbian Exposition Illustrated,* June, 1892, 85. After the Woman's Library opened, one English woman complained that the English books "will be

found in, I am sorry to say, a rather dark corner," but added the manuscripts were displayed "in cases in the centre of the room." Quoted from an article in *Englishwoman's Review* in "World's Fair Letter," *Woman's Tribune*, August 5, 1893, 136.

83. Maud Howe Elliott, "The Library," in *Art and Handicraft in the Woman's Building of the World's Columbian Exposition, Chicago, 1893*, ed. Elliott (Paris: Goupil, 1893), 111. Elliott wrote: "The first page of Adam Bede, with an affectionate note of dedication to George Lewes, signed Marian Lewes . . . is one of the most interesting objects in the World's Fair." Here and in the following paragraphs, names of authors represented in the library have been gleaned from Edith Clarke's *List of Books Sent by Home and Foreign Committees to the Library of the Woman's Building* (Chicago, 1894).

84. "Work of the Women," *Chicago Daily Tribune*, May 21, 1892; untitled article, *World's Columbian Exposition Illustrated*, June 1892, 85.

85. Josefa Humpal Zeman, "The Women of Bohemia," in Eagle, *Congress of Women*, 129. Zeman's figures were estimated; for more accurate totals see table 2.1 in this chapter.

86. Willard, "Woman's Department of the World's Fair," 458.

87. Palmer tells this story in Palmer to Jennings, June 18, 1894, box 6.5, vol. 17, BLM Papers. See also Madame Fanny Zampini Salazar, "Women in Modern Italy," in Eagle, *Congress of Women*, 162.

88. Weimann, *Fair Women*, 135–40; Johnson, *History of the World's Columbian Exposition*, 1:214–15. See also *World's Columbian Exposition Illustrated*, June 1892, 85. According to Weimann, "the Mexicans sent only one book, commissioned especially for the Fair: a collection of poetry by Mexican women" (*Fair Women*, 375), but this volume is not listed in the library's inventory of books. Possibly it was displayed elsewhere in the Woman's Building.

89. Weimann notes that Palmer reported earlier that "the Chinese deeply feel the humiliation of the Exclusion Laws" (138), a response that may have been a factor in the small number of books sent to the library from China (evidently by a Christian missionary).

90. "World's Fair Notes," *Woman's Journal*, January 14, 1893, 9. See also Edith E. Clarke, "'Women in Literature at the Fair, from the Standpoint of a Librarian and a Cataloger,' 4, Paper Read before the Chicago Library Club, Jan. 1894," in BLM Papers. On Japan's masculinist presence at the fair, see Lisa K. Langlois, "Japan—Modern, Ancient, and Gendered at the 1893 Chicago World's Fair," in Boisseau and Markwyn, *Gendering the Fair*, 56–74; on *Japanese Women*, a book produced by the Japanese Woman's Commission (but not included in the library's bibliography), see 64, 67, 70.

91. "Writings by Women," *Chicago Daily Tribune*, July 9, 1892; "World's Fair Notes," *Woman's Journal*, August 26, 1893, 269. See also Adkinson, "Bertha Honore Palmer," 129; *Daily Columbian*, May 1, 1893. The text of the circular sent to foreign committees appears in Arthur B. Farquhar, ed., *Pennsylvania and the World's Columbian Exposition* (Harrisburg: E. K. Meyers, n.d.), 179.

92. Palmer to Byse, April 20, 1892, box 4, vol. 13, BLM Papers. Edith Clarke's final bibliography lists no entries for Switzerland. Other would-be exhibitors manifested different entrepreneurial tendencies. In a response to a request from Marguerite A. Hamm of New York City to set up "a booth" for "selling papers and periodicals" written by "women of note," Palmer wrote on May 12, "I fear that such a privilege shall not be allowed." Palmer to Hamm, May 12, 1892, box 4, vol. 13, BLM Papers.

93. "The Fair of Fairs," *Los Angeles Times*, October 15, 1892; Palmer quoted in *Connecticut at the World's Fair*, 207.

94. New York's commitment to comprehensiveness was not entirely consistent. For example, E. D. E. N. Southworth had published more than sixty volumes of fiction by 1893 (as indexed in *American Fiction, 1774–1910* [Gale Cengage]), but only four of these were included in the Woman's Building Library.

95. Blanche Bellamy, "General Introduction," in *Woman and the Higher Education*, ed. Anna C. Brackett, Distaff Series (New York: Harper and Brothers, 1893), vi.

96. "Report of the Woman's Library," April 25, 1893, box 4, vol. 23, BLM Papers.

97. Handy, *Official Directory*, 81, 82.

98. Frances L. Gilbert, "Literature," in *Official Catalogue of the Illinois Women's Board* (Chicago: W. B. Conkey, 1893), 3; *World's Columbian Exposition Illustrated*, November 1892, 234.

99. Weimann, *Fair Women*, 389. For more on the contribution of Illinois women, see Bernice E. Gallagher, *Illinois Women Novelists in the Nineteenth Century: An Analysis and Annotated Bibliography* (Urbana: University of Illinois Press, 1994); and Bernice E. Gallagher, "Illinois Women's Novels in the Woman's Building Library," *Libraries & Culture* 41.1 (Winter 2006): 109–32.

100. Bagley quoted in "World's Fair Doings," *Woman's Journal*, December 19, 1891, 410; *Report of the Iowa Columbian Commission* (Chicago: Iowa Columbian Commission, 1893), 188–95.

101. *Report of the Iowa Columbian Commission*, 192–94. See also Weimann, *Fair Women*, 128–32.

102. "Preparing for the Fair," *Chicago Daily Tribune*, September 3, 1892. The Michigan building that was ultimately constructed did include a 25-square-foot library of Michigan authors put together by University of Michigan faculty; see Weimann, *Fair Women*, 388–89. On Minnesota, see Leo J. Harris, "The Search for Marian Shaw," in *World's Fair Notes: A Woman Journalist Views Chicago's 1893 Columbian Exposition* ([St. Paul]: Pogo Press, 1992), 78.

103. "Kansas Books," *Woman's Journal*, April 15, 1893, 119. See also *Report of the Kansas Board of World's Fair Managers, 1893*, 2nd ed. (Topeka: Press of the Hamilton Printing Co., 1894), 42–52.

104. On libraries in the state buildings of Nebraska, Texas, and Virginia, see Handy, *Official Directory*, 90, 99, 100.

105. *Connecticut at the World's Fair*, 207, 219–20, 221; Mrs. J. G. Gregory, ed., *Selections from the Writings of Connecticut Women* (Norwalk: Literary Committee, Connecticut Board of Lady Managers for the Columbian Exposition, 1893). See also "Connecticut Female Authors: Specimens of Their Work to Be Sent to the World's Fair," *New York Times*, May 21, 1893.

106. *Connecticut at the World's Fair*, 281–82.

107. Ibid., 281–82. See also Weimann, *Fair Women*, 365.

108. Margaret Tufts Yardley, ed., *The New Jersey Scrap Book of Women Writers*, 2 vols. (Newark: Advertiser Printing House, 1893), 1:iii–vii.

109. *Report of the Massachusetts Board of World's Fair Managers* (Boston: Wright and Potter, 1894), 176; "Women's Work at Columbian Exposition," *Woman's Journal*, January 9, 1892, 16.

110. "Massachusetts Woman's Columbian Exposition Exhibit," *Woman's Journal*, April 1, 1893, 104. See also "Windows from Women," *Boston Daily Globe*, April 25, 1893. Exceptions to the one-book-per-author rule included Maria Hildred Parker, Elizabeth Palmer

Peabody, Clara Louise Burnham, Annie Fields, Mary J. Lincoln, Martha Perry Lowe, Mary Peabody Mann, Edna Dean Proctor, Eleanor Putnam, Sarah Elizabeth Titcomb, and Eliza Orne White.

111. Fanny Purdy Palmer, *A List of Rhode Island Literary Women (1726–1892) with Some Account of Their Work* (Providence: Rhode Island Women Commissioners of the World's Columbian Exposition, 1893).

112. "Woman's Share in the World's Progress," *Woman's Tribune*, January 16, 1892, 12. See also Mary Stuart Smith, "The Virginia Woman of Today," in Eagle, *Congress of Women*, 411.

113. "World's Fair Notes," *Woman's Journal*, May 21, 1892, 163; Farquhar, *Pennsylvania and the World's Columbian Exposition*, 63; information on Philadelphia women in "World's Fair Notes," *Woman's Journal*, May 1, 1893, 137.

114. "World's Fair Notes," *Woman's Journal*, February 27, 1892, 70.

115. "World's Fair Notes," *Woman's Journal*, April 30, 1892, 139. See also William Stephenson, "How Sallie Southall Cotten Brought North Carolina to the Chicago World's Fair of 1893," *North Carolina Historical Review* 58 (October 1981): 364–83; Eileen L. McGrath, "Bruce Cotten," *Dictionary of Literary Biography*, vol. 187, 2nd series (Detroit: Gale, 1997), 45–50. In part because of this experience, Bruce Cotten later decided to collect North Caroliniana, which he subsequently donated to the University of North Carolina. We are indebted to Robert Anthony, curator of the North Carolina Collection at UNC, for bringing this information to our attention.

116. "Women Moving for the World's Fair," *Woman's Journal*, August 22, 1891, 274; "World's Fair Notes," *Woman's Journal*, July 2, 1892, 214.

117. *Utah at the World's Columbian Exposition* (Salt Lake City: World's Fair Commission, 1894), 20; Andrea G. Radke-Moss, "Mormon Women, Suffrage, and Citizenship at the 1893 Chicago World's Fair," in Boisseau and Markwyn, *Gendering the Fair*, 102–3. In a summary report submitted January 1, 1894, the Board of Lady Managers of the Utah World's Fair Commission especially noted that in the Woman's Building "our ladies were represented by the books 'Songs and Flowers from the Wasatch,' being selections of verse from our noted poets, exquisitely illustrated in water colors and handsomely bound. Also, a volume of essays and a history of the churches and charities of Utah" (88). For more information see Radke-Moss, "Mormon Women, Suffrage, and Citizenship."

118. *A List of Books by California Writers, Issued by the San Francisco Women's Literary Exhibit* (San Francisco: San Francisco World's Fair Association, 1893). This 52-page bibliography includes both men and women of the state.

119. Ella Sterling Cummins, *The Story of the Files: A Review of Californian Writers and Literature* (San Francisco: World's Fair Commission of California, 1893).

120. *World's Columbian Exposition Illustrated*, June 2, 1892, 85; Minutes, April 28, 1892, v, BWM Papers; Ralph, "Woman's Triumph," 698. See also Willard, "Woman's Department of the World's Fair," 467.

121. Benjamin Cummings Truman, *History of the World's Fair: Being a Complete Description of the World's Columbian Exposition from its Inception* (Chicago: Mammoth Publishing, 1893), 111. See also Johnson, *History of the World's Columbian Exposition*, 1:231–32.

122. "Address at Dedicatory Ceremonies of the Exposition, Manufactures Building, October 21, 1892," in Board of Lady Managers, World's Columbian Exposition, *Address and Reports of Mrs. Potter Palmer* (Chicago: Rand, McNally, 1894), 114–15, 119. For accounts of the dedication ceremony, see Weimann, *Fair Women*, 215–23; Burg, *White City*, 105–6; Badger, *Great American Fair*, 83–85; Truman, *History of the World's Fair*, 111–14; and

Johnson, *History of the World's Columbian Exposition,* 1:277–80. Palmer's address "received little attention from the general press save an occasional slur," a *Woman's Tribune* editorial noted, "because it said so little about Columbus and so much about woman." *Woman's Tribune,* October 29, 1892, 212.

3. Empire Building

1. Nancy Huston Banks, "Woman's Work," *World's Columbian Exposition Illustrated,* July 1891, 14–15. Jeanne Madeline Weimann, *The Fair Women: The Story of the Woman's Building, World's Columbian Exposition, Chicago, 1893* (Chicago: Academy Chicago, 1981), 107, 125.

2. *Report of the Board of General Managers of the Exhibit of the State of New York at the World's Columbian Exposition* (Albany: James B. Lyon, 1894), 25; "Woman's Work at the Fair," *New York Times,* December 3, 1891.

3. *Report of the Board of General Managers of the Exhibit of the State of New York,* 32–33; and Florence C. Ives, "Report of the Board of Women Managers," ibid., 164, 176. See also Weimann, *Fair Women,* 121–22; and Christopher Robert Reed, *"All the World Is Here!" The Black Presence in the White City* (Bloomington: Indiana University Press, 2000), 18.

4. Palmer to Wheeler, March 16, 1892, box 4, vol. 12, BLM Papers. See also Weimann, *Fair Women,* 224.

5. Quoted in Amelia Peck, "Candace Wheeler: A Life in Art and Business," in Amelia Peck and Carol Irish, *Candace Wheeler: The Art and Enterprise of American Design, 1875–1900* (New York: Metropolitan Museum of Art, 2001), 65.

6. Ibid., 3–4.

7. Candace Wheeler, "The New Woman and Her Home Needs," *Christian Union,* June 25, 1891, 845. In an oft-cited article, Ellen Jordan traced the introduction of the phrase "New Woman" to an 1894 exchange in the *North American Review.* See Ellen Jordan, "The Christening of the New Woman: May 1894," *Victorian Newsletter* 63 (Spring 1983): 19–21.

8. The inspiration for the Society of Decorative Arts had been an exhibit of the Royal School of Art Needlework at the 1876 Centennial Exhibition, where Wheeler began to devise an American counterpart: "a woman-run business that would benefit women" by providing instruction and a sales outlet for needlecrafts and other applied arts. See Candace Wheeler, *Yesterdays in a Busy Life* (New York: Harper, 1918), 209–17, 222; and Peck, "Candace Wheeler," 20–34. On the Woman's Exchange, see Wheeler, *Yesterdays in a Busy Life,* 223–28 and Peck, "Candace Wheeler," 34–38.

9. Minutes, April 28, 1892, v, BWM Papers. See also Peck, "Candace Wheeler," 69.

10. Minutes, June 8, 1892, 8–9, 13, BWM Papers; "Women at the Fair," *Brooklyn Eagle,* July 31, 1892. For the exact date when the New York Board of Women Managers first learned the library would be located on the second rather than first floor, see Ives, "Report of the Board of Women Managers," 170.

11. Ives, "Report of the Board of Women Managers," 162–63.

12. Minutes, July 19, 1892, viii–x, BWM Papers; Ives, "Report of the Board of Women Managers," 170; "World's Fair Notes," *Woman's Journal,* August 6, 1892, 252.

13. Minutes, July 19, 1892, viii–x, BWM Papers; Ives, "Report of the Board of Women Managers," 170.

14. Minutes, September 6, 1892, xvi, BWM Papers.

15. Sorosis was established in 1868, the Buffalo Graduates' Association in 1876. Each had experience in supporting libraries going back decades. See Jane Cunningham Croly, *History of the Women's Club Movement in America* (New York: Henry G. Allen, 1898), 15–34, 879–80.

16. Minutes, September 7, 1892, 24–26, BWM Papers.

17. Ives, "Report of the Board of Women Managers," 171; and "World's Fair Notes," *Woman's Journal,* October 15, 1892, 332.

18. Minutes, September 7, 1892, 32–33, BWM Papers; Ives, "Report of the Board of Women Managers," 176.

19. Ives, "Report of the Board of Women Managers," 29, 30.

20. Ibid., 159. See also Weimann, *Fair Women,* 126–27, 355–56.

21. Ives, "Report of the Board of Women Managers," 171. For examples of appeals outside of New York, see "Living Female Authors," *Davenport (Iowa) Tribune,* November 2, 1892; and "For a Woman's Library," *Chicago Daily Tribune,* November 2, 1892.

22. Minutes, October 4, 1892, 13; October 12, 1892, 17 BWM Papers.

23. "Report of Mrs. Bellamy, Chairman of the Committee on Women's Work in Literature," appended to Minutes, November 1, 1892, 29–31, BWM Papers.

24. BLM Executive Committee Minutes, October 26, 1892, box 1, BLM Papers.

25. BLM Executive Committee Minutes, October 31, 1892, box 6, BLM Papers; "Resolutions Adopted by the Executive Committee," October 31, 1892, box 8, BLM Papers. On December 13 the committee in charge of the library resolved "that the Librarian of the Woman's Building must be selected from the class of professionals in that line." Minutes, December 13, 1892, box 1, vol. 6, BLM Papers. It is possible that the BLM had the library in mind at this time because Candace Wheeler had visited the building then under construction to survey the room for decoration. See Weimann, *Fair Women,* 227.

26. Rules for library in "For Women to Obey," *Chicago Daily Tribune,* December 24, 1892; rules for librarian in Minutes, December 13, 14, 16, and 20, 1892, box 1, vol. 6, BLM Papers.

27. Bellamy to Palmer, November 14, 1892, Misc. boxes, October 1892–April, 1893, BLM Papers. See also the 73-page "Record of Female Authors" prepared by Fanny Goodale for the New York counties of Oneida, Jefferson, Herkimer, Madison, and Essex, Oneida Historical Society, Utica, N.Y.

28. Bellamy to Palmer, November 14, 1892. Florence Ives later reported that "hundreds, possibly thousands, of women, in various parts of the State aided in different branches of the work" of the New York board's Literary Committee. See Ives, "Report of the Board of Women Managers," 171.

29. Minutes, November 15, 1892, 41–42, BWM Papers.

30. Ibid. ("I have only evenings"); Minutes, December 6, 1892, 47, BWM Papers ("was accomplishing a great deal").

31. See Anne Ruggles Gere, *Intimate Practices: Literacy and Cultural Work in U.S. Women's Clubs, 1880–1920* (Urbana: University of Illinois Press, 1997), 116.

32. Minutes, November 15, 1892, 33, 38, BWM Papers. The description of Mary Trautmann is Sara Hallowell's. See Weimann, *Fair Women,* 186.

33. Minutes, December 6, 1892, 43–44, 4, 50, BWM Papers; Margaret A. Sangster, "A Peep at the Past," *Harper's Bazar,* September 23, 1893, 783.

34. Board Minutes, December 19, 1892, box 1, vol. 6, BLM Papers.

35. Minutes, January 11, 1893, 53–55, BWM Papers.

36. Board Minutes, December 20, 1892, box 1, vol. 6, BLM Papers.

37. All quotations in this and the following paragraph are from Board Minutes, December 20, 1892, box 1, vol. 6, BLM Papers. See also Weimann, *Fair Women,* 359.

38. Bellamy to Trautmann, n.d., Misc. boxes, Oct. 1892–April, 1893, BLM Papers. One reason why the New York delegation may have been so unwilling to compromise was that they had also taken responsibility for preparing a library exhibit of all New York authors for the New York State Building, which was installed on May 26, 1893. Clara Stranahan and Blanche Bellamy had been integral in putting this collection together. For a description of the installation ceremony, see "Harriet Beecher Stowe Bust," *Boston Daily Globe,* May 27, 1893.

39. Minutes, January 10, 1893, 58–59, BWM Papers.

40. Minutes, January 11, 1893, 48–49, BWM Papers.

41. Ibid., 53–55.

42. Trautmann's comments are in Minutes, January 11, 1893, 53–55, BWM Papers; "Folios for the World's Fair," *New York Times,* February 19, 1893. See also "Women at Chicago," *Los Angeles Times,* January 29, 1893; and Caroline Garland, "Some of the Libraries at the Exposition," *Library Journal* 18 (August 1893): 284.

43. Palmer to Miss Dodd, March 2, 1893, box 6, vol. 15, BLM Papers. See also Garland, "Some of the Libraries at the Exposition," 284.

44. Garland, "Some of the Libraries at the Exposition," 284. None of this ire was evident in a report on Massachusetts women's contributions to the Woman's Building that appeared in "Windows from Women," *Boston Daily Globe,* April 25, 1893.

45. Minutes, February 14, 1893, 66, BWM Papers.

46. Wheeler, *Yesterdays in a Busy Life,* 341–42.

47. Minutes, March 7, 1893, 76–77, BWM Papers.

48. The prolific translator was probably Isabel Florence Hapgood, whose translations of works by Victor Hugo, Leo Tolstoy, Nikolai Gogol, and others were cataloged in the library's official *List of Books Sent by Home and Foreign Committees to the Library of the Woman's Building, Chicago, 1893,* compiled by Edith Clarke (Chicago, 1894).

49. Minutes, March 22, 1893, 88–89, BWM Papers.

50. Ibid.; Ives, "Report of the Board of Women Managers," 171–72. See also "Women's Work for the World's Fair," *Far and Near* 3 (May 1893): 142; "New York Woman's Exhibit," *Chicago Daily Tribune,* April 6, 1893; and "The Woman's Library," *Syracuse Evening Herald,* April 15, 1893.

51. Wheeler, *Yesterdays in a Busy Life,* 345–46. For photographs of some of the library's decorative pieces, see Peck and Irish, *Candace Wheeler,* 214, 236–37.

52. Minutes, May 2, 1893, 104–5, BWM Papers; Ives, "Report of the Board of Women Managers," 177.

53. See Ives, "Report of the Board of Women Managers," 171, 172.

54. Minutes, May 2, 1893, 104–5, BWM Papers; Weimann, *Fair Women,* 362. In a review of a Distaff Series volume, the *New York Times* identified the books as "the first written, edited, set up, and bound by women." See "Philanthropy in Literature," *New York Times,* September 3, 1893.

55. Blanche Bellamy, "New York Literary Exhibit,' in *Art and Handicraft in the Woman's Building of the World's Columbian Exposition, Chicago, 1893,* ed. Maud Howe Elliott (Paris:

Goupil, 1893), 115–17. The official *List of Books* in the Woman's Building Library includes only sixteen volumes by Child. Her controversial novel *Hobomok* is a notable absence. The thirty-one volume set of Child's work mentioned by Bellamy was most likely displayed separately.

56. Weimann, *Fair Women*, 361–62; Bellamy, "New York Literary Exhibit," 117–18. With the exception of three works written in German by the German-born Therese Albertina Louise von Jakob (Mrs. Edward Robinson), who wrote under the name "Talvi," the foreign-language books Bellamy cites are translations by Anglo-American women.

57. E. C. Hovey to Bertha Palmer, September 9, 1891, Misc. boxes, February–December 1891, BLM Papers.

58. Palmer to Hovey, September 16, 1891; Palmer to Davis, September 16, 1891, both in box 3, vol. 9, BLM Papers. For background information on Hovey's connection to the ALA, see Wayne A. Wiegand, *Politics of an Emerging Profession: The American Library Association, 1876–1917* (New York: Greenwood Press, 1986), 61.

59. Palmer to Parker, June 14, 1892, box 4, vol. 13, BLM Papers.

60. Palmer to the American Library Association, June 24, 1892; Secretary to Bertha Palmer to Mr. Dawson (Secretary of the Director General of the Exposition), July 7, 1892, both in box 4, vol. 13, BLM Papers.

61. Hill to Palmer, July 15, 1892, Misc. boxes, January–September 1892, BLM Papers.

62. Dewey was also president of the Library Bureau, and thus the employer of W. E. Parker, who had offered to help Palmer find a female librarian for the Woman's Library. See Wayne A. Wiegand, *Irrepressible Reformer: A Biography of Melvil Dewey* (Chicago: American Library Association, 1996), esp. 235–37. It is probable that Parker contacted Dewey about Palmer's need for a librarian.

63. Sophonisba Breckinridge estimated in 1933 that 75 percent of the public libraries in the United States owed their origins to the organizing efforts of a local women's club. See Breckinridge, *Women in the Twentieth Century* (New York: McGraw Hill, 1933), 93.

64. Palmer to Dewey, July 19, 1892, box 4, vol. 13, BLM Papers.

65. Palmer to Hill, July 15, 1892, box 4, vol. 13, BLM Papers.

66. Palmer to Dewey, January 31, 1893, box 3, Dewey Papers.

67. Palmer to Dewey, February 6, 1893, box 3, vol. 15, BLM Papers.

68. Quotations in this and the following two paragraphs are from Dewey to Palmer, February 15, 1893, box 3, Dewey Papers.

69. See Handy, *Official Directory*, 206. By the end of the fair the World's Congress Auxiliary had sponsored 1,238 separate sessions, at which 5,978 speeches and papers were presented. David F. Burg, *Chicago's White City of 1893* (Lexington: University Press of Kentucky, 1976), 238.

70. Hill to Dewey, April 29, 1892, box 2, Dewey Papers; Hill to George Watson Cole, April 30, 1892, George Watson Cole Papers, American Antiquarian Society, Worcester, Mass. (hereafter cited as Cole Papers); Hill to Richard Rogers Bowker, May 10, 1892, Richard R. Bowker Papers, Manuscripts and Archives Division, New York Public Library, Astor, Lenox and Tilden Foundations. The ALA's experiences in preparing for the 1893 World's Fair are described in more detail in Wiegand, *Politics of an Emerging Profession*, 40–74; and Wiegand, *Irrepressible Reformer*, 214–16.

71. H. P. James to Dewey, June 16, 1892; Hill to Dewey, June 16, 1892; F. M. Crunden to Dewey, June 17, 1892; Cutter to Dewey, June 19, 1892, June 20, 1892; Dewey to "Members

of the ALA Columbian Exposition Committee, June 22, 1892; Crunden to Dewey, June 26, 1892, all in box 3, Dewey Papers; Cutter to C. Alex Nelson, n.d. (attached to letter dated April 1, 1893), William Frederick Poole Papers, Newberry Library, Chicago.

72. Hild to Dewey, August 8, 1892; Dewey to "Standing Committee," September 5, 1892; Dewey to Hild, September 5, 1892; Hill to Dewey, September 9, 1892; Crunden to Dewey, September 12, 1892; James to Dewey, September 19, 1892, box 3, Dewey Papers.

73. Undated document titled "ALA Columbia Meeting, 1893, by Melvil Dewey," box 3, Dewey Papers. See also *Library Journal* 18 (February 1893): 44–45.

74. Palmer to Dewey, February 28, 1893, box 6, vol. 15, BLM Papers (also in box 3, Dewey Papers).

75. *World's Columbian Exposition Illustrated,* February 1893, 282–83.

76. Palmer to Reed, March 11, 1893; Palmer to Sage, March 20, 1893, both in box 6, vol. 15, BLM Papers.

77. See Budd L. Gambee, "Fairchild, Mary Salome Cutler (1855–1921)," and Joan M. Costello and Edward G. Holley, "James, Hannah Packard (1835–1903)," in *Dictionary of American Library Biography,* ed. Bohdan Wynar (Littleton, Colo.: Libraries Unlimited, 1978), 167–70 and 264–66.

78. Dewey to Palmer, March 22, 1893, box 3, Dewey Papers.

79. Dewey to Plummer, April 10, 1893, box 3, Dewey Papers. Dewey already knew Plummer would be at the fair, since she was scheduled to supply an educational exhibit. See "Pratt Institute Graduates," *Brooklyn Eagle,* February 5, 1893.

80. Palmer to Dewey, March 23, 1893, box 6, vol. 15, BLM Papers (also in box 3, Dewey Papers); Dewey to Palmer, March 24, 1893, box 3, Dewey Papers.

81. Dewey to Palmer, March 28, 1893, box 3, Dewey Papers. Although Clarke served as Poole's cataloger at the Newberry, she did not have a very high opinion of him. She complained that the Chicago Library Club "lack[ed] enthusiasm and outspokenness at our meetings" because Poole tended to dominate. Clarke to George Watson Cole, February 28, 1892, Cole Papers.

82. Clarke to Dewey, April 3, 1893; Dewey to Clarke, April 5, 1893, both in box 3, Dewey Papers.

83. Palmer to Clarke, April 11, 1893, box 6, vol. 15, BLM Papers.

84. Circular from Dewey titled "The Woman's Library at the World's Fair," dated April 12, 1893; Dewey to Coe, April 13 1893, both in box 3, Dewey Papers.

85. Coe to Dewey, April 13, 1893; Plummer to Dewey, April 15, 1893; West to Dewey, April 15, 1893, box 3, Dewey Papers. West did, however, contribute two works to the library: her *Bibliographical List of Works on Political Economy in Milwaukee Public Library* (n.p.) and her *History of Milwaukee Public Library* ([1893]), which makes no mention of the Linderfelt affair.

86. Undated document, box 3, Dewey Papers. Penciled in at the bottom of this draft is the notation "Registry of those interested for use at Albany."

87. Clarke to Dewey, April 16, 1893, box 3, Dewey Papers.

88. Dewey to Clarke, April 21, 1893, box 3, Dewey Papers.

89. Dewey to Palmer, April 15, 1893; Dewey to Plummer, April 15, 1893; Plummer to Dewey, April 20, 1893; Dewey to Plummer, April 21, 1893; Dewey to Palmer, April 21, 1893; Dewey to Plummer, April 25, 1893; and Dewey to Palmer, April 26, 1893, box 3, Dewey Papers.

90. Dewey to Mrs. Julia C. B. Dorr, May 12, 1893; see also Titcomb to Dewey, May 9, 1893; and Dewey to Titcomb, May 13, 1893, box 3, Dewey Papers.

91. BLM Executive Committee Minutes, April 25, 1893, box 1, vol. 6, BLM Papers; Clarke to Dewey, May 11, 1893, box 3, Dewey Papers. See also "Report of the Woman's Library," copy found in box 8, vol. 23, BLM Papers.

92. The quotation describing Eagle is from Enid Yandell and Laura Hayes, *Three Girls in a Flat* (Chicago: Knight, Leonard, 1892), 60; remaining quotations are from BLM Minutes, April 28, 1893, Misc. boxes, BLM Papers. A *Chicago Daily Tribune* reporter noted "the difficulty [the women who were arranging the library] have experienced in getting their cases in readiness." "It Is Near Readiness," *Chicago Daily Tribune*, April 30, 1893. See also Weimann, *Fair Women*, 238, 239.

93. On women who wanted to exhibit in state buildings see Weimann, *Fair Women*, 284–89.

4. Grand Opening

1. For a detailed description of the opening day ceremonies, see David F. Burg, *Chicago's White City of 1893* (Lexington: University Press of Kentucky, 1976), 109–13; and Rossiter Johnson, *A History of the World's Columbian Exposition Held in Chicago in 1893*, 4 vols. (New York: D. Appleton, 1897–1898), 1:343–45.

2. *Report of the President to the Board of Directors of the World's Columbian Exposition: Chicago, 1892–1893* (Chicago: Rand, McNally, 1898), 211; see also Robert Muccigrosso, *Celebrating the New World: Chicago's Columbian Exposition of 1893* (Chicago: Ivan R. Dee, 1993), 79–80.

3. "Woman's Building," *Daily Columbian*, May 2, 1893.

4. All descriptions and quotations from Palmer's speech in this and the following paragraphs are from *Addresses and Reports of Mrs. Potter Palmer, President of the Board of Lady Managers, World's Columbian Exposition* (Chicago: Rand, McNally, 1894), 131–41. A transcript of the speech also appears in Benjamin Cummings Truman, *History of the World's Fair: Being a Complete Description of the World's Columbian Exposition from Its Inception* (Chicago: Mammoth Publishing, 1893), 173–83. See also Jeanne Madeline Weimann, *The Fair Women: The Story of the Woman's Building, World's Columbian Exposition, Chicago, 1893* (Chicago: Academy Chicago, 1981), chap. 11.

5. Toward the end of the fair, Logan made her criticisms public. See "Criticized by Mrs. Logan," *Chicago Daily Tribune*, September 8, 1893; and "Replies to Mrs. Logan's Criticisms, *Chicago Daily Tribune*, September 9, 1893.

6. Logan quoted in Weimann, *Fair Women*, 313; Ellen M. Henrotin, "An Outsider's View of the Women's Exhibit," *Cosmopolitan*, September 1893, 561; "World's Fair Buildings," *American Architect*, November 5, 1892, 86. See also Weimann, *The Fair Women*, 313–23 and Burg, *White City*, 143.

7. Madame Léon Grandin, *A Parisienne in Chicago: Impressions of the World's Columbian Exposition*, trans. Mary Beth Raycraft (Urbana: University of Illinois Press, 2010), 128; Helen Keller, *The Story of My Life* (New York: Grosset and Dunlap, 1902), 220; undated Chicago *Record* article quoted in "Editorial Notes," *Woman's Journal*, August 12, 1893, 249, 250.

8. Isabel Bates Winslow, "Woman's Work at the World's Fair," *Far and Near* 4 (December

1893): 31–32; Elizabeth Kingsbury, ed., *Tales of An Amateur Adventuress: The Autobiography of Esther Gray* (Cincinnati: Editor Publishing, 1988), 101; and Helen Watterson, "Women's Excitement over 'Woman,'" *Forum* 16 (September 1893): 75.

9. Winslow, "Woman's Work," 31–32; Dora M. Morrell, "About Going to the Fair," *Far and Near* 4 (May 1893): 17–18.

10. "Editor's Outlook: The Queens of the World's Fair," *Chautauquan* 17.4 (July 1893): 474; Candace Wheeler, *Yesterdays in a Busy Life* (New York: Harper and Brothers, 1918), 346; Marian Shaw, *World's Fair Notes: A Woman Journalist Views Chicago's 1893 Columbian Exposition* ([St. Paul]: Pogo Press, 1993), 63; Marietta Holley, *Samantha at the World's Fair* (New York: Funk and Wagnalls, 1893), 285, 255–56.

11. Dewey to Garland, May 4, 1893; Garland to Dewey, May 6, 1893, and May 10, 1893 (quotation), box 3, Dewey Papers.

12. Handy, *Official Directory*, 205; Weimann, *Fair Women*, 328; see also Johnson, *History of the World's Columbian Exposition*, 1:220–21; *Connecticut at the World's Fair: Report of the Commissioners from Connecticut of the Columbian Exhibition of 1893 at Chicago. Also Report of the Work of the Board of Lady Managers of Connecticut* (Hartford: Case, Lockwood, and Brainard, 1898), 211; and Weimann, *Fair Women*, 329–31. In the first four months of the fair the dormitory housed 12,210 women.

13. Clarke to Dewey, May 5, 1893, box 3, Dewey Papers. Plummer corroborated Clarke's complaints. She wrote Dewey on May 8 that she had found the library "in a very incomplete state," and that Clarke was "now getting the catalogue made under great disadvantages." Plummer to Dewey, May 8, 1893, box 3, Dewey Papers.

14. Dewey to Clarke, May 9, 1893, box 3, Dewey Papers. See also Dewey to James, May 9, 1893; and Clarke to Dewey, May 11, 1893, box 3, Dewey Papers. That Dewey intended to use the women staffing the library to promote his brand of librarianship was always obvious. For example, on June 2, 1893, May Seymour, one of Dewey's subordinates at the New York State Library, sent "one hundred NYSL yearbooks and 200 small circulars" to Palmer for the librarians to distribute to visitors. Seymour to Palmer, June 2, 1893, box 3, Dewey Papers.

15. Edith Clarke, draft of "The Library in the Woman's Building," box 3, Dewey Papers.

16. Ibid.

17. Lucy Monroe, "Chicago Letter," *Critic*, June 3, 1893, 374.

18. All quotations in this and the following paragraph are from Edith Clarke, *Woman in Literature at the Fair, from the Standpoint of a Librarian and Cataloger* (privately printed; copy held by the Chicago History Museum), 7–9. See also Weimann, *Fair Women*, 367–68.

19. Dewey to Clarke, May 15, 1893, box 3, Dewey Papers.

20. Garland to Dewey, May 18, 1893, box 3, Dewey Papers.

21. Ibid., and Garland to Dewey, May 23, 1893; Margaret Tomes to Dewey, May 25, 1893, box 3, Dewey Papers.

22. All quotations in this paragraph are from Dewey to Garland, June 26, 1893; and Garland to Dewey, June 29, 1893, box 3, Dewey Papers.

23. Clarke to Dewey, May 18, 1893, box 3, Dewey Papers. Final records indicate that Edith Clarke worked April 25–30, all of May and June, and September 1–19; Caroline Garland, May 15–July 22; Mary Titcomb, June 3–30; Ellen Coe, June 20–July 30; Florence Woodworth, July 15–August 19; Ada Alice Jones, July 19–August 19; Helen Giles, September 1–18, Elizabeth Clarke, August 21–December 7; Mary Sargent, September 1–30; and Mary Loomis and Mary L. Davis, October 1–31. See "Expenses of Committee on Library," n.d., box 8, vol. 23, BLM Papers.

24. "The Bust Is Presented," *Chicago Tribune*, May 27, 1893; "Harriet Beecher Stowe Bust," *Boston Globe*, May 27, 1893. The quotations on Stowe and Child are from Laura E. Richards, "Woman in Literature," in *Art and Handicraft in the Woman's Building at the World's Columbian Exposition, Chicago, 1893*, ed. Maud Howe Elliott (Paris: Goupil, 1893), 102. (Richards and Elliott were both daughters of another prominent abolitionist writer, Julia Ward Howe.) The quotation on Sigourney is from Angela Sorby, "Symmetrical Womanhood: Poetry in the Woman's Building Library," *Libraries & Culture* 41.1 (Winter 2006): 16. On Wheeler's abolitionism, see Peck, "Candace Wheeler," 5–6, 14; and Wheeler, *Yesterdays in a Busy Life*, 36–38.

25. "As Uncle Tom: Fred Douglass Assists at Unveiling of the Harriett Beecher Stowe Bust," *Aberdeen Daily News*, May 26, 1893. According to this article, "Mr. Douglass heard of the proposed ceremony and asked to be permitted to stand as Uncle Tom." The reporter (or source) for this story was likely Matilda Joslyn Gage, whose son-in-law published the *Aberdeen Daily News*. See also "Fred Douglass as Uncle Tom: Unveiling of a Bust of Mrs Stowe at the Women's Building," *Chicago Daily Record*, May 25, 1893.

26. "World's Fair Letter," *Woman's Tribune*, June 3, 1893, 100. See also "Bust of Harriet Beecher Stowe," *Duluth News-Tribune*, May 29, 1893. Hooker described in Enid Yandell and Laura Hayes, *Three Girls in a Flat* (Chicago: Knight, Leonard, 1892), 59.

27. For an insightful analysis of other ways late nineteenth-century readers reinterpreted *Uncle Tom's Cabin*, see Barbara Hochman, *Uncle Tom's Cabin and the Reading Revolution* (Amherst: University of Massachusetts Press, 2011).

28. "Exposition Notes," *The Columbian Woman*, 22.

29. Quoted in Weimann, *Fair Women*, 530.

30. Ibid.

31. Yandell and Hayes, *Three Girls in a Flat*, 77.

32. The text of these speeches can be found in May Wright Sewall, ed., *The World's Congress of Representative Women*, 2 vols. (Rand, McNally, 1894), 1:433–37 (Harper) and 2:696–729 (Williams, Cooper, Coppin, Early, and Brown). See also Weimann, *Fair Women*, 545; Reid Badger, *The Great American Fair: The World's Columbian Exposition and American Culture* (Chicago: N. Hall, 1979), 105–6; Burg, *White City*, 239–49; Ann Ruggles Gere, *Intimate Practices: Literacy and Cultural Work in U.S. Women's Clubs, 1880–1920* (Urbana: University of Illinois Press, 1997), 137–38. For further discussion of these events, see Christopher Robert Reed, *"All the World Is Here!" The Black Presence in the White City* (Bloomington: Indiana University Press, 2000); Mary Jo Deegan, introduction to *The New Woman of Color: The Collected Writings of Fannie Barrier Williams, 1893–1918* (Dekalb: Northern Illinois University Press, 2002), xxix–xxi; Anna Julia Cooper, *The Voice of Anna Julia Cooper: Including "A Voice from the South" and Other Important Essays, Papers, and Letters*, ed. Charles Lemert and Esme Bhan (Lanham, Md.: Rowman and Littlefield, 1998), 201; and Vivian M. May, *Anna Julia Cooper, Visionary Black Feminist: A Critical Introduction* (New York: Routledge, 2007), 21.

33. James to Annie Dewey, January 25, 1893; James to Annie Dewey, May 10, 1893, box 20A, Dewey Papers; and Melvil Dewey to James, May 17, 1893, box 3, Dewey Papers.

34. Ellen M. Coe did, however, report on behalf of the ALA in the May 18 "Report Congress." See *Programme of the World's Congress of Representative Women* (Chicago: World's Congress Auxiliary, Department of Woman's Progress, 1893), 26.

35. For Rogers's remarks, see Mary Kavanaugh Oldham Eagle, ed., *The Congress of Women Held in the Woman's Building, World's Columbian Exposition, Chicago, U.S.A., 1893* (Chicago:

W. B. Conkey, 1894), 587; for Greene's remarks see 46–47. See also Johnson, *History of the World's Columbian Exposition*, 1:223–24, and Eagle, introduction to *Congress of Women*, n.p. In this introduction to her volume on the Congress of Women, Eagle regretfully acknowledges that a few papers that should have been included in the volume were unavailable to her (13).

36. Adelaide Hasse, "Women and Libraries," *Woman's Journal*, July 15, 1893, 222. See also Mary Biggs, "Librarians and the 'Woman Question': An Inquiry into Conservatism," *Journal of Library History* 17 (Fall 1982): 409–28. Gayle Gullett argues that the voices of the female working class were also absent from the Congress. See her "'Our Great Opportunity': Organized Women Advance Women's Work at the World's Columbian Exposition of 1893," *Illinois Historical Journal* 87 (Winter 1994): 259–76.

37. The "Congress of Libraries" program is described in *Library Journal* 18 (June 1893): 191. See also Giulia Sacconi-Ricci, "Observations on the Various Forms of Catalogs Used in Modern Libraries, with Special Reference to a System of Mechanical Binding," *Library Journal* 18 (October 1893): 423–27. In a chapter titled "The Library" that she wrote for a collection of essays published after the fair closed, Maud Howe Elliott indicated that "Mr. Melville [*sic*] Dewey . . . gives, as the result of his experience, the statement that our young women are better fitted for this work than their brothers. We learn from him that there is an ever-increasing demand for women librarians." Maud Howe Elliott, "The Library," in Elliott, *Art and Handicraft in the Woman's Building*, 111.

38. "World's Fair Letter," *Woman's Tribune*, July 7, 1893, 116. The incident involving breastfeeding is mentioned in Ishbel Ross, *Silhouette in Diamonds: The Life of Mrs. Potter Palmer* (1960; repr., New York: Arno Press, 1975), 92.

39. Quotations taken from a paper read before the Chicago Library Club in January, 1894. See Clarke, *Women in Literature at the Fair*, 2–3, 6. Since a permanent Woman's Library was not established after the fair closed, Higginson donated his collection to the Boston Public Library (see chapter 2). Higginson quotation is from Horace G. Wadlin, *The Public Library of the City of Boston: A History* (Boston: Boston Public Library, 1911), 154.

40. Garland, "Some of the Libraries at the Exposition," *Library Journal* 18 (August 1893): 284–85.

41. Ibid., 285.

42. "At the Fair," *Chicago Record*, May 12, 1893.

43. Minutes, June 20, 1893, 110–13, BWM Papers.

44. Minutes, August 8, 1893, 130, BWM Papers.

45. Press Committee report, July 21, 1893, box 8, vol. 23, BLM Papers.

46. How aware BLM members were of the catalog's status is difficult to discern. In her essay on the library, published after the fair closed, Maud Howe Elliott reported that "the catalogue, which has been very carefully prepared, will prove one of its most interesting features." Elliott, "The Library," 113.

47. Dewey to Palmer, August 28, 1893, box 3, Dewey Papers.

48. Loomis to Dewey October 21, 1893; Dewey to Loomis, October 23, 1893, both in box 3, Dewey Papers; Palmer to Jones, October 27, 1893; and Palmer to Mrs. S. G. Cooke of the Administration Building, October 27, 1893, both in box 6, vol. 16, BLM Papers. Palmer acknowledged this November 11 report in Palmer to Lockwood, November 15, 1893, box 6, vol. 16, BLM Papers. Dewey referred to Palmer's missive as "a remarkable letter," since responsibility for submitting a voucher "was never mentioned to me before." He nonetheless asked Edith Clarke to draw up a report and submit it to him so he could

certify and forward it to Palmer. See Dewey to Clarke, November 6, 1893, box 3, Dewey Papers. See also "Report of the Library Committee," October 23, 1893, box 8, vol. 23, BLM Papers.

49. Minutes, Executive Committee, October 28, 1893, box 1, vol. 6, BLM Papers; entry for October 28, 1983, Sallie Cotten Diary, Sallie Southall Cotten Papers #2613, Southern History Collection, Wilson Library, University of North Carolina, Chapel Hill.

50. James Clifford, "Museums as Contact Zones," in *Representing the Nation: A Reader: Histories, Heritage and Museums,* ed. David Boswell and Jessica Evans (London: Routledge, 1999), 440.

51. Clifford, "Museums as Contact Zones," 438, 446.

5. "To Read Her Is a Liberal Education"

1. Candace Wheeler, *Yesterdays in a Busy Life* (New York: Harper and Brothers, 1918), 357.

2. Candy Gunther Brown, "Publicizing Domestic Piety: The Cultural Work of Religious Texts in the Woman's Building Library," *Libraries & Culture* 41.1 (Winter 2006): 40.

3. Blanche Bellamy, "General Introduction," in *Woman and the Higher Education,* ed. Anna C. Brackett, Distaff Series (New York: Harper and Brothers, 1893), vi.

4. "Philanthrophy in Literature," *New York Times,* September 3, 1893. On the Distaff Series, see also Amelia Peck and Carol Irish, *Candace Wheeler: The Art and Enterprise of American Design, 1875–1900* (New York: Metropolitan Museum of Art, 2001), 69–70.

5. As Brown observes, "The prominence in the [Woman's Building Library] of at least two of the best represented authors, Frances Willard and Julia Ward Howe, might also be explained in part by these women's roles in sponsoring the Woman's Building.'"Publicizing Domestic Piety," 38.

6. On the World's Congress of Representative Women session of the American Protective Society of Authors, see *Publishers' Weekly* 43 (June 3, 1893): 851.

7. Sarah J. Lippincott, "A Statement of Fact," in *The World's Congress of Representative Women: A Historical Résumé for Popular Circulation of the World's Congress of Representative Women,* ed. May Wright Sewall, 2 vols. (Chicago: Rand, McNally, 1894), 2:891–94. Wheeler's comments on Anthony and Howe can be found in *Yesterdays in a Busy Life,* 355–56. Wheeler noted particularly Howe's "uncommonness": "She could not give you a cup of tea in her own house in Boston . . . without in a certain sense handing it down to you," she remarked (356).

8. On Field, see Gary Schornhorst, *Kate Field: The Many Lives of a Nineteenth-Century Journalist* (Syracuse, N.Y.: Syracuse University Press, 2008), 217–23. For Shaw's World's Fair dispatches and a biographical sketch, see Marian Shaw, *World's Fair Notes: A Woman Journalist Views Chicago's 1893 Columbian Exposition,* biographical sketch by Leo J. Harris ([St. Paul]: Pogo Press, 1992).

9. The *Programme of the World's Congress of Representative Women* includes the names of many of these women. Contemporary biographies of many of them can be found in Frances E. Willard and Mary Livermore, eds., *A Woman of the Century: Fourteen Hundred-Seventy Biographical Sketches Accompanied by Portraits of Leading American Women in All Walks of Life,* 2 vols. (1893; repr., Bowling Green Station, N.Y.: Gordon Press, 1975). Summaries and analyses of novels in the Woman's Building Library by Illinois women can be found in Bernice E. Gallagher, *Illinois Women Novelists in the Nineteenth Century: An Analysis and*

Annotated Bibliography (Urbana: University of Illinois Press, 1994). In particular, see entries on fair insiders Mary Hartwell Catherwood, Caroline Corbin, Elizabeth Morrison Boynton Harbert, Mary French Sheldon, Rebecca Ruter Springer, and Celia Parker Woolley.

10. Alan Trachtenberg, *The Incorporation of America: Culture and Society in the Gilded Age* (New York: Hill and Wang, 1982), 231. Consistent with this aim is Susan K. Harris's observation (based on Nina Baym's research) that one of the assumptions of nineteenth-century book reviewers was that a good novel should "present models of order to counter what [Lydia Maria] Child refers to 'as the present disorderly state of the world.'" Susan K. Harris, *19th-Century American Women's Novels: Interpretative Strategies* (Cambridge: Cambridge University Press, 1990), 19; and Nina Baym, *Novels, Readers, and Reviewers: Responses to Fiction in Antebellum America* (Ithaca: Cornell University Press, 1984), 173–95.

11. On the use of "the new woman" and "new womanhood," see the discussions of Candace Wheeler in chapter 4 and Annie Nathan Meyer later in this chapter. The Woman's Building Library contained an article titled "The New Womanhood" by Anna M. Fullerton, M.D. Later in the decade, suffragist Anna Howard Shaw, who spoke on "The Fate of Republics" at the Congress of Women, expanded the "New Woman" dialogue with her speech "The New Man," in which she called for "equal pay for equal quality and quantity of work." See Will A. Linkugel and Martha Solomon, *Anna Howard Shaw: Suffrage Orator and Social Reformer* (New York: Greenwood Press, 1991), 32, 129.

12. The faith in the continuous advancement of humanity and civilization resonates with several popular theories of the time, including Herbert Spencer's social Darwinism, social evolutionary theory, and Unitarianism's emphasis on the progressive advancement of human spirituality. For a discussion of these ideas in connection with Unitarianism, see Lee Schweninger, *The Writings of Celia Parker Woolley (1848–1918), Literary Activist* (Lewiston, N.Y.: Edwin Mellen Press, 1998), especially chap. 2 and the epilogue.

13. The phrase is Trachtenberg's (*Incorporation of America*, 217). On Wheeler and the Aesthetic movement, see Mary Warner Blanchard, *Oscar Wilde's America: Counterculture in the Gilded Age* (New Haven: Yale University Press, 1998), chap. 2, and Kathleen D. McCarthy, *Women's Culture: American Philanthropy and Art, 1830–1930* (Chicago: University of Chicago Press, 1991), chap. 2.

14. Abby Morton Diaz, *Only a Flock of Women* (Boston: D. Lothrop, 1893), 1. The daughter of Ichabod Morton, an abolitionist who briefly belonged to the Brook Farm Community, Diaz was an author, lecturer, teacher, and reformer. She was a founder of the Woman's Educational and Industrial Union of Boston and served on the Home Advisory Council of the World's Congress of Representative Women.

15. The content analysis figures cited in this chapter are derived from a bibliographical database covering the American portion of the Woman's Building Library (archived at ePublications@Marquette). They represent the basic outlines of the content areas of the library, rather than a statistically exact measure, as they do not account for about 800 unclassified books, out of a total of 4,855 records. These unclassified books are either absent from WorldCat and other sources used to develop the database, or their records lack Dewey numbers in WorldCat and other sources consulted. The figures also do not distinguish between juvenile books and works for adults.

16. By 1850 women and girls constituted the largest segment of the market for belles lettres in the United States, and by the early 1870s women were producing nearly three-fourths of all the novels published in the United States. See Nina Baym, *The Shape of Hawthorne's Career* (Ithaca, N.Y.: Cornell University Press, 1976), 17–18; and Susan Coul-

trap-McQuin, *Doing Literary Business: American Women Writers in the Nineteenth Century* (Chapel Hill: University of North Carolina Press, 1990), 2.

17. Other DDC categories that fall within the "Literature" class are "Rhetoric and collections of literature" (67 volumes in the American section identified), "American literature in English" (60 volumes identified), "American miscellaneous writings" (34 volumes), and "German fiction" (34 volumes). For comparative percentages in the ALA model library, see 222n49.

18. Jane Tompkins, *Sensational Designs: The Cultural Work of American Fiction, 1790–1860* (New York: Oxford University Press, 1986), xi. For an illuminating survey of late nineteenth-century poetry included in the library, see Angela Sorby, "Symmetrical Womanhood: Poetry in the Woman's Building Library," *Libraries & Culture* 41.1 (Winter 2006): 5–34.

19. Frances Willard, *How to Win: A Book for Girls* (Chicago: Woman's Temperance Publication Association, 1886), 103; Elizabeth Boynton Harbert, *Amore* (Chicago: New Era, 1892), 96, 99; Elizabeth Cady Stanton, "Preface," in Helen H. Gardener, *Pray You, Sir, Whose Daughter?* (New York: R. F. Fenno, 1892), vi–vii; WCTU lecturer quoted in Alison M. Parker, "'Hearts Uplifted and Minds Refreshed': The Woman's Christian Temperance Union and the Production of Pure Culture in the United States, 1880–1930," *Journal of Women's History* 11.2 (1999): 141. In *Pray You, Sir, Whose Daughter?* Gardener, a suffragist who gave three addresses at the World's Congress of Representative Women, argues for legislation to raise the age of consent and protests the economic dependence imposed on women. Boynton served on the Committee on a World's Congress of Representative Women and moderated a congress session devoted to the National Columbian Household Economic Association.

20. Frances E. W. Harper, *Iola Leroy; or, Shadows Uplifted* (1892; repr. Boston: Beacon, 1987), 236. Palmer's dedication speech is cited in 237n4.

21. See, for example, Elizabeth Harbert Boynton's *Amore* (1892) and *Out of Her Sphere* (1871) on women's rights; Harriet Newall Kneeland Goff's *Was It an Inheritance? Or Nannie Grant* (1876) on temperance; Harriette A. Keyser's *On the Borderland* (1882) on mental illness; and Alice Wellington Rollins's *Uncle Tom's Tenement* (1888) on economic oppression. Anna E. Dickinson and Harriet Newall Kneeland Goff (see chapter 6) both wrote novels exposing racially motivated violence and advocating African American rights.

22. Lillie Devereux Blake, *Fettered for Life; or, Lord and Master: A Story of Today* (New York: Sheldon, 1874), 254. See also May Rogers, "The Novel as Educator of the Imagination," in *The Congress of Women, Held in the Woman's Building, World's Columbian Exposition,* ed. Mary Kavanaugh Oldham Eagle (Chicago: Monarch Book Company, 1894), 586–89. For a look at Louisa May Alcott's account of how shared reading of two texts in the Woman's Building Library—Rose Terry Cooke's *Happy Dodd; or, "She hath done what she could"* (1878) and Helen Stuart Campbell's *Prisoners of Poverty: Women Wage-Workers, Their Trades and Their Lives* (1887) —prompted members of a literary club to engage in community service, see Sarah Wadsworth, "Social Reading, Social Work, and the Social Function of Literacy in Louisa May Alcott's 'May Flowers,'" in *Reading Women: Literary Figures and Cultural Icons from the Victorian Age to the Present,* ed. Janet Badia and Jennifer Phegley (Toronto: University of Toronto Press, 2005), 149–67.

23. These novelists share something of the transitional quality Angela Sorby identifies in the postsentimental "genteel idealist" poets represented in the Woman's Building Library. See Sorby, "Symmetrical Womanhood." For further commentary on the library's novelist-reformers, see Sarah Wadsworth, "Refusing to Write Like Henry James: Women

Reforming Realism in *Fin-de-siècle* America," *European Journal of American Studies* 2011 (2), http://ejas.revues.org/9067.

24. For example, Lee Schweninger, in *The Writings of Celia Parker Woolley*, suggests that Woolley's "social purpose and artistic intentions are one in [*sic*] the same" (109) and that Woolley "use[d] the novel as a vehicle to analyze and explore social concerns such as the place of religion and the status of women in nineteenth-century America" (75).

25. Celia Parker Woolley, "The East and the West, Once More," *Dial*, October 16, 1893, 217, quoted in Schweninger, *Writings of Celia Parker Woolley*, 49–50.

26. The Woman's Christian Temperance Union (many of whose publications appeared in the Woman's Building Library) attempted to implement this blending of literary and moral aims on a large, institutional scale through their Department for the Promotion of Purity in Literature and Art, which, Alison M. Parker observes, "defined a cultural hierarchy that prioritized morality as a crucial component of aesthetics, and then created those cultural products it deemed superior according to this standard of purity." According to this view, "that 'which was not morally sound could not be aesthetically pleasing.'" Parker, "'Hearts Uplifted and Minds Refreshed,'" 137–38.

27. See Baym, *Woman's Fiction*. Elsewhere, Baym writes, "We may discover in time that representations of female selves as privatized and domesticated beings are actually minority strands in nineteenth-century American women's literature, owing their prominence to present-day preoccupations." Nina Baym, *American Women Writers and the Work of History, 1790–1860* (New Brunswick, N.J.: Rutgers University Press, 1995), 4. In the Woman's Building Library, the domestic strand is so interwoven with others that its precise proportion would be impossible to determine. Nevertheless, the library's contents tend to support Baym's suggestion.

28. See Nancy T. Gilliam, "A Professional Pioneer: Myra Bradwell's Fight to Practice Law," *Law and History Review* 5.1 (Spring 1987): 105–33. As Gilliam notes, "In 1860, there were no female attorneys in the United States; the 1870 census would list five. A decade later there would be seventy-five women lawyers in this country" (107). Authors of legal texts in the Woman's Building Library include Mary L. Rice, Lelia Josephine Robinson, and M. B. R. Shay, along with Bradwell.

29. See Baym, *American Women Writers and the Work of History*, and Wanda M. Corn, *Women Building History: Public Art at the 1893 Columbian Exposition* (Berkeley: University of California Press, 2011).

30. Harris, *19th-Century American Women's Novels*, 24; Scott E. Casper, *Constructing American Lives: Biography and Culture in Nineteenth-Century America* (Chapel Hill: University of North Carolina Press, 1999), 78. The most important reasons for the growth in women's biographies, Casper argues, were "the increase in women's reading and writing associated with the evangelical revivalism of the 1830s and new, middle-class forms of activity that offered women new avenues into prominence as agents of reform and as subjects of biography" (78).

31. Alison Booth, *How to Make It as a Woman: Collective Biographical History from Victoria to the Present* (Chicago: University of Chicago Press, 2004), 213–14. Group biographies of women in the Woman's Building Library include the two-volume *Pen-Portraits of Literary Women by Themselves and Others*, edited by Helen Gray Cone and Jeannette L. Gilder, Lydia Maria Child's *Biographies of Good Wives* (1846), Jesse Clement's *Noble Deeds of American Women* (1851), Sarah J. Hale's *Biography of Distinguished Women* (1876), *Worthy Women of Our First Century* (1877), by Sarah Butler Wister and Agnes Irwin, and Sarah K. Bolton's

Successful Women (1888), which includes the earliest known biography of Candace Wheeler (Peck, "Candace Wheeler," 76). Ellet's three-volume *The Women of the American Revolution* was "the first study [of the Revolutionary War] to be based wholly on authenticated primary sources" and is still regarded as "a landmark document in social history." Quotations on Ellet are from Cathy N. Davidson and Linda Wagner-Martin, eds., *Oxford Companion to Women's Writing of the United States* (New York: Oxford University Press, 1995), 274–75. See also Casper, *Constructing American Lives,* 158–78, 306–9.

32. Mary Florence Taney, *Kentucky Pioneer Women: Columbian Poems and Prose Sketches* (Cincinnati: Robert Clarke, 1893), n.p. On the practice of writing the lives of deceased relatives, see Casper, *Constructing American Lives,* 15, 115–19.

33. Mary Stuart Smith, *Lang Syne; or, The Ward of Mount Vernon: A Tale of the Revolutionary Era* (New York: J. B. Alden, 1890), 97.

34. Flora Adams Darling, "Daughters of the Revolution, 1776–1812," in *The Columbian Woman,* ed. Mrs. Rollin A. Edgerton (Chicago, 1893), 7.

35. Smith, *Lang Syne,* 133. In her study of religious texts in the *Woman's Building Library,* Candy Gunther Brown observes a similar interest in texts such as memoirs and biographies that "simultaneously exalted women's religious character and provided examples of pious women who had stretched the boundaries of the domestic sphere." Brown, "Publicizing Domestic Piety," 45.

36. [Annie Nathan Meyer], *Helen Brent, M.D.: A Social Study* (New York: Cassell, 1892), 93–94; Casper, *Constructing American Lives,* 78.

37. Susan Griffin, "Women, Anti-Catholicism, and Narrative in Nineteenth-Century America," in *The Cambridge Companion to Nineteenth-Century American Women's Writing* (Cambridge: Cambridge University Press, 2001), 157; Robert H. Abzug, *Cosmos Crumbling: American Reform and the Religious Imagination* (New York: Oxford University Press, 1994), 4. Candy Gunther Brown's research further substantiates the primacy of religion in contemporary print culture, as well as its preponderance and significance in the Woman's Building Library. Working with an earlier version of the library database, Brown identified 1,593 American titles "explicitly religious in content" (36).

38. Among these are Caroline M. Sawyer's translation of *Leaves of Antiquity; or, The Poetry of Hebrew Tradition,* by Johann Gottfried von Herder (1847) and Matilda Coxe Stevenson's *The Religious Life of the Zuni Child* (1887). Also of note are Elizabeth A. Reed's *Hindu Literature; or, The Ancient Books of India* (1890) and *Persian Literature: Ancient and Modern* (1893).

39. Beverly Zink-Sawyer, *From Preachers to Suffragists: Woman's Rights and Religious Conviction in the Lives of Three Nineteenth-Century American Clergywomen* (Louisville, Ky.: Westminster John Knox Press, 2003), 3, 20–21, 23.

40. This text was almost certainly written by the New England minister, temperance worker, and suffragist Phebe Hanaford, although the absence of complete bibliographical data makes attribution difficult. The text was most likely an unpublished manuscript (possibly a lecture) or a pamphlet.

41. As Zink-Sawyer notes, "most gender battles of the nineteenth-century . . . were fought against the backdrop of biblical, ecclesiastical, and theological issues" (*From Preachers to Suffragists,* 8). On Gage see Leila R. Brammer, *Excluded from Suffrage History: Matilda Joslyn Gage, Nineteenth-Century American Feminist* (Westport, Conn.: Greenwood Press, 2000), 18; for a detailed summary and analysis of *Woman, Church, and State,* see 80–91. On Blackwell, see Elizabeth Cazden, *Antoinette Brown Blackwell: A Biography* (Old West-

bury, N.Y.: The Feminist Press, 1983). Other ordained Columbian Woman writers include Augusta Cooper Bristol and Mary L. Moreland.

42. Schweninger, *Writings of Celia Parker Woolley*, 57–58.

43. See Brown, "Publicizing Domestic Piety," 40–43, for a breakdown of denominations represented in the Woman's Building Library. Brown observes, for example, that the Presbyterian Board of Publication was "the best-represented publisher in both the religion database [a subset of the library]" and the entire library (40). Weimann points out that more than a third of the groups represented in the Organizations Room had religious affiliations. Jeanne Madeline Weimann, *The Fair Women: The Story of the Woman's Building, World's Columbian Exposition, Chicago, 1893* (Chicago: Academy Chicago, 1981), 499.

44. Schweninger, *Writings of Celia Parker Woolley*, 53.

45. Ibid., 4–5, 23.

46. Ibid., 80; on Woolley's contribution to the printed history of the Chicago Woman's Club, see 22.

47. Celia Parker Woolley, *Love and Theology* (Boston: Ticknor, 1887), 13, 38–39, 45, 47, 250–51, 63. On the novel's early success see Schweninger, *Writings of Celia Parker Woolley*, 27.

48. Woolley, *Love and Theology*, 436, 439.

49. Ibid., 26–27, 138.

50. Willard, *How to Win*, 20.

51. As Susan K. Harris observes, "the desire for an education is one of the most common themes evinced in nineteenth-century women's literature." Harris, *19th-Century American Women's Novels*, 27.

52. *The Columbian Woman*, 5; Dewey quoted in "World's Fair Letter," *Woman's Tribune* 10 (July 29, 1893). In her memoir, the novelist and illustrator Mary Hallock Foote confessed less enthusiastically that "education pursued one there till the mind became glutted and one longed to go away and look at the Javanese dancers." Rodman W. Paul, ed., *A Victorian Gentlewoman in the Far West: The Reminiscences of Mary Hallock Foote* (San Marino, Calif.: Huntington Library, 1972), 357. Her remark resonates with Henry Adams's observation that "education ran riot" at the exposition. Quoted in Robert W. Rydell, "The Chicago World's Columbian Exposition of 1893: 'And Was Jerusalem Builded Here?'" in *Representing the Nation: A Reader: Histories, Heritage and Museums*, ed. David Boswell and Jessica Evans (London: Routledge, 1999), 280. For a firsthand account of the education one young man received at the exposition, see G. L. Dybwad and Joy V. Bliss, eds., *White City Recollections: The Illustrated 1893 Diary of Friend Pitts Williams' Trip to the World's Columbian Exposition* (Albuquerque: The Book Stops Here, 2003).

53. Celia Parker Woolley, *A Girl Graduate* (Boston: Houghton, Mifflin, 1889), 299, 240–41.

54. Woolley, *A Girl Graduate*, 251, 257, 196.

55. Harris, *19th-Century American Women's Novels*, 27.

56. Woolley, *A Girl Graduate*, 359, 293.

57. Harris, *19th-Century American Women's Novels*, 26.

58. Quoted in Schweninger, *Writings of Celia Parker Woolley*, 27, from *Coldwater (Mich.) Republican*, February 19, 1889.

59. Woolley, *A Girl Graduate*, 24, 388.

60. For a discussion of Springer's novels, see Bernice E. Gallagher, *Illinois Women's Novelists in the Nineteenth Century* (Urbana: University of Chicago Press, 1994), 167–72.

61. See Enid Yandell and Laura Hayes, *Three Girls in a Flat* (Chicago: Knight, Leonard, 1892), 115–25.

62. For more about Pool, see "A Brief Sketch of the Life of Maria Louise Pool," at www. burrows.com/poolbio.html. We are grateful to John Burrows for acquainting us with Pool's work. On sex radicalism, see Joanne E. Passet, *Sex Radicals and the Quest for Women's Equality* (Urbana: University of Illinois Press, 2003), esp. 19–38 (on Nichols), 96–111 (on Woodhull), and 112–21 (on Waisbrooker).

63. Quotations from Grace Farrell, afterword to *Fettered for Life; or, Lord and Master: A Story of To-Day*, by Lillie Devereux Blake (1874; New York: Feminist Press at City University of New York, 1996), 387, 413. According to Farrell, "*Fettered for Life* is a subversive, rather than simply a reform novel"; as she explains, reform novels reveal "how social institutions do not live up to an ideal, [but] do not subvert these institutions at all." On the other hand, "subversive novels not only reveal social ills, but also challenge underlying cultural presumptions" (387). *Woman's Place To-day*, according to Elinore Hughes Partridge, "created a sensation in the contemporary press and did much to awaken women into active workers for suffrage" (quoted in Farrell, afterword to *Fettered for Life*, 417). On the NAWSA exhibit in the Organizations Room, see Weimann, *Fair Women*, 494.

64. Grace Farrell, *Lillie Devereux Blake: Retracing a Life Erased* (Amherst: University of Massachusetts Press, 2002), 4. The quotation on Blake's platform presence is from Leila R. Brammer, *Excluded from Suffrage History: Matilda Joslyn Gage, Nineteenth-Century Feminist* (Westport, Conn.: Greenwood Press, 2000), 6. See also Lori D. Ginzburg, *Women and the Work of Benevolence: Morality, Politics, and Class in the Nineteenth-Century United States* (New Haven: Yale University Press, 1990), 188. See Grace Farrell, "Beneath the Suffrage Narrative," *Canadian Review of American Studies* 36.1 (2006), 45–65, and Farrell, afterword to *Fettered for Life*, 417, for a synopsis of how Blake was "systematically marginalized" by the NAWSA; and Farrell, *Lillie Devereux Blake*, 145–48, on Blake's role in connection with Barnard.

65. Farrell, afterword to *Fettered for Life*, 393. For Blake, Farrell observes, "gender is socially constructed and historically contingent" (393). Blake's anonymous 1863 essay "The Social Condition of Woman" articulates her view that "the characteristics of 'true womanliness' are the result not of nature but of training" (afterword to *Fettered for Life*, 292).

66. Blake, *Fettered for Life*, 53.

67. Ibid., 64.

68. Weimann, *Fair Women*, 122, 381, 391, 377; see 376–90 for a detailed discussion of the exhibit. See also BLM Secretary's Report, n.d., vol. 8, BLM Papers; Florence C. Ives, "Report of the Board of Woman Managers," in *Report of the Board of General Managers of the Exhibit of the State of New York at the World's Columbian Exposition* (Albany: James B. Lyon, 1894), 181–82.

69. Farrell, afterword to *Fettered for Life*, 394.

70. On Kellogg, see Chester M. Destler, "The Influence of Edward Kellogg upon American Radicalism, 1865–96," *Journal of Political Economy* 40.3 (June 1932): 338–65. Larcom and Goddard had both previously contributed to the *Lowell Offering*. See Judith A. Ranta, *Women and Children of the Mills: An Annotated Guide to Nineteenth-Century American Textile Factory Literature* (Westport, Conn.: Greenwood Press, 1999), 299. Goddard's *Trojan Sketch Book* also contained contributions by a number of other female writers, some of whom may have been working-class writers as well. The volume, titled "Sketches," by the New Century Guild of Working Women was, apparently, unpublished and has not been located.

In *Thoughts of Busy Girls,* the working-class perspectives represented are mediated through the organization of a benevolent society as well as through Dodge's editorial control.

71. Thomas J. Jablonsky, *The Home, Haven, and Mother Party: Female Anti-Suffragists in the United States, 1868–1920* (Brooklyn, N.Y.: Carlson Publishing, 1994), xxv. Other texts by prominent "Antis" in the Woman's Building Library include Jeannette L. Gilder's *Pen-Portraits of Literary Women,* four volumes of fiction by Molly Elliot Seawell, *Two Modern Women: A Novel* (1890) by Kate Gannett Wells, six volumes by Kate Douglass Wiggin, eight volumes authored or edited by Helen Kendrick Johnson, and Kate Field's *Charles Albert Fechter* (1882) and *Kate Field's Washington* (1882).

72. Maud Howe Elliott, "The Library," in *Art and Handicraft in the Woman's Building of the World's Columbian Exposition, Chicago, 1893,* ed. Elliott (Paris: Goupil, 1893), 109. On Deland's popularity, see also Diana C. Reep, *Margaret Deland* (Boston: Twayne Publishers, 1985), preface, [ix]; 15–16.

73. Reep, *Margaret Deland,* preface, [xi], [ix]. Reep writes in her preface that Deland "was later accused of advocating free love, approving of adultery, being a pacifist, and attacking women's rights—all because of her fiction" ([ix]). *John Ward, Preacher* sold well—six editions in five months (Willard and Livermore, *A Woman of the Century,* 1:238). This was "partly because of the vicious attacks on it. Ministers preached against its 'attack on Christianity'; the Boston YWCA refused to put a copy in its library; Professor Edward Gardiner of the Massachusetts Institute of Technology was forced to leave a dinner party after revealing that the Delands were friends. Publisher Henry O. Houghton just laughed, 'Abuse will help the sales.'" Reep, *Margaret Deland,* 9; see also Deland, *Golden Yesterdays,* 223–25.

74. Margaret Deland, *John Ward, Preacher* (Boston: Houghton, Mifflin, 1888), 178.

75. Ibid., 40, 42, 87–88, 191, 427.

76. Deland, *Golden Yesterdays,* 5, 215–16, 220.

77. Deland, *John Ward, Preacher,* 191, 391, 402, 405.

78. Ibid., 9–11.

79. Ibid., 462, 472.

80. Annie Nathan Meyer, *It's Been Fun: An Autobiography* (New York: H. Schuman, 1951), 215. Other American Jewish women we have identified in the Woman's Building Library include Harriet Lieber Cohen, Mary M. Cohen, Mrs. Lee Cohen Harby, Frances Hellman, Rebekah Hyneman, Emma Lazarus, Cornelia Kahn, Ruth Ward Kahn, Rosalie Kaufman, Simha Cohen Peixotto, and Alice Hyneman Rhine. The library also contained two texts that document the contribution of Jewish Americans to abolition and racial justice: Kate R. Pickard's *The Kidnapped and the Ransomed* (1856) and Harriet Newell Kneeland Goff's *Other Fools and Their Doings* (1880). See chapter 6.

81. Lynn D. Gordon, "Annie Nathan Meyer and Barnard College: Mission and Identity in Women's Higher Education, 1889–1950," *History of Education Quarterly* 26.4 (Winter 1986): 517. In *Barnard Beginnings* (Boston: Houghton Mifflin, 1935), Meyer tells how she launched the campaign to found the women's branch of Columbia following a conversation with and suggestion from Melvil Dewey, then Columbia's librarian. See also Meyer, *It's Been Fun,* 166–68; and, for a discussion of the controversy over Meyer's role in the founding of Barnard, Gordon, "Annie Nathan Meyer and Barnard College."

82. Meyer, *It's Been Fun,* 271, 268. According to Meyer, *Black Souls* was the first play to portray African Americans as "ladies and gentlemen, college professors, instead of the usual Mammies, faithful servants of ne'er-do-wells" (268).

83. In her autobiography Meyer writes of *Woman's Work in America:* "Although at the

time, there were several other such compilations, George William Curtis, the distinguished critic, stated that it was the only book of its kind to be taken seriously. The then President of Vassar spoke of its thoroughness and breadth; the United States Commissioner of Education called it a great book." *It's Been Fun*, 218.

84. Ibid., 202–6, 16; Gordon, "Annie Nathan Meyer and Barnard College," 512.

85. Harris, *19th-Century American Women's Novels*, 30.

86. Other women doctors identified in the Woman's Building Library are M. Imogene Bassett, Frances N. Baker, Alice Bennett, Alice B. Condict, C. R. Conkey, Rachel Brooks Gleason, Cornelia Kahn, C. M. Kennedy, Clara Marshall, Sarah J. McNutt, Marie J. Mergler, Eliza C. Minard, Eliza M. Mosher, Sarah Linton Phelps, Mary P. Sawtelle, Alice B. Stockham, and Anita Tyng. The presence of the work of so many female doctors, along with texts by professional scientists such as Rachel Holloway Lloyd, Hellen Abbott Michael, and Margaretta Palmer, and a host of books on botany, zoology, and geology contributes to the knowledge of American women's professional scientific endeavors, along with a "growing awareness that a broad range of nonprofessional and quasi-professional scientific activities were pursued by U.S. women" in the nineteenth century. Nina Baym, *American Women of Letters and the Nineteenth-Century Sciences: Styles of Affiliation* (New Brunswick, N.J.: Rutgers University Press, 2002), 6; for a useful discussion of "Women of Letters and Medical Science" (including several of the physicians represented in the Woman's Building Library), see 174–84.

87. [Meyer], *Helen Brent, M.D.*, 20–21; Meyer, *It's Been Fun*, 5. Like Candace Wheeler, Meyer wrote of the "new womanhood" prior to the date commonly cited as the debut of the phrase "New Woman"; Meyer, *It's Been Fun*, 5.

88. [Meyer], *Helen Brent, M.D.*, 126, 109, 104–5.

89. Meyer, *It's Been Fun*, 218, 3.

90. [Meyer], *Helen Brent, M.D.*, 38–40.

91. Ibid., 40, 54, 27, 30, 129–30.

92. Ibid., 53, 135, 195–96. Meyer did not shrink from treating delicate topics. Of *Helen Brent, M.D.*, she wrote, "it was ahead of its day; for it handled with great frankness the theme of social evil. . . . One critic declared its place was in a doctor's office or laboratory, not in the library of a lay person" (218). In her autobiography she also recalls her "unpublished novel written about thirty-five years ago . . . about a woman who craved maternity, but who did not want either marriage or just sleeping with man. She had her child by artificial insemination, a theme which shocked two publishing houses to the marrow, but which today is written of quite casually in the daily newspapers." Meyer, *It's Been Fun*, 3. On Meyer's treatment of controversial racial issues, see *It's Been Fun*, 271.

93. Caroline Fairfield Corbin, *Rebecca; or, A Woman's Secret* (Chicago: Clarke, 1868), 155.

94. Caroline Corbin, *Letters from a Chimney-Corner: A Plea for Pure Homes and Sincere Relations between Men and Women* (Chicago: Fergus Printing, 1886), 9, 29, 34–35, 47. Corbin's treatment of this unique womanly power was singled out for praise in several reviews. *Rebecca* "treats the Woman Question with rare delicacy and strength," noted the *New Covenant*. "Every woman who reads the book will be grateful to the author for the grand womanliness of each of its women, and for the contribution its temper and spirit make to the question of Woman's Position." Quoted in advertisement included in the back matter of Corbin's juvenile novel *Belle and the Boys* (Chicago: Jansen, McClurg, 1880).

95. In *Letters from a Chimney-Corner*, Corbin explained, "It has been a continuous labor of my life for more than thirty years, to become familiar with all accessible facts and con-

ditions bearing upon those relations which consign women to infamy and desecrate the home" (40–41). On the "social purity" movement see Ginzburg, *Women and the Work of Benevolence,* 202–3.

96. Jane Jerome Camhi, *Women Against Women: American Anti-Suffragism, 1880–1920* (Brooklyn, N.Y.: Carlson Publishing, 1994), 238–39, 85. Corbin wasn't the only author represented in the Woman's Building Library who worried about the impact of socialism on women's role. In *The Republic of the Future, or Socialism a Reality* (New York: Cassell, 1887), Anna Bowman Dodd expresses concern that men will lack sentiment and affection for "men-women—who are neither mothers nor housekeepers" (42) in her fictitious twenty-first-century American socialist republic, where men and women do the same work and children are brought up by the state. Corbin elaborated her views on socialism and suffrage in her pamphlets *The Position of Women in the Socialist Utopia* (1901) and *Socialism and Christianity, with Reference to the Woman Question* (1905), both published by the Illinois Association Opposed to the Extension of Suffrage to Women.

97. Quotations are from the "Third Annual Report of the Illinois Association Opposed to the Extension of Suffrage to Women" (1906), quoted in Camhi, *Women Against Women,* 85–86.

98. Caroline F. Corbin, "The Higher Womanhood," in Eagle, *Congress of Women Held in the Woman's Building,* 326.

99. Harper, "Woman's Political Future," in *The World's Congress of Representative Women,* ed. May Wright Sewall, 2 vols. (Chicago: Rand, McNally, 1894), 1:433–34; Jablonsky, *The Home, Heaven, and Mother Party,* xxvi.

100. Marietta Holley, *Samantha at the World's Fair* (New York: Funk and Wagnalls, 1893), 255–56.

101. As Farrell notes, "Reformers saw the complex interrelationship among [a range of] social issues and those that particularly affected women's lives, and often they devoted their time to more than one major issue." Farrell, afterword to *Fettered for Life,* 386.

102. Michel Foucault, "Texts/Contexts: Of Other Spaces," trans. Jay Miskowiec, in *Grasping the World: The Idea of the Museum,* ed. Donald Preziosi and Claire J. Farago (Aldershot, England: Ashgate, 2004), 374.

103. Farrell, afterword to *Fettered for Life;* Corbin, *Rebecca,* 8.

6. Ghosts and Shadows

1. Annie Nathan Meyer, *It's Been Fun: An Autobiography* (New York: H. Schuman, 1951), 165.

2. Ibid.

3. Rosemarie K. Bank, "Representing History: Performing the Columbian Exposition," *Theatre Journal* 54.4 (December 2002): 591. Invoking Foucault's theory of the heterotopia, Bank proposes a more nuanced view of the fair than that suggested by the "binary negation" of this "dream scenario" and its "flip side": "the demon scenario" of "exhibits and interpretations that produced intensely racist, sexist, and ethnist effects" (591). James C. Davis observes that "while there are empirical reasons for the whiteness of the White City (a mere 1.3 percent of Chicago was black in 1890), its racial makeup was no demographic accident but the result of a systematic effort." See Davis, "'Stage Business' as Citizenship: Ida B. Wells at the World's Columbian Exposition," in *Women's Experience of Modernity,*

1875–1945, ed. Ann L. Ardis and Leslie W. Lewis (Baltimore: Johns Hopkins University Press, 2003), 191.

4. Candace Wheeler, *Yesterdays in a Busy Life* (New York: Harper and Brothers, 1918), 11.

5. Hazel Carby, *Reconstructing Womanhood: The Emergence of the Afro-American Woman Novelist* (New York: Oxford University Press, 1987), 5.

6. "*Towards the Gulf:* A Brief Sketch of Its Author," New Orleans *Times-Democrat,* January 30, 1887; John Q. Anderson, "Folklore in Two Northeast Louisiana Novels," *Louisiana Folklore Miscellany* 2.1 (August 1961): 40. See also Kate Stone, *Brokenburn: The Journal of Kate Stone, 1861–1968,* ed. John Q. Anderson (Baton Rouge: Louisiana State University Press, 1955); and "A Literary Secret Out," *New York Times,* January 31, 1887. The identity of the author, recorded in Edith Clarke's *List of Books Sent by Home and Foreign Committees to the Library of the Woman's Building* (Chicago, 1894) simply as "Buckner," was obscure enough to later generations that a 1982 reprint of the novel was published with no author's name entered either on the title page or in the Library of Congress Cataloging-in-Publication data. The striking parallel between the names (and nicknames) of the Morris sisters and that of Buckner's protagonist, Alabama (Bamma) Morant (née Muir), raises tantalizing questions. Did Buckner conceive of her heroine as an imaginary sister separated from her siblings by an invisible yet seemingly impenetrable racial barrier? Might there have been an even closer relationship between Missie Morris and Bamma Morant—that of alter ego, model, half sister, or other blood relative?

7. Lafcadio Hearn, "Essays on American Literature," New Orleans *Times-Democrat,* January 2, 1887, repr. in *Essays on American Literature,* ed. Sanki Ichikawa (Tokyo: Hokuseido Press, 1929), 233, 228. Hearn praises Buckner's tale as "weird with an exotic weirdness." For Hearn, Buckner's use of characterization and point of view to convey Bamma's "terror" and her husband's "tortured imagination" creates "a sensation of nightmare," while her telling the story "in the plainest and quietest way imaginable" contributes to what he construes as Buckner's scrupulous avoidance of "race-feeling" and "visible personal sentiment" (231–32). Conflating point of view with authorial bias, two more recent readings take a less positive view of *Towards the Gulf;* see Thomas H. Fick and Eva Gold, "Race, Region and the Reconstruction of the Southern Gentleman: The American Race Melodrama in Buckner's *Towards the Gulf,*" *Southern Quarterly* 35.3 (Spring 1997): 29–41; and Debra J. Rosenthal, "The White Blackbird: Miscegenation, Genre, and the Tragic Mulatta in Howells, Harper, and the 'Babes of Romance,'" *Nineteenth-Century Literature* 56.4 (March 2002): 495–517.

8. [William Dean Howells], "Editor's Study," *Harper's New Monthly Magazine* 74 (April 1887): 827–28.

9. Grace Farrell, in *Lillie Devereux Blake: Retracing a Life Erased* (Amherst: University of Massachusetts Press, 2002), offers an eloquent meditation on "how authoritative proclamations, however softly whispered, can erase a woman from history" (4).

10. The quotation is from Rosenthal, "The White Blackbird," 501.

11. [Alice Mississippi Morris Buckner], *Towards the Gulf: A Romance of Louisiana* (New York: Harper and Brothers, 1887), 11, 113.

12. Jill Bergman, "Natural Divisions/National Divisions: Whiteness and the American New Woman in the General Federation of Women's Clubs," in *New Woman Hybridities: Femininity, Feminism, and International Consumer Culture, 1880–1930,* ed. Ann Heilmann and Margaret Beetham (London: Routledge, 2004), 236.

13. Frances E. W. Harper, *Iola Leroy; or, Shadows Uplifted* (1892; repr., Boston: Beacon, 1987), 262.

14. Quoted in Ann Massa, "Black Women in the 'White City,'" *American Studies* 8.3 (1974), 320.

15. Robert W. Rydell, "The Chicago World's Columbian Exposition of 1893: 'And Was Jerusalem Builded Here?'" in *Representing the Nation: A Reader: Histories, Heritage and Museums,* ed. David Boswell and Jessica Evans (London: Routledge, 1999), 281; Toni Morrison, *Playing in the Dark: Whiteness and the Literary Imagination* (Cambridge: Harvard University Press, 1992), 46.

16. Morrison, *Playing in the Dark,* 22, 11.

17. Perhaps Edith Clarke's efforts to record and preserve biographical statistics on the authors represented in the library filled in some of the blanks. In her *List of Books Sent by Home and Foreign Committees to the Library of the Woman's Building,* however, the race and ethnicity of contributors are not made evident.

18. Kathleen Brogan, "American Stories of Cultural Haunting: Tales of Heirs and Ethnographers," *College English* 57.2 (February 1995): 163. See also Kathleen Brogan, *Cultural Haunting: Ghosts and Ethnicity in Recent American Literature* (Charlottesville: University Press of Virginia, 1998).

19. Buckner, *Towards the Gulf,* 110.

20. "Report of the Board of Woman Managers," in *Report of the Board of General Managers of the Exhibit of the State of New York at the World's Columbian Exposition* (Albany: James B. Lyon, 1894), 187.

21. Minutes, September 7, 1892, 20–21, BWM Papers. It is possible that the omission of the Pocahontas portrait was merely "an unaccountable oversight," as indicated in "Report of the Board of Woman Managers" (187). Perhaps, however, Candace Wheeler felt the portrait would detract from the library's decorative fireplace. It is also possible, although less likely, that she resented the rejection of her daughter's portrait of Lowell. Although references to the Pocahontas portrait in the Woman's Building Library appear in contemporary reports, we have found no photograph of the library in which the portrait is visible.

22. Minutes, October 4, 1892, 13, BWM Papers. Wellcome made a fortune in pharmaceuticals (with which his name is still associated) and became an art collector and philanthropist. After the Columbian Exposition, his copy of *Pocahontas* was displayed in the U.S. Capitol, and in 1899 he presented it to the Senate (see note 27 below).

23. For an insightful discussion of the larger context in which "American progress was used to justify white supremacy and to define white New Womanhood" (225), see Bergman, "Natural Divisions/National Divisions," and Louise Michelle Newman, *White Women's Rights: The Racial Origins of Feminism in the United States* (New York: Oxford University Press, 1999).

24. Bank, "Representing History," 592–93, 596. On the "development of the white race in America," Bank is quoting Rossiter Johnson's *A History of the World's Columbian Exposition Held in Chicago in 1893,* 4 vols. (New York: D. Appleton, 1898), 2:356.

25. Rydell, "Chicago World's Columbian Exposition of 1893," 274, 285; Caroline F. Corbin, "The Higher Womanhood," in *The Congress of Women Held in the Woman's Building, World's Columbian Exposition, Chicago, U.S.A., 1893,* ed. Mary Kavanaugh Oldham Eagle (Chicago: Monarch Book Company, 1894), 326.

26. Erik Trump, "Primitive Woman—Domestic(ated) Woman: The Image of the Primitive Woman at the 1893 World's Columbian Exposition," *Women's Studies* 27.3 (1998), 11,

21. On the anthropological exhibits in the Woman's Building, see also Jeanne Madeline Weimann, *The Fair Women: The Story of the Woman's Building, World's Columbian Exposition, Chicago, 1893* (Chicago: Academy Chicago, 1981), 394–404; and Bank, "Representing History," 595.

27. The European coloring in the portrait most likely derives from the black-and-white engraving that served as the painter's model. See description and image provided by U.S. Senate curatorial office at www.senate.gov/artandhistory/art/artifact/Painting_31_00014.htm.

28. "Personalities," *Chemist and Druggist*, February 24, 1894, 272.

29. Bank, "Representing History," 595.

30. Bergman, "Natural Divisions/National Divisions," 224. As James C. Davis notes, "the authors of 'The Reason Why' sought to make this absence [of African Americans at the World's Columbian Exposition] conspicuous to white fairgoers." Davis, "'Stage Business' as Citizenship," 191.

31. Rebecka Rutledge Fisher, "Cultural Artifacts and the Narrative of History: W. E. B. Du Bois and the Exhibiting of Culture at the 1900 Paris Exposition Universelle," *Modern Fiction Studies* 51.4 (Winter 2005): 742. The African American exhibit at the Paris exposition was an award-winning exhibit that "provided, perhaps for the first time in the history of world's fairs, a broad opportunity for African Americans to represent themselves at such an event."

32. Brogan, "American Stories of Cultural Haunting," 163–64.

33. Davis, "'Stage Business' as Citizenship," 192.

34. [Buckner], *Towards the Gulf*, 206. Our parsing of Buckner's phrase owes a debt to Toni Morrison's *Beloved* (1987; New York: Alfred A. Knopf/Everyman's Library, 2006), and the substantial body of criticism that references Morrison's turn of phrase in "This is not a story to pass on" (316).

35. Bank, "Representing History," 600.

36. Ibid., 595 ("conflation of real and faux"); James William Buell, *The Magic City* (1893; repr. New York: Arno Press, 1974), [n.p.] ("uncivilized peoples"). For examples of what Buell terms "characters" or "types of the Midway," see photographs in *The Magic City*.

37. Davis, "Stage Business as Citizenship," 198. Davis elaborates, "Frederick Douglass identifies the racism of 'exhibit[ing] the Negro as a repulsive savage' in "The Reason Why,' and recent historians have argued further that the racialization of the Fair's spaces served to confirm white supremacist thinking and to justify imperialism."

38. Ina Coolbrith, "The Captive of the White City," *Songs from the Golden Gate* (Boston: Houghton Mifflin, 1895), 58. As Bank points out, Rain-in-the-Face "had petitioned the Fair Managers for (and been denied) control over or influence in Native American representations on the fairgrounds" (599).

39. Bank, "Representing History," 603. Bank interprets the Wild West Show as "serv[ing] both as site and counter-site for the histories offered by the Columbian Exposition and its Congresses." As she points out, "the show underscored the presence, rather than the absence, of Indians and the frontier" (603).

40. Rydell, "Chicago World's Columbian Exposition of 1893," 293; Robert Muccigrosso, *Celebrating the New World: Chicago's Columbian Exposition of 1893* (Chicago: Ivan R. Dee, 1993), 150.

41. Bank, "Representing History," 595. As Bank argues, "The White City and its Midway can be seen as a heterotopia of contesting sites—the 'real,' the faux, and the simulated; the

educational, the aesthetic, and the entertaining; the State-sponsored, Fair-sponsored, and the commercially produced. The World Congresses reflecting the ideologies driving the White City may also profitably be viewed as heterotopic performances rather than unitary or utopic/dystopic spaces" (599). Davis points out that "'sham' public spheres like the 1893 Fair were not simply a 'sham,' for they served to enact and naturalize a mode of social segregation and economic and political subordination as much as to reflect an existing one" ("Stage Business as Citizenship," 196). Proctor's cowboy and Indian statues are pictured in Buell, *The Magic City.*

42. Enid Yandell and Laura Hayes, *Three Girls in a Flat* (Chicago: Knight, Leonard, 1892), 76.

43. Trump, "Primitive Woman—Domestic(ated) Woman," 18; Nancy Huston Banks, "Woman's Marvellous Achievements," in Henry Davenport Northrop, *The World's Fair as Seen in One Hundred Days* (Philadelphia: National Publishing, 1893), 644. French visitor Madame Léon Grandin found the Indian women's exhibit to be one of the most interesting displays in the Woman's Building, with its elegant pottery and fine handcrafted objects. See Madame Léon Grandin, *A Parisienne in Chicago: Impressions of the World's Columbian Exposition,* trans. Mary Beth Raycraft (Urbana: University of Illinois Press, 2010), 128.

44. Nor would they have found much evidence of the nation's Hispanic heritage, aside from celebrations of Queen Isabella. Maria Ampara Ruiz de Burton's novels *Who Would Have Thought It* (1872) and *The Squatter and the Don* (1885) were absent; and although the library included French fiction published in Louisiana and German fiction from New York and Pennsylvania, it shows little evidence of Spanish influence, aside from a few recipes in Spanish contributed to Carrie Shuman's World's Fair cookbook by Lady Managers from New Mexico and a few novels set in the Southwest by Anglo-American writers, such as Helen Hunt Jackson's *Ramona,* Evelyn Raymond's *Monica the Mesa Maiden,* Marian Calvert Wilson's *Manuelita: The Story of San Xavier del Bac* (1891), and Augusta Jane Evans's *Inez: A Tale of the Alamo* (1855). See Carrie V. Shuman, comp., *Favorite Dishes: A Columbian Autograph Souvenir Cookery Book,* ed. Bruce Kraig (1893; repr., Urbana: University of Illinois Press, 2001), 67, 72, 110, 129, 177, 190. On the novels *Inez, Ramona,* and *Monica the Mesa Maiden,* see Nina Baym, *Women Writers of the American West, 1833–1927* (Urbana: University of Illinois Press, 2011), 15–16, 191–92, and 203, respectively. The few writers of Native American heritage we were able to identify (Eldridge and the Ray sisters, who were of mixed African American and Native American ancestry) are discussed later in this chapter. To be sure, a few short pieces by Native American or Hispanic women may have been buried in magazines, newspapers, scrapbooks, miscellanies, or among the numerous pamphlets. If Josephine Barnaby's eight-page pamphlet *The Present Condition of My People* (1880) was included in the collection, however, it was not indexed in the library's official *List of Books* (although other ephemera are listed). *The Literary Voyageur or Muzzeniegun,* which published the work of Jane Johnston Schoolcraft, does not appear in the *List of Books.*

45. Sarah Winnemucca Hopkins's *Life among the Piutes* was edited by Mary Peabody Mann. Although it was, therefore, eligible for inclusion in the Massachusetts collection, it does not appear in the *List of Books.*

46. See Boisseau, "White Queens," and Trump, "Primitive Woman—Domestic(ated) Woman." The one exception referred to here is Edmonia Lewis's sculpture *The Wooing of Hiawatha.*

47. Other early American texts in the library include Charlotte Lennox's *The Female Quixote, Euphemia,* and translation of *Memoirs of Maximilian de Bethune,* Sarah Wister's

Amusing Scenes of the Revolution, Susanna Rowson's *The History of Charlotte Temple,* Hannah Adams's *A View of Religion, in Two Parts,* Anne MacVicar Grant's *Letters from the Mountains* and *Memoirs of an American Lady,* and Mercy Otis Warren's *Poems.*

48. Mrs. [Susannah Willard] Johnson, *A Narrative of the Captivity of Mrs. Johnson, Containing an Account of Her Sufferings during Four Years with the Indians and French* ([Walpole, N.H.]: David Carlisle Jr., 1796), 8, 76.

49. Margaret Hosmer, *The Child Captives: A True Tale of Life among the Indians of the West* (Philadelphia: Presbyterian Board of Publication, 1870), 219–20. On the Presbyterian Board of Publication and other denominational publishers, see Candy Gunther Brown, "Publicizing Domestic Piety: The Cultural Work of Religious Texts in the Woman's Building Library," *Libraries & Culture* 41.1 (Winter 2006): 40–42.

50. Hosmer, *Child Captives,* 143–44, 208, 146.

51. The inherent contradictions in Hosmer's construction of white Christian nationhood repeatedly surface only to be ignored or denied. One of the preoccupations of *The Child Captives,* for example, is the authenticity and vulnerability of whiteness. When a lawless white man, a fugitive from justice, colors his skin "red" (122) in order to pass as Native American, members of the tribe he lives among are hoodwinked while a white boy immediately notices the line on the man's face where the red tint ends. A young female captive who is transformed into a "wild white girl" (188) through her long residence among Native Americans similarly reveals the instability of the text's racial constructs. And, when a sympathetic Indian "could not have been kinder or more sympathetic had he been as fair as alabaster" (207), Hosmer's text undermines the universality of whiteness as an index of value even as it attempts to reinforce it.

52. Margaret Hosmer, *Chumbo's Hut; or, The Laguna School* (Philadelphia: Presbyterian Board of Publication, 1879), 8.

53. Ibid., 231.

54. On Kinzie's "engagingly liberal" *Wau-Bun,* see Baym, *American Women Writers and the Work of History,* 111–12; and Margaret Beattie Bogue, "As She Knew Them: Juliette Kinzie and the Ho-Chunk, 1830–1833," *Wisconsin Magazine of History* 85.2 (December 2001): 44–57; on Holley's *Once Their Home,* see Baym, *Women Writers of the American West,* 154–55.

55. Of Custer's friendship with Wheeler, Amelia Peck writes: "Mrs. Custer was given the job of corresponding with women whose work the [Society of Decorative Art] had turned down for sale, and apparently she excelled at this delicate task, handling it with considerable tact. Wheeler grew to admire her . . . and the two became lifelong friends." "Candace Wheeler: A Life in Art and Business," in Amelia Peck and Carol Irish, *Candace Wheeler: The Art and Enterprise of American Design, 1875–1900* (New York: Metropolitan Museum of Art, 2001), 27.

56. Custer, *Following the Guidon,* 38, 41–43. Sherman Alexie evokes the slaughter of these ponies as a scene of "cultural haunting" in his novel *Reservation Blues* (New York: Atlantic Monthly Press, 1995). For further discussion of Custer, see Baym, *Women Writers of the American West,* 140–41.

57. Karen Woods Weierman, *One Nation, One Blood: Interracial Marriage in American Fiction, Scandal, and Law, 1820–1870* (Amherst: University of Massachusetts Press, 2005), 63.

58. Annie Nathan Meyer, "Woman's Place in the Republic of Letters," in *The World's Congress of Representative Women,* ed. May Wright Sewall (Chicago: Rand, McNally, 1894), 141–42.

59. Mary Gardiner Horsford, *Indian Legends and Other Poems* (New York: J. C. Derby; Boston: Phillips, Sampson; Cincinnati: H. W. Derby, 1855), 27.

60. Martha Perry Lowe, *The Story of Chief Joseph* (Boston: D. Lothrop, 1881), 36, 39. According to Lowe, she based her poem on a narrative by Chief Joseph published in the *North American Review* with an introduction by William Hobart Hare, an Episcopal bishop stationed in Niobrara in the Dakotas: "An Indian's Views of Indian Affairs," *North American Review* 128 (April 1879): 412–33.

61. Biographical details on Tekakwitha are drawn from American National Biography Online. Beatified by Pope John Paul II in 1980, Kateri Tekakwitha was the first Native American to be declared "Blessed" by the Roman Catholic Church.

62. Allan Greer, "Natives and Nationalism: The Americanization of Kateri Tekakwitha," *Catholic Historical Review* 90.2 (April 2004): 267. For a more extended account, see Greer's *Mohawk Saint: Catherine Tekakwitha and the Jesuits* (Oxford: Oxford University Press, 2005).

63. Greer, "Natives and Nationalism," 266.

64. J. W. Powell, introduction to *Second Annual Report of the Bureau of Ethnology to the Secretary of the Smithsonian Institution, Washington* (Washington, D.C.: Government Printing Office, 1883), xxix–xxx. On the intersections of social evolutionary discourse and nineteenth-century women's rights, see Newman, *White Women's Rights,* 8–14.

65. Rydell, "Chicago World's Columbian Exposition of 1893," 285; Will Roscoe, *The Zuni Man-Woman* (Albuquerque: University of New Mexico Press, 1991), 9. According to Roscoe, the work of Cushing and Stevenson "still dominates the field of Zuni studies" (viii).

66. Darlis A. Miller, *Matilda Coxe Stevenson: Pioneering Anthropologist* (Norman: University of Oklahoma Press, 2007), xvi. On Stevenson's role at the fair, see 101–2.

67. One of the best-known examples of ethnographic verse by a nineteenth-century American woman writer is Lydia Sigourney's *Pocahontas* (1841). Although this verse romance was (surprisingly) absent from its shelves, Sigourney had a conspicuous presence in the Woman's Building Library. Given her close association with Pocahontas as a poetic subject, the portrait of her displayed in the library forms a kind of companion piece to Wellcome's *Pocahontas.* On ethnographic verse, see John O'Leary, "'Tribes of the Eagle, the Panther, and Wolf': Nineteenth-Century Ethnographic Verse in the United States and Beyond," *Nineteenth-Century Contexts* 30.3 (September 2008): 261–74.

68. See Edna Dean Proctor, "Columbia's Emblem," in *Columbia's Emblem, Indian Corn: A Garland of Tributes in Prose and Verse,* ed. Candace Wheeler (Boston: Houghton Mifflin, 1893), 9–11.

69. Eliza Ruhamah Scidmore, *Alaska: Its Southern Coast and the Sitkan Archipelago* (Boston: D. Lothrop, 1885), 26, 62, 100, 89.

70. Leslie Marmon Silko, "Books: Notes on Mixtec and Maya Screenfolds, Picture Books of Preconquest Mexico," in *Yellow Woman and a Beauty of the Spirit: Essays on Native American Life Today* (New York: Simon and Schuster, 1996), 162; Amelia V. Katanski, *Learning to Write "Indian": The Boarding School Experience and American Indian Literature* (Norman: University of Oklahoma Press, 2005), 65. For an extended analysis of *Stiya,* see Katanski, *Learning to Write "Indian,"* 64–82. For a scathing account of a Pueblo family's response to *Stiya,* see Silko, "Books," 161–65. As Silko points out, "Books like *Stiya,* purportedly written by Indians about Indian life, still outnumber books actually written by Indians" (165).

71. Amelia Stone Quinton, "The Indian," in *The Literature of Philanthropy*, ed. Frances A. Goodale (New York: Harper and Brothers, 1893), 128, 122.

72. Mary E. Dewey, in *Historical Sketch of the Formation and Achievements of the Women's National Indian Association in the United States* (1900), denounced the reservation system as resulting in no "broad and wholesome civilization" so long as it enforced "permanent imprisonment and segregation." See Valerie Sherer Mathes, "Nineteenth-Century Women and Reform: The Women's National Indian Association," *American Indian Quarterly* 14.1 (Winter 1990): 5. On Quinton and the WNIA, see also Weimann, *Fair Women*, 500.

73. Katanski, *Learning to Write "Indian,"* 3; Mathes, "Nineteenth-Century Women and Reform," 3.

74. Robin Jones, "Elaine Goodale Eastman," in *The Oxford Companion to Women's Writing in the United States*, ed. Cathy N. Davidson and Linda Wagner-Martin (New York: Oxford University Press, 1995), 268; Elaine Goodale Eastman, "The Indian—A Woman among the Indians," in Goodale, *Literature of Philanthropy*, 139.

75. Silko, "Books," 165, 155. "The Metaphysics of Indian Hating" forms part of the title of chapter 26 of Melville's novel *The Confidence Man*. Ginzberg's phrase is from Lori D. Ginzberg, *Women and the Work of Benevolence: Morality, Politics, and Class in the Nineteenth-Century United States* (New Haven: Yale University Press, 1990), 2.

76. [Buckner], *Towards the Gulf,* 54–64.

77. Ibid., 84, 300.

78. Florence C. Ives, "Report of the Board of Woman Managers," in *Report of the Board of General Managers of the Exhibit of the State of New York at the World's Columbian Exposition* (Albany: James B. Lyon, 1894), 176–77; "Work of Colored Women: Some Excellent Exhibits Made by Them at the World's Fair," *New York Times,* June 10, 1893. Information about Howard and the exhibit in this and the following paragraphs is drawn from these sources and from Weimann, *Fair Women*, 121–22, and Christopher Robert Reed, *"All the World Is Here!" The Black Presence in the White City* (Bloomington: Indiana University Press, 2000), 111–12. Other African American exhibits at the fair, each of which included a few representations of the culture of print, could be found at booths operated by the Hampton Institute, Wilberforce University, and Atlanta University.

79. Ives, "Report of the Board of Women Managers," 177. Ives's report describes the piece as a "statuette of Hiawatha by Edmonia Lewis"; its ownership by the Boston YMCA identifies it as *The Wooing of Hiawatha*. See Kirsten Pai Buick, *Child of the Fire: Mary Edmonia Lewis and the Problem of Art History's Black and Indian Subject* (Durham: Duke University Press, 2010), 66, 117–24, 238n96.

80. Anna Julia Cooper, *A Voice from the South* (New York: Oxford University Press, 1988), 276; I. Garland Penn, "The Progress of the Afro-American since Emancipation," in Ida B. Wells, ed., *The Reason Why the Colored American Is Not in the World's Columbian Exposition: The Afro-American's Contribution to Columbian Literature* (1893), ed. Robert W. Rydell (Urbana: University of Illinois Press, 1999), 60–61; Hallie Q. Brown, "Discussion of the Same Subject by Hallie Q. Brown of Alabama," in *The World's Congress of Representative Women: A Historical Résumé for Popular Circulation of the World's Congress of Representative Women*, ed. May Wright Sewall, 2 vols. (Chicago: Rand, McNally, 1894), 2:726. In her overview of the Woman's Building exhibits, Frances Willard noted that "Edmonia Lewis, the colored sculptor, exhibits a number of statuettes." See Frances Willard, "Woman's Department of the World's Fair," in *The World's Fair: Being a Pictorial History of the Columbian Exposition*, ed. William E. Cameron (Chicago: Columbia History Company, 1893), 469.

81. Naurice Frank Woods Jr., "An African Queen at the Philadelphia Centennial Exposition 1876: Edmonia Lewis's 'The Death of Cleopatra,'" *Meridians: Feminism, Race, Transnationalism* 9.1 (2009): 67. Many critics have observed that Lewis's representations of Native Americans conform to Eurocentric models. See, for example, Kirsten Pai Buick, "The Ideal Works of Edmonia Lewis: Invoking and Inverting Autobiography," *American Art* 9.2 (Summer 1995): 4–19; and Buick, *Child of the Fire*, chap. 3. See also Juanita M. Holland, "Mary Edmonia Lewis's Minnehaha: Gender, Race, and the 'Indian Maid,'" *Bulletin of the Detroit Institute of Arts* 69 (1995): 32, on Lewis's five sculptural interpretations of Longfellow's *The Song of Hiawatha*. In Buick's view, Lewis's "decision to obliterate 'color'" was "influenced by the Cult of True Womanhood, which crossed all racial boundaries" ("Ideal Works of Edmonia Lewis," 12).

82. These titles appear in Daniel Murray, *Preliminary List of Books and Pamphlets by Negro Authors for Paris Exposition and Library of Congress* (Washington, D.C.: Government Printing Office, 1900).

83. Alison Booth, *How to Make It as a Woman: Collective Biographical History from Victoria to the Present* (Chicago: University of Chicago Press, 2004), 215. Booth is quoting Randall K. Burkett's introduction to the 1988 Oxford University Press reprint of Hallie Q. Brown's *Homespun Heroines*.

84. The Grimké sisters had drawn sharp criticism not only for their opposition to slavery but also for violating the cultural prohibition against women publicly addressing mixed-gender audiences.

85. Stowe quoted in J. Matthew Gallman, introduction to *What Answer?* by Anna E. Dickinson (New York: Prometheus Books, 2003), 7.

86. In her preface, Holland describes her country as a place "where a refined[,] cultivated people were thrown down in extreme poverty in the midst of a coarse African race, whom slavery barely rescued from cannibalism." Annie Jefferson Holland, *The Refugees: A Sequel to "Uncle Tom's Cabin"* (Austin, Tex.: published for the author, 1892), 5. Although self-published, the novel, which also rails against the Federal government and "the white-skinned scum of society" (109), was issued through the support of local schools and businesses, several of which ran ads at the end of the volume.

87. [Harriet Newell Kneeland Goff], *Other Fools and Their Doings; or, Life among the Freedmen* (New York: J. S. Ogilvie, 1880), 234. We are grateful to Hamburg historian Wayne O'Bryant for verifying the general accuracy of Goff's account.

88. France E. Willard and Mary A. Livermore, eds., *A Woman of the Century: Fourteen Hundred-Seventy Biographical Sketches Accompanied by Portraits of Leading American Women in All Walks of Life*, 2 vols. (1893; repr., New York: Gordon Press, 1975), 1:322.

89. Albert Tricomi, "Dialect and Identity in Harriet Jacobs's Autobiography and Other Slave Narratives," *Callaloo* 29.2 (Spring 2006): 621.

90. For an extended analysis of *Memoirs of Elleanor Elldridge* and *Elleanor's Second Book*, see Sarah C. O'Dowd, *A Rhode Island Original: Sarah Whipple Green McDougall* (Lebanon, N.H.: University Press of New England, 2004), chap. 2. For further analysis of African American texts in the library, see Amina Gautier, "African American Women's Writing in the Woman's Building Library," *Libraries & Culture* 41.1 (Winter 2006): 55–81. We are greatly indebted to Gautier for her groundbreaking work.

91. Gautier, "African American Women's Writing," 64.

92. On the genteel idealist poets in the library see Angela Sorby, "Symmetrical Woman-

hood: Poets in the Woman's Building Library," *Libraries & Culture* 41.1 (Winter 2006): 5–34 (quotation on 21); for Sorby's analysis of Ray see 24–25. Like Lewis, who, as Woods notes, sometimes "translated African American themes into neoclassical sculpture," some of Ray's later poems have African American subjects, including Frederick Douglass and Paul Laurence Dunbar. Woods, "An African Queen at the Philadelphia Centennial Exposition," 72.

93. Surprisingly, given that Foote was born in New York, her autobiography was not among the New York books. Nor was it contributed by Ohio, the state she eventually made her home, but rather by Pennsylvania.

94. As her modern editor notes, Foote "demonstrated her sisterhood with feminists touched by mid-nineteenth-century perfectionism in her attacks on general evils like racial bigotry and male authoritarianism and on specific social institutions like capital punishment." William L. Andrews, introduction to *Sisters of the Spirit: Three Black Women's Autobiographies of the Nineteenth Century* (Bloomington: Indiana University Press, 1986), 4.

95. The African American exhibit featured one other volume, *Tones and Undertones*, by a Miss M. R. Lyons, the only text not duplicated in the New York section of the Woman's Building Library.

96. Christensen was a folklorist who wrote a paper on African American spirituals and shouts that was presented at the Columbian Exposition. According to Monica M. Tetzlaff, "Christensen believed she should use the profits from the sale of her book on behalf of African Americans. Starting with a modest sum, she worked with other Whites and Blacks to found the Port Royal Agricultural School for African Americans in 1902. See "Christensen, Abigail Mandana ('Abbie') Holmes (1852–1938)," in *American Folklore: An Encyclopedia*, ed. Jan Harold Brunvand (New York: Garland, 1996), 296. See also Monica Maria Tetzlaff, *Cultivating a New South: Abbie Holmes Christensen and the Politics of Race and Gender, 1852–1938* (Columbia: University of South Carolina Press, 2002). For a discussion of Aunt Jemima in the context of Ida B. Wells's "act of counterpublicity" at the World's Columbian Exposition, see Davis's "Stage Business as Citizenship."

97. Orra Langhorne, *Aunt Pokey's Son: A Story of the New South* ([Lynchburg, Va.]: I. P. Bell, 1890), 2. Although the pamphlet form of *Aunt Pokey's Son* is quite rare, the story initially ran as a two-part serial in the *Southern Workman* (August–September 1885), where Earle could feasibly have encountered it. For a wide array of Langhorne's *Southern Workman* columns, see Orra Langhorne, *Southern Sketches from Virginia, 1881–1901*, ed. Charles E. Wynes (Charlottesville: University Press of Virginia, 1964).

98. Victoria Earle (Mrs. W. E. Matthews), "Aunt Lindy: A Story Founded on Real Life," in *Afro-American Women Writers, 1746–1933: An Anthology and Critical Guide,* ed. Ann Allen Shockley (Boston: G. K. Hall, 1988), 185. Republished as a 16-page illustrated pamphlet in 1893, *Aunt Lindy* first appeared in the *A.M.E. Church Review* in 1891. See Dickson D. Bruce Jr., "Confronting the Crisis: African American Narratives," in *A Companion to American Fiction, 1865–1914,* ed. Robert Paul Lamb and Gary Richard Thompson (Oxford: Blackwell, 2005), 283. For a brief biographical sketch of Victoria Earle (Matthews), see Heidi Stauffer, "Victoria Earle Matthews, 1861–1898," in *Encyclopedia of African American Women Writers,* ed. Yolanda Williams Page (Westport, Conn.: Greenwood Press, 2007), 391–92; and Shockley, *Afro-American Women Writers,* 181–83. See also Hallie Q. Brown, *Homespun Heroines and Other Women of Distinction* (1926; New York: Oxford University Press, 1988), 208–16.

99. Earle (Matthews), "Aunt Lindy," 188–89.

100. Margaret Tufts Yardley, ed., *The New Jersey Scrap Book of Women Writers* (Newark: Board of Lady Managers of New Jersey, 1893), 296; Esther "Hetty" Saunders, *I Love to Live Alone: The Poems of Esther "Hetty" Saunders*, ed. Donald L. Pierce (Salem, N.J.: Salem County Historical Society, 2001), 8, 11–12. Reference to dictation seems odd: Pierce notes that she "learned to read and write and is said to have read all of the books that were available in the . . . household" where she lived (8). In addition, the major manuscript source of Saunders's poetry is a copybook believed to be written in her own hand.

101. In Donald L. Pierce's modern edition, *I Love to Live Alone*, this poem is titled "On the Prospect of Moving from Claysville to James Woodnutts" (13–15). Pierce traces the initial publication of "The Hill of Age" to *The Select Miscellany* (Philadelphia, 1900). Since the *New Jersey Scrap-Book* was published in 1893, this Columbian edition reestablishes the poem's date of first publication. Biographical details on Saunders are taken from Sibyl E. Moses, *African-American Women Writers in New Jersey, 1836–2000: A Biographical Dictionary and Bibliographic Guide* (New Brunswick: Rutgers University Press, 2006), 141, and Pierce's introduction to *I Love to Live Alone*.

102. See Frances E. W. Harper, "Woman's Political Future," in Sewall, *World's Congress of Representative Women*, 1:435–37. For a detailed study of all seven of the African American women who spoke at the Columbian Exposition, see Temple Bryonny Tsenes-Hills, "I Am the Utterance of My Name: Black Victorian Feminist Discourse and Intellectual Enterprise at the Columbian Exposition, 1893" (Ph.D. diss., Loyola University Chicago, 2004). For a brief account of Williams's and Cooper's addresses at the exposition, see Elizabeth Ammons, *Conflicting Stories: American Women Writers at the Turn into the Twentieth Century* (New York: Oxford University Press, 1991), 24–25. For a succinct discussion of the participation of African Americans in the Congress of Women, see Michelle Rief, "Thinking Locally, Acting Globally: The International Agenda of African American Clubwomen, 1880–1940," *Journal of African American History* 89.3 (Summer 2004): 204. On Harper, see also Gautier, "African-American Women's Writings," 67–79, and Melba Joyce Boyd, *Discarded Legacy: Politics and Poetics in the Life of Frances E. W. Harper, 1825–1911* (Detroit: Wayne State University Press, 1994).

103. Boyd, *Discarded Legacy*, 92–108.

104. Frances E. Watkins Harper, *Sketches of Southern Life* (1872; repr., Philadelphia: Ferguson Bros., 1891), chap. 2. *Moses: A Story of the Nile* also includes a short story titled "The Mission of the Flowers."

105. [Buckner], *Towards the Gulf*, 114, 314, 113; Gautier, "African American Women's Writing," 79. Debra Rosenthal makes the case that between *Towards the Gulf* and *Iola Leroy* there are two degrees of separation: William Dean Howells, she argues, reworked aspects of *Towards the Gulf* in his novel *An Imperative Duty* (1891), and Harper revises elements of Howells's novel in *Iola Leroy*, which "uncouples the 'tragic' from the 'mulatta' and restores [the] heroine to life, bounty, and racial uplift." Rosenthal, "The White Blackbird," 516.

106. Harper, *Iola Leroy*, 231, 249, 282.

107. According to the newspaper sketch on *Towards the Gulf* published shortly after the novel's release, "the revelation of Bamma's relationship to the planter, by her resemblance to the old portrait in the deserted house" was "an absolute occurrence" drawn from life. See "*Towards the Gulf*: A Brief Sketch of Its Author."

108. [Buckner], *Towards the Gulf*, 214–15.

109. Ibid., 216.

110. "The scholarship that looks into the mind, imagination, and behavior of slaves is valuable," Toni Morrison writes in *Playing in the Dark.* "But equally valuable is a serious intellectual effort to see what racial ideology does to the mind, imagination, and behavior of masters"(11–12). Just as Buckner's novel invites this kind of critical investigation on a textual level, the Woman's Building Library invites a parallel inquiry at the institutional level.

111. Howells, "Editor's Study," 828; [Buckner], *Towards the Gulf,* 312.

112. See, for example, Teresa A. Goddu, *Gothic America: Narrative, History and Nation* (New York: Columbia University Press, 1997); Kathleen Brogan, *Cultural Haunting: Ghosts and Ethnicity in Recent American Literature* (Charlottesville: University of Virginia Press, 1998); and Justin D. Edwards, *Gothic Passages: Racial Ambiguity and the American Gothic* (Iowa City: University of Iowa Press, 2003).

113. [Buckner], *Towards the Gulf,* 110.

114. Brogan, "American Stories of Cultural Haunting," 152, 164.

7. "I Will Write for the People"

1. Maud Howe [Elliott], *Atalanta in the South: A Romance* (Boston: Roberts Bros., 1886), 324.

2. In *Atalanta in the South,* Therese Caseneuve "had always spoken of herself as belonging to the African race" from the moment she discovered "that her blood was tainted by that inferior strain" (323). The plots of *Towards the Gulf* and *Atalanta in the South* diverge in other important ways as well. In the latter novel, Therese and Fernand Thoron, unable to marry, become lovers, and Therese is, as a consequence, degraded. Defending her honor as well as her secret (and his own), Therese's half-brother, Robert Feuardent (the planter's legitimate son), kills Fernand in a duel, a murder for which Therese feels responsible.

3. On "reversion of type," see [Alice Mississippi Morris Buckner], *Towards the Gulf: A Romance of Louisiana* (New York: Harper and Brothers, 1887), 287–90.

4. Howe [Elliott], *Atalanta in the South,* 317.

5. Simon Pokagon, a Potawatomi chief who distributed copies of "The Red Man's Rebuke" inscribed on birch bark at the Columbian Exposition, used very similar imagery in his essay "The Future of the Red Man," originally published in the journal *Forum* in August 1897. Of the future assimilation of Native Americans, which he predicted would follow the passing away of reservations and tribal relations, Pokagon wrote: "Through intermarriage the blood of our people, like the waters that flow into the great ocean, will be forever lost in the dominant race; and generations yet unborn will read in history of the red men of the forest, and inquire, 'Where are they?'" "The Future of the Red Man," in *The American 1890s: A Cultural Reader,* ed. Susan Harris Smith and Melanie Dawson (Durham, N.C.: Duke University Press, 2000), 220.

6. Hazel V. Carby, introduction to *Iola Leroy; or, Shadows Uplifted,* by Frances Ellen Watkins Harper (1892; repr., Boston: Beacon, 1987), xiv. In his review of *Towards the Gulf* Lafcadio Hearn wrote that the title "has at once the fault and the merit of possessing a double meaning—at least to Americans." For Hearn, a French translation of the novel could render a "truer signification" in the title *Vers l'Abime* ("Toward the Abyss"). Lafcadio Hearn, *Essays on American Literature,* ed. Sanki Ichikawa (Tokyo: Hokuseido Press, 1929), 233.

7. Smith and Dawson, *The American 1890s,* 75, 8.

8. Martha Banta, *Imaging American Women: Idea and Ideals in Cultural History* (New York: Columbia University Press, 1987), xxix.

9. Timothy Mitchell, "Orientalism and the Exhibitionary Order," in *The Visual Culture Reader*, ed. Nicholas Mirzoeff (London: Routledge, 1998), 294.

10. Banta, *Imaging American Women*, xxxi.

11. Henry Adams, *The Education of Henry Adams* (1918; New York: Modern Library, 1931), 343.

12. Regionalism—one of the most important literary developments of late nineteenth-century America—is a mode frequently associated with women writers. See, for example, Judith Fetterley and Marjorie Pryse, *Writing Out of Place: Regionalism, Women, and American Literary Culture* (Urbana: University of Illinois Press, 2003); Elizabeth Ammons, "Going in Circles: The Female Geography of Jewett's *Country of the Pointed Firs*," *Studies in the Literary Imagination* 16.2 (Fall 1983): 83–92; and Sandra A. Zagarell, "Narrative of Community: The Identification of a Genre," *Signs* 13.3 (Spring 1988): 498–527.

13. See, for example, the pulpy and exploitative *An I.D.B. in South Africa* (1888), by Louise Vescelius Sheldon; Mrs. R. Duin Douglass's *A Romance of the Antipodes* (1890); and Laura Coates Reed's *West and East: An Algerian Romance* (1892).

14. See Mary Peabody Mann, *Juanita: A Romance of Real Life in Cuba Fifty Years Ago* (Boston: D. Lothrop, 1887) and Frances Hammond Pratt, *La Belle Zoa; or, The Insurrection of Hayti* (Albany, N.Y.: Weed, Parsons, 1854).

15. Caroline Earle White, *Love in the Tropics: A Romance of the South Seas* (Philadelphia: J. B. Lippincott, 1890), iii–iv.

16. The western states contributed only a small quantity of regional fiction. Nevertheless, a great deal of Western fiction was contributed by other states, the birth-states or homes of women who emigrated to the West, or merely visited the West and later wrote fiction based on their travels. Many of these writers are discussed in Nina Baym, *Women Writers of the American West, 1833–1927* (Urbana: University of Illinois Press, 2011). The absence of Constance Fenimore Woolson is surprising, considering that at least four states might have claimed her, including New York, whose collection was claimed to include all women writers born in or resident of the state. Possibly Woolson's expatriate status—she lived in Europe from 1879 until her death in 1894—placed her beyond the purview of these states' literary committees. Unexpectedly, given Woolson's absence from the library's *List of Books*, her novel *East Angels* received praise in a Columbian essay by Maud Howe Elliott's sister. See Laura E. Richards, "Women in Literature," in *Art and Handicraft in the Woman's Building of the World's Columbian Exposition, Chicago, 1893*, ed. Maud Howe Elliott (Paris: Goupil, 1893), 108. May Rogers also praised Woolson's *For the Major* in her Congress of Women speech, "The Novel as an Educator of the Imagination."

17. Roughly half the fiction (of all kinds) contributed by states of the Midwest and the Old Southwest (including Louisiana, Arkansas, and Missouri) was published within these regions. Of the relatively small body of fiction contributed by states in the Far West, roughly 60 percent were published in Boston, with the remainder emanating from Chicago, Portland, and San Francisco. If Helen Hunt Jackson is excluded from the sample, nearly all of the works of fiction contributed by the western states were published in the West.

18. See, for example, Fetterley and Pryse, *Writing Out of Place*, 169–73. Although some might dispute the label "regionalist" as applied to some of the fiction considered in this chapter, the texts we identify as regionalist are deeply imbued with a sense of region. Many of the texts in the Woman's Building Library announce their regional identification in subtitles, such as "A Story of the Blue Grass Country" and "A Story of Tuna Valley."

19. In the regional historical mode, the novelist imagines the region's past in order to trace, recover, and preserve the traditions and heritage of its people at a time of rapid change and apparent weakening of the autonomy, insularity, and distinctiveness of the region. For more on historical fiction in the Woman's Building Library, see Emily B. Todd, "The Woman's Building Library and History," *Libraries & Culture* 41.1 (Winter 2006): 153–61. For further discussion of the regional reform novel, see Sarah Wadsworth, "Refusing to Write Like Henry James: Women Reforming Realism in *Fin-de-siècle* America," *European Journal of American Studies*, 2011 (2), http://ejas.revues.org/9067.

20. Sharon Macdonald and Roger Silverstone, "Rewriting the Museum's Fictions: Taxonomies, Stories and Readers," in *Representing the Nation: A Reader: Histories, Heritage and Museums,* ed. David Boswell and Jessica Evans (London: Routledge, 1999), 425–26, 431. Drawing on Michel de Certeau and others, Macdonald and Silverstone illustrate the concept of stories as the museum's "new fictions" by explicating a permanent gallery called "Food for Thought" in Britain's National Museum of Science and Industry.

21. Maud Howe Elliott, "The Library," in Elliott, *Art and Handicraft in the Woman's Building,* 109–10. As we saw in chapter 6, New Hampshire contributed a copy of Frances Harper's *Iola Leroy.* The rest of the state's collection consisted of two detective novels by Mary R. Platt Hatch (*The Missing Man* and *The Bank Tragedy*) and Harriet McEwan Kimball's *Poems.* Regional responses to the Woman's Building Library include a *Brooklyn Eagle* article noting that eight hundred of the books were "written by women now or heretofore of Brooklyn" and a *New York Times* report that "in the great department of woman's work . . . the great Empire State occupies a position that is at once gratifying to her sons and daughters, and calculated to increase her already great importance in the eyes of the world." "The Eagle To-day," *Brooklyn Eagle,* June 27, 1893; and "New-York Women at the Fair," *New York Times,* May 4, 1893.

22. Edith Clarke, draft of "The Library in the Woman's Building," box 3, Dewey Papers; Fetterley and Pryse, *Writing Out of Place,* 12.

23. On the popularity of the reunion-through-marriage plot see Karen A. Keely, "Marriage Plots and National Reunion: The Trope of Romantic Reconciliation in Postbellum Literature," *Mississippi Quarterly* 51 (Fall 1998): 621–48. In *Atalanta in the South,* Elliott embellishes the North–South reconciliation theme by depicting white Northerners coming to the aid of Southerners in a city afflicted by fever and famine. After a "fair Northern girl" dies "having given her life to succor the sick and dying of a stranger city," she writes: "O South! Can there be any bitterness left in your hearts against a North which has laid so white a sacrifice before the awful demon of the pestilence that laid your fairest cities desolate? One such pure life—and there were many such given—should efface the memory of a Gettysburg and a Shiloh" (320–21).

24. Howe [Elliott], *Atalanta in the South,* 305, 298. As one character declares, "If I were President of these United States I should legislate to the end of amalgamating the too-cold Northern and the over-hot Southern blood. In two generations we should have the finest race of people . . . that has existed in this world since the day when Adam broke his alliance with the brutes and called himself man, and their master" (305).

25. Ibid., 209–10. For Elliott's evocation of an Indian camp, see 232–39.

26. Ibid., 298.

27. Elizabeth Holbrook, *Old 'Kaskia Days: A Novel* (Chicago: Schulte Publishing, 1893), dedication page.

28. Ibid., 40–41, 270, 5, 122, 82, 85, 89, 101. Holbrook's depiction of a New Orleans

throng has an analog in Buckner's *Towards the Gulf.* Troubled by the problem of race, John Morant ventures to the French Market, where he views with sinking heart "the kaleidoscopic stream pouring through the heavy archways, going out and coming in, always grinding the same grist, light and dark, dark and light, white and yellow, yellow and white . . ." (301).

29. Holbrook, *Old 'Kaskia Days,* 47, 148, 47, 61, 29–30, 200. See also Frederick Jackson Turner, "The Significance of the Frontier in American History" (1893), in *A Documentary History of the United States,* ed. Richard D. Heffner, 4th ed. (New York: Mentor/New American Library, 1985), 191.

30. Ibid., 5–6, 294–95.

31. Ibid., 6.

32. "Recent Fiction," *Overland Monthly and Out West Magazine,* March 1892, 333. On the land laws, the reviewer noted: "These were framed with extreme liberality, giving every married man a claim to six hundred and forty acres, or a section one mile square; but requiring one half of the grant to be entered in his wife's name. No single man could hold more than three hundred and twenty acres. The result of this provision, which was framed with the object of protecting women, was in some cases most disastrous. Every man that had not a wife already set about finding one immediately. Women were scarce, and children of only fourteen, sometimes even eleven, years were married to men twice their own age" (333).

33. Turner, "Significance of the Frontier," 184.

34. Mary P. Sawtelle, *The Heroine of '49: A Story of the Pacific Coast* (San Francisco: Francis, Valentine, 1891), 224. The Pilgrims' landing formed a leitmotif at the World's Columbian Exposition. In her novel *Elsie at the World's Fair* (1894; Nashville: Cumberland House, 2000), Martha Finley uses the landing of the Pilgrims at Plymouth Rock to explore a different side of American history. When the characters visit the Florida Building, which was modeled on Old Fort Marion (its foundations laid in 1620, "the same year of the landing of the Pilgrims in Massachusetts"), they note that "it took 150 years of toil by exiles, convicts, and slaves to construct [it]" (53). Similarly, at the Congress of Representative Women Anna Howard Shaw used the painting *The Landing of the Pilgrim Fathers* as a device to focus her critique in her speech "The Fate of the Republics," and Lillie Devereux Blake paid tribute to the "Pilgrim Mothers" in her speech "Our Forgotten Foremothers." Anna Howard Shaw, "The Fate of Republics," and Lillie Devereux Blake, "Our Forgotten Foremothers," in *The Congress of Women Held in the Woman's Building, World's Columbian Exposition, Chicago, U.S.A., 1893,*" ed. Mary Kavanaugh Oldham Eagle (Chicago: Monarch Book Company, 1894), 156, 32.

35. Sawtelle, *Heroine of '49,* 213, 221, 237.

36. Sawtelle's textual response to Southern slavery lacks the compassion of her response to the Umpquas' displacement. Although her heroine declares herself an "abolitionist," determined to fight against the enslavement of women, the novel bemoans the fighting that took place during the Civil War in order to free a "handful of Negro slaves" (148).

37. Sawtelle, *Heroine of '49,* n.p. Copy in Charles Deering McCormick Library of Special Collections, Northwestern University. This is the last ad in the book. It informs readers that "the county is rapidly filling up with intelligent and prosperous people" and "the overland trains of the Canadian Pacific Railway arrive and depart daily from New Whatcom."

38. Ibid., 180, 187–88, 184–85.

39. A number of critics have posited connections between regionalism and the foreign Other associated with immigration and imperialism. See, for example, Stephanie Foote,

Regional Fictions: Culture and Identity in Nineteenth-Century American Literature (Madison: University of Wisconsin Press, 2001); and Amy Kaplan, "Nation, Region, and Empire," in *The Columbia History of the American Novel,* ed. Cathy N. Davidson et al. (New York: Columbia University Press, 1991), 240–66.

40. Esther Jerman Baldwin, *Must the Chinese Go? An Examination of the Chinese Question,* 3rd ed. (New York: H. B. Elkins, 1890), 5.

41. Frona Eunice Wait, *Wines and Vines of California: A Treatise on the Ethics of Wine-Drinking* (San Francisco: Bancroft, 1889), 19.

42. Other texts in the Woman's Building Library that employ the popular device of juxtaposing characters from different classes include three Columbian Women's texts: Frances Willard's *How to Win: A Book for Girls* (1888), Helen H. Gardener's *Pray You Sir, Whose Daughter?* (1892), and Blanche Fearing's poem *In the City by the Lake; in Two Books: The Shadow and the Slave Girl* (1892).

43. Kate Gannett Wells, *Two Modern Women: A Novel* (Philadelphia: J. B. Lippincott, 1890), 42.

44. Ibid., 228. For Wells's biography, see Mary M. Huth, "Kate Gannett Wells, Anti-Suffragist," *University of Rochester Library Bulletin* 34 (1981): 3–23, available at www.lib.rochester.edu/index.cfm?PAGE=3562.

45. Sawtelle, *Heroine of '49,* 224.

46. Mary W. Blanchard, "Anglo-American Aesthetes and Native Indian Corn: Candace Wheeler and the Revision of American Nationalism," *Journal of American Studies* 27.3 (1993): 377, 379–81, 384. For further discussion of Wheeler's aesthetics, see Mary Warner Blanchard, *Oscar Wilde's America: Counterculture in the Gilded Age* (New Haven: Yale University Press, 1998), chap. 2; and Kathleen D. McCarthy, *Women's Culture: American Philanthropy and Art, 1830–1930* (Chicago: University of Chicago Press, 1991), chap. 2.

47. The quotation is from Turner, "Significance of the Frontier," 184.

48. Gail Bederman, *Manliness and Civilization: A Cultural History of Gender and Race in the United States, 1880–1917* (Chicago: University of Chicago Press, 1995), 31.

49. Robert W. Rydell, "The Chicago World's Columbian Exposition of 1893: 'And Was Jerusalem Builded Here?'" in Boswell and Evans, *Representing the Nation,* 281, 295.

50. John Coleman Adams, "What a Great City Might Be—A Lesson from the White City," in Smith and Dawson, *The American 1890s,* 389 (originally published in *New England Magazine* 14 [March 1896]: 3–13); Bederman, *Manliness and Civilization,* 35. Here Bederman is talking about the absence of people of color from the management and exhibits of the White City. Although responses to the multiethnic crowds at the fair vary, even a visitor wholly invested in the ideology of types felt the need to expand what Martha Banta calls the late nineteenth-century "canon of types." "Studying this infinite stream of humanity," John Ames Mitchell (architect, novelist, and cofounder of *Life* magazine) concluded that "new types seem to have sprung into existence for the sole purpose of appearing at the fair." J. A. Mitchell, "Types and People at the Fair," in Francis Davis Millet et al., *Some Artists at the Fair* (New York: C. Scribner's Sons, 1893), 43. For a more critical reading of "types" at the fair, see "Sketches of American Types," a series of six essays by the novelist and journalist Octave Thanet (Alice French), published in *Scribner's* from March to September 1894 and excerpted in Smith and Dawson, *The American 1890s,* 86–93.

51. Candace Wheeler, *Yesterdays in a Busy Life* (New York: Harper and Brothers, 1918), 349–50, 354.

52. Ibid., 355. In a letter to Lucy Stone, Antoinette Brown Blackwell described a similar

response: "The Parliament of Religions was a grand demonstration in favor of toleration and an underlying unity for all. It was like a new Pentacost." Blackwell, who wrote that she enjoyed "the freedom of the place," found the exposition "a curious study of human nature." Quoted in Elizabeth Cazden, *Antoinette Brown Blackwell: A Biography* (Old Westbury, N.Y.: The Feminist Press, 1983), 233.

53. Wheeler, *Yesterdays in a Busy Life,* 350–55.

54. Ibid., 33–34.

55. Blanchard, "Anglo-American Aesthetes and Native Indian Corn," 389; Candace Wheeler, "Decorative Art," *Architectural Record* 4 (April–June 1895): 410, 412; Wheeler, *Yesterdays in a Busy Life,* 351. "A style or development of art founded upon national gifts or preferences and instinct with living motives is more likely to become permanent and general," Wheeler writes in "Decorative Art," "than a more or less accidental graft perfected by a different race under widely different conditions" (413).

56. James Clifford, "Museums as Contact Zones," in Boswell and Evans, *Representing the Nation,* 441. Wheeler's response to race is complex. As the child of abolitionists in a county where abolitionism was not popular, she had been scorned by other children as "the nigger queen." Later, during the draft riots that raged in New York City in 1863, she sheltered several African Americans in her neighborhood and was prepared to defend them with firearms. Although she was politically progressive and in some respects an activist, her autobiography is nevertheless laced with racial stereotypes and a benevolence tinged with condescension.

57. Toni Morrison, *Playing in the Dark: Whiteness and the Literary Imagination* (Cambridge: Harvard University Press, 1992), 7.

58. The phrase, echoed in the 1900 novel *Contending Forces* by the African American novelist Pauline Hopkins, comes from Hamlin Garland's "The Local Novel," in *Crumbling Idols: Twelve Essays on Art Dealing Chiefly with Literature, Painting and the Drama* (Chicago: Stone and Kimball, 1894), 70–71. In this companion piece to Garland's Columbian Exposition address "Local Color in Fiction" at the World's Congress of Authors, Garland advocated "a literature from the plain people" (74).

59. Morrison, *Playing in the Dark,* 7; Macdonald and Silverstone, "Rewriting the Museum's Fictions," 427.

Epilogue

1. Another death saddened many a week before the fair closed. Lucy Stone, who delivered a speech on "The Progress of Fifty Years" at the Congress of Women, died on October 19.

2. "World's Fair Notes," *Woman's Journal,* July 8, 1893, 210; Henry Davenport Northrop, *The World's Fair as Seen in One Hundred Days* (Philadelphia: National Publishing, 1893), 163. See also *World's Columbian Exposition Illustrated,* August 1893, 148.

3. Candace Wheeler, "Decorative Art," *Architectural Record* 4 (April–June 1895): 410; Jeanne Madeline Weimann, *The Fair Women: The Story of the Woman's Building, World's Columbian Exposition, Chicago, 1893* (Chicago: Academy Chicago, 1981), 259.

4. "Work of the Women," *Chicago Daily Tribune,* October 6, 1894; Alice Freeman Palmer, "Some Lasting Results of the World's Fair," *Forum* 16 (December 1893): 518; *History of the World's Fair* quoted in Weimann, *Fair Women,* 278; Marietta Holley, *Samantha at the World's Fair* (New York: Funk and Wagnalls, 1893), 243–44.

5. Kate Field, "Women and the Fair," *Chicago Daily Tribune,* November 12, 1893; Jennifer Jolly, "History in the Making: A Columbian Exposition Scrapbook," in *The Scrapbook in American Life,* ed. Susan Tucker, Katherine Ott, and Patricia P. Buckler (Philadelphia: Temple University Press, 2006), 79–96; and "The Equal Rights Association," *Massilon Independent,* September 7, 1893.

6. R. S. Dix, "At the Columbian Exposition: The Story of a Second Day's Visit," *Leslie's Weekly,* October 5, 1893, 218.

7. "Expenses of Committee on Library," October 20, 1893, box 8, vol. 23, BLM Papers; see also Weimann, *Fair Women,* 584. Many governments proudly enumerated titles and authors in the Woman's Building Library in their own publications. See, for example, the *Official Special Catalogue of the Austrian Section of the World's Columbian Exposition, Chicago, 1893* (Vienna: John Vernay, 1893), 105.

8. "Expenses of Committee on Library."

9. Executive Committee Minutes, October 27, 1893, box 1, vol. 6, BLM Papers. See also "World's Fair Yesterday," *Chicago Herald,* August 1, 1893; untitled article, *Stevens Point (Wisc.) Journal,* October 14, 1893; "World's Fair Notes," *Woman's Journal,* August 26, 1893, 269; and entry for July 30, 1893, Sallie Cotten Diary, folder 15, Sallie Southall Cotten Papers #2613, Southern History Collection, Wilson Library, University of North Carolina, Chapel Hill (hereafter cited as Cotten Diary). See also Hubert Howe Bancroft, *The Book of the Fair: An Historical and Descriptive Presentation of the World's Science, Art, and Industry, as Viewed through the Columbian Exposition at Chicago in 1893,* 2 vols. (Chicago: Bancroft, 1895), 1:289; and Maud Howe Elliott, "The Library," in *Art and Handicraft in the Woman's Building of the World's Columbian Exposition, Chicago, 1893,* ed. Elliott (Paris: Goupil, 1893), 111.

10. Minutes, January 17, 1894, 65, BWM Papers.

11. Minutes, November 17, 1893, 132–33, BWM Papers.

12. Palmer to Madame E. Ankaravard, n.d., box 6.5, vol. 17, BLM Papers.

13. Quoted in Henry Davenport Northrop, *The World's Fair as Seen in One Hundred Days* (Philadelphia: National Publishing, 1893), 165.

14. In her autobiography Mary Hallock Foote recalled an episode that reflects this resistance. Although "the men did not want us on their juries," Foote writes, Bertha Palmer "decreed that on each of the juries of selection and awards a woman should be appointed by her Board to serve with the same honors and emoluments as the men." A highly respected illustrator as well as a popular writer of sketches set in the Far West, Foote was asked to serve as an art juror. Foote thought about declining, then decided she "could not refuse $500 and expenses to Chicago" and a chance to visit a son there she had not seen for two years. Unfortunately, she was erroneously appointed to the awards jury for etching rather than black-and-white illustration (her forte). Not wanting to be a "fraud," Foote gamely learned all she could about etching in the space of a week so that she could carry out her official responsibilities. Mary Hallock Foote, *A Victorian Gentlewoman in the Far West: The Reminiscences of Mary Hallock Foote,* ed. Rodman W. Paul (San Marino, Calif.: Huntington Library, 1972), 357–58.

15. Rossiter Johnson, *A History of the World's Columbian Exposition Held in Chicago in 1893,* 4 vols. (New York: D. Appleton, 1897–1898), 1:231–38; untitled article, *Daily Columbian,* July 1, 1893.

16. Undated article from *Chicago Herald* quoted in *Woman's Journal,* September 30, 1893, 312.

17. Cotten Diary, July 21, 1893, and August 12, 1893.

18. Dewey to Meredith, June 26, 1893, box 3, Dewey Papers. See also Meredith to Dewey, June 23, 1893. On June 29 Dewey informed Hannah P. James, "I think there is no doubt that you will be appointed as judge in the library matters on behalf of the woman managers. This will be a great honor which you have earned by your good work, and your trustees would be very unhappy if you were not to accept it." Dewey to James, June 29, 1893, box 3, Dewey Papers. Hannah P. James and J. S. R. James of the People's Palace Library in London were not related to each other.

19. Palmer to Cooke, November 16, 1893, box 6, vol. 16, BLM Papers.

20. Palmer to Jennings, June 18, 1894, box 6.5, vol. 17, BLM Papers.

21. Ibid.

22. Meredith to Dewey, April 26, 1894, box 3, Dewey Papers. See also Palmer to John Hoyt, June 13, 1894; Palmer to Hoyt, June 18, 1894; Palmer to A. T. Britton, July 27, 1894; Palmer to Meredith, July 27, 1894; BLM Secretary to E. R. L. Gould, August 13, 1894, all in box 6.5, vol. 17, BLM Papers; and Florence Ives, "Report of the Board of Women Managers," in *Report of the Board of General Managers of the Exhibit of the State of New York at the World's Columbian Exposition* (Albany: James B. Lyon, 1894), 170.

23. Minutes, January 17, 1894, 64–65, 75, BWM Papers; *Report of the Board of General Managers of the Exhibit of the State of New York,* 118; Christopher Robert Reed, *"All the World Is Here!" The Black Presence in the White City* (Bloomington: Indiana University Press, 2000), 111–12; and Ives, "Report of the Board of Women Managers," 162, 164.

24. Palmer to Coe (c/o Melvil Dewey), March 10, 1894, box 6, vol. 16; Palmer to Coe, April 2, 1894, box 6.5, vol. 17. Palmer describes her meeting with Clarke in Palmer to Lockwood, May 4, 1894, box 6.5, vol. 17. See also Palmer to Lockwood, February 3, 1894, box 6, vol. 16; Palmer to Lockwood, April 18, 1894, box 6.5, vol. 17.

25. Obviously, the BLM considered the catalog less important than the physical collection itself and the manner in which it was exhibited. Ironically, its inability or unwillingness to conform to the practices of the emerging profession of librarianship may also have substantially undermined their efforts to pass down to future generations an enduring record of women's writing. Clarke's bibliography, with a preface dated August 8, 1894, was published as *List of Books Sent by Home and Foreign Committees to the Library of the Woman's Building, World's Columbian Exposition, 1893.*

26. Minutes, May 22, 1894, 137–40, BWM Papers.

27. Minutes, May 28, 1894, box 1, vol. 6, BLM Papers.

28. University of the State of New York, *New York State Library: 79th Annual Report, 1896* (Albany: University of the State of New York, 1897), 16.

29. Weimann, *Fair Women,* 369.

30. Ibid., 391–92.

31. Virginia Grant Darney, "Women and World's Fairs: American International Expositions, 1876–1904" (Ph.D. diss., Emory University, 1982), 143; *The Official Catalogue of the Cotton States and International Exposition* (Atlanta: Claflin and Mellichamp, 1895, 123–24. See also *The Cotton States and International Exposition and South, Illustrated* (Atlanta: The Illustration Company, 1896), 51–54.

32. I. Garland Penn, "Awakening of a Race," *Atlanta Constitution,* September 22, 1895. See also *Cotton States and International Exposition and South,* 55–61.

33. Daniel Murray, comp., *Preliminary List of Books and Pamphlets by Negro Authors for Paris Exposition and Library of Congress* (Washington, D.C.: Library of Congress, n.d.), 2.

A handwritten note in the Library of Congress copy of this pamphlet, dated June 26, 1902, reads: "DM says only 155 of the 224 books orig. shipped to Paris have been returned." An additional handwritten notation records "211 listed / 519 sent to exhibit." After the Paris exposition, Murray continued to develop his bibliography, which ultimately included 1,400 works. See David Levering Lewis, "A Small Nation of People: W. E. B. Du Bois and Black Americans at the Turn of the Twentieth Century," in Library of Congress, *A Small Nation of People: W. E. B. Du Bois and African American Portraits of Progress* (New York: HarperCollins, 2003), 27–28.

34. For a summary, see Mary Frances Cordato, "Representing the Expansion of Woman's Sphere: Women's Work and Culture at the World's Fairs of 1876, 1893, and 1904" (Ph.D. diss., New York University, 1989), 430–45; and Darney, "Women and World's Fairs," ii. See also Mary Pepchinski, "Woman's Buildings at European and American World's Fairs, 1893–1939," in *Gendering the Fair: Histories of Women and Gender at World's Fairs,* ed. TJ Boisseau and Abigail M. Markwyn (Urbana: University of Illinois Press, 2010), 187–207. On the transition from gender separation to integration, see also Estelle Freedman, "Separatism as Strategy: Female Institution Building and American Feminism, 1870–1930," *Feminist Studies* 5.3 (Autumn 1979): 519–22; and Kathleen D. McCarthy, *Women's Culture: American Philanthropy and Art, 1830–1930* (Chicago: University of Chicago Press, 1991).

35. Quoted in Ishbel Ross, *Silhouette in Diamonds: The Life of Mrs. Potter Palmer* (1960; repr., New York: Arno Press, 1975), 99. The full text of Palmer's speech can be found in Board of Lady Managers, World's Columbian Exposition, *Addresses and Reports of Mrs. Potter Palmer* (Chicago, Rand, McNally, 1894), 149–58.

36. James Clifford, "Museums as Contact Zones," in *Representing the Nation: A Reader: Histories, Heritage and Museums,* ed. David Boswell and Jessica Evans (London: Routledge, 1999), 452.

37. On female institution building, see Freedman, "Separatism as Strategy."

38. The phrase "jury of woman's peers" is from Palmer's speech at the dedication ceremony, "Address at Dedicatory Ceremonies of the Exposition, Manufactures Building, October 21, 1892," in Board of Lady Managers, *Addresses and Reports of Mrs. Potter Palmer,* 114–19; Freedman, "Separatism as Strategy," 517.

39. Anne Ruggles Gere, *Intimate Practices: Literacy and Cultural Work in U.S. Women's Clubs, 1880–1920* (Urbana: University of Illinois Press, 1997), 100.

40. Holley, *Samantha at the World's Fair,* 255.

Index